Pope John's Council

Pope John's Council

Part Two of

Liturgical Revolution

by Michael Davies

PO Box 217 | Saint Marys, KS 66536

Originally and simultaneously published in Great Britain by Augustine Publishing Co., Devon and in the United States by Angelus Press.

Library of Congress Cataloging-in-Publication Data

Davies, Michael, 1936-
  Pope John's Council / by Michael Davies. -- 2nd ed.
    p. cm. -- (The liturgical revolution ; pt. 2)
  Includes bibliographical references and index.
  ISBN 1-892331-36-5 (alk. paper)
    1. Vatican Council (2nd : 1962-1965)   I. Title. II. Series: Davies, Michael, 1936-   . Liturgical revolution ; pt. 2.
BX8301962 .D35 2006
262'.52--dc22

                                        2005027807

©2007 by Angelus Press
All rights reserved. No part of this book may be reproduced or transmitted in any form or by any means, electronic or mechanical, including photocopying, recording, or by any information storage and retrieval systems without permission in writing from the publisher, except by a reviewer, who may quote brief passages in a review.

ANGELUS PRESS
PO Box 217
Saint Marys, Kansas 66536
Phone (816) 753-3150
Fax (816) 753-3557
Order Line 1-800-966-7337
www.angeluspress.org

ISBN: 978-1-892331-36-6

SECOND EDITION
TENTH PRINTING–August 2021

Printed in the United States of America

Acknowledgments

Grateful acknowledgment is made to the following publishers for their permission to reproduce excerpts from the works listed below, all rights reserved:

THE AMERICA PRESS: *The Documents of Vatican II*, edited by W. Abbott, S.J. (1966).

FRANCISCAN HERALD PRESS: *The Decomposition of Catholicism* by L. Bouyer (1970).

HAWTHORN BOOKS: *The Rhine Flows into the Tiber* by R. M. Wiltgen (1967).

HODDER & STOUGHTON: *Crown of Thorns* by Cardinal Heenan (1974).

MOWBRAYS: *Rome and Canterbury through Four Centuries* by B. & M. Pawley (1974).

UNA VOCE, Scottish Branch: *Athanasius and the Church of Our Times*, by Monsignor R. Graber (1974). Published by Scottish Una Voce, 6 Belford Park, Edinburgh EH4 3DP.

Contents

Errata   xxi

Author's Introduction   xxiii

I   Pope John Is Inspired   1
Pope John claims that God inspired him to call an ecumenical council—Lack of enthusiasm in the Curia—Previous councils condemned the chief errors of their times—Vatican II did not—It has produced no good fruits—Evidence that the post-conciliar Church is engaged in a process of self-destruction—The evils now afflicting the Church are a result of the Council itself—Pope John completely failed to foresee the results of his decision to call a council—He had envisaged no more than a glorified Synod of Rome—Most of the Fathers shared Pope John's illusions—Vatican Council II differed from its predecessors by being "pastoral" in nature, and in promulgating no infallible doctrinal or moral teaching binding upon the Church—By 1968 Pope Paul lamented the fact that the Church was undergoing a process of self-destruction—Statistics which prove this—The testimonies of Professor James Hitchcock, Father Louis Bouyer, Archbishop Lefebvre, and Cardinal Ratzinger.

II   The Church Before the Council   21
Pope John pays tribute to the vitality of the pre-conciliar Church—This was manifested not simply in preaching the Gospel but in an unprecedented concern for the material needs of all mankind—Weaknesses in the pre-conciliar Church were normally exaggerations of valid aspects of the Faith—These weaknesses analysed

by Dietrich von Hildebrand—Considerable room for liturgical renewal on the lines advocated by the papally-approved Liturgical Movement—A Modernist fifth column existed within the pre-conciliar Church—The Council created the climate for it to emerge—The conciliar documents cannot be absolved from all responsibility for the present crisis—This view was shared by Dietrich von Hildebrand—Monsignor George A. Kelly documents the healthy state of American Catholicism before the Council and its collapse in the aftermath of Vatican II.

III   Blitzkrieg   35

Most bishops were unprepared for the Council—Few clearly understood their role—A group of liberal-minded bishops from Rhineland countries came to the Council with a definite plan for reforming the Church in accordance with their own ideas—particularly to replace the true concept of Catholic ecumenism, as laid down by Pope Pius XI in *Mortalium Animos* 1928, with a policy of "unity at any price"—The conciliar "experts" (*periti*) were more influential than the bishops—The Rhine group overthrows the established election procedure and initiates a campaign to secure the election of its own candidates to the influential conciliar commissions—The election is a triumph for the Rhine group, which quickly expands when its success initiates a bandwagon movement.

IV   Mopping Up   47

The Rhine Group consolidates by changing the rules of procedure and securing the appointment of its members to more key positions—A single *peritus* could impose his views on the Council if he could gain the support of the German bishops—Additional elections are held and every successful candidate is a Rhine member—the Rhine Group achieves total control—Archbishop Lefebvre insisted that the present crisis is a direct result of the Council.

Contents

V   Liberal Shock Troops   55
The *periti* are the shock troops of the Rhine Group—Vatican II is the Council of the *periti*—The preparatory schemata (draft documents) for the Council are scrapped at the behest of the *periti*—Cardinal Heenan testifies that the *periti* were able to introduce ambiguous formulas into the official conciliar documents—The bishops did not realise what the experts were planning—Cardinal Heenan feared what would happen if the *periti* obtained the power to interpret the Council to the world—The *periti* secured this power by taking control of the post-conciliar commissions invested with the authority to interpret and implement the official documents—The first four preparatory schemata are rejected contrary to the rules of the Council—The importance of the Council as an event which enabled liberal—Catholics from all over the world to organise themselves and plan their campaign—There is now a "parallel magisterium" of the experts which is imposing its will upon the Church—The nature of the liberal conspiracy—Some of the Council *periti* became the most vociferous opponents of Catholic teaching on faith and morals—The relevance of St. Pius X's encyclical *Pascendi* Gregis to the present crisis.

VI   Time Bombs   81
Archbishop Lefebvre warned against time-bombs in the Council documents—These are passages capable of a modernistic interpretation after the Council—A prominent theologian denies that such passages exist—Archbishop Lefebvre's view is confirmed by spokesmen of all shades of Catholic and Protestant opinion—The documents themselves prove him to be correct—Passages from some documents are examined in detail to demonstrate this—On 6 August 2000, the Congregation for the Doctrine of the Faith (CDF) published the *Declaration on the Unicity and Salvific Universality of Jesus Christ and the Church (Dominus Jesus)* which included an authoritative interpretation of the term "subsists" as used by the Second Vatican Council.

VII   The Prefabricators   119
The press has never had such an influence on any Council as upon Vatican II—Father Bouyer claims that the Council surrendered itself to the dictatorship of the journalists—The liberal journalists fabricate a myth—This myth has now become generally accepted as the true story of the Council—A small liberal elite is able to pass off its own policies as public opinion—Contrary views are excluded from the establishment press—The liberal bishops and *periti* co-operate closely with the liberal journalists—The importance of IDOC—Xavier Rynne insists that the Council has initiated a second Pentecost—The myth of Vatican II is fabricated—Close co-operation between journalists and liberal Fathers—The humiliation of Cardinal Ottaviani—Another illustration of the relevance of *Pascendi Gregis*.

VIII   The Background to Protestantism   143
The history of Protestantism is one of fragmentation—Every Protestant is his own Pope—The rejection of papal authority by the Protestant Reformers initiated a process which can only end in Rationalism—Nonetheless many individual Protestants lead exemplary Christian lives—The ecumenical movement is not a movement towards Protestantism but towards Rationalism—Cardinal Manning explains how Protestant rationalism in Germany infected catholic academics—Cardinal Heenan confirms that Rationalism is now rampant within the Catholic Church—Catholic and Protestant liberals unite in grovelling before the world—They envisage the first duty of a Christian to be constructing an earthly paradise—The Dutch catechism—The errors of "liberation theology"—Ecumenical dialogue with Protestants is shown to be both futile and dangerous—The only true basis for Catholic ecumenism is to invite Protestants to abandon their errors and return to the one, true Church founded by Jesus Christ.

IX   Protestant Pressures   161

The effects of Vatican II have exceeded the wildest hopes of Protestants—Protestants claim that the Council marked the end of the Counter-Reformation—Protestant satisfaction with the Council must be a cause for concern for Catholics—Strong Protestant influence during the Council guaranteed with the establishment of the Secretariat for Christian Unity as a body completely independent of the Curia—The presence of the Protestant observers at the Council had an inhibiting effect upon the Fathers—Some Fathers made speeches on behalf of the observers—The observers exert considerable influence behind the scenes—Their influence can be seen in the wording of the documents—As a result of the Council the Catholic Church has been drawn into an ecumenical policy of appeasement in which unity is sought at the expense of truth—No matter how sincere Catholic ecumenists may be their policies can only end in disaster—Evangelisation has been replaced by dialogue—Many clerics find ecumenical dialogue to be a pleasant and undemanding alternative to evangelisation—The greater the progress of ecumenism, the greater the decline of all the denominations concerned—Protestants claim that Catholic involvement in the ecumenical movement is now irreversible—Where the immediate future is concerned this view may well be correct—A vast new ecumenical bureaucracy has come into being—Liturgical changes praised by Protestants—The Mass in its new form is no longer a cause of dissension—Catholics motivated by charity for their separated brethren will spare no effort to bring them into communion with the Vicar of Christ—This is the only valid basis for Catholic ecumenism.

X   Mother of the Church   181

The treatment of Our Lady during the Council illustrates the extent of Protestant influence—A separate document on Our Lady is opposed by Protestants as increasing her importance—The Fathers from the Eastern Churches support the separate schema—The Irish Mariologist Father Michael O'Carroll wrote: The greatest theological system on our Lady's universal mediation is from an Orthodox theologian, Theophanes of Nicea (d. 1381)—The Fathers eventually voted to relegate the schema on Our Lady to the Constitution on the Church by only seventeen votes—Protestant observers express satisfaction that disaster has been avoided—Protestants object to the title *Mediatrix of All Graces*—A compromise is reached, *Mediatrix is* retained but the words *of all Graces* are dropped—In a written intervention, Cardinal Spellman asked whether such titles used by the Supreme Pontiffs could be passed over simply "because they would be rather difficult for Protestants to understand—The task of an ecumenical council is to teach the members of the Church, rather than those outside of it—Protestants object to the title *Mother* of *the Church*—It is dropped but Pope Paul proclaims Our Lady as Mother of the Church on his own authority—Protestants and the liberal Fathers are enraged—The Chapter on Our Lady in its final form has much to commend it—Despite the extent to which their demands were met the Protestant observers are far from satisfied.

XI   The Dogmatic Constitution On Divine Revelation—*Dei Verbum*   197

Dei Verbum, the Dogmatic Constitution on Divine Revelation, is considered by some commentators to be the supreme achievement of the Council—It was one of the most hotly contested documents of the Council—The liberal and ecumenical majority of Fathers attempted to undermine the role of oral tradition as an authentic source of revelation—Trent and Vatican I teach infallibly that there are two sources of revelation—This is also the consensus of the earlier and later Church Fathers—Protestants insist that sacred Scripture is the sole source of revelation—This fundamental incompatibility between Catholic and Protestant teaching posed a great problem for those bishops and *periti* at Vatican II for whom the ecumenical dimension of the council took precedence over all else—The preliminary schema drawn up by the pre-conciliar Theological Commission and presented for discussion by Cardinal Ottaviani had as the title of its first chapter "Two Sources of Revelation"—It came under fierce attack from Father Schillebeeckx, and was one of the four preliminary schemata that he demanded successfully should be rewritten—Bishop Emile de Smedt of Bruges condemns the schema as lacking notably in the ecumenical spirit and harmful—as there could be no formal rejection of the teaching of Trent or Vatican I on the two sources the only viable tactic for the liberals was to emphasise the role of Scripture at the expense of oral tradition—In the newly written schema all mention of "sources" was suppressed—The International Group of Fathers and other bishops dedicated to the defence of tradition were determined that the traditional and infallible teaching on the two sources of revelation should be stated explicitly in this dogmatic constitution—The minority of traditional Fathers eventually secured several specific affirmations of the fact that there are two sources of revelation—Pope Paul intervened in the interests of orthodoxy—The finalised version of Chapter II contains a number of clear affirmations of the place of oral tradition as an authentic source of divine revelation—Despite the fact that the treatment given to oral tradition in *Dei Verbum* is greatly overshadowed by that given to sacred Scripture we must be grateful to the International Group of Fathers and to Pope Paul VI for ensuring that the doctrine of the two sources is stated specifically, and orthodoxy upheld.

XII The Status of the Documents 209

A distinction must be made between the official documents and the background to their promulgation—The Council did not intend any of its teaching to be infallible—Vatican II is only infallible when citing previous infallible definitions—Cardinal Heenan explains that Vatican II deliberately limited its objectives—These were primarily pastoral—Only binding definitions of general councils are infallible—An infallible pronouncement is simply one that is protected from error. There are no definitions in this technical sense in the teaching of Vatican II except where it quotes already existing infallible papal or conciliar teaching—Bishop Butler explains that Vatican II gave us no new dogmatic definitions—Pope Paul VI states unequivocally that the documents of Vatican II promulgate no infallible teaching—A Catholic has no right to refuse to accept officially promulgated conciliar teaching simply because it is not infallible—There is a considerable difference in the degree of assent demanded by the different conciliar pronouncements—There are accepted principles which a Catholic can use to help him discriminate—We can never be compelled to accept an interpretation of a conciliar document which conflicts with traditional teaching—It will be found that most post-conciliar abuses cannot be specifically justified by reference to an official document—Most abuses derive from what are claimed to be interpretations or implementations of the official documents—But the Council cannot be absolved from all responsibility for abuses due to the atmosphere it generated and deficiencies in some of its documents—We should accept the conciliar documents with prudence and reserve, and interpret them in the light of tradition.

XIII Left Turn   233

Pope Pius XII's policy of confrontation with Communism was been replaced by one of dialogue—This resulted in continual concessions on the part of the Church—The Communist tactic of the "outstretched hand" analysed—Communists use dialogue as a weapon to make their attainment of power easier—Evidence that a more sympathetic attitude to Communism displayed by a General Council would help Russia's bid for world conquest—Since the Council many Catholics did not simply cease to oppose Communism but did all in their power to advance it—The betrayal of Cardinal Mindszenty—Orthodox observers attend the Council on condition that there will be no fresh condemnation of Communism—The Vatican's new Ostpolitik was based on a disastrous illusion and had disastrous results—The Council was prevented from condemning atheistic Communism by a process of calculated fraud—No Catholic was obliged to support the Holy

Contents

See in its Ostpolitik—By 1975 evidence of second thoughts on the part of the Vatican was available.

XIV   Pernicious Adversaries   257

Bishop Graber's book reveals the extent of the Masonic conspiracy against the Church—The liberals ridicule any Catholic who suggests that there is such a conspiracy—The liberals are helped by Catholics suffering from conspiracy mania—The Popes have taught that Catholicism and Masonry are fundamentally irreconcilable—No Catholic can ever be a Mason—This prohibition is incorporated into Canon Law—It is lifted in 1974—The Sacred Congregation for the Doctrine of the Faith declared on 26 November 1983 that the Church's negative judgement in regard to Masonic associations remains unchanged since their principles have always been considered irreconcilable with the doctrine of the Church and therefore membership in them remains forbidden—The faithful who enrol in Masonic associations are in a state of grave sin and may not receive Holy Communion—The Masons, like the Communists, make no secret about their intentions—They no longer intend to destroy the Church but to make use of it by infiltrating it—Father Arrupe, he Jesuits General, warned that the mentality and the cultural environment of the modern world is atheistic and even crosses the ramparts and enters the very territory of the City of God, insidiously influencing the minds of believers (including even religious and priests) with its hidden poison, and producing its natural fruits in the Church: naturalism, distrust, rebellion—In his encyclical *Humanum Genus* (1884) Pope Leo XIII warned that "the partisans of evil seem to be drawing closer together and, as a body, appear to be animated with extraordinary energy, under the leadership and with the assistance of the widely diffused and strongly organised associations known as Freemasonry. No longer concealing their designs, they are now, with the greatest audacity, preparing to rise up against God Himself. They are planning the utter destruction of Holy Church publicly and openly, with the intention of completely despoiling the Christian Nations of the benefits procured for them by Jesus Christ—There is a strong case for believing Archbishop Bugnini to have been a Mason—The Council and post-conciliar developments go a long way towards meeting Masonic objectives—Some Masons are far from satisfied with the Council Documents—The importance of not going beyond the evidence when positing the conspiracy theory—Most liberals are not sinister but silly.

XV The Enigma of Pope Paul   277

It is necessary to be in communion with the Vicar of Christ to be a member of the Mystical Body of Christ—Some Catholics manifest an understandable but exaggerated loyalty to the person of the pope and act as if his every decision were inspired by God—Such an attitude is historically indefensible—Infallibility is not an assistance attached to the person of the pope but a quality inherent in his office—Papal primacy is exercised only when the Universal Church is its end, and even then only when the teaching concerns faith or morals—The idea that the pope cannot be criticised is a post-Reformation attitude—Dietrich von Hildebrand pointed out how mistaken is the attitude that practical decisions of the pope are accepted in the same way as *ex cathedra* definitions—Cardinal Manning explains the true nature of infallibility—Those who believe that the pope is inerrant devised incredible theories to explain the fact that Pope Paul permitted measures which harmed the Church—The Pope's behaviour can be explained in the light of his attachment to the philosophy of Integral Humanism—The nature of Integral Humanism—The role of Jacques Maritain—Pope Paul a disciple of Maritain—The spirit of Integral Humanism pervades the Constitution on the Church in the Modern World—Pope Paul's speech at the United Nations an endorsement of Integral Humanism—The Abbé de Nantes and Pope Paul—Pope Paul and Communism—The Pope was not pro-Communist but refused to follow an anti-Communist policy—His policy of dialogue furthered the ends of Communism—The communists of Rome paid tribute to him upon his death—Pope Paul criticised the policies of some Western Governments—The Pope and Modernism—He upheld authentic Catholic teaching in principle but allowed it to be undermined in practice—The Pope and Protestantism—His anxiety for dialogue contributed to the spirit of false ecumenism which is harming the Church—His error in designating the Church of England as a "sister Church"—He conducted secret negotiations with Anglicans during the Pontificate of Pope Pius XII—Protestants hoped for his election when Pope John died—His apology to Protestants for Catholic responsibility for the sin of schism is considered of monumental importance—His interventions during the Council did not please Protestants—He is attacked for his *Credo* and his encyclicals *Mysterium Fidei* and *Humanae Vitae*—Some of his policies were not developments but reversals of the teaching of his predecessors—Pope Paul was willing to dialogue with anyone except Catholic traditionalists—A tribute to Paul VI appeared in the Italian Masonic journal *Rivista Massonica* which stated for us it is the death of him who has put an end to the condemnation of Clement XII and of his successors. For the first time in the history of modern Masonry, the head of the largest religion in the West dies not in a state of hostility towards Freemasons.

XVI   Planting the Time Bombs   327

The Liturgy Commission was dominated by liberals—The reforms envisaged coincided not simply with Protestant demands but with the principles of the Jansenist Synod of Pistoia—They also correspond with the principles of the anti-liturgical heresy condemned by Dom Guéranger—The retention of Latin a key issue in the debate—Cardinal Montini was opposed to a vernacular Canon—Few Fathers imagined that Latin would virtually disappear from the liturgy—Father Bouyer claims that the interpretation of the Liturgy Constitution is a betrayal not simply of what the Council Fathers' intentions but of the Liturgical Movement—Protestants and liberals are well satisfied with the constitution—Liberals obtain control of the post-conciliar commission charged with implementing the constitution—The constitution is disciplinary not doctrinal in character and does not involve the Church's infallibility.

XVII Unearthing the Time Bombs   341
The *Constitution on the Sacred Liturgy* (CSL) could have been the means of implementing a liturgical renewal—It was used to initiate a revolution—The importance of Pope Pius XII's Encyclical *Mediator Dei*—The nature of the liturgy—The seeds of the liturgical evolution found in the preface and first chapter of the CSL—Any drastic change in existing rites is contrary to the entire tradition of the Church—Their claim that the liturgy must be adapted to the circumstance and needs of modern times provides a mandate for a permanent liturgical revolution—The CSL does not include the word "transubstantiation"—Contrast between the CSL and Pope Paul's *Mysterium Fidei*—*The* need for the active participation of the people to be considered before all else also provides a mandate for liturgical revolution—Analysis of other vaguely worded articles—The recommendation to adapt the liturgy to different groups, regions and people provides an additional mandate for revolution—As early as 1965 some priests cast aside all restraint and celebrated Mass as it suited them—The *Consilium* charged with reforming the liturgy condemned this but took no effective action to prevent abuses—Its eventual policy was to legalise the abuses by incorporating them into the official reform—The virtual abolition of Latin—The CSL ignored—The dismissal of Archbishop Bugnini may be a sign of hope.

XVIII Counting the Cost   377
Neither the Council nor its teaching captured the interest of the ordinary Catholic—Even the self-appointed "intelligentsia" sometimes have little first-hand knowledge of the official documents—An estimate of the material cost of the Council—The cost to the life of the Church can never be calculated—"When they create a wilderness, they call it a renewal".

Contents

Appendix I—The General Councils of the Church — 381

Appendix II—Chronology of the Council — 383

Appendix III—The Press and
the First Vatican Council — 387

Appendix IV—Liberal Mythology — 393

Appendix V—The Declaration *Dominus Jesus*
Regarding the Term *Subsistit* — 403

Appendix VI—Sillonism — 421

Appendix VII—Salleron on Maritain — 429

Appendix VIII—The Anti-liturgical Heresy — 447

Appendix IX—The Fruits of Vatican II — 453

Bibliography — 467

Index — 471

ERRATA

Although Michael Davies does a very good job showing the time bombs of the Council, we cannot but write this caveat concerning his treatment of ecumenism, especially pages 97-98 (calling the Orthodox authentic churches with formal apostolic succession) and 403-408 (commenting on *Dominus Jesus*).

Ecumenism was center stage at Vatican II. The Council theologians had introduced various *diminutions* of the Catholic Church, gradually losing her traditional equivalence to the kingdom of God and to the Church of Christ. Other traps were used also at the Council with the introduction of new concepts essential to the ecumenical arsenal: the *elementa Ecclesiae* and the broad use of the term "church" to designate schismatic and heretical groups.

1. FROM *VESTIGIA* TO *ELEMENTA ECCLESIAE*

For the ecumenists, the religious groups truly shared in the treasures of Christ's Church. Here was their reasoning: if rudiments of truth and grace in the individual who was outside the visible Catholic Church justified his belonging to Her, why couldn't something similar occur for communities? Isn't the faith that saves the protestant individual nourished by the Sacred Scripture proposed by his community? Didn't grace come to him though the baptism which his community gave him in good faith?

Yet, in spite of such thinking, this open door is false. For, if theology calls the rudiments "vestigial," it is exactly because they are but traces or ruins of the Church, which in sects are dead and inactive as opposed to the live, sanctifying principle suggested by the term "elements". The seed of the Faith that a few souls among them might possess tends to be choked by the heresies which the community upholds. The true faith of the Protestant person is in fact in contradiction with the formal principle of his sect, which is using the elements of truth as bait for a substantial error. Likewise, the sacraments might be valid, but they do not impart the fruit of grace which is needed to be called true (St. Thomas Aq. III q. 82 a. 7). The apostolic succession in schismatic sects that have preserved the validity of the sacrament of Holy Orders is purely material. Besides, the episcopal sees were usurped and lack jurisdiction.

2. FROM RELIGIOUS COMMUNITIES TO CHURCHES

But things were not meant to stagnate. The ecumenists wished to qualify the religious sects with the name of "churches". Following its collegial, democratic orientation, Vatican II especially emphasized the notion of "particular Churches" within the universal Church (*Lumen Gentium* # 23). Likewise, these particular Churches were called sacraments, and such "sacramental" qualification of the church, which is realized in every Eucharistic assembly, promotes the ecumenical agenda. This ambiguity allows the name of true "Churches" to be given to those communities which, although separate from the Catholic hierarchy, nonetheless preserve the "ecclesiastic elements" of the Eucharist and the priesthood.

The Declaration *Dominus Jesus,* although published firstly to mitigate many Catholics' excessive ecumenical enthusiasm, did not hesitate to grant the title of "true particular Churches" to other communities. "The Churches which, while not existing in perfect communion with the Catholic Church, remain united to her by means of the closest bonds, that is, by apostolic succession and a valid Eucharist, are true particular Churches. Therefore, the Church of Christ is present and active also in these Churches, even though they lack full communion with the Catholic Church..." (No. 17)

However, this new ecclesiology held to this day by the Congregation of the Doctrine of Faith is founded on an erroneous principle. It pretends that the Church of Christ is the Catholic Church only because it enjoys the quantitative and material plenitude of the means of salvation. But the unity of the Church is not a material composition of a greater or lesser number of elements; it demands a formal principle. This formal principle, which will always be lacking to all separated communities, no matter how many Church "elements" they may have, is a supernatural principle because it is divinely instituted. It is the social order of the exterior profession of the true faith and of true worship, produced by the hierarchical government of the pope, supreme head, and of the bishops, subordinate heads. The sacraments, Holy Scripture, and the dogmas are as such hierarchical realities, received by divine authority through the Pope, or they are nothing worthwhile.

—Angelus Press

Author's Introduction

The text of this book was unchanged for the first four printings. This seventh edition has been so extensively revised that it is not unreasonable to describe it as a new book. It contains one new chapter and one new appendix. Several more of the existing chapters have been so extensively revised as to virtually constitute new ones. The original list of recommended publications has been removed as many of the items mentioned in it are now unobtainable. The original appendix documenting the collapse of Catholicism in the West since Vatican II has been replaced by an extensive new appendix (Appendix IX) showing that beyond any possible doubt there have been no good fruits emanating from the Council, and that every aspect of Catholic life subject to statistical verification has been subjected to a catastrophic decline.

The most significant event relating to Vatican II since this book was first published in 1977 was the convocation by Pope John Paul II of an extraordinary synod of bishops in Rome in November 1985, to assess the impact of the Council upon the life of the Church. National hierarchies submitted reports upon the effectiveness of the conciliar reforms in their own countries. Where English-speaking hierarchies were concerned, the result was as predictable as that of an election in the former Soviet Union. The submission of the English bishops was possibly the most fatuous, but only marginally more inane than that of the hierarchy of the United States. It was claimed that we are in the midst of a second Pentecost of such magnitude that the first was a non-event in comparison. Everyone everywhere is engaged in incessant dialogue and ceaseless renewal. The only blot upon the idyllic post-conciliar landscape is the presence of Catholics expressing "an extreme minority view". These Catholics, whose crime is fidelity to the Magisterium of the Church and her most venerable traditions, are denounced by the English bishops for manifesting "a lack of tolerance and a certain new fundamentalism".

Sadly, the Extraordinary Synod itself endorsed this attitude of fatuous optimism. A God-given opportunity to face up to the facts of the post-conciliar debacle and initiate a return to Tradition was rejected. In its final report the Fathers of the Synod proclaimed:

> The reason for the summoning of this synod was to celebrate, reaffirm the meaning, and carry forward the work of the Second Vatican Council. We are grateful to see that, with God's help, we have achieved these aims. We have celebrated Vatican II wholeheartedly together, as a grace of God and gift of the Holy Spirit, from which many spiritual benefits have issued for the universal Church, for particular Churches, and for the people of our time. In the same mind and with joy we have affirmed the meaning of Vatican II as a lawful and valid expression of the deposit of faith contained in sacred Scripture and in the living tradition of the Church. For this reason we decided to go forward on the same path that the Council pointed out.

Author's Introduction

One can only remark that this is precisely the reaffirmation one might expect from a synod of lemmings determined to go forward on the same path to self-destruction taken by their predecessors twenty years previously. A far more realistic assessment of the post-conciliar epoch, and one which coincides exactly with that expressed in this book when it was first published, was expressed by Cardinal Joseph Ratzinger, Prefect of the Congregation for the Doctrine of the Faith, and published in the English edition of *L'Osservatore Romano* on 24 December 1984:

> Certainly the results [of Vatican II] seem cruelly opposed to the expectations of everyone, beginning with those of Pope John XXIII and then of Pope Paul VI: expected was a new Catholic unity and instead we have been exposed to dissension which, to use the words of Pope Paul VI, seems to have gone from self-criticism to self-destruction. Expected was a new enthusiasm, and many wound up discouraged and bored. Expected was a great step forward, and instead we find ourselves faced with a progressive process of decadence which has developed for the most part precisely under the sign of a calling back to the Council, and has therefore contributed to discrediting it for many. The net result therefore seems negative. I am repeating here what I said ten years after the conclusion of the work: it is incontrovertible that this period has definitely been unfavourable for the Catholic Church.

Cardinal Ratzinger's realistic assessment of post-conciliar Catholicism won him no friends within the Catholic media. In an editorial comment on the English bishops' submission, *The Tablet* was able to gloat over the fact that "There is no reflection here of the views of Cardinal Ratzinger. On the contrary, his gloomy assessment of the state of the Church today, leading him to deplore the record of the last twenty years, and to call for a `restoration', is often explicitly opposed" (3 August 1985). *The Tablet* had already attacked Cardinal Ratzinger for his "pessimism" in its 13 July issue, and, by an interesting coincidence, the 3 August issue, praising the English bishops' submission, also included a letter to the editor from Bob Santamaria, undoubtedly the greatest Australian layman of this century. Mr. Santamaria's letter was a response to *The Tablet*'s attack on Cardinal Ratzinger. He pointed out that since the Second Vatican Council, in France, Italy and Holland, over eighty per cent of Catholics do not practise their faith. In his own country of Australia, Mass attendance has plummeted from fifty-three per cent in 1960 to twenty-five per cent in 1985. Mr. Santamaria commented:

> If we project these figures into the future, short of a religious miracle, what figures are we seriously entitled to expect ten years from now? Facts cannot be "optimistic" or "pessimistic". Facts can only be true or false. If these facts are false, let them be shown to be so. If they are true let us not conclude our assessment with the monumental absurdity that, in proportion as Catholics vote with their feet and empty once-full churches, the Holy Ghost is "renewing" what is visibly ceasing to exist.

By 2004 Mass attendance in Australia had sunk to thirteen per cent.

An argument which has been used frequently by proponents of the post-conciliar reforms is *post hoc non ergo propter hoc*, i.e., because the decline has followed the Council it is not necessarily a result of the Council. What these people fail to face up to is the fact that the reforms allegedly implementing the Council were intended to initiate a renewal, and a renewal must necessarily involve expansion and not decline. What would these people have replied had their reforms resulted, for example, in a massive increase in Mass attendance, and Catholics who did not like the liturgical changes had replied: *"Post hoc non ergo propter hoc"*?

There is a respect in which the Church can be compared to any great manufacturing company, and I hope that making this comparison will not appear too irreverent. The object of any manufacturer is to persuade the public to buy its product in preference to that of its competitors. Let us imagine that the chief executives of, say, the Ford Motor Company, decided to give the company and its products a totally new image. In order to achieve this they made radical alterations in the appearance of Ford cars, threw out all their tried and tested marketing methods, and promoted their restyled vehicles in a completely new manner. Imagine then, that sales plummeted, and not only did they win practically no new customers, but lost a huge proportion of their established clients, in some countries as many as eighty per cent. It would be an understatement to claim that these executive officers would have lacked credibility had they denied any connection between their new marketing policies and the collapse of their company. Imagine the reaction had the same executives not only tried to exculpate their new policies from any responsibility for the collapse, but denied that any collapse had taken place, despite the fact that in country after country Ford factories were closing down, and that sales were at the lowest level ever. Let us go one step further and image that they refused to abandon the disastrous policies they had adopted, refused to return to their traditional methods, but intended "to go forward on the same path" that had led to the self-destruction of Ford Motor Company. One can only conclude that under such circumstances their next shareholders' meeting would be somewhat stormy. No, Mr. Santamaria is correct. It is a monumental absurdity to claim that as once full churches empty, "the Holy Ghost is 'renewing' what is visibly ceasing to exist".

Father Kenneth Baker, Editor of the *Homiletic and Pastoral Review*, has gone as far as to claim that the "product" marketed by the "executives" of the Catholic Church in the United States is no longer the "product" marketed before Vatican II. In the editorial to his January 1983 edition he wrote: "We are witnessing the rejection of the hierarchical Church founded by Jesus Christ to be replaced by a Protestant American Church separated from Rome". This judgment is radical and severe, but it is one which faithful Catholics throughout the West could apply to what is taking place in their own countries. One of the most significant comments upon the fruits of Vatican II appeared in the 10 October 1982 issue of the *National Catholic Register*, which was dedicated to the twentieth anniversary of the Council, which had opened formally on 11 October 1962. The article was written by Michael Novak, who is mentioned several times in this book, and was, at the time of the Council, an ultra-liberal. He now appears to have undergone a conversion to moderate conservatism, and is something of a scourge of the American bishops. Novak recollected his euphoria at the opening of the Council, and his conviction that the world would for evermore be different and better:

> Is it only that I am now older? For my thoughts about the Church today are not of growth but of decline; not of more intense orthodoxy, but of growing dissension and deliberate heterodoxy; not of more devout moral living, but of growing slackness and surrender to the world on the world's own terms. Vatican II was supposed to renew the Church. At least in some measure, it seems to have diluted, divided and weakened it.

Author's Introduction

In the March 1985 issue of his journal, *Christian Order*, Father Paul Crane, S.J., spelled out precisely what is taking place in the post-conciliar Church: "What confronts the Church today is a new body of belief and moral practice, propagated from within the Church itself by those who call themselves Catholics. In fact, a new religion, a new faith, not in God primarily, but in man. Man-centred rather than God-serving". The June 1986 issue of the *Homiletic and Pastoral Review* included an article by Cardinal Ratzinger in which he deplored the emergence of a new concept of the People of God in which "God" means only the people themselves, and in the liturgy the people celebrate only themselves.

Lest any reader should feel despondent after reading the seventh edition of this book, it is worth recalling that we have Our Lord's promise that His Church will endure until He comes again in the manner He constituted it, as a visible hierarchically governed body founded upon the Rock of Peter. The Church founded by Our Lord cannot fail. It is indefectible. The gates of hell will never prevail against it, even though violent storms may seem to submerge it for a time, and Peter himself may appear to waver. The Church may be reduced in influence. Whole countries may fall away from the faith never to return, as has happened in the past, but the Church itself will and must continue to stand until the end of time, *"ad finem saeculorum usque firma stabit"*, to quote the comforting words of the First Vatican Council in its Dogmatic Constitution *Pastor Aeternus*. The duty of faithful Catholics in these times is to avoid despair, and at all costs to remain within the barque of Peter. Pope Leo XIII warned us in his encyclical *Satis Cognitum* that "the Church of Christ, therefore, is one and the same forever: those who leave it depart from the will and command of Christ, the Lord. Leaving the path of salvation they enter on the path of perdition".

Pope John's Council

To conclude on a note of hope, Our Lady of Fatima promised that in the end her Immaculate Heart will triumph. More than ever, here in this valley of tears, we must make her our most gracious advocate, and the advocate of the Church of which she is the Mother.

Michael Davies
15 August 2004
The Assumption of Our Blessed Lady

I

Pope John Is Inspired

The Universe is the Catholic weekly with the largest circulation in Britain. In its edition of 20 October 1972 it carried a brief report which stated:

> The tenth anniversary of the opening of the Second Vatican Council passed almost unnoticed. Pope Paul briefly referred to it in a routine speech as a living factor in the spiritual history of the Church and of the world, and destined to grow in importance. But there were no celebrations to mark the day, 11 October 1962, when Pope John XXIII inaugurated the Council in a magnificent ceremony which captured the imagination and inspired the hopes of the world. Pope Paul made only a ninety-second reference to the anniversary when he greeted hundreds of pilgrims at his weekly general audience in a Vatican meeting hall.

Pope John was quite certain that his decision to convene the Council was inspired by God: "We had decided, under the inspiration of God, to convene an ecumenical council".[1]

It is important to note that as used here the word "ecumenical" (*oecumenical*) has nothing to do with the movement for Christian unity. There are numerous forms of synod or council recognised within the Church—diocesan, national, patriarchal, of the East or of the West. The highest form is the ecumenical council to which bishops and others entitled to vote are convoked from the whole world (the Greek word *oikoumenikos*). There had been twenty of these councils prior to Vatican II, from Nicea in 325 to Vatican I in 1869. They must be presided over by the pope or his legates, and their definitions, if confirmed by the pope, bind all Christians.[2]

According to Pope John, the inspiration to call an ecumenical council came to him during a conversation with Cardinal Tardini towards the end of 1958. The Pope "asked his Secretary of State what might be done to give the world an example of peace and concord among men, and an occasion for hope, when suddenly there sprang to his own lips the words, 'A Council'!"[3] This was, he explained later, "an impulse of divine providence".[4] Pope John's "divinely inspired" plan was revealed to the Sacred College of Cardinals "on that memorable 25 January 1959, the feast of the Conversion of St. Paul, in the basilica dedicated to him. It was completely unexpected, like a flash of heavenly light, shedding sweetness in eyes and hearts".[5]

There was, in fact, a distinct lack of enthusiasm on the part of the cardinals; and when Pope John asked them for their reaction to his "inspiration", not one of them had a word to say. He later admitted his disappointment: "Humanly speaking we could have expected that the cardinals, after hearing our allocution, might have crowded round to express approval and good wishes". However, he put the most favourable possible explanation on their failure to reply, which he described as "a devout and impressive silence".[6]

Pope John's belief that his Council had been summoned in response to a divine inspiration was shared by his successor. Pope Paul VI included the following words in his opening address to the second session:

Pope John Is Inspired

> O dear and venerated Pope John, may gratitude and praise be rendered to you for having resolved—doubtless under divine inspiration—to convoke this Council in order to open to the Church new horizons and to tap the fresh spring water of the doctrine and grace of Christ and let it flow over the earth.[7]

There is, of course, no obligation for any Catholic to believe that Pope John's inspiration came from God. He may easily have been a good and holy pope who may possibly be canonised—but those familiar with the lives of the saints also know that it is often to the most saintly members of the Church that Satan addresses his most subtle temptations.

In a pastoral letter addressed to his clergy in 1870, explaining the background to the events at the First Vatican Council, Cardinal Manning quoted with approval the words of Cardinal Pallavicini that "to convoke a general council, except when absolutely demanded by necessity, is to tempt God".[8] He later adds that: "Each several council was convened to extinguish the chief heresy, or to correct the chief evil, of the time".[9] Cardinal Manning had made the same point in an earlier pastoral and explained as regards ecumenical councils that:

> The first six were convened to condemn heresies, the seventh to condemn the Iconoclasts, the eighth for the cause of Photius, the ninth for the recovery of the Holy Land, the tenth against the claims of anti-popes, the eleventh against the Waldenses, the twelfth against heresies and for the Holy Land, the thirteenth against the usurpation of the Emperor Frederick II, the fourteenth against the errors of the Greeks, the fifteenth against various heresies, the sixteenth for the reunion of the East, the seventeenth for the healing of schisms and for questions of

public law, the eighteenth against the great Lutheran heresy, and for the correction of moral evils.[10]

There can be no doubt at all that atheistic Communism is the chief evil of our own time, but it is an evil which the Council made a particular point of *not* condemning. This is a paradox which will be examined in detail in Chapter XIII.

Needless to say, no matter what the source of inspiration for the Council, once it had been convoked the Holy Ghost would, at the very least, have prevented it from teaching formal heresy in its officially promulgated documents.* Perhaps the influence of the Holy Ghost is most manifest in the fact that the Council differed from its predecessors by being "pastoral" in nature, and in promulgating no infallible doctrinal or moral teaching binding upon the Church. The status of the conciliar documents will be examined in Chapter XII. As will be made clear in this chapter, the fact that these documents contain no formal heresy* by no means implies that they invariably explain the faith in the clearest possible manner or that, indeed, it might not have been far better had the Council never been convoked.

"*A fructibus eorum cognoscetis eos*—By their fruits you shall know them. Do men gather grapes of thorns, or figs of thistles? Even so, every good tree bringeth forth good fruit; and the evil tree bringeth forth evil fruit. A good tree cannot bring forth evil fruit; neither can an evil tree bring forth good fruit" (Mt. 7:16-19). No rational person can deny that up to the present Vatican II has produced no good fruits. The reforms enacted in its name, according to Archbishop Marcel Lefebvre, "have contributed and are still contributing to the demolition of the Church, the ruin of the priesthood, the destruction of the Sacrifice and the sacraments, the disap-

---

* There is an argument that can be made that the expression "formal heresy" cannot be applied to a text but only to a person.

Pope John Is Inspired

pearance of religious life, as well as to the emergence of a naturalist and Teilhardian doctrine in universities, seminaries, the religious education of children—a teaching born of Liberalism and Protestantism, and condemned many times by the Solemn Magisterium of the Church".[11]

Even Pope Paul came to speak in very different terms from those of his opening address to the second session. By 1968 he had reached the stage of lamenting the fact that the Church was engaged in a process of self-destruction (*autodistruzione*.)[12] On the Feast of SS. Peter and Paul, 1972, he went so far as saying that somehow or other Satan himself had found an opening into the Church, where he was spreading doubt, disquiet, and dissatisfaction to the extent that any profane prophet giving vent to his views in a newspaper is listened to with greater care than the Church. "We thought", he complained, "that after the Council there would be a day of sunshine for the history of the Church; instead we found new storms". He continued: "There is uncertainty; people seek to open gulfs rather than to bridge them. How did this happen? We will confide this thought to you—that there was an adverse power, the Devil, whom the Gospel calls the mysterious enemy of man, something preternatural which came to suffocate the fruits of the Vatican Council".

This judgement by the Pope provides a striking justification of an assessment made by James Hitchcock, a disillusioned liberal professor, in a book first published in 1971:

> There are many curiosities in the history of the Church in the post-conciliar years, and not the least is the fact that so few progressives have noticed the extent to which the "reactionaries'" predictions prior to the Council have been proven correct and that their own expectations have been contradicted. They continue to treat the conservatives as ignorant, prejudiced, and out of touch with reality. Yet the progressives' hope for "renewal" now seems

largely chimeric, a grandiose expectation, an attractive theory, but one which failed of achievement. In the heady days of the Council it was common to hear predictions that the conciliar reforms would lead to a massive resurgence of the flagging Catholic spirit. Laymen would be stirred from their apathy and alienation and would join enthusiastically in apostolic projects. Liturgy and theology, having been brought to life and made relevant, would be constant sources of inspiration to the faithful. The religious orders, reformed to bring them into line with modernity, would find themselves overwhelmed with candidates who were generous and enthusiastic. The Church would find the number of converts increasing dramatically as it cast off its moribund visage and indeed would come to be respected and influential in worldly circles as it has not been for centuries. In virtually every case the precise opposite of these predictions has come to pass...in terms of the all pervading spiritual revival which was expected to take place, renewal has obviously been a failure....Little in the Church seems entirely healthy or promising; everything seems vaguely sick and vaguely hollow. No one can predict with any certainty that the Church will have a visible existence by the end of the century.[13]

Let us examine just one of the examples cited by Professor Hitchcock, who tells us that following the Council it was presumed that: "The religious orders, reformed to bring them into line with modernity, would find themselves overwhelmed with candidates who were generous and enthusiastic". The generous and enthusiastic candidates who were to overwhelm the religious orders would, of course, have been their seminarians. The future of any religious order depends on the number of seminarians it attracts to guarantee its future. In 1965 there were 3,559 Jesuit seminarians;

in 2000 there were 389, a decline of 89 per cent. There were 2,251 Franciscan O.F.M. seminarians in 1965; in 2000 there were 60, a decline of 97 per cent. There were 912 Christian Brothers novices in 1965; in 2000 there were 7, a decline of 99 per cent. There were 1,128 Redemptorist seminarians in 1965; in 2000 there were 24, a decline of 98 per cent. The Oblates of Mary Immaculate had 914 seminarians in 1965, in 2000 there were only 13, a decline of 99 per cent. The La Salette Fathers had 552 seminarians in 1965, and only 1 in 2000—a decline of 99 per cent. Every major religious order in the United States mirrors these statistics for seminarians, indicating not an influx of generous and enthusiastic candidates, but that not one of the major religious orders for men has a viable future.[14]

Professor Hitchcock warned that no one could predict with any certainty that the Church would have a visible existence by the end of the twentieth century. That century is now over, and Professor Hitchcock was presumably referring to the Church in the advanced Western countries. It still has a visible existence in those countries, but is declining at an alarming and depressing rate, as will be made clear in Appendix IX. In view of Our Lord's promise that His Church will endure until He comes again, is it possible that, in fact, the Church could disappear in these countries? Father Robert Southard explains:

> The Catholic Church will survive on this planet till the end of time, believing, teaching and practising essentially what Christ wills of her. To guarantee this, He has promised us the abiding presence of the Father, the Holy Spirit and Himself. But we must understand this promise correctly. The Church in this or that particular place can be destroyed. There are limits to Christ's promise. It applies to the Church as a whole, not to every member or parish or diocese; not even to nations as a whole.[15]

In his book *Open Letter to Jesus Christ*, Father Henri Bruckberger, O.P., warns that "the Church can very well find itself reduced to a very small number one day, to a handful of inflexible faithful held in contempt by all, lying in a dungeon. This would still be the Church, Your beloved Spouse, in the midst of the universal apostasy".[16]

It is certainly no exaggeration to claim that the present trend in the West is towards universal apostasy. Two American sociologists, Father Andrew Greeley and William McCready—both liberals—claimed the results of a survey on Catholic life in the U.S.A. since the Council up to 1972 made it clear that "American Catholicism as it was known before 1960 seems to be finished". They found that the decline in Mass attendance had reached "catastrophic proportions" and could think of no other time in the course of human history when so many people—particularly older people—so decisively removed themselves from "canonically required ecclesiastical practices". In questions of doctrine and morality they found Catholics and Protestants are becoming virtually indistinguishable, and that the prospects of a significant proportion of the young continuing to regard themselves as Catholics are remote in the extreme. "The remarkable thing is that no outside foe destroyed us", they remark, "we destroyed ourselves".[17] The pattern described by these sociologists is common, in varying degrees, to most Western countries. A spokesman for the French hierarchy lamented the fact that "France is being swept by a tidal-wave of unbelief".[18] Cardinal Marty conceded that in the years following the Council, up to 1975, Mass attendance in the parish churches of Paris had declined by the staggering figure of 54 per cent.[19] It fell from 41 per cent of the population in France in 1964 to 8 per cent in 2002, and where young people are concerned only 2 per cent now assist at Mass.[20] The decline in vocations has been even more serious—the number of men studying for the priesthood having dropped by 83 per cent between 1963 and 1973.[21] In Great Britain and the United States the decline is equally catastrophic as has been shown above and as will be made clear in Appendix IX. "One does not need to be a prophet to realise that without a dramatic reversal of the present trend there will be no future for the Church in the English-speaking countries", wrote Cardinal Heenan of Westminster in 1972.[22]

In his opening speech to the Council, Pope John had used stern words towards those whom he designated as "prophets of gloom who are always forecasting disaster". He claimed that even the ashes of St. Peter and his other holy predecessors thrilled "in mystic exultation" at his Council which, "now beginning, rises in the Church like daybreak, a forerunner of most splendid light. It is now only dawn". But, as Professor Hitchcock has shown, the predictions of the "reactionaries", Pope John's "prophets of gloom", have been proven correct.

Professor Hitchcock is not alone in this judgement. Father Louis Bouyer is one of the most distinguished living Catholic scholars, and prior to the Council had been regarded as a priest of liberal views. He was a prominent figure in the liturgical movement and had expected great things from the Council, especially from the Liturgy Constitution—as his book *The Liturgy Revived* (1964) makes clear. By 1968 he was completely disillusioned, and published *The Decomposition of Catholicism*, in which he stated: "Unless we are blind, we must even state bluntly that what we see looks less like the hoped-for regeneration of Catholicism than its accelerated decomposition".[23] He reveals that some progressives even hail signs of this decomposition as the first fruits of renewal: "A French weekly which calls itself 'Catholic' went so far recently as to inform us that the post-conciliar renewal had not really penetrated the Spanish Church, using as a criterion the fact that the number of priestly and religious vocations has not decreased very far in that country!"[24] It is hardly surprising that Holland is depicted as being in the forefront of renewal when such criteria are used. In 1957 there were 420 ordinations. By 1971 there was not even one ordination to the secular priesthood, while in the preceding year 271 priests had died and 243 had abandoned their vocations.[25]

In his opening speech to the Council, Pope John had explained that:

> The greatest concern of the Ecumenical Council is this: that the sacred deposit of Christian Doctrine should be guarded and taught more efficaciously…to transmit that doctrine pure and integral, without any attenuation or distortion, which throughout twenty centuries, notwithstanding difficulties and contrasts, has become the common patrimony of men. It is a patrimony not well received by all, but always a rich treasure available to men of good will.[26]

There is no reason to suppose that he was not totally sincere in this aim. "I often wonder" wrote Cardinal Heenan in 1968, "what Pope John would have thought had he been able to foresee that his Council would provide an excuse for rejecting so much of the Catholic doctrine which he wholeheartedly accepted". Pope Paul may have had this in mind when on 3 April 1968 he spoke to an international audience composed largely of students:

> The word of Christ is no longer the truth which never changes, ever living, ever radiant and fruitful, even though at times beyond our understanding. It becomes a partial truth…and is thus deprived of all objective validity and transcendent authority. It will be said that the Council authorised such treatment of traditional teaching. Nothing is more false, if we are to accept the word

Pope John Is Inspired

of Pope John who launched that *aggiornamento* in whose name some dare to impose on Catholic dogma dangerous and sometimes reckless interpretations.[27]

Pope John had hoped that, as a result of his Council, the old truths would be expressed in new ways which, while preserving their essential meaning, would aid the Church in the mission entrusted to her by Christ, of evangelising the world—a world increasingly influenced by secular modes of thought. As Pope Paul conceded in his Opening Speech to the 1967 Synod of Bishops, the opposite has happened:

> We refer to the immense dangers on account of the present age's cast of mind alienated from religion. They are so full of snares, so that in the very bosom of the Church there appear works by several teachers and writers who, while trying to express Catholic doctrine in new ways and forms, often desire rather to accommodate the dogmas of faith to the secular modes of thought and expression than be guided by the norms of the teaching authority of the Church.[28]

This warning against enemies within the Church echoes that of St. Pius X when he condemned Modernism in *Pascendi Gregis.* In this encyclical he wrote of "the partisans of error" who attack the Church "in her very bosom". The key aim of the original Modernists was also, "to accommodate the dogmas of faith to secular modes of thought".[29]

Pope Paul was correct in denying that the Council authorised such treatment of traditional teaching, but the conciliar documents did leave the way open for it. Although he complained that the devil had found an opening which enabled him to enter the Church and suffocate the fruits which should have sprung from Vatican II, it was the Council itself which provided the breach in the ramparts of the

City of God through which the "mysterious enemy of man" wormed his way into "the very bosom" of the Church to initiate the process of decomposition which, as Father Bouyer has observed, is accelerating.

There are a good many sincere and exemplary Catholics who, like the Pope, believe that the paradox of the actual as opposed to the intended fruits of the Council can be solved by making a distinction between the so-called "Spirit of Vatican II" and the conciliar documents themselves. Adherence to these documents, they claim, would have brought about an unprecedented renewal. Once again it must be stressed that a good tree *cannot* bring forth bad fruit. There was no "spirit" of Trent or Vatican I working in a contradictory sense to the expressed intentions of these councils because their documents are *not* open to such an interpretation. No one has been able to misuse Pope Paul's *Mysterium Fidei* (his encyclical on the Eucharist) or his *Credo of the People of God*, as instruments for undermining traditional teaching, because these documents are not open to an unorthodox interpretation.

Professor Van der Ploeg, O.P., a distinguished Dutch biblical scholar, claimed unequivocally that: "The rise of neo-modernism is historically connected with the Second Vatican Council".[30] Dr. Rudolph Graber, Bishop of Regensburg, explained that:

> Certainly the texts are formulated orthodoxly, in places nothing short of classically, and it will be our task for a long time to come to arm ourselves with the words of the Council to fight against its being undermined by the famous "spirit" of the Council. But since the Council was aiming primarily at a pastoral orientation and hence refrained from making dogmatically binding statements or disassociating itself, as previous Church Assemblies had done, from errors and false doctrines by means of

clear anathemas, many questions now took on an opalescent ambivalence which provides a certain amount of justification for those who speak of the spirit of the Council.[31]

This viewpoint was expressed even more strongly by Archbishop Lefebvre, selected by Pope John as a member of the Council's Central Preparatory Commission, and one of the more tireless defenders of orthodoxy during the Council itself: "This Council, then, is not a Council like the others, and for that reason we have a right to judge it prudently and with some reservation. We have no right to say that the crisis through which we are going is wholly unrelated to the Council, that it is simply a misrepresentation of the Council".[32] The Archbishop insists that: "A tree is judged by its fruits".[33] Pope Paul himself admitted that Vatican II was a council that was different in his General Audience of Wednesday, 6 August 1975, when he said: "Differing from other councils, this one was not directly dogmatic but doctrinal and pastoral".

The Church is at present undergoing what must certainly be her worst crisis since the Arian heresy. There is hardly an aspect of traditional Catholic dogma, morality, or practice which has not been questioned, ridiculed, or contradicted "within the bosom of the Church". The liturgy above all has been reduced to a condition which varies from banality to outright profanity and sacrilege. The question to be answered is whether these are the fruits of the Council itself, not the fruits which the majority of the Fathers intended or even expected but, nevertheless, the direct result of the Council. Is there, in fact, a causal connection between Vatican II and the so-called "Spirit of Vatican II", as Archbishop Lefebvre, Bishop Graber, and Father Van der Ploeg claim? In order to show that "the rise of neo-modernism is historically connected" with the Council, that the documents themselves contain that "opalescent ambivalence" which justified "those who speak of the 'spirit' of the Council", it is necessary to study not only the documents themselves, but the manner in which they were formulated. Such a study will reveal that it was Pope John's Council itself which, as Cardinal Heenan put it, "provided an excuse for rejecting so much of the Catholic doctrine which he wholeheartedly accepted".

Although, perhaps mercifully, Pope John did not live to see the full extent of the devastation in the Lord's vineyard initiated by his Council, there can be no doubt that he had lost most of his illusions before his death between the first and second sessions. Cardinal Heenan made this clear in the second volume of his own autobiography. He explained that Pope John could not possibly have foreseen the results of his decision to hold a council, and that he did not fully appreciate the significance of the events he was setting in motion.[34] According to the Cardinal, most of the Council Fathers shared the Pope's illusion that they "had come together as brothers in Christ for a short convivial meeting. Pope John and the Fathers were quickly brought to a sense of reality".[35] The Pope had "imagined the Council as a glorified synod of Rome which would provide the bishops with the chance of reunion in the home of their common father. Pope John saw the Council as an episcopal safari".[36] However, the Cardinal explains that before the end of the first session, "He (Pope John) must have thought of his Council less like a safari than a siege".[37]

When Pope Paul gave his annual address to Rome's Lenten preachers on 2 March 1976 he came closer than ever before to conceding that it was indeed the Council which had initiated the process of devastation in the vineyard of the Lord.[38] While insisting that the Council had "perfected the doctrine on the Church to such an extent as not to leave any hesitation about the identity of her theological mystery" he also referred to the fact that it had brought forth "sources of new and inexhaustible beauty". It is in this "newness" that the Pope located the origin of the two "temptations" which are tearing the Church apart today—one leading to Protestantism and the other to Marxism. "This same newness seems to have fostered the outbreak of doubts and restlessness that the legacy of contestation of the Reformation had deposited in the subconscious of some scholars and not a few faithful". This is a very precise description of the effect the Council has had upon the Church, and one which will be returned to frequently throughout this book. The evils which are rampant in the post-conciliar Church existed beneath the surface in the pre-conciliar Church. The temptations of Protestantism and Marxism, to which the Pope refers, together with that of Modernism, lay in the subconscious of many Catholics, particularly in the countries bordering upon the Rhine. In others it had passed the subconscious stage and they were simply biding their time. The Council created the conditions which enabled these tendencies to surface, to be proclaimed with arrogance, and codified as a new orthodoxy.

The Pope warned the Lenten preachers that the first temptation (to Protestantism) "has shaken the community cohesion of the Church". He continued:

> It has questioned the system of her authority, it has weakened the brotherly and filial obedience characteristic of Catholic morals, it has fostered an ambiguous pluralism, often similar to private judgement, disintegrating the unity of faith, morality and discipline. The other temptation (towards Marxism) has given preference to the horizontal, that is the temporal and social view of our religion, over the vertical and global one, and it has sometimes thought that it could make the Christian profession effective by inserting the class struggle in the

exercise of charity and brotherhood—in fact even preferring it—as an irreplaceable energy, derived from an inevitable and selfish economic necessity, supported by a partial materialistic rationality.

Although year by year throughout the pontificate of Pope John Paul II, every aspect of Catholic life in the Western world subject to statistical verification showed a consistent and abysmal decline, Pope John Paul II refused to accept that the Second Vatican Council has been anything but an unqualified success and a great blessing for the Church. In his sermon for Pentecost 2001, he rendered homage to Pope John XXIII on the occasion of the thirty-eighth anniversary of his death:

> The Second Vatican Council, announced, convoked, and opened by Pope John XXIII, was conscious of this vocation of the Church. One can well say that the Holy Spirit was the protagonist of the Council from the moment the Pope convoked it, declaring that he had welcomed as coming from above an interior voice that imposed itself upon his spirit. This "gentle breeze" became a "violent wind" and the conciliar event took the form of a new Pentecost. "It is, indeed, in the doctrine and spirit of Pentecost", affirmed Pope John, "that the great event which is an ecumenical council draws its substance and its life".[39]

On 5 March 2000, *The Catholic Times* (London) reported Pope John Paul II as stating that the little seed planted by Pope John XXIII has become "a tree which has spread its majestic and mighty branches over the vineyard of the Lord". He added that: "It has given us many fruits in these thirty-five years of life, and it will give us many more in the years to come".

Pope John Is Inspired

With all the respect that is due to the Vicar of Christ, the fact that there has been no renewal cannot be changed simply because he would like a renewal to have taken place. If the fruits of Vatican II are to be compared to a tree, Matthew Chapter 7, verses 16-19, which has already been cited, comes to mind immediately: *"A fructibus eorum cognoscetis eos*—By their fruits you shall know them".

Cardinal Joseph Ratzinger takes a very different view of the fruits of the Council than the Pope he has served so loyally, and he has had the courage and integrity to make his views public. In a statement published in the 24 December 1984 English edition of *L'Osservatore Romano,* he wrote:

> Certainly the results (of Vatican II) seem cruelly opposed to the expectations of everyone, beginning with those of Pope John XXIII and then of Pope Paul VI: expected was a new Catholic unity and instead we have been exposed to dissension which, to use the words of Pope Paul VI, seem to have gone from self-criticism to self-destruction. Expected was a new enthusiasm, and many wound up discouraged and bored. Expected was a great step forward, instead we find ourselves faced with a progressive process of decadence which has developed for the most part under the sign of a calling back to the Council, and has therefore contributed to discrediting it for many. The net result therefore seems negative. I am repeating here what I said ten years after the conclusion of the work: *it is incontrovertible that this period has definitely been unfavourable for the Catholic Church* [my emphasis].

In his opening speech to the Council in 1962 Pope John XXIII has already been cited as describing his council as a new dawn for the Church, rising, he claimed, like daybreak, "a forerunner of most splendid light". Did that "most splendid light" actually appear to dazzle the world with its brilliance? The answer can be found in the Autumn 1997 issue of the excellent American journal, *The Latin Mass*, which contains an interesting anecdote related by a deacon who had been teaching in a high school in the United States. He was somewhat surprised when a pupil approached him one day after class and said, "Sir, what exactly was the aim of Vatican II?" The deacon gave what he thought was a very good answer, one which he was sure would have pleased Pope John XXIII. "Aggiornamento," he explained, "was the purpose—to bring the Church up to date, but not in the sense that the Church wanted to make itself like the modern world, but to find better ways of preaching the Gospel in the modern world". The deacon was somewhat disconcerted when the pupil pondered for a few moments, and then replied, "Sir, it didn't work, did it?"

Notes

[1] Apostolic Letter *Rubricarum Instructum*, 25 July 1960.
[2] For an explanation of the term "definition" see Chapter XII. It is important to realise that only the definitions of general councils are binding upon the faithful.
[3] XR-1, p. 1.
[4] Apostolic Constitution *Humanae Salutis*, 25 December 1961, convoking the Second Vatican Council. Abbott, p. 705.
[5] Opening Speech to the Council, 11 October 1962, Abbott, pp. 711-12.
[6] XR-1, p. 2.
[7] XR-2, p. 349.
[8] PP, III, p. 24.
[9] PP, III, p. 35.
[10] PP, II, pp. 80-81.
[11] Declaration of 21 November 1974. See *Apologia* I, pp. 38-40.
[12] *L'Osservatore Romano*, 8 December 1968.
[13] DFRC, pp. 22-23.
[14] K. C. Jones, *Index of Leading Catholic Indicators: The Church Since Vatican II* (St. Louis, 2003), pp. 83-101.
[15] *Homiletic and Pastoral Review*, April 1974, p. 32.
[16] *Lettre ouverte à Jésus-Christ* (Paris, 1973), p. 45.
[17] *America*, 28 October 1972.
[18] *The Universe*, 19 January 1973.
[19] *The Tablet*, 11 October 1975, p. 978.
[20] *La Croix*, 24 and 25 December 2002. The same report reveals

the alarming facts that in 1962, 52 per cent of priests were under 50 years of age. In 2000 it was only 11 per cent. In 1960, 595 priests were ordained. In 2000 the figure was 142.
21. Report issued by the French National Centre for Vocations and cited in the *Irish Catholic* of 20 March 1975.
22. *Times Literary Supplement*, 22 December 1972.
23. *The Decomposition of Catholicism*, English edition (Chicago: Franciscan Herald Press, 1969), p. 1.
24. DC, p. 2.
25. *Christian Order*, May 1973, p. 281.
26. Abbott, pp. 713, 715.
27. *The Tablet*, 18 May 1968, p. 489.
28. *Ibid.*, 7 October 1967, p. 1036.
29. PG, pp. 13, 14, 22, 23, 31.
30. *Catholic Priests' Association Newsletter*, Vol. III, 1973, p. 15.
31. ACT, p. 66.
32. ABS, p. 137.
33. *Ibid.*, p. 71.
34. CT, p. 352.
35. *Ibid.*, p. 343.
36. *Ibid.*, p. 354.
37. *Ibid.*
38. *L'Osservatore Romano* (English edition), 25 March 1976, p. 3.
39. *Documentation Catholique*, 1 July 2001, No. 2251.

II

The Church Before the Council

Despite the abysmal state of the post-conciliar Church, which should be evident to anyone with eyes to see and ears to hear, there are still those who claim that we are living in a period of exhilarating renewal in happy contrast with the moribund Church of pre-conciliar days. It seems that even in this age of sophisticated and instant communication there is still truth in the old saying: there are none so blind as those who will not see. Thus, in an editorial published on Friday, 2 April 1976, the London *Universe* was able to proclaim that "the Holy Father is leading the Church forward to a new age of spirituality" and to reproach Archbishop Lefebvre for his "refusal to move forward with the Church of the seventies". It would have been interesting had the editor of *The Universe* added a few words on precisely where he thought the Church of the seventies was moving. He clearly considered that his paper was in the vanguard of this movement, and this is something with which no one could disagree. *The Universe* had a weekly circulation of 311,512 in 1963, which had declined to 61,000 by 2003—a decrease of 81 per cent.

However, those Catholics who are old enough to remember the unrenewed Church will agree wholeheartedly with the comments made by one Council Father during the debate on collegiality. Patriarch Ignace Pierre XVI Batanian,

Pope John's Council

Armenian Patriarch of Cilicia, insisted that a tree must be judged by its fruits and added that "the Church, notwithstanding the calamities that plague the world, is experiencing a glorious era, if you consider the Christian life of the clergy and of the faithful, the propagation of the faith, and the salutary universal influence possessed by the Church in the world today".[1] Pope John XXIII most certainly did not believe the Church to be in any sort of decline when he convoked the Council. Indeed, when he issued his apostolic constitution *Humanae Salutis* convoking Vatican II, he made a special point of paying tribute to the vitality of the Church as it then existed. "It has", he said, "followed step by step the evolution of peoples, scientific progress, and social revolution".

> It has opposed decisively the materialistic ideologies which deny faith. Lastly, it has witnessed the rise and growth of the immense energies of the apostolate of prayer, of action in all fields. It has seen the emergence of a clergy constantly better equipped in learning and virtue for its mission; and of a laity which has become ever more conscious of its responsibilities within the bosom of the Church, and, in a special way, of its duty to collaborate with the Church hierarchy. To this should be added the immense suffering of entire Christian communities, through which a multitude of admirable bishops, priests, and laymen seal their adherence to the faith, bearing persecutions of all kinds and revealing forms of heroism which certainly equal those of the most glorious periods of the Church.[2]

When Pope John wrote this in 1961 who could have imagined that his Council would be prevented from condemning atheistic Communism, which was responsible for this immense suffering?—and prevented from condemning it by a process of calculated fraud perpetrated by some of its members, an incident which will be fully documented in Chapter XIII.

In the same apostolic constitution, Pope John pointed out the contrast between "a world which reveals a grave state of spiritual poverty and the Church of Christ, which is still so vibrant with vitality". A Church vibrant with vitality in 1961, according to Pope John XXIII, and a Church in a process of self-destruction in 1968, according to Pope Paul VI. Who would have believed that a debacle of such proportions could occur in so short a time? The Arian and Protestant heresies were gradual processes compared with this. The answer can only be found, as Pope Paul claimed, by the entry of the enemy of man into the Church, an entry which the Prince of this world made through the window to the world opened by Pope John. "I am certain", remarked Cardinal Felici, Secretary General to the Council, "that when in the Council I pronounced the ritual words *'Exeant Omnes'* (Everyone out), which all remember, one who did not obey was the devil....He is always where confusion triumphs, to stir it up and take advantage of it".[3]

It is fashionable for Catholic liberals to decry the pre-conciliar Church as concerned with little more than personal piety, and completely indifferent to injustice and suffering in the world. This is a monstrous travesty of the truth as every adult Catholic must surely know. Never in the history of our planet has so much concern been shown for the material needs of all humanity as that displayed by the Catholic Church in the twentieth century. All over the world selfless priests, members of religious orders, and lay Catholics had established countless schools, hospitals, orphanages, homes for old people; wherever need existed, Catholic relief agencies could be found ministering to the hungry, the homeless, the victims of famine, pestilence, or earthquakes. But in the pre-conciliar Church there was never any confusion about what the prime duty of the Church was—to preach the Kingdom of God—and when the Kingdom of God is preached all else will follow. There can be no doubt that the service rendered to the material needs of men, incalculable though this most certainly was, pales into insignificance beside the spiritual solace brought by the Church to hundreds of millions of men and women of all races and all nations: the beauty and comfort of her liturgy, the grace of her sacraments, the inspiration of her teaching—these gave meaning to a life which for millions would otherwise have been meaningless; they gave the strength to endure a life that would otherwise have been unendurable. And above all, the Church was concerned with the truth, the truth that is Christ, the truth that is His Gospel, the truth that we have a Father in heaven Who loves us, Who sent His Son to die for us so that we can live with Him forever in the happiness of heaven

It would, however, be wrong to portray the pre-conciliar Church as devoid of any fault. Dietrich von Hildebrand was most certainly one of the greatest lay-theologians and philosophers of the twentieth century, certainly the greatest in the English-speaking world. He was, in fact, described by Pope Pius XII as *the* twentieth-century doctor of the Church. In 1965 he wrote *Trojan Horse in the City of God*, which was the first detailed critique to appear in English of the sickness which had infected the Church after the Council and initiated the process of decomposition. Dr. von Hildebrand's book remains a primary source for those concerned at what is happening to the Church and is invaluable not only for its diagnosis of what is wrong in the Church today, but for the extent of its positive teaching and its evocation of the true Catholic ethos. Not only is no attempt made to hide the fact that the pre-conciliar Church did have faults, but some of the more important ones are analyzed in great depth. As Dr. von Hildebrand shows, these deficiencies generally involved some valid aspect of the faith which had been exaggerated to the point where a redress of balance was needed. He writes:

> There certainly were many abuses of authority in religious orders and seminaries which led to a depersonalization of religious life and sometimes even to a blunting of conscience. By making formal obedience the most important virtue, by blurring the essential difference between moral virtues and mere disciplinary correctness, by over-emphasising things which, because of the *parvitas materiae*, were trivial, those in authority produced a state of affairs in which the personality of the religious or seminarian was in danger of being emptied and in which the sense of a hierarchy of values was almost inevitably deadened.

He explains that only something which has value can be abused, and that under no circumstances can an abuse be corrected by abolishing whatever it is of value that is being abused. The liberal Catholic has, he shows, made the correction worse than the abuse by doing "away with sacred authority and holy obedience" and failing "to grasp the meaning and beauty of holy obedience, the inner freedom which it bestows on the obedient, the glorious self-donation it implies".[4]

The extent of this devalued concept of obedience before the Council is reflected in the almost total lack of resistance on the part of priests and religious to the revolution imposed upon the Church in the name of Vatican II. Those who had initiated the revolution were only too well aware of the fact that, provided their innovations could be imposed from above, they could expect to encounter very little effective opposition from priests and religious, and this meant virtually no opposition at all. This in itself highlights another defect of the pre-conciliar Church, its all-pervasive clerical dominance. The prevailing attitude was that the role of the laity was to follow whatever lead the clergy gave them—and only too often in the history of the Church the lead given by the clergy, the higher clergy in particular, has been to heresy and apostasy, something made clear during the Arian heresy and the English Reformation. It is now only too apparent that very few laymen realised that every individual Catholic has a duty derived from his baptism and confirmation to uphold the faith; and that upholding the faith does not consist simply of behaving as an automaton programmed to carry out any and every clerical command. The same is true of rank and file priests and religious with regard to their superiors. Monsignor Lefebvre considered that:

> Satan's masterstroke is to have succeeded in sowing disobedience to all Tradition through obedience. The most typical example of these established facts is that of the *aggiornamento* of the religious orders. Through obedience, monks and nuns are made to disobey the rules and constitutions laid down by their founders, laws which they swore at their profession to obey. Here comes the profound disorder which reigns in the bosom of these societies and in the bosom of the Church. Obedience in this case should be a categorical refusal. Authority, even a legitimate authority, cannot command a bad and reprehensible act. No one can force us to transmute our vows into simple promises. No one can force us to become Protestants or Modernists. The results of such blindness are tragically clear. [5]

The prevailing attitude among so many of the clergy is to accept a particular belief or practice, not because it has an inherent and enduring truth or value, but because it happens to be the current policy. Thus the very clergy who would have denounced (and rightly so) any layman who had attended a Protestant service before the Council, will now denounce any layman who suggests that the faith could be in any way compromised by attending such services. Attendance at Protestant services, although a matter of discipline, most certainly involves vital doctrinal principles. Thus a matter touching upon the very nature of the Church Christ founded is seen in itself as something neutral; all that matters is the current instruction issued by whoever is one rank higher up the hierarchical scale. Needless to say, these remarks apply to the more conservative and orthodox priests and laity—the liberals, true to the essence of liberalism, never have the least qualm at doing what seems best to them at the time.

There was also a definite need for a widespread liturgical renewal in the pre-conciliar Church—but a renewal on the lines advocated by the liturgical movement approved by Pope St. Pius X. The pseudo-renewal which has followed Vatican II has nothing in common with the authentic spirit of the papally approved liturgical movement, as Father Louis Bouyer, one of its leading advocates, has testified.[6] True liturgical renewal would not have involved discarding the traditional liturgy to be replaced by a continually evolving and ecumenically inspired series of gimmicks; it would have involved utilising the existing liturgy to its fullest potential, and this potential was infinite.

In a parish where the liturgy came alive the parish came alive. In Mesnil St. Loup in France, for example, between the years 1849 and 1903, the saintly Père Emmanuel transformed his parish into what could truly be described as a religious community, mainly through bringing his people to know, to love, and to play their proper part in the liturgy—above all by the use of Gregorian chant. If Père Emmanuel's peasant parishioners could sing Latin vespers in their church each evening—joyfully and easily—then any parish could have done the same. If such parishes had been the rule rather than the only too rare exception, then the history not only of the Church but of the world would have been different.

What has been written here with regard to the need for liturgical renewal in no way conflicts with the reference to the beauty and dignity of the pre-conciliar liturgy made earlier in this chapter. While there were some cases of priests who tended to "gabble" their Mass in a manner which made it unedifying, the majority conformed to the rubrics and this, in view of the nature of the traditional Mass, made it impossible for it not to be an impressive and inspiring ceremony. I well remember how, as a convert with wide experience of very vocal and emotional evangelical Protestant services, as well as several varieties of Anglican liturgy, the first experience of real *worship* that I encountered was at a low Mass in a working class parish. Only the server made the responses in the packed church, few present had a missal, but the atmosphere of reverence and, at the consecration, of palpable adoration was something which I had never experienced before and which I shall never forget. But at the same time it must be admitted that the liturgical life of most of these worshippers would have been confined to attendance at one such low Mass each week—and when the endless riches offered to them in the liturgical treasury of the Church are considered, this was clearly a state of affairs open to a great deal of improvement.

Finally, when considering the state of the Church before the Council, mention must be made of the Modernist fifth column, the "pernicious adversaries" condemned by St. Pius X in his encyclical *Pascendi Gregis*, men lodged within the "very bosom" of the Church, determined to destroy her "vital energy" and "utterly to subvert the very Kingdom of Christ". Much will be written of these pernicious adversaries during the course of this book, adversaries whose advance St. Pius X and his successors had been able to contain, but whose presence they had been unable to eliminate from the Mystical Body within which, like some malignant virus, they waited for the right conditions to enable them to proliferate and infect the entire organism. Before the Council the Church was, indeed, as Pope John claimed, "vibrant with vitality"; there are few signs of vitality in the decomposing body of the post-conciliar Church—but the forces which drained her vitality away existed long before the Council created the climate which enabled them to launch the attack which has come near to destroying the "vital energy" of the Church, in the Western countries at least.

Those who have read Dr. von Hildebrand's *Trojan Horse in the City of God*, one of the small number of books which every concerned Catholic should own, will find that he makes a distinction between the official documents of the Council and the so-called "Spirit of Vatican II". He says a great deal in praise of the Council itself, its aims, and its documents. However, as his book was written in 1965 such an attitude is hardly surprising. In my own case, the realisation that not only the Council itself as an event, but even its official documents, cannot be absolved from responsibility for the present deplorable state of the Church, did not come until 1972 when I read the Abbé de Nantes's very radical criticisms of the conciliar texts.[7] Until this point, as I could prove by citing many articles and pamphlets, that, like Dr. von Hildebrand, I had always taken the line that the Council documents were beyond reproach and that the present chaos was the result of their being contradicted or ignored. Indeed, it was with the object of establishing, if only for my own benefit, that the criticisms made by the Abbé de Nantes could not be justified, that I began to study the documents more closely, and one can hardly deny that he made it quite clear that these documents are most certainly far from being the irreproachable and even sublime restatement of Catholic truth which so many of us had at first taken them to be. This view was confirmed when I had the good fortune to obtain a copy of Father Wiltgen's book *The Rhine Flows into the Tiber*. When I read Father Wiltgen's book in 1973, and discovered the background to the formulation of the Council texts, a clear pattern began to emerge, a definite and logical progression from the circumstances in which the documents were formulated, the documents themselves, and the events which followed the Council.

In view of the manner in which my own enthusiasm for the Council had been modified, I wrote to Dr. von Hildebrand and asked him if his own views had undergone any changes, particularly with regard to such instances as his praise for the official documents and "the greatness of the Second Vatican Council" found on page one of his book. He informed me that he had indeed greatly modified his views concerning the documents of the Second Vatican Council, and that while there are still certain points in them which he welcomes, though only a few, a more detailed study has revealed that such harmful tendencies as horizontalism, communitarianism, and false ecumenism can be detected in some of the documents. This was not apparent to him in 1965 when he wrote his book, and it would have been hard not to react positively to the official documents when contrasting them with the deplorable books, articles, and lectures of priests and theologians who claimed to be interpreting the "Spirit of the Council". Dr. von Hildebrand authorised me to mention the fact that he modified his opinion concerning Vatican II. His letter, dated 22 April 1976, reads as follows:

> Dear Friend in Christ,
> I was very pleased about your words concerning my position toward the documents of Vatican Council II. I consider the Council—notwithstanding the fact that

it brought some ameliorations—as a great misfortune. And I stress time and again in lectures and articles that fortunately no word of the Council—unless it is a repetition of former definitions *de fide*—is binding *de fide*. We need not approve—on the contrary we should disapprove. Unfortunately, Maritain said in his last book: the two great manifestations of the Holy Spirit in our times are Vatican Council II and the foundation of the state of Israel.

I read the chapter of your book and I am completely satisfied.

Hoping to meet you some day, I am united with you in *caritate Christi* and in the fight against Modernism.

Yours affectionately,

Dietrich von Hildebrand.

Monsignor George A. Kelly is one of America's best known writers on Catholic issues. He is author of more than twenty-five books and Director of the Institute of Advanced Studies in Catholic Doctrine at St. John's University, New York. His book *The Battle for the American Church* provides invaluable documentation on the state of the Church before the Council in the United States, which closely resembled that of the Church in all English-speaking countries The title of his book shows that he is under no illusion as to the fact that what is taking place within Catholicism at present; it is nothing less than total war.[8]

Monsignor Kelly documents the transformation of a relatively small Church in the United States, composed in the main of underprivileged immigrants, to the most important and influential religious body in that country. By 1950 there were 60,000 priests with 25,000 seminarians in training and 150,000 religious educating 5,000,000 youth in Catholic schools from kindergarten to university with 5,000,000 more young people under catechetical instruction.[9]

What kind of Catholics were they? The first large census study in Florida of 50,000 American Catholics (completed in 1944) indicates that the Catholicisation process that had begun one century earlier was complete. The religious behaviour of Catholics matched the Church's highest expectations: 75 per cent of married Catholics attended Mass every Sunday; 50 per cent received Communion at least monthly; 85 per cent made their Easter duty; 85 per cent of the single people went to Mass every Sunday regardless of whether they were 19, 29, 39, 49, or over; 50 per cent of the single people received Communion monthly regardless of age. The college-educated Catholics were more regular in Mass attendance than anyone else, went to Communion more often, and had the largest families.[10] Monsignor Kelly produces other statistics to illustrate the progress of American Catholicism before Vatican II; for example, what can only be described as the explosion of the Catholic School system. In the Diocese of Chicago alone, school enrolment rose from 120,000 in 1913 to 427,000 in 1960, and in New York for the same period from 111,000 to 352,000.[11]

The overwhelming majority of the Catholic people had been reached effectively by the Church's manifold structures. They were practising Catholics. The leaders of the Church—bishops, priests, religious, lay apostles—won the loyalty of the great majority of Catholics in major matters involving Catholic doctrine and Church policy. The institutional Church also presided over the emergence of a Catholic elite—mainly through its colleges, seminaries, and lay apostolic movements for social justice, international peace, family life, and spiritual perfection. These movements owed their existence to the impetus given them by the Holy See from Leo XIII onwards. As a *tour de force* by a religious group, the institutional and community accomplishments

The Church Before the Council

of the American Church were unsurpassed in Catholic history. [12]

The author then placed the reality of the alleged postconciliar renewal before us: by 1976 as many as 10,000,000 Catholics stopped regular attendance at Sunday Mass—a 30 per cent decline. (In some metropolitan archdioceses only 30 per cent of the Catholic population goes to Mass every Sunday.) The declines were more severe among the young, including those receiving a complete Catholic education, and surprisingly among middle-class women in the middle years of life, who hitherto were exemplars of Catholic piety. A once-proud Catholic school system was down almost 2,000,000 in enrolment. The number of babies baptised had dropped by almost 500,000. There were almost 50,000 fewer converts.[13] Catholic attitudes toward the Church and its teaching had radically changed. From remarkable conformity in belief and practice, researchers in 1976 found that three out of four Catholics approved sexual intercourse for engaged couples; eight out of ten approved of contraception; seven out of ten approved of legalised abortion; four out of ten did not think the Pope is infallible.[14]

No Catholic who loves his Church, because it is the one ark of salvation founded by Our Lord Jesus Christ to perpetuate His saving presence in the world, can read such statistics without profound sorrow, and it will be made clear in Appendix IX that since 1979 the collapse of every aspect of Catholic life subject to statistical verification has accelerated in the most disastrous manner. The disintegration of the Church in the United States is not an isolated phenomenon. The collapse has been far more extensive in France and Holland, and the same pattern is found in such countries as Germany, Belgium, Great Britain, Australia and New Zealand. Monsignor Kelly began his book by stating:

A guerilla-type warfare is going on inside the Church, and its outcome is clearly doubtful. The Pope and the Roman Curia are fending off with mixed success the attacks of their own theologians who, in the name of scholarship, demand more radical accommodation with Protestant and secular thought. The issues at stake are the correctness of Catholic doctrine and the survival of the Catholic Church as a significant influence in the life of her own communicants....The Catholic Church gives the clearest example of what happens to a public institution when someone tampers with its basic tenets.[15]

This, then, is what the battle is about—it is a battle for the survival of the Catholic Church in the West. Our Lord promised that the gates of Hell would not prevail against His Church, but he did not guarantee its survival in any country or group of countries—witness North Africa or Scandinavia. The situation has been reached where, in fact, it is those who wish to uphold orthodoxy who are the guerillas fighting an uphill battle against a powerfully entrenched liberal Establishment.

Notes

[1] RFT, p. 113.
[2] Apostolic Constitution *Humanae Salutis*, 25 December 1961. Abbott, p. 703.
[3] Radio interview on the tenth anniversary of the Council, cited in *The Laity* (New Delhi, 1973), p. 45.
[4] *Trojan Horse in the City of God* (Chicago, 1969), pp. 30-31.
[5] ABS, p. 103.
[6] DC, p. 99.
[7] *Contre Réforme Catholique* (10260 St-Parres-les-Vaudes, France), French edition: Numbers 51 to 61 inclusive; English edition, No. 22 and subsequent editions.
[8] G. Kelly, *The Battle for the American Church* (New York: Doubleday, 1979).
[9] BAC, p. 455.
[10] *Ibid.*
[11] *Ibid.*
[12] *Ibid.*, 456.
[13] *Ibid.*, pp. 456-57.
[14] *Ibid.*, p. 457.
[15] *Ibid.*, p, vii.

III

Blitzkrieg

Many of the Council Fathers, perhaps most, arrived in Rome for the first session of Vatican II without any clear idea as to why they were there, and without any definite plan as to what they intended to achieve. They could well have sung, as did the British troops who found themselves in France in 1914, "We're here because we're here because we're here!"

"Looking back", writes Cardinal Heenan, "it is easy to see how psychologically unprepared bishops were for what happened during the first session. Most of us arrived in Rome in October 1962 without any idea of the anti-Italian mood of many Europeans....The conciliar Fathers for the most part shared Pope John's illusion that the bishops of the world had come together as brothers in Christ for a short convivial meeting".[1]

Bishop Lucey of Cork and Ross (Ireland) wrote that certain "hierarchies came to the Council knowing what they wanted and having prepared a way to get it, others came feeling their way".[2] Prominent among those who knew what they wanted were the German-speaking, Dutch, and French hierarchies. Xavier Rynne, who reported on the Council for the *New Yorker*, notes with satisfaction that before the Council had even been announced, there had been pressure in these countries

> for a modernization of the way in which the Church faces its internal problems. Some groups were openly agitating for a reorganization, if not abolition, of the Roman Curia. Others wanted changes in the laws and regulations affecting marriage and education, the Mass, the sacraments, liturgical ceremonies, the inquisitorial and condemnatory procedures of the Holy Office, clerical dress, and the unseemly pomp of prelatial vestiture and a redefinition of the rights and prerogatives of bishops and laymen in the Church's structure.[3]

The extent to which these aims have now been achieved is the most evident fact of life in the post-conciliar Church. Indeed, the ease with which total victory was achieved surprised even the progressives themselves. To quote Xavier Rynne again: "They had come to the first session of the Council hoping that they might win some concessions. They returned home conscious that they had obtained complete victory. And they were confident that numberless other victories were yet to come".[4]

In an address to the U.S. Bishops' Press Panel, at the end of the first session, Father Hans Küng, the Swiss *peritus* (expert), "asserted jubilantly that what had once been the dream of an *avant-garde* group in the Church had 'spread and permeated the entire atmosphere of the Church due to the Council'".[5]

A key aim of the European *avant-garde* (obsession might be a more accurate word) had been to replace the true concept of Catholic ecumenism, as laid down by Pope Pius XI in *Mortalium Animos*, with a policy of "unity at any price". The atmosphere in Germany as the Council began was well summed up in a letter to *The Tablet* by Father F. J. Ripley, one of England's best-known priests. He warned against "the desire now manifest in Germany to present the Catholic mysteries in terms traditionally associated with Protestantism", and continued:

> Many visitors to Germany recently have been shocked by certain elements of the new approach. An eminent Australian asked a parish priest how he encouraged his people to visit the Blessed Sacrament since he had removed it from the high altar to an obscure side-chapel. "I don't", he said. All who have spoken to me after visits to Germany have been, to express it very mildly, disturbed by what they saw there. As another priest put it: "They are talking about sweeping away useless accretions to the liturgy; but they are in reality attacking perfectly legitimate developments which have meant much to the piety of the faithful. Pius XII warned against this very thing in *Mediator Dei*".
>
> Yet another visitor, an American priest, summed up his impression of Catholic scholarship in Germany like this: "I guess they're waging a total war against tradition". Nor is it confined to the liturgy. Some speak of "the tragic definition of the Assumption", which came perilously near to being the "death blow of the Ecumenical Movement". Others want us to drop reference to tradition as a source of revelation. And alongside all this is a calculated refusal to try to make individual converts on the excuse that conversion work will impede progress towards unity—again a practical reversal of the policy of the Church since apostolic times.[6]

It is important to note that this letter was published in 1962, and was not written with the benefit of hindsight. It is hardly necessary to point out the extent to which the situation which Father Ripley described as existing in Germany in 1962 has spread throughout the West since the Council, and practices which he then criticised as aberrations are now recommended to us by the Vatican. The 1969 General Instruction to the new Mass recommended "that the Blessed Sacrament be reserved in a special chapel well suited for private prayer".[7] In certain respects England could now claim to have stolen a march on the Germans as Catholics and Anglicans not only share the same churches in some places but even a common tabernacle.

Cardinal Heenan has explained how completely unaware the British and American bishops were of the extent to which so many of their European counterparts had been infected by what he later termed "ecumania". He writes:

> We did not know what the Dutch were thinking and were quite unprepared for the later discovery that some Dutch Catholics had made almost a religion of ecumenism. Impatient of any dogmatic differences, they were ready to barter any doctrine in the cause of external unity. When the Secretariat for Christian Unity was first set up, there were not less than four members from Holland. This did not seem significant at the time, because the rest of the Church was unaware of the vast religious change in Holland since the war.
>
> Looking back, it is quite clear that the English-speaking bishops were quite unprepared for the kind of council the rest of the northern Europeans were planning. The Americans were even less prepared than the British. They made no contribution at all to the first session, which was largely a probing battle between the old and the new theological ideas.[8]

It will soon become clear that Cardinal Heenan's warlike metaphor was well chosen—for a battle did take place. In a review of one of the first books to appear on the Council, one English Father, Abbot (later Bishop) Butler, criticised it for failing "to convey to one who was not present at those fateful debates the passion of the drama that was being enacted in them".[9] Dr. John Moorman, leader of the Anglican delegation, affirmed that those in the "observers' box" were aware that during the Council "there was a very real division among the Fathers, a deep feeling that two big forces were coming to grips and that this was not just a clash of opinions but of policies and even of moralities".[10]

The tactic used by the Germans and their allies can best be described by comparing it with a technique which they introduced into military warfare, that of the *Blitzkrieg*. Time and again they shattered and demoralised their opponents by the efficient use of the pressure group methods used in political takeovers. It is doubtful whether any hierarchy but the German would have had the efficiency, the organization, and the resources necessary to initiate and sustain such a campaign. It will be shown in Chapter V that the proponents of neo-modernism, referred to by Pope Paul in Chapter I, were found principally among the *periti* (experts) rather than among the bishops themselves. The conciliar documents were not so much the work of the bishops, who voted for them, as of the experts who prepared them, and as whose mouthpieces so many of the bishops were contented to act. Some of these *periti* had been under suspicion of unorthodoxy during the reign of Pope Pius XII. His encyclical *Humani Generis* shows how clearly this great pontiff appreciated the growing strength and menace of the neo-modernist fifth column within the Church. Many of the *periti* have become notorious since the Council for their opposition to Catholic teaching on various points of faith and morals, men such as Charles Davis (who has formally apostatised), Hans Küng, Gregory Baum, Edward Schillebeeckx, and Bernard Häring.

Another factor of great importance in assessing the conduct of most Council Fathers is that probably the majority of those who supported the German bishops did so because it seemed the fashionable thing to do, because everyone else seemed to be taking this line. There was once a popular song entitled *Everybody's doing it*! When everybody is doing it the normal reaction is to do it too; and even those who have been consecrated as bishops remain only too human in many respects—as any Church historian will confirm. If a bandwagon begins to roll along, it takes great strength of character to refrain from leaping upon it. "When the vote came round", wrote Archbishop Dwyer of Portland, Oregon, an American Father, wise after the event, "like wise Sir Joseph Porter, KCB, 'We always voted at our party's call; we never thought of thinking for ourselves at all'. That way you can save yourself a world of trouble".[11]

On the other hand, it would be unrealistic not to recognise the fact that there must have been some Council Fathers well aware of the direction the policies they advocated would take the Church, and who were happy to co-operate with the *periti* because they shared the same theological outlook. The "business sessions" of the Council were called general congregations. The first of these took place on 13 October 1962. Archbishop Lefebvre wrote: "From its very first day the Council was besieged by the forces of the progressives. We experienced it, felt it, and when I say 'we', I refer to the majority of Council Fathers at that time. We were convinced that something abnormal was happening in the Council".[12] Cardinal Heenan testifies that: "The first general congregation had scarcely begun when the northern bishops went into action".[13] Their objective was to win control of the ten conciliar commissions, which would mean virtual control of the Council itself.

After the Mass with which the first general congregation had begun, each of the Fathers received three printed booklets. The first contained a list of all the Fathers eligible for election to the ten commissions; the second listed those who had taken part in the preparatory commissions; the third contained ten pages, one for each commission. There were sixteen blank spaces on each page for each Father to complete with the names of the candidates he thought most suitable for the sixteen elective places on each commission. The commissions would have twenty-four members in all—an additional eight would be nominated by the Pope.

The German bishops realised that if the Fathers voted on the basis of a general list containing the names of all eligible candidates they would be unlikely to dominate the commissions. They decided that it would suit them far better if each hierarchy could put forward a list of candidates from its own ranks for each commission. This would mean that rather than voting for a candidate simply on his individual merits he would be considered as the representative of a hierarchy, or a group of hierarchies. The Germans were in a position to form the largest block and would be in a position to ensure the election of a substantial number of candidates (not necessarily German-speaking) who were sympathetic to their policies. A meeting was held in the house of Cardinal Frings of Cologne at which a plan to secure the adoption of this procedure was adopted. It was decided to use a non-German Father to put their proposals forward, and Cardinal Liénart, president of the French episcopal conference, agreed to do this. Cardinal Heenan describes what happened at the first general congregation after the three booklets had been distributed:

> Cardinal Liénart, Bishop of Lille, rose to make a speech of protest. It would be absurd to vote immediately for members of the commissions, he said, because as yet the Fathers were unacquainted with each other. It would be much wiser and fairer to allow time for bishops to ex-

change information and discuss the merits of the proposed candidates. If votes were taken at once bishops would be voting for men with whom they were unfamiliar even by name. The qualifications and worth of individual bishops are usually not known outside their own country of origin. The Cardinal proposed that the various hierarchies should consider what talents they could offer and then pass on to the other hierarchies the names of their strongest candidates. As soon as the French cardinal sat down his German friend, Cardinal Frings, Archbishop of Cologne, rose to second the proposal. This drew a sustained burst of applause from the Fathers who evidently thought that the Council had been saved from disaster. The reaction of the bishops was unmistakable, and the Secretary General thought it superfluous to put Cardinal Liénart's motion to the vote. The first General Congregation of the Second Vatican Council was suspended after exactly fifteen minutes.[14]

Blitzkrieg tactics indeed!

Cardinal Heenan also reveals that in preparing their lists: "The bishops from the north acted in concert from the very beginning and were in frequent touch with their English brethren".[15] Henri Fesquet, religious affairs correspondent for the French daily *Le Monde*, was one of the liberal journalists who played such an influential part in conditioning both the Council Fathers and the Catholic public to accept the liberal takeover, a process which will be described in detail in Chapter VII. In his book *Journal du Concile*, he described these events as a "demolition exercise" (*entreprise de démolition*) by a group of "modern-minded bishops" (*évêques avancés*).[16] He confirms that: "It needed only two or three determined bishops to modify fairly considerably the proceedings of the Council".[17]

The military metaphors used by some of the commentators cited in this chapter are amply justified by the jubilant comment of a Dutch bishop, who called to a friend as he left St. Peter's: "That was our first victory!"[18] The spirit in which the liberals had come to the Council was clear; the party mentality, the "us versus them" attitude was already manifest. Similar comments were made by liberal Fathers emerging from St. Peter's after another "victory", and recounted with great relish and approval by Robert Kaiser: "Now the gloves are off"—"The big fellow (Cardinal Bea) got 'em and I got 'em too".[19]

The German bishops had prepared the ground for victory by persuading the Council to accept their proposals for electing members to the commissions—but to achieve victory it was necessary to get their candidates elected. To continue with the *blitzkrieg* analogy, the Stukas had done their work, now it was time for the Panzers to move in.

"Then", wrote Cardinal Heenan, "began the well-known process of lobbying".[20] In his diary for 13 October 1962 he records that he received visits from the Bishop of Bruges (Belgium), who came as an emissary from the German bishops. He gave the then Archbishop Heenan some names that the Germans, Dutch, and Belgians intended to back, and explained that "a final list was being drawn up at a meeting then in progress at the Anima College (German house of studies) under the presidency of Cardinal Frings. This list would be available at nine o'clock the next day. Meanwhile, many names had been given and it was hoped to make the list fairly international. It would attract the vote of missionaries—e.g., the Congo has many Belgian bishops".[21]

Archbishop Lefebvre recorded the stupefaction of the Fathers when, on 14 October, each one was presented with a printed list of candidates containing names which most of them had never heard of but for whom they eventually voted. "The compilers of the lists knew these bishops well.

Need I say that they all thought on the same lines".[22] Cardinal Heenan explains that: "Even using every spare moment it was impossible to learn enough about sixteen people for each of the commissions. It was, therefore, inevitable that the bishops gave votes for some candidates knowing little about them beyond their names".[23]

The manoeuvres which resulted in the liberal take-over of the ten commissions have been documented in detail in Father R. M. Wiltgen's authoritative study, *The Rhine Flows into the Tiber*.[24] This is certainly the most objective and complete account of the Council yet written. Allegations were made that the Roman authorities bought up copies to prevent the contents being known, but Father Wiltgen, in a letter to the Latin Mass Society of Australia dated 15 May 1975, stated that this was quite untrue. He explains in his book how the Rhine Group, i.e. the German bishops and their allies, quickly expanded to include the bishops of Austria, Switzerland, Holland, Belgium, and France. A Dutch-born bishop of an African diocese was instrumental in organising a list of bishops from both French and English-speaking Africa, which he put at the disposal of the Rhine Group, thus assuring it of many extra votes. Liberal-minded bishops from other countries were contacted both as candidates and supporters. A handpicked list of 109 candidates was designed to ensure Rhine Group representation on all the commissions and, in a success which exceeded anything they had thought possible, seventy-nine of their candidates were elected. And when the Pope appointed his own nominees to bring the number of each commission up to twenty-four, he included eight more Rhine candidates among them. Eight out of every ten candidates put forward by the European Alliance, as the Rhine Group was called, received a commission seat. In the liturgical commission the alliance received twelve out of the sixteen seats. This was reduced to a majority of fourteen to eleven after the papal nominations.

"After this election", writes Father Wiltgen, "it was not too hard to foresee which group was well enough organised to take over the leadership at the Second Vatican Council. The Rhine had begun to flow into the Tiber".[25] This success had been obtained because, in contrast with other hierarchies, "the alliance was able to operate effectively because it knew beforehand what it wanted and what it did not want".[26]

Notes

[1] CT, p. 343.
[2] *Catholic Standard* (Dublin), 14 September 1973.
[3] XR-1, p. 10.
[4] RFT, p. 63
[5] *Ibid.*, p. 59.
[6] *The Tablet*, 17 November 1962, p. 1111.
[7] *General Instruction on the Roman Missal*, No. 276.
[8] CT, p. 339.
[9] *The Tablet*, 31 August 1963, p. 935.
[10] VO, p. 112.
[11] Archbishop R. J. Dwyer, *Twin Circle*, 26 October 1973.
[12] ABS, pp. 69.
[13] CT, p. 343.
[14] *Ibid.*, pp. 343-4.
[15] CT, p. 344.
[16] JC, p. 165.
[17] *Ibid.*, p. 20.
[18] *Ibid.*, p. 17.
[19] IC, p. 160.
[20] CC, p. 10.
[21] CT, p. 349.
[22] ABS, p. 70.
[23] CT, pp. 344-45.
[24] RFT, pp. 17-19.
[25] *Ibid.*, p. 19.
[26] *Ibid.*, p. 63.

IV

Mopping Up

Despite the overwhelming success of its initial *blitzkrieg*, the Rhine Group still had a great deal of mopping up to do. There were isolated pockets of resistance to be disposed of, areas of the conciliar administration which needed to be brought under its total control. With these objectives in mind, the Rhine bishops and their *periti* were busy between the first and second sessions of the Council. During this period, there had, of course, been a change of pontiff, Pope John having died on 3 June 1963, after an agonising illness. This was a merciful relief, according to Cardinal Heenan, for "Pope John was spared the agony of seeing the Catholic Church in decline. At the time of John's death there was no hint of impending disintegration. The neo-modernists and Catholic anarchists who changed his successor into a man of sorrows were yet to appear....Jesus wept over Jerusalem and John would have wept over Rome if he had foreseen what would be done in the name of his council".[1] Note carefully the Cardinal's use of the term "disintegration".

The Rhine Group planned its strategy for the second session at a meeting in Munich and at the widely publicised Fulda Conference in Germany from 26 to 29 August 1963. This conference has also been referred to as the "Fulda Conspiracy".[2] Four cardinals and seventy archbishops from ten countries took part—the Scandinavian bishops had joined the alliance by then. As a result of this meeting, every member of the Rhine Group arrived at the second session with a 480-page plan of campaign!

The influence of the *periti* will be examined in the next chapter, but even at this point it is important to note once again that, in general, policies were formulated by the "experts" and then proposed and voted for by the Fathers who acted as their mouthpieces. Father Wiltgen remarks:

> Since the position of the German-language bishops was regularly adopted by the European alliance (the Rhine Group), and since the alliance position was regularly adopted by the Council, a single theologian might have his views accepted by the whole Council if they had been accepted by the German-speaking bishops.[3]

In order to win total control of the Council, the Rhine Group needed to ensure that the procedural rules were altered. These were denounced by Xavier Rynne as "highly contrived to assure domination of the proceedings at all stages by the Curial party".[4] How this alleged curial domination could be reconciled with the liberal triumph during the first session is hard to explain, particularly as Xavier Rynne himself concedes that it "had exceeded the hope of the progressives".[5]

The principal complaint, according to Rynne, was that the cardinals presiding over the conciliar commissions had "powers that were too vast and arbitrary—again a reflection on the Curia. Not enough use was made", said the critique, "of the Council experts or *periti*, who not infrequently found themselves virtually excluded from any participation in the work".[6]

Pope Paul decided to revise the procedural rules on "the advice of certain venerable Council Fathers".[7] The

Rhine Group demands were largely met, particularly useful to them being the transfer of a great deal of power to four Cardinal Moderators who would be responsible for "directing the activities of the Council and determining the sequence in which topics would be discussed at the business meetings".[8] The Pope's own sympathies were made clear when he selected well-known liberals to fill three of the four posts—Cardinals Döpfner, Lercaro, and Suenens. They were, as Henri Fesquet remarked, "universally known for their reformist ardour"; and Father Wiltgen points out that as the fourth Cardinal, Agagianian, "was not a forceful person, the three liberal Cardinal Moderators often had 100-per-cent control".[9]

Another procedural change useful to the Rhine Group made it possible for as few as five members on any commission to substitute another form of any amendment proposed. By an interesting coincidence, the Rhine Group had a minimum of five members on every commission![10] It was also made possible for *periti* to speak in the Council debates under certain circumstances.[11] Father Wiltgen writes:

> It was clear at this point how the discussions would develop. There would be strong German influence which would make itself felt in nearly every Council decision and statement of any importance. In every Council commission, German and Austrian members and *periti* would be highly articulate in presenting the conclusions reached at Munich and Fulda. With the Munich and Fulda conferences, the drastic changes that Pope Paul had made in the rules of procedure, and the promotion of Cardinals Döpfner, Suenens, and Lercaro to the position of Moderators, domination by the European Alliance (the Rhine Group) was assured.[12]

The second session opened on 29 September 1963. By mid-November the Rhine Group aimed at nothing less than total control. "The European Alliance by this time had full control of the Council majority and was confident that it could replace all conservative members on the Council commissions if only it were given the opportunity".[13] It wished to impose its own *diktat*, under the slogan of freeing the commissions from curial control! In response "to the requests of many Council Fathers", writes Father Wiltgen, the Pope agreed to allow additional members to be elected to the commissions, and the Rhine Group set about "drawing up an unbeatable international list". He continued:

> This work was greatly facilitated since...the European alliance had expanded into a world alliance. In point of fact, the origins of the world alliance went back to the beginning of the first session, and from that time it was always under the dominating influence of the European alliance.
>
> The world alliance during the first session was an undercover group...who met periodically. From the beginning of the second session, when they considered themselves strong enough to act more openly, they held meetings at *Domus Mariae* each Friday evening and saw their membership grow to twenty-four bishops and archbishops, who represented approximately sixty-five episcopal conferences....
>
> Although not juridically organised, the world alliance was able to determine the policy of the controlling liberal majority.[14]

The election for the additional commission members took place on 28 November, and all the candidates elected to office came from the list prepared by the world alliance! "After this election", comments Father Wiltgen, "there was no longer need for anyone to doubt the direction in which the Council was headed".¹⁵ The commissions were controlled, according to Archbishop Lefebvre, by a "majority of members imbued with an ecumenism which, according to their own statement, is not only no longer Catholic, but bears a remarkable resemblance to the Modernism condemned by St. Pius X, and that, as Paul VI noted in his Encyclical *Ecclesiam Suam*, is once more coming to life".¹⁶

Monsignor Lefebvre was particularly critical of the unwillingness of the Council to formulate clear definitions for the Fathers to vote upon:

> We have asked repeatedly for a definition of Collegiality. No one has yet succeeded in defining it. We have asked repeatedly for a definition of ecumenism. We are told through the mouths of the commission secretaries and rapporteurs themselves: *"But we are not holding a dogmatic council, we are not making philosophical definitions. This is a pastoral council aimed at the Church as a whole. Consequently, it is pointless to frame here definitions which would not be understood"*. But it is surely the height of stupidity to think that we can meet and yet fail to define the very terms we are discussing [emphasis in original].¹⁷

The Archbishop adds that it is his sincere belief that the crisis in the Church today originated in the Council:

> *I sincerely believe that it is the Council which is at the back of all this* since many of the bishops, above all especially those chosen to be members of the commissions, were people who had been formed in an existentialist philosophy, but had never studied Thomistic philosophy, and so do not know what a definition is. For them there is no such thing as essence; nothing is defined any longer, one expresses or describes something but never defines

> it. *Moreover, this lack of philosophy was patent throughout the whole Council.* I believe this to be the reason why the Council was a mass of ambiguities, vagueness, and sentimentality, things which now clearly admit all interpretations and have left all doors open [emphasis in original].[18]

The Archbishop contrasts the documents of Vatican II with those of previous councils:

> All councils save this last have been dogmatic councils. Those dogmatic councils gave us the exact expression of Tradition, the exact terms of what the Apostles taught. That is unalterable. The decrees of the Council of Trent are unalterable because they are infallible. They were written and proclaimed as embodying the faith coming down to us by Tradition and this by an official act of the Church. They are wholly free from errors. We must believe them. But the last council, which was a pastoral council (as the popes themselves have repeatedly said), was averse from being dogmatic, and its propositions may therefore be discussed. These propositions are not infallible because the popes would not invoke their infallibility. That is exceedingly important.[19]

There is little point in devoting more space to documenting the manner in which the progressive stranglehold on the Council was extended and tightened. The story is told in great detail in Father Wiltgen's book. What now needs to be done is to examine the manner in which the liberals used their power—and in order to do this it is necessary to take a closer look at the *periti*, for it was on behalf of these "experts" that the Rhine Group had won its victories.

Notes

[1] CT, p. 389.
[2] RFT, p. 81.
[3] *Ibid.*, p. 80.
[4] XR-II, p. 27.
[5] *Ibid.*
[6] XR-II, pp. 27-28.
[7] RFT, p. 82.
[8] *Ibid.*
[9] JC, p.171; RFT, p. 83.
[10] RFT, p. 83.
[11] *Ibid.*, p. 84.
[12] *Ibid.*
[13] RFT, p. 128.
[14] *Ibid.*, p. 129-30.
[15] *Ibid.*, p. 130.
[16] ABS, p. 81.
[17] *Ibid.*, p. 106.
[18] *Ibid.*, pp. 109-110.
[19] *Ibid.*, p. 161.

V

Liberal Storm Troops

Douglas Woodruff, one of England's outstanding Catholic scholars, was editor of *The Tablet* during Vatican II. In one of his reports on the Council he remarks: "For in a sense this Council has been the Council of the *periti*, silent in the *aula*, but so effective in the commissions and at bishops' ears".[1] This is an exceptionally perceptive comment, and it would be hard to improve on "the Council of the *periti*" as a one-phrase description of Vatican II. Father Wiltgen has already been cited as explaining how a single *peritus* could impose his views upon the whole Council if he could win the approval of the German bishops.[2] Bishop Lucey of Cork and Ross (Ireland) stated that the *periti* were more powerful than most bishops even though they had no vote "because they had the ear of a cardinal or the head of a national group of bishops, and they were influential in the drafting of Council documents. The expert...is the person with power".[3] Indeed, as Cardinal Heenan reveals, there were occasions on which the Fathers were so overwhelmed with material to read concerning the drafts for conciliar documents, and particularly with amendments to them which could run into hundreds of pages, that they "were called upon to cast their votes before they could possibly have studied the text and context, much less the implications, of the amendments".[4] However silent the *periti* may have been in the *aula*, they certainly had no qualms about making themselves heard during private meetings of the commissions. Cardinal Heenan mentions one such meeting in which: "The only discord came from the advisers (*periti*) in attendance. A German theologian addressed us in a voice often rising to a scream".[5]

Periti power cannot be illustrated better than by referring to the fate of the preparatory schemata (drafts for the conciliar documents) prepared on the instructions of Pope John XXIII. They were totally orthodox and in full accord with the traditional teaching of the Church. They were the fruit of an intensive two-year effort by 871 scholars ranging from cardinals to laymen. Monsignor Vincenzo Carbone, of the General Secretariat, was able to claim with perfect accuracy that no other Council had had a preparation "so vast, so diligently carried out, and so profound".[6] Archbishop Lefebvre wrote:

> I took part in the preparations for the Council as a member of the Central Preparatory Commission. Thus, for two years I was present at all its meetings. It was the business of the Central Commission to check and verify all the preparatory schemata issued by all the committees. Consequently, I was well placed for knowing what was to be put forward during the Council. This work was carried out very conscientiously and with a concern for perfection. I possess the seventy-two preparatory schemata and can state, speaking generally, in these seventy-two schemata the doctrine of the Church was absolutely orthodox and that there was hardly any need for retouching. There was, therefore, a very fine piece of work for presentation to the Council—schemata in conformity with the Church's teaching, adapted to some extent to our era, but with prudence and wisdom.[7]

Liberal Storm Troops

After these two years of conscientious work, what actually happened at the Council will seem quite incredible. On 13 July 1962, Pope John decreed that the first seven preparatory schemata should be sent to the Council Fathers throughout the world. The first four were dogmatic constitutions entitled: *Sources of Revelation, Preserving Pure the Deposit of Faith, Christian Moral Order,* and *Chastity, Matrimony, the Family, and Virginity.* The titles alone were sufficient to send any self-respecting liberal screaming to his psychiatrist! The fifth schema came into a very different category. It concerned the liturgy and was known as the "Bugnini schema" as Father Annibale Bugnini was its principal author, and it enjoyed the wholehearted approval of the bishops and *periti* from the Rhine countries who had inserted their own ideas into it. The first four schemata were anathema to the liberals who resolved that they should not even be discussed. The Dutch hierarchy issued a commentary which was printed in Latin, French, and English and was distributed to the Fathers from all countries as they arrived at the Council. This commentary contained a strong attack on the first four schemata and suggested that they should be rewritten completely, and that the liberal-inspired liturgy schema should be considered first. Most of the Fathers had arrived in Rome with no preconceived ideas and were thus liable to accept well-argued suggestions presented to them by those who already had definite aims and definite plans to implement them. A majority voted in favour of both these demands.

It so happened that a majority vote was not enough. To quote Monsignor Lefebvre again:

> It was laid down in the Council's rules that a two-thirds majority was needed for the rejection of a preparatory schema. Now in the sixth or seventh meeting of the Council, a vote was taken on the preparatory schemata to decide on their study or rejection. Two-thirds of

the votes were therefore needed for their rejection. As it happened, there were sixty per cent against and forty per cent in favour. The two-thirds majority was lacking so, under the rules of the Council, there should naturally have been a study of the schemata. It should be said that there already existed at that time a powerful, extremely powerful, body, well organised by the cardinals from the Rhineland, and their perfectly equipped secretariat. They brought pressure on Pope John, saying to him: "It is inadmissible to ask us to study schemata which did not carry a majority. They must be rejected outright". Pope John XXIII sent us word that given the fact that less than half the members of the meeting had voted for the schemata, all were rejected. After a fortnight we were left without any preparation. It was really inconceivable.[8]

Once again the liberals had known what they wanted and how to obtain it. The conservative Fathers had about as much chance of stopping them as did the Polish cavalry who drew their sabres and charged the German panzers in 1939. And the result? The Bugnini liturgy schema was brought forward to be first on the list for discussion—and as for the four schemata condemned by the Dutch bishops, Monsignor Lefebvre wrote:

> Now you know what happened at the Council? A fortnight after its opening not one of the prepared schemata remained, not one! All had been turned down, all had been condemned to the wastepaper basket. Nothing remained, not a single sentence. All had been thrown out.[9]

Father Wiltgen comments that this was the third important victory won by the Rhine Group. "Although the first two victories—the postponement of elections and the placing of hand-picked candidates on the Council commissions—were given extensive coverage, this third victory passed unnoticed".[10] The most astonishing aspect of this scandalous affair, the relegation to the wastepaper basket of a preparation "so vast, so diligently carried out, so profound", is that it really took place in response to the wishes of a single *peritus*. Yes, just one "expert" had the power and influence to secure the rejection of the most meticulous conciliar preparation in the entire history of the Church, the painstaking work of 871 scholars! Although the commentary which secured the rejection of the preparatory schemata was circulated in the name of the Dutch bishops, as Father Wiltgen reveals, it was the work of just one man, "Father Edward Schillebeeckx, O.P., a Belgian-born professor of dogmatics at the Catholic University of Nijmegen, who served as the leading theologian for the Dutch hierarchy".[11] This instance alone more than substantiates Father Wiltgen's assertion concerning the power a single *peritus* could wield. However, although most of the Council Fathers tended to ride the band-wagon, the majority were orthodox and would not have voted for any document containing evident heresy. The tactic of some *periti* was simple. They proposed to insert ambiguous phrases into the conciliar texts which they could exploit after the Council provided they could gain control of the post-conciliar commissions. To his credit, Father Schillebeeckx disapproved of these tactics. He was an extreme liberal and he wished the texts to state the extreme liberal position openly. Father Congar, another well-known liberal, had also objected to a conciliar text being deliberately ambiguous. These revelations were in the Dutch weekly *De Bazuin* on 23 January 1965.[12] Some examples of ambiguous wording in conciliar documents will be provided in the next chapter and also in Chapter XIII.

Cardinal Heenan was well aware of the manner in which the *periti* could phrase the official texts with a view to manipulating them for their own purposes after the Council.

> There are hundreds of papers in the Vatican archives which presumably will reveal to scholars of the future the proceedings in secret commission meetings. The more significant activities within commissions have not yet been fully revealed. The framing of amendments for the vote of the Fathers was the most delicate part of a commission's work. A determined group could wear down opposition and *produce a formula patient of both an orthodox and modernistic interpretation* [my emphasis].[13]

During the debate on the pastoral constitution *Gaudium et Spes*—The Church in the Modern World—Cardinal Heenan warned the Fathers to scrutinise texts with great care before voting upon them because of the danger that "the mind of the Council will have to be interpreted to the world by the *periti* who helped the Fathers of the commission to draw up the documents. God forbid that this should happen! I fear *periti* when they are left to explain what the bishops meant....It is of no avail to talk about a College of Bishops if *periti* in articles, books and speeches contradict and pour scorn on what a body of bishops teaches".[14] He cites the Liturgy Constitution as an example of a text which was open to an interpretation very different from that intended by the Fathers who passed it by an almost unanimous vote.

> At the close of the first session little had been decided but many ideas had been ventilated. The subject most fully debated was liturgical reform. It might be more accurate to say that the bishops were under the impression that the liturgy had been fully discussed. In retrospect it is clear that they were given the opportunity of discuss-

ing only general principles. Subsequent changes were more radical than those intended by Pope John and the bishops who passed the decree on the liturgy. *His sermon at the end of the first session shows that Pope John did not suspect what "was being planned" by the liturgical experts* [my emphasis].¹⁵

Cardinal Heenan warned the Council Fathers of the possible consequences if they did not scrutinise the documents with sufficient care. Tragically, his warning went unheeded. He had also warned of the consequences which would ensue if the *periti* interpreted the Council to the world—and this is precisely what has happened. The confidence of the liberals that they would dominate the post-conciliar commissions was more than justified. Indeed, the five post-conciliar commissions were created *as a result of pressure from the Rhine Group* which "feared that the progressive measures adopted by the Council might be blocked by conservative forces near the Pope once the Council Fathers had all returned home".¹⁶ The members of these commissions were "chosen with the Pope's approval, for the most part from the ranks of the Council *periti*. The task of the commissions is to put into effect the Council decrees concerned, with the co-ordinating commission to co-ordinate their work and, when necessary, to interpret the Council constitutions, decrees and declarations".¹⁷ "God forbid that this should happen"! Cardinal Heenan had warned—but happen it did. Pope Paul himself stated that, where difficult questions were concerned: "It would be left to the post-conciliar commissions to explain these principles more fully and to work out their practical implementation".¹⁸ "To work out their practical implementation"—to quote Cardinal Heenan again:

> There is a certain poetic justice in the humiliation of the Catholic Church at the hands of the liturgical anarchists.

> Catholics used to laugh at Anglicans for being "high" or "low"....The old boast that the Mass is everywhere the same and that Catholics are happy whichever priest celebrates is no longer true. When on 7 December 1962 the bishops voted overwhelmingly (1,922 against 11) in favour of the first chapter of the Constitution on the Liturgy, they did not realise that they were initiating a process which after the Council would cause confusion and bitterness throughout the Church.[19]

Confusion and bitterness throughout the Church—these are fruits of the "practical implementation" of the Liturgy Constitution which no Catholic who loves the Church, who loves the Mass, who loves the faith of his fathers, has been able to escape.

When certain conciliar texts are interpreted in a manner which appears to be in direct conflict with Catholic teaching and tradition, the natural reaction is to exclaim: "But that couldn't have been intended!" As far as the intention of the majority of Council Fathers is concerned, such a judgement would probably be correct—but as regards the periti who drafted the documents the opposite is true. The best insight into the real views of these "experts" can be obtained not by reading conservative criticisms of them, but by examining their own activities and writings since the Council.

It is necessary to make a distinction between the teaching of the Council, as contained in its official documents (unsatisfactory as these may be in places as Dietrich von Hildebrand has testified), and the Council as an event. The effects of the Council derive less from the former than from the latter. Not least among the consequences of the Council as an event was that liberal theologians from all over the world were brought together in Rome (at very great expense, borne ultimately by the ordinary faithful) where they were able to get to know each other, to organise themselves, and to formulate policies at their leisure and in great comfort. An Anglican observer remarked that: "If Christian unity were no more than a question of prodigal sons returning to their father's house...many of us would be tempted to go there tomorrow if the standard of living is anything like what we saw".[20]

Another result of the Council as an event is that the liberal European *periti* were able to "convert" previously conservative theologians from such countries as the U.S.A., and not only theologians but bishops too! Bishop William Adrian of Nashville, Tennessee, echoing Archbishop Lefebvre, wrote:

> As the Council developed, some of the originally somnolent American bishops, catching fire from their alert European colleagues, became the able engineers of liberal proposals, going beyond the Europeans in ferocious, vituperative attacks on the Roman Curia. Yet, however brilliant the American *periti* may have been, they got their ideas from the European Catholic liberals, and some conservative Americans, following their second-rate *periti*, joined the revolutionary group to bring about whatever their mentors thought best. The European *periti*, who really imposed their theories upon the bishops, were themselves deeply imbued with the errors of Teilhardism and situation ethics, which errors ultimately destroy all divine faith and morality and all constituted authority. They make the person the centre and judge of all truth and morality irrespective of what the Church teaches. It is the root of the evil of this disrespect for authority, divine and human. These liberal theologians seized on the Council as the means of decatholicising the Catholic Church while pretending only to de-Romanise it. By twisting words and using Protestant terminology and ideas they succeeded in creating a mess whereby many Catholic priests, religious, and laymen

have become so confused that they feel alienated from Catholic culture.[21]

Under Pope Pius XII, the liberal theologians had been on the defensive, but now, as a result of the Council, the situation has been reversed. Pope John, like Count Frankenstein, brought into existence a creature he could not control. "As the Council progressed Pope John grew more and more depressed", writes Cardinal Heenan.[22] Doubtlessly, like Count Frankenstein, Pope John did what he did with the best of intentions, but now it is the Magisterium which is on the defensive. So many bishops are obsessed by one fear and one fear only, that of appearing "reactionary". Once again, Cardinal Heenan has summed up the situation perfectly:

> We bishops are exercising the Magisterium with an unsure touch. To question brash theological opinion has become increasingly hazardous. No wise bishop courts popularity for its own sake but, if only to preserve his authority with his clergy and people, he wanted to eschew the reputation of being reactionary. Unfortunately, if a bishop criticises dangerous opinions he is said to be obscurantist. The Magisterium is thought unenlightened whenever it questions novel interpretations of Catholic doctrine.[23]

In his book *The Decline and Fall of Radical Catholicism*, Professor James Hitchcock has fully documented the manner in which the new liberal establishment has taken control of the Church in the United States. The situation he describes is equally true, in varying degrees, for the other Western countries. Pope Paul expressed his anguish, his anxiety, his insistence on orthodoxy. Cardinal Heenan commented:

Liberal Storm Troops

The Pope may be badly advised and physically weak, but he contrives to make his voice clearly heard and more often than not he displays a deep anxiety. Constantly he returns to the theme of the erroneous teaching of theology. Unfortunately, his condemnations are made in general terms. Since nobody knows which theologians are being condemned, it is impossible for bishops to take any action.[24]

Despite his frequent appeals for orthodoxy, Pope Paul was quite unable to exercise any effective control over the new and militant "parallel magisterium" of the "experts", either as individuals or as the corporate body into which Vatican II moulded them. "Jesus wept over Jerusalem", remarks Cardinal Heenan, "and John would have wept over Rome if he had foreseen what would be done in the name of his Council. It was no wonder that Pope Paul wept".[25] He added that after the Council: "A bitter attack on the Catholic Church was mounted by her own children".[26] And the leaders of this attack came from among the *periti*, the shock troops of the liberal forces.

It is customary for liberals to write off any suggestions of an organised conspiracy on their part as little more than the paranoid ravings of the theologically illiterate who are unable to adapt. Professor Joad, the "father" of all radio and T.V. pundits, would have said: "It all depends on what you mean by a conspiracy". With the evidence that is available, it would be an exaggeration to claim to be able to prove that, as a body, these men were motivated by a conscious and malicious desire to destroy the Church. What they are doing is using every means at their disposal to impose their view of what the Church should be upon the mass of the faithful. Professor Hitchcock notes that:

> What is often called the "revolt of the laity" in the Church is in reality closer to a revolt of the experts, who use a democratic rhetoric to mask an elitist conception of religious reform. These experts have a constituency—a minority of the educated laity in a few of the more advanced Western nations—who support them enthusiastically, look to them for leadership the bishops cannot provide, and sometimes urge them on to greater daring. The remainder of the Church is, in varying degrees, indifferent, uninformed, bewildered, sceptical, wary, fearful, or hostile concerning these same experts.[27]

Robert Hoyt, editor of the ultra-liberal *National Catholic Reporter*, did go as far as conceding that:

> There *is* a liberal conspiracy, in the sense John Courtney Murray used the word, of a "breathing together" (*conspiratio*); liberal theologians dominate the public prints, the catechetical training centers, the publishing houses, the professional associations, much of the Catholic bureaucracy. They praise each other's books, award each other contracts, jobs, awards, and perquisites. There wasn't anything sinister in all this; it wasn't planned, it just happened. [28]

To provide just one early example, Hans Küng (wasting no time) brings out a book on the Council in 1963. By May of that year the German edition had appeared with an introduction by Cardinal Koenig who lavished praise on Dr. Küng and hoped that "this book and the challenge which it presents will be received with understanding and spread far and wide". Cardinal Liénart did the same for the French edition, and when Cardinal Bea was awarded an honorary doctorate by Boston University he made a special point of paying tribute to Dr. Küng.[29] Similar examples will be cited in Chapter VII.

The reality and the extent of the liberal conspiracy, in the sense in which it has just been explained, was demonstrated convincingly by Father Albert J. Nevins in *Our Sunday Visitor*, the Catholic paper with the largest circulation in the United States.[30]

> There is no doubt that collusion exists among the Modernists. It is evident in the *tenor of the whole attack being made on the papacy. It is obvious in the direction* given to Catholic religious education. It appears in joint simultaneous and identical statements. Perhaps the best example was in the large displays which appeared in the nation's press denouncing Pope Paul and his encyclical *Humanae Vitae* almost as soon as it appeared. These advertisements of protest contained 423 signatures. Who thought up the protest? What group frantically phoned and contacted the 423 persons who signed the protest? Who raised the money to pay for the campaign? Who did actually circulate the protests? The 423 signers did not just happen to come together on their own; there were instigators, plotters, and pseudo-Catholics working in collusion. Of course, the 423 signers were not all inside the clique. Most of them were used. But there were sinister forces behind the protest, forces willing to spend money to attack Pope Paul and his encyclical on human life.

Such organised protests were not, of course, confined to the United States. England had its famous (or infamous) fifty-six priests who signed a letter dissenting from *Humanae Vitae* which was published in *The Times* on 2 October 1968. A similar letter signed by dissenting laymen was published in *The Tablet* on 5 October.[31] It is interesting to note that at least one-third of the priests who signed *The Times* manifesto have now left the priesthood.

It is of great significance that among the most prominent agitators against *Humanae Vitae* were some of the most prominent *periti* of Vatican II. Karl Rahner is included in their number. He informed Catholics that they were not being disobedient if they ignored the Sovereign Pontiff when he reiterated in *Humanae Vitae* a point of consistently taught Catholic moral teaching, that contraception is intrinsically evil, which had been particularly emphasised by recent popes. Father Rahner gave the following advice:

> If a Catholic Christian, after sufficient proof of his conscience, believes that he has arrived, after full reflection and self-criticism, at a position which dissents from the papal norm and follows it in his married life under the observance of these principles which have already been alluded to frequently as commonly Christian, *then* such a Catholic needs to fear no subjective guilt or to consider himself as formally disobedient to the Church authority.[32]

The immediate problem posed by such a viewpoint is that if such principles can be applied to the question of contraception then why not to other aspects of traditional Catholic morality? The obvious answer is that they have been and are being applied with increasing frequency and audacity to almost every aspect of traditional morality. Indeed, it would be hard to find any attack upon Catholic teaching on faith or morals which cannot rustle up some *periti* in support—not even excluding the campaign for women priests, "gay liberation", or *de facto* divorce.[33] Even more serious than the attitude of the *periti* is that of some bishops, even entire episcopal conferences. An extremely ambivalent attitude towards the teaching of *Humanae Vitae* was taken by the German, French, Dutch, and Belgian bishops—Rhine Group stalwarts, of course—and also by the Canadian hierarchy which was clearly working overtime to outstrip its European counterparts in adopting the most liberal policies. In a letter professing to offer "pastoral guidance", it instructs confessors to inform those who have rejected the encyclical "that whoever honestly chooses that course which seems right to him does so in good conscience".[34] It is evident that there can be no objective standards of morality if this principle is accepted as a general norm.

The liberal consensus is clearly developing along the lines that papal teaching is a very important factor which a Catholic must take into account when reaching a decision on a moral question—but it is not the only factor, and he is not bound to conform with it providing he gives it careful consideration. Robert McAfee Brown, a Protestant observer at the Council, saw important ecumenical implications in this new attitude:

> Need a Protestant ask for more? Most Protestants would be quite willing to consider what the pope says as one item in terms of which they reach their own decisions, and many in fact do so now. In the sense, then, *Humanae Vitae* may inadvertently be a great gift to the ecumenical movement, for its reception shows conclusively that traditional views of papal authority are now being radically updated, and that loyal and committed Catholics feel no greater sense of being bound to questionable doctrine [sic] than do Protestants.[35]

Dr. McAfee Brown's assessment of the direction in which the Catholic liberals were heading needs to be taken very seriously. He realised that they were approaching, if they had not already arrived at, the classic liberal position consistently condemned by the popes and which is also the basis of Freemasonry—the denial of "the existence of any teacher who ought to be believed by reason of the authority of his office".[36] The major Protestant denominations have long been affected by liberalism, indeed it is the inevitable result of their rejection of papal authority. Liberalism, naturalism, and rationalism have been gaining an ever stronger foothold within the Catholic Church, largely via German Protestantism, and the efforts of a long line of pontiffs to contain the attack were eventually rendered ineffective when the floodgates burst as a result of the Council. The problem now is not to discover where in the West these principles can be found but to discover a country or even a diocese in which they are not accepted as the norm.

Once again the importance of the Council as an event must be stressed. The liberal success lay not so much in incorporating their ideas into the official documents, although they were not without success in this respect, as the next chapter will show, but in the fact that most of the bishops and theologians who came to the Council went away with a changed outlook, an outlook conditioned by the atmosphere and the debates during Vatican II.

Two of the principal means of co-ordinating and extending the influence of the new liberal establishment were the IDO-C organization and the review *Concilium*. Reference to IDO-C will be made in Chapter VII. It would not have been unfair to describe *Concilium* as the official mouthpiece of the conciliar "experts". Its editorial board included most of those given "instant hero" status by the liberal press during the Council, and whose every word was revered as an oracle inspired by whoever it is that inspires liberals.[37] The co-operation between the *periti* and the press will be examined in detail in Chapter VII. It is no exaggeration to claim that the IDO-C/*Concilium* establishment constituted a parallel magisterium which rivalled that of the pope as far as practical authority was concerned. As early as 1968, Cardinal Heenan commented:

> The Ordinary Magisterium of the Pope is exercised in his writings and allocutions. But today what the Pope says is by no means accepted as authoritative by all Catholic theologians. An article in the periodical *Concilium* is at least as likely to win their respect as a papal encyclical. The decline of the Magisterium is one of the most significant developments in the post-conciliar Church.[38]

The audacity with which some *periti* have attacked the most fundamental articles of our faith, and the contempt with which they reject any censure from the Holy See, almost defies credibility. The scandal their views and their acts have given to the ordinary faithful cannot be calculated, and equally scandalous is the manner in which the Holy See allows them to say and do what they wish with impunity from any sanction. Any teacher or parent is well aware of what will happen if children are allowed to break rules and the adult charged with their care does no more than say that they must stop what they are doing while allowing them to continue. Hans Küng is probably the most obvious example. The Sacred Congregation for the Doctrine of the Faith issued a declaration, approved by the Pope, on 14 February 1975, listing several opinions in his works which "to varying degrees, are in conflict with the doctrine of the Catholic Church which must be professed by all the faithful". The declaration expressed regret that he had declined several invitations "to explain in writing how such opinions did not contradict Catholic doctrine". He had already declined an earlier order to explain his views in person, as he was "too busy" to come to Rome. No action was taken to discipline Father Küng in any way, or to deny him the status of an approved teacher of Catholic doctrine. Apart from listing what the Sacred Congregation suggested politely appeared to be his errors, the matter was closed. "This declaration for the time being concludes the action of the Sacred Congregation for the Doctrine of the Faith on this matter". In a brief and contemptuous rejoinder issued on 20 February, Dr. Küng stated: "I shall not let myself be prevented from further performing my theological service to mankind in an ecumenical spirit".[39] But this was by no means the end of the story, and, as will be documented below, in 1979 the Congregation for the Doctrine of the Faith would deprive Küng of his *missio canonica*, his authority to teach as a Catholic theologian.

For Catholic liberals at that time no praise could be too high for Dr. Küng and his fellow *periti*. Robert Kaiser wrote in ecstatic terms of "theologians like Karl Rahner, Joseph Ratzinger, Yves Congar, M. D. Chenu, Henri de Lubac, Edward Schillebeeckx, Hans Küng. All of them were theologians on the march, men well equipped with the ideas that dovetailed neatly into the needs of pastors around the world. The joint effort of bishops and theologians together in group conferences and dinner conversations had an incalculable effect".[40] Mr. Kaiser failed to inform his readers exactly where he thought his favoured theologians were marching. It is worth noting that all the theologians he mentions, with the exceptions of Fathers de Lubac and Ratzinger, were members of the editorial board of *Concilium* in 1968. Father Ratzinger tried to group theologians of his own moderately progressive views together in what is seen as an opposition movement to the *Concilium* group and helped to found a rival journal, *Communio*.

It is hard to believe that St. Pius X did not have some of the Vatican II *periti* in mind when he wrote *Pascendi Gregis* on the doctrines of the Modernists. (It must be stressed that throughout this chapter only *some* of the *periti* have been referred to, subsequent chapters will show that a number were totally orthodox and did all in their power to ensure that the conciliar documents reflected traditional teaching.) *Pascendi Gregis* even refers to the conditioned reflex of pained surprise, still affected by liberal theologians, that anyone (the Pope included) should venture to question either their theology or their motives. This encyclical has never been more relevant than at the present time—not the least for the fact that all the so-called "new insights" of contemporary theologians will be found listed there, and condemned as already very old liberal-Protestantism. St. Pius X wrote:

> Although they express their astonishment that We should number them amongst the enemies of the Church, no one will be reasonably surprised that we should do so, if, leaving out of account the internal disposition of the soul, of which God alone is the Judge, he considers their tenets, their manner of speech, and their action. Nor indeed would he be wrong in regarding them as the most pernicious of all the adversaries of the Church. For, as We have said, they put into operation their designs for her undoing, not from without but from within. Hence, the danger is present almost in the very veins and heart of the Church, whose injury is the more certain from the very fact that their knowledge of her is more intimate. Moreover, they lay the axe not to the branches and shoots, but to the very root, that is, to the faith and its deepest fibres. And once having struck at this root of immortality, they proceed to diffuse poison through the whole tree, so that there is no part of Catholic truth which they leave untouched, none that they do not strive to corrupt. Further, none is more skilful, none more astute than they, in the employment of a thousand noxious devices; for they play the double part of rationalist and Catholic, and this so craftily that they easily lead the unwary into error; and as audacity is their chief characteristic, there is no conclusion of any kind from which they shrink or which

they do not thrust forward with pertinacity and assurance....Finally, there is the fact which is all but fatal to the hope of cure that their very doctrines have given such a bent to their minds, that they disdain all authority and brook no restraint; and relying upon a false conscience, they attempt to ascribe to a love of truth that which is in reality the result of pride and obstinacy.[41]

On 18 December 1979, to the outrage and dismay of Liberal Catholics and Protestants, the Congregation for the Doctrine of the Faith withdrew Küng's *missio canonica*, his authority to teach, stating that he could "no longer be considered a Catholic theologian nor function as such in a teaching role". *The Universe* (London) reported the news in its 21 December issue in the following terms:

The Pope Silences Dr. Küng
by Ronald Singleton

Rome. Professor Hans Küng, the Church's most controversial theologian, was on Tuesday forbidden to teach theology. The Pope on Tuesday approved a censure by the Congregation for the Doctrine of the Faith on the 51-year-old, Swiss-born Father Küng, theology professor at Tübingen, West Germany. The Vatican announced: "Professor Küng may no longer teach theology and may no longer be considered to be a Catholic theologian. We are obliged to declare that in his writings he fell short of integrity and the truth of Catholic faith". Father Küng has continually declined to be questioned by the Congregation "until I am assured of receiving a fair trial". The announcement was simultaneously confirmed by the president of the West German Episcopal Conference, Cardinal Höffner, leader of West German "conservatives". The Professor was shocked. Neither he nor his advocates expected such a move, made swiftly and with no warning....

Father Küng was born on 19 March 1928. He was ordained at Rome's Pontifical German College on 10 October 1954, and the following day celebrated his first Mass in St. Peter's. He is a priest of the Basle diocese in Switzerland. In 1970, he published a powerful, theological argument against the doctrine of papal infallibility. The investigation of his writings has been conducted for years. More than 20,000 Swiss Catholics signed a petition asking the Congregation to treat him with "justice and impartiality". He has criticised persistently dogmas and traditions such as the apostolic succession of the bishops, the sinlessness of Mary and rules on priestly celibacy. His 720-page book, *On Being a Christian*, was a first edition best-seller of 150,000 copies. Father Küng is under no obligation to resign from Tübingen University. It is a state institution.

As subsequent events made only too clear, the Pope had by no means silenced Hans Küng; in fact, the action taken against him prompted this far-from-taciturn Swiss cleric to a degree of unprecedented loquacity. The removal of Küng's mandate to teach as a Catholic theologian also prompted liberal theologians in a number of countries to considerable loquacity in defence of a colleague they clearly regarded as a martyr for truth. Similar support came from his many Protestant admirers who had come to imagine that the Catholic Church no longer objected to Protestantism, as Küng had been allowed to preach Protestant theology for so many years in his official capacity as a Catholic theologian. Küng was soon to embark on a triumphal international tour to receive in person the fulsome tributes of his admirers, and to express his contempt for the Vatican and for the teaching of the Church, sometimes even within

Catholic institutions. The 14 January 1982 issue of *The Wanderer* reported that on 7 December 1981 Küng gave a lecture to a standing-room only audience at the University of Notre Dame, the foremost Catholic university in the United States. He was introduced by Father Richard McBrien, Chairman of the Theology Department at the University, as "a fellow Catholic theologian", a statement which can only be described as an insolent and cynical rejection of the judgement of the Sacred Congregation. Needless to say, the audience considered Father McBrien's statement highly amusing, and he received loud applause. McBrien himself is the author of a two-volume work, *Catholicism*, which should, in fact, be entitled *Modernism*. It is a menace to the faith of any Catholic who reads it, but is now a standard textbook in many English-speaking seminaries, and receives praise from bishops. It is hardly necessary to remark that under no circumstances whatsoever would Archbishop Lefebvre have been permitted to speak at Notre Dame University, or on any other Catholic campus in the English-speaking world. Liberal-Catholic belief in academic freedom is restricted to those propagating views acceptable to liberal Catholics.

The decision to act against Hans Küng was a courageous one on the part of Cardinal Seper and Pope John Paul II. They knew it would incite the fury of liberal Catholics and Protestants. It would be churlish for traditional Catholics to withhold their gratitude for this decision, but at the same time they could observe quite reasonably that it was long overdue and that the only sanction imposed upon Father. Küng, the withdrawal of his *missio canonica,* was far too mild, even ludicrously mild. Archbishop Lefebvre, who had never questioned a single defined teaching of the Church, had been suspended *a divinis,* and forbidden to offer Mass in public, while Küng, who had questioned such fundamental dogmas as papal infallibility and the nature of the priesthood, incurred no such sanctions.

Liberal Storm Troops

Some Interesting Reactions

It should be noted that Küng's contempt for the authority of the Holy See was such that, unlike Monsignor Lefebvre, he refused to appear before the Sacred Congregation to explain his case in person. Reference has already been made to the fact that Küng received considerable support from Protestants and liberal Catholics. The World Council of Churches stated that the Pope's decision could not be regarded as an internal affair of the Catholic Church since it had immediate ecumenical repercussions. This is a most interesting point of view! The supreme authority in the Catholic Church is no longer entitled to say who shall or shall not represent the Church as an official teacher without first consulting the World Council of Churches! Dr. Stuart Blanch, the Anglican Archbishop of York, claimed that Küng was a great theologian who put the whole world in his debt in a courageous if sometimes provocative attempt "to explain the Gospel in intellectual categories more appropriate to our time". In a charming act of ecumenical courtesy, the Anglican *Church Times* asked whether Pope John Paul II "is going to turn out to be the Ayatollah of the West" (11 January 1980). He did not!

The liberal Catholic establishment was equally indignant. *The Tablet* fulminated against the removal of Küng's *missio canonica* in an editorial which compared this action to the pattern of "life under a Communist regime". It praised Küng as a "noble thinker", and actually demanded the abolition of the Sacred Congregation for the Doctrine of the Faith. I showed this editorial to Cardinal Seper during a meeting which I had with him on Easter Monday 1980. The Cardinal was highly amused, and remarked that *The Tablet* was a journal that "used to be Catholic".

Fifty Swiss theologians announced that they were "profoundly disturbed...our faith in the Vatican is shaken".

Seventy American and Canadian theologians informed the world that: "We publicly affirm our recognition that Professor Küng is indeed a Catholic theologian". The directors of *Concilium*, mouthpiece of the parallel magisterium of liberal theologians, insisted that they did not see "any well-founded reason not to consider our colleague Hans Küng as a Catholic theologian".

The question of "human rights" was raised by many of Küng's defenders, but not one of them explained why an individual has the right to represent any organization, religious or secular, and publicly repudiate its most fundamental principles. Some of Küng's defenders stated that while they did not necessarily agree with his theology they defended his right to teach it. Nothing was heard from these zealous defenders of human rights and free speech when Archbishop Lefebvre was condemned and persecuted, indicating that their concern for these issues was, to put it mildly, somewhat selective. What, above all, the condemnation of Küng made clear is the complete contempt for the authority of the Holy See by the theological establishment throughout the world, men who despite their open and insolent support for Küng, were almost all accredited teachers in Catholic institutions. There can be no doubt whatsoever that this contempt for legitimate ecclesiastical authority, which was virtually unheard of before Vatican II, is the direct result of the Council, a striking manifestation of the so-called spirit of the Council which now pervades and is destroying the Church throughout the countries of the Rhine and the English-speaking world.

Notes

[1] *The Tablet*, 27 November 1965, p. 1318.
[2] RFT, p. 80.
[3] *Catholic Standard* (Dublin), 17 October 1973.
[4] CC, p. 17.

5 CT, p. 356.
6 RFT, p. 22.
7 ABS, p. 132-33. Father Wiltgen puts the number of preparatory schemata as seventy-five, which were eventually reduced to twenty, RFT, p. 22.
8 ABS, pp. 133.
9 *Ibid.*
10 RFT, p. 24.
11 *Ibid.*, p. 23.
12 *Ibid.*, p. 242.
13 *The Tablet*, 18 May 1968, p. 489.
14 RFT, p. 210.
15 CT, p. 367.
16 RFT, pp. 287-8.
17 *The Tablet*, 22 January 1966, p. 114.
18 OC, p. 309.
19 CT, p. 367.
20 VO, p. 23.
21 *The Wanderer*, 1 August and 8 August 1969.
22 CT, p. 353.
23 *The Tablet*, 18 May 1968, p. 488.
24 *The Tablet*, 22 January 1966, p. 114. OR, 18 May 1968, p. 488.
25 CT, p. 389.
26 *Ibid.*, p. 399.
27 DFRC, p. 48.
28 *National Catholic Reporter*, 10 July 1970, p. 15.
29 *The Tablet*, 25 May 1963, p. 576.
30 *Our Sunday Visitor*, 1 September 1974.
31 The texts of these letters and the names of the signatories were published in the Dossier on IDO-C published by *Approaches* but now out of print.
32 *National Catholic Register*, 18 September 1968, p. 7.
33 For examples, see: *The Remnant*, 18 November 1974, p. 11; G. Baum's article entitled "Homosexuals" in *Commonweal*, Vol. XCIX, No. 19, pp. 479-82; and Dale Francis in *Twin Circle*, 8 November 1974.
34 *The Catholic Voice*, 2 October 1968, p. 24.
35 ER, p. 346.
36 Pope Leo XIII, Encyclical Letter *Humanum Genus*. See Chapter XIV for a more detailed treatment.
37 *Concilium* was still being published in 2004. Details can be found on Internet Explorer.
38 *The Tablet*, 18 May 1968, p. 488.
39 The full texts of all the relevant documents appear in the London *Catholic Herald* of 28 February 1975.
40 IC, p. 139.
41 PG, pp. 4-5.

VI

Time Bombs

"There were time bombs in the Council", wrote Archbishop Lefebvre.[1] These "time bombs" were, of course, the ambiguous passages inserted in the official documents by the liberal Fathers and *periti*; passages which could weaken the presentation of traditional teaching by abandoning the traditional terminology, by omissions, or even by ambiguous phraseology which could seem to favour, or at least be compatible with, a non-Catholic interpretation after the Council. To repeat a remark by Cardinal Heenan, cited in the previous chapter: "A determined group could wear down opposition and produce a formula patient of both an orthodox and modernistic interpretation". Archbishop Lefebvre went to the extent of describing the Council as "a mass of ambiguities, vagueness and sentimentality, things which now clearly admit all interpretations and have left all doors open".[2] He has been criticised for such statements, even by some priests who are as far from having Modernist sympathies as he is himself. Father Edward Holloway was an English theologian to whom all Catholics owe a debt of gratitude for the lead he has given in exposing and rejecting the ambiguities, inexactitudes, and vaguely expressed feelings of the Agreed Statements on the Eucharist and Ministry (*sic*) produced by the Catholic–Anglican Joint International

Commission. He is quite adamant that Monsignor Lefebvre's criticisms of the conciliar documents are unjustified. "With all respect", he writes, "it is not true that the decrees of the Council 'lack definition' and proceed along courses alien to the traditional definitions and emphasis of the Church in preceding councils...they do express clearly the nature and purposes, the doctrines and the structures of the Church, and do it without ambiguity".[3] It would, of course, be necessary to write an almost endless series of books to vindicate either of these views, not simply examining the final format of the documents but comparing them with the original schemata which they replaced. To give just one example, the Constitution on the Church includes a passage stating that:

> Religious submission of will and mind must be shown in a special way to the authentic teaching authority of the Roman Pontiff, even when he is not speaking *ex cathedra*. That is, it must be shown in such a way that his Supreme Magisterium is acknowledged with reverence, the judgements made by him are sincerely adhered to, according to his manifest mind and will. His mind and will in the matter may be made known chiefly either from the character of the documents, from his frequent repetition of the same doctrine, or from his manner of speaking.[4]

"There you are!" Father Holloway could point out, "a very fine passage. What more could you want? It proves my point".

But it must be borne in mind that Archbishop Lefebvre was appointed by Pope John as a member of the Central Preparatory Commission which made a laborious examination of all the original schemata as they were prepared. He could have informed Father Holloway that the original schema contained an almost identical passage but with the addition of these words which are, of course, a quotation from *Humani Generis*: "And when the Roman Pontiffs go out of their way to pronounce on some subject which has hitherto been controverted, it must be clear to everybody concerned that, in the mind and intention of the Pontiffs concerned, this subject can no longer be regarded as a matter of free debate among theologians".[5] This passage was removed from the revised schema. A group of bishops submitted an emendation asking that it should be replaced, but their suggestion was not accepted.[6]

"There you are!" Monsignor Lefebvre could reply. "It proves my point".

It could be argued that the deleted passage is contained implicitly in the one that remains. It is hardly possible to adhere sincerely to the manifest mind and will of the Sovereign Pontiff while making his decision a matter for free debate. Nonetheless, what a fine quotation the one from *Humani Generis*, had it remained in the Constitution on the Church, would have been to cite against the theologians who expressed their public dissent from *Humanae Vitae*. Once again, it could be argued that it can still be used against them as it is of great authority, coming from an encyclical—but how much notice is taken of "pre-conciliar" encyclicals? Had this passage remained in the Constitution on the Church these theologians could have been accused of defying the explicit teaching of Vatican II—the Council of which they all claim to be the most zealous disciples. Father Holloway did concede that there are elements which can be picked out "which mean different things to different interpreters especially in the light, or the twilight, of the Council debates". But he insists that taken within their context and clarified by the footnotes they can be interpreted "only in a sense consistent with tradition if the interpreter is honest to the Constitution as a *conciliar* document. There is no *conciliar* sense of any document of a general council, which abstracts or derogates from the explicit sense the Pope gives to the document". The final sentence in particular is totally correct, and in Chapter XII, dealing with the status of the documents, some stress is laid upon the fact that where an apparent ambiguity occurs we have a duty to interpret it, and insist that it is interpreted, in a sense consistent with the traditional teaching of the Church. The so-called "Spirit of Vatican II" is certainly based upon a misinterpretation of the documents in the sense that the Holy Ghost could not have intended a general council to promulgate unorthodox teaching. This remains true even if the passage concerned is being interpreted by the *periti* who drafted it in the sense that they intended—for it is the sense intended by the legislator and not those who helped him to produce his legislation which is legally binding. But this in no way weakens Archbishop Lefebvre's charge of ambiguity—and, as this chapter will make clear, he is by no means alone in making it. The fact that a particular passage *ought* to be interpreted only in one way does not alter the fact that it *can* be interpreted in another. When a Protestant praises some aspect of a Vatican II document as a step towards Protestantism it can be argued that he is in error as this cannot be the case—but prior to this Council, Catholic teaching had been stated so clearly and so explicitly that no such impression could have been given. Only one interpretation, the orthodox Catholic interpretation, was possible. *The Concise Oxford Dictionary* defines ambiguity as an "expression capable of more than one meaning". Readers must decide for themselves whether such ambiguity does exist in the Council documents, and also whether or not there was a change of emphasis with regard to certain basic doctrines of such an extent that Protestants in good faith imagine the Church is approaching the point of accepting their position. In some cases Protestant claims pass beyond ambiguity and express the clear teaching of certain documents.

There can be little doubt that Professor Oscar Cullmann was one of the most distinguished scholars among the Protestant observers at the Council, a man of such stature and integrity that he merits the respect of Catholics of every shade of opinion. It would be a rash commentator indeed who could dismiss Professor Cullmann's opinion lightly, and the extent to which his opinions coincide with those of Archbishop Lefebvre is a factor which requires the most careful consideration. He insists that:

> The definitive texts are for the most part compromise texts (*textes de compromis*). On far too many occasions they juxtapose opposing viewpoints without establishing any genuine internal link between them. Thus every affirmation of the power of bishops is accompanied in a manner which is almost tedious by an insistence upon the authority of the Pope....There is nonetheless as the basis of all these documents an intention of renewal from which reforms can emerge after the Council.
>
> This is the reason why, even while accepting that these are compromise texts, I do not share the pessimism of those who subscribe to the slogan that: "Nothing will come out of the Council!" *All the texts are formulated in such a manner than no door is closed and that they will not present any future obstacle to discussions among Catholics or dialogue with non-Catholics, as was the case with the dogmatic decisions of previous councils* [my emphasis].[7]

The importance of Professor Cullmann's assessment of the ambiguous nature of the Conciliar texts can only be enhanced when it is considered that there can be very few Catholics whose knowledge of either the Council or its texts even approaches his own.

An equally impressive testimony to Monsignor Lefebvre's thesis comes from Peter Hebblethwaite. Until he left the priesthood to marry he was editor of the Jesuit journal *The Month*, once one of the most reputable journals in the English-speaking Catholic world, but now reduced to the status of little more than a purveyor of very tedious liberal party-line hand-outs. Hebblethwaite concedes that much of the post-conciliar malaise springs from the fact that the disputants are literally talking at cross-purposes. The Council laid down admirable (*sic*) principles which were resisted by some while others developed and extended them. But it has produced compromise texts, and where it could not solve a difficulty, it hopefully set the contrasting positions alongside each other. The result is that the conciliar texts are capable of different readings:

> Thus it is perfectly possible to read the Council as the reassertion of Vatican I's intransigent teaching on the power of the papacy; one can quote chapter and paragraph to that effect. But there is another reading equally possible which stresses that the Pope exercises his office of unity in the context of the world's bishops ('collegiality'). If the first reading leads back into the fortress and pulls down the drawbridge, the second makes ecumenical progress possible.[8]

A French theologian, at the opposite end of the theological spectrum to Mr. Hebblethwaite, selected Chapter 5 of the schema on ecumenism for particular censure in view of its "scarcely credible incoherence". According to this theologian, Father de Broglie-Revel, S.J., a professor of dogmatic theology at the Gregorian University, certain passages in this chapter "subscribed without any reservation to the most extreme theses of liberalism". He claimed that "this incoherence was intended, in reality, to cover up an equivocation, for it was a question of attempting an impossible compromise between liberal principles and the teaching of Pope Pius IX".[9]

A Protestant observer who considered the official documents to be ambiguous was David F. Wells, Associate Professor of Church History at the Trinity Evangelical Divinity School in Illinois. His book *Revolution in Rome* was reviewed by the distinguished New Zealand theologian Father G. H. Duggan in *Faith*, the bi-monthly journal which Father Holloway edits. "In all honesty", writes Father Duggan, "we must admit, I think, that the author is on target when he points to certain ambiguities in the documents of Vatican II, *ambiguities which the 'progressive' theologians have exploited to the full*"[10] (my emphasis). This is a very similar judgement to that of Bishop Graber cited in Chapter I. Archbishop Lefebvre explained that the majority of Council Fathers had not imagined for one moment that the Council documents would be used in this way, and that it was the scheme of only a group of bishops and *periti*.[11] Cardinal Heenan confirmed that few of the bishops realised what the experts were planning.[12] Archbishop Lefebvre cited a false ecumenism which aimed at minimising anything in the documents which might offend the Orthodox and above all the Protestants as the principal motive behind the ambiguous terminology.[13] Cardinal Heenan made the same point in much stronger language:

> In the Council there was a small group of what our separated brethren call ecumaniacs. These sincere but simple men see an ecumenical aspect in everything. Owing to this preoccupation with ecumenism, the word itself became a catch-phrase in the Council. No topic came up for discussion but it was examined for ecumenical content. The wilder ecumenists used a theological geiger counter to detect any statement of Catholic belief that might not be fully acceptable to non-Catholics.[14]

This preoccupation with appeasement rather than truth was not unopposed. Bishop Luigi Carli of Segni "maintained that certain Council Fathers had carried their ecumenical preoccupation to excess. It was no longer possible, he charged, to speak about Our Lady; no one might be called heretical; no one might use the expression 'Church Militant'; and it was no longer possible to call attention to the inherent powers of the Catholic Church".[15] The Servite Bishop Giocondo Grotti from Brazil asked:

> Does ecumenism consist in confessing or in hiding the truth? Ought the Council to explain Catholic doctrine, or the doctrine of our separated brethren?...Hiding the truth separates both us and those separated from us. It hurts us because we appear as hypocrites. It hurts those separated from us because it makes them appear weak and capable of being offended by the truth.[16]

The justification for this lack of precision was that the Council was pastoral and not dogmatic. "The Second Vatican Council was unique in yet another way", wrote Cardinal Heenan. "It deliberately limited its own objectives. There were to be no specific definitions. Its purpose from the first was pastoral renewal within the Church and a fresh approach to those outside".[17] Archbishop Lefebvre stressed the fact that:

> The Council steadily refused to give exact definitions of the matters under discussion. It is this rejection of definitions, this refusal to examine philosophically and theologically the questions under discussion which meant that we could do no more than describe them, not define them. Not only were they not defined, but very often in the course of discussions on the subjects, the traditional definition was falsified. I believe that is why we are now

confronted with a whole system which we cannot manage to grasp and can keep in check only with difficulty, because the traditional definitions, the true definitions, are no longer accepted.[18]

Cardinal Ruffini expressed particular concern at the fact that the Decree on Ecumenism failed to provide any adequate definition of the word "ecumenism" itself—a factor which he considered dangerous as the word is used in a different sense by Catholics and Protestants.[19] Cardinal Heenan stated that:

> The Second Vatican Council had no set theme. Anything with a pastoral or ecumenical significance could find a place on its agenda. That is why its treatment of certain questions is bound to be inadequate. We are now able to recognise that a constitution of a council should contain only those questions already sufficiently mature before the Council began. No question is ripe for conciliar decision until theologians have studied it in deliberate and unhurried fashion. Only after long thought and prayer should the Fathers be called upon to give a verdict in solemn Council. But this process was not possible in Vatican II.[20]

Monsignor Lefebvre referred to the difficulty of obtaining precise definitions of the terms under discussion. When asked to define such terms as "collegiality" or "ecumenism" the commission secretaries would reply: "'This is a pastoral Council aimed at the world as a whole. Consequently it is pointless to frame here definitions which would not be understood'. But surely it is the height of stupidity to think that we can meet and yet fail to define the very terms we are discussing".[21]

The original draft of the Dogmatic Constitution on the Church stated that the Church, existing on earth as a structured society, *is* the Catholic Church.[22] This was changed to: "This Church constituted and organised in the world as a society, *subsists* in the Catholic Church...".[23] Now what does "subsists" mean and why was the change made? Some orthodox commentators, no doubt in all sincerity, claimed that "is" and "subsists" mean the same thing. Once again, the question must be put: if so, why was the change made? Gregory Baum interpreted it in precisely the modernistic sense which Cardinal Heenan had said was possible. "Instead of simply identifying the Church of Christ with the Catholic Church, the Constitution rather says more carefully that the Church of Christ 'subsists' in the Catholic Church. The body of Christ is present in the Catholic Church, but, at the same time, without losing its historical and incarnate character, transcends it...".[24]

Pope Pius XII, however, made the simple identification of the Church of Christ with the Catholic Church in his encyclicals *Mystici Corporis Christi* and *Humani Generis*, and in doing so was faithfully reflecting the traditional teaching of the Church. An Anglican observer quoted Gregory Baum's explanation of "subsists in" with great approval and claimed with complete assurance that: "The Council has, therefore, admitted that the Church of Christ is something bigger than the Roman Catholic Church".[25] However, the Decree on the Catholic Eastern Churches states:

> That Church, Holy and Catholic, which is the Mystical Body of Christ, is made up of the faithful who are organically united in the Holy Spirit through the same faith, the same sacraments, and the same government, and who combining into various groups held together by a hierarchy, form separate Churches or rites.[26]

The teaching of Pius XII is thus taught specifically by the Council. As Alice in Wonderland expressed it: "Curiouser and curiouser".

On 6 August 2000, the Congregation for the Doctrine of the Faith (CDF) published the Declaration on the Unicity and Salvific Universality of Jesus Christ and the Church (*Dominus Jesus*) which included an authoritative interpretation of the term "subsists" as used by the Second Vatican Council. It is unlikely in the extreme that this was the interpretation intended by the *periti* who drafted the Constitution on the Church, but whatever their intention may have been the clarification of the CDF represents the official teaching of the Church:

> The interpretation of those who would derive from the formula *subsistit in* the thesis that the one Church of Christ could subsist also in non-Catholic Churches and ecclesial communities is therefore contrary to the authentic meaning of *Lumen Gentium*. The Council instead chose the word *subsistit* precisely to clarify that there exists only one "subsistence" of the true Church, while outside her visible structure there only exist *elementa Ecclesiae*, which—being elements of that same Church—tend and lead toward the Catholic Church.

This authoritative interpretation means that no Catholic can accept the Gregory Baum thesis. A more detailed exposition of the *Dominus Jesus* ruling is included as Appendix V.

The Dogmatic Constitution on the Church, *Lumen Gentium*, contains a great deal of traditional and orthodox Catholic terminology well calculated to inspire confidence. Such confidence is likely to be weakened, however, when it is realised how pleasing the document is to both Catholic ecumaniacs as well as to Protestants. If the document is as sound as it appears, then why do those who reject Catholic teaching praise it? The answer can only be found by comparing it with previous statements which were anathema to those who reject the unique claims of the Catholic Church, particularly the decrees of Trent and Vatican I. Father (now Cardinal) Avery Dulles, who wishes to relegate the Immaculate Conception of our Blessed Lady to the status of an optional belief, in order to facilitate union with Protestants who reject this doctrine, is full of enthusiasm for *Lumen Gentium*. He is particularly pleased at the contrast with the original schema which he saw as influenced "by centuries of anti-Protestant polemics" and with a "heavy emphasis on the hierarchical and juridical aspects of the Church, including the supremacy of the pope". In contrast with this, the revised constitution is praised because: "Avoiding rigid definitions and scholastic or juridical subtleties, the Council shows a marked preference for vivid and biblical language....The tone of the document is, moreover, strongly ecumenical".[27]

Dr. A. C. Outler, a Protestant commentator, was equally enthusiastic about the difference between the original and the revised texts. He categorises the original as "an ominous sample of what has been called 'the siege mentality of preconciliar Rome'".[28] Where the finalised text is concerned, he is certain that Protestants "will find little here that offends and much that edifies".[29]

The section on collegiality is particularly ambiguous. Dr. McAfee Brown, a Protestant observer at the Council, and subsequently one of the world's best-known professional ecumenists, interpreted this section of the document as follows:

> Teaching authority is henceforth to be understood as *collegial* authority—the pope as head of the college and not simply *primus inter pares*, but not fully defined save in relation to the college, and the bishops as members of the college, a college not fully defined save as the college

of which the pope is head. The doctrine is carefully and tentatively worded—so that both "liberal" and "conservative" can read it and take heart—but it is clear that it contained the kernel of a doctrinal breakthrough with momentous implications, leading as it will to a kind of theological and structural decentralization of power in the Catholic Church. Certain practical implications are observable already: the pope has appointed a "synod of bishops" to meet with him from time to time to assist the rule of the church, and the documents promulgated at Vatican II were promulgated not by the pope alone, as was true at Vatican I, but by "Paul, bishop, servant of the servants of God, together with the Fathers of the Sacred Council".[30]

Pope Paul himself was so concerned about the possible ambiguity of the explanation of collegiality that he felt bound to intervene by adding an explanatory note which, although not an integral part of the constitution itself, was published in the Acts of the Apostolic See. It sets forth "in more technical and juridical language how certain points in the text are to be understood".[31] In particular, this appendix represents the clear intention of the Pope to uphold the authority of the papal primacy as defined by Vatican I. However, while it certainly does this, it does not clarify precisely what collegiality is and hence confusion remains to this day. Unfortunately, because this clarification comes in an appendix, and not in the text of the Constitution itself, it lacks the prestige attached to teaching actually contained within a dogmatic constitution but, equally and unfortunately, it was nevertheless instrumental in obtaining overwhelming support for the constitution because it went "far to remove the lingering doubts of some Council Fathers and thus pave the way for the almost unanimous acceptance which the Constitution on the Church finally received".[32] Dr. S. Mc-

Crea Cavert, a Protestant commentator, is full of praise for the Decree on Ecumenism:

> The promise of a new era is especially evident in the new way in which the decree speaks of non-Catholic Christians...instead of dogmatically insisting on their return to Rome as the only possible movement towards unity, the decree is concerned with a movement toward Christ. From a Protestant angle, this fresh orientation is of the highest consequence and is pregnant with creative possibilities".[33]

Is such an interpretation consistent with the decree itself? Technically the answer must be that it is not. As Father Holloway rightly insisted, conciliar documents must be interpreted in a sense that conforms to tradition. But this does not alter the fact that the *periti* have worded it in such a way that Protestants, whose sincerity we have no right to question, believe that such an interpretation is consistent with the decree. It states, for example, that:

> For men who believe in Christ and have been properly baptised are brought into a certain, though imperfect, communion with the Catholic Church....They therefore have a right to be honoured by the title Christian, and are properly regarded as brothers in the Lord by the sons of the Catholic Church. Moreover some, even very many, of the most significant elements or endowments which together go to build up and give life to the Church herself can exist outside the visible boundaries of the Catholic Church: the written word of God; the life of grace; faith, hope and charity, along with other interior gifts of the Holy Spirit and visible elements. All of these, which come from Christ and lead back to Him, belong by right to the one Church of Christ.[34]

Time Bombs

The words, "by right" were added to the final sentence by Pope Paul VI. It is fascinating to examine the footnotes to the Abbott edition of the Council documents and to see the nineteen occasions on which Pope Paul intervened by adding clarifications to the text precisely to avoid ambiguity. To give just one more example, the decree stated: "And yet everyone, though in different ways, longs that there may be one visible Church of God". The Pope amended the text to read: "And yet *almost* everyone..." because, of course, some Protestants deny that Christ founded a visible Church.[35]

Dr. McAfee Brown attached the very greatest importance to Article I of the decree, in which: "It affirms, from a Catholic standpoint, that the Holy Spirit works *through* Protestant 'churches and ecclesial communities', and not just *in spite of* them. God gives his gifts to the separated brethren in their corporate ecclesial life, and not merely in their encounters with God".[36] Does the decree actually state this? It does indeed, but adds immediately (Nevertheless...) a carefully worded qualification which will not have been pleasing to Protestants:

> It follows that these separated Churches and Communities, though we believe they suffer from defects already mentioned, have by no means been deprived of significance and importance in the mystery of salvation. For the Spirit of Christ has not refrained from using them as means of salvation which derive their efficacy from the very fullness of grace and truth entrusted to the Catholic Church.[37]
>
> *Nevertheless*, our separated brethren, whether considered as individuals or as Communities and Churches, are not blessed with that unity which Jesus Christ wished to bestow on all those whom He has regenerated and vivified into one body and newness of life—that unity which the holy Scriptures and the revered tradition of

the Church proclaim. For it is through Christ's Catholic Church alone, which is the all-embracing means of salvation (*generale auxilium salutis*)[38] that the fullness of the means of salvation can be obtained. It was to the apostolic college alone, of which Peter is the head, that we believe Our Lord entrusted all the blessings of the New Covenant, in order to establish on earth the one Body of Christ into which all those should be fully incorporated who already belong in any way to God's People.[39]

Dr. McAfee Brown also expressed satisfaction at the fact that "non-Catholic liturgical actions are described in such a way that 'these actions can truly engender a life of grace, and can rightly be described as providing access to the community of salvation'".[40] The decree does not in fact say this. It reads: "The brethren divided from us also carry out many of the sacred actions of the Christian religion. Undoubtedly, in ways that vary according to the condition of each Church or Community, these actions can truly engender...". This is a typical example of the ambiguity condemned by Archbishop Lefebvre. The passage does not refer to which of the sacred actions of the Christian religion are referred to, and who the separated brethren are who carry them out. The Orthodox Eastern Churches, for example, celebrate seven valid sacraments, have a beautiful liturgy, great devotion to Our Lady, and theological teaching which in most important respect corresponds to that of the Catholic Church. The Orthodox liturgy receives specific mention for its sublimity:

> Everybody also knows with what love the Eastern Christians enact the sacred liturgy, especially the celebration of the Eucharist, which is the source of the Church's life and the pledge of future glory. In this celebration the faithful, united with their bishop and endowed with an

outpouring of the Holy Spirit, gain access to God the Father through the Son, the Word, made flesh, who suffered and was glorified. And so, made "partakers of the divine nature" (2 Pet. 1:4), they enter into communion with the most holy Trinity. Hence, through the celebration of the Eucharist of the Lord in each of these Churches, the Church of God is built up and grows in stature, while through the rite of concelebration their bond with one another is made manifest....Although these Churches are separated from us, they possess true sacraments, above all—by apostolic succession—the priesthood and the Eucharist, whereby they are still joined to us in a very close relationship.[41]

Dr. Cavert complains about the ambiguity of the document in one place. The decree stops short of referring to all Protestant denominations as "Churches" and refers to them as "Churches and ecclesial communities". "This", he comments, "apparently implies a difference between 'Church' and 'ecclesial community'. What is this difference? Non-Catholics still need further light as to how far the Catholic Church goes in acknowledging the reality of the Church beyond its own borders".[42]

Dr. Cavert was extremely naive in asking what distinction the decree makes between Churches and ecclesial communities. It should first be made clear what a church is, making a distinction between a local Church and the Universal Church. A local church, written sometimes with an upper case "C" and some times with a lower case, is a diocese. There is the church of New York, the church of Paris, the church of Milan, the church of Madrid. To be an authentic local church it is necessary to have clergy with valid orders, apostolic succession, and a valid Eucharist, all of which are possessed by the Orthodox churches (dioceses). But does authenticity require communion with the Pope?

Many readers will be surprised to learn that it does not. The local churches of Moscow, Constantinople, and Athens are undoubtedly authentic local churches even though, as the decree states, "these churches are separated from us"—"separated" being a euphemism for schismatic (separated and schismatic having the same meaning).

In his Apostolic Letter *Arcano Divinae Providentiae*, 8 September 1868, Pope Pius IX invited the bishops of the churches of the Oriental Rite not in communion with Rome to be present at the First Vatican Council on an equal basis with the bishops of the Latin Rite in communion with Rome. "Not in communion" is evidently another euphemism for schismatic. Pope Pius wrote:

> Since We must ceaselessly devote all Our efforts and thoughts to looking after the salvation of all who acknowledge and adore Christ Jesus, We turn Our eyes and Our paternal heart toward those churches that were once joined closely with this Apostolic See, and that were highly praised for their holiness and sacred teaching, and that produced abundant fruits of divine glory and the salvation of souls. But now, through the nefarious arts and machinations of him who incited the first schism in heaven, these churches are, to our great sorrow, cut off and separated from communion with the holy Roman Church, which has spread through the whole world....Since, with the advice of our venerable Brethren, the Cardinals of the holy Roman Church, we have recently announced and convoked an Ecumenical Synod, to be celebrated in Rome next year beginning on the eighth day of December dedicated to the Immaculate Conception of the Virgin Mary, Mother of God, We again direct our voice to you. With still greater earnestness of heart, We implore, remind, and beseech you, so that you may wish to come to this general synod, just as your

predecessors assembled at the Second Council of Lyons, held by Blessed Gregory IX, Our memorable predecessor; and at the Council of Florence, celebrated by Eugene IV, Our predecessor of happy memory.

It is sad to relate that the Orthodox Churches declined this gracious invitation. Pope Pius sent a very different Apostolic Letter, *Iam Vos Omnes*, 13 September 1868, to all Protestants and other non-Catholics on the occasion of Vatican I. This letter took a very different approach to that sent to the Orthodox Churches, making it clear to Protestants that they are in a state of grave doctrinal error and form no part of the Church founded by Our Lord:

> We, on the occasion of the coming Council, cannot refrain from addressing Our apostolic and paternal words to all who acknowledge the same Christ Jesus as Redeemer, and who glory in the Christian name, but who do not profess the true faith of Christ or follow the communion of the Catholic Church. We do this, so that in all zeal and charity We may strongly advise, exhort, and beseech them to consider seriously and to take heed whether or not they are following the road prescribed by Christ the Lord, which leads to eternal salvation.
>
> No one can indeed doubt that Christ Jesus Himself, in order that He might apply the fruits of His redemption to all generations of men, established here on earth upon Peter His unique Church, that is, the one, holy, Catholic, apostolic Church; and that He conferred on her all the power necessary to guard integral and inviolate the deposit of faith, and to hand on the same faith to all peoples, races, and nations; so that through Baptism all men might be admitted into His Mystical Body, and so that in them might be preserved always and perfected this new life of grace, without which no one can ever merit and

attain eternal life; so that also the same Church, which constitutes His Mystical Body, may endure and flourish in her own true nature, always firm and unchanged until the end of the world, and may provide all her children with the means of salvation.

Let each one ponder and meditate carefully about the condition of the various religious groups that disagree among themselves and that are separated from the Catholic Church, which without intermission since the time of Christ the Lord and His apostles has always exercised, through His legitimate sacred shepherds, and still exercises at the present time the divine power transmitted to her by the Lord Himself. If he does so, he must easily persuade himself that no single one of these groups, or all of them together, constitute and are in any manner that one Catholic Church which Christ the Lord erected, established, and willed; and that these groups can in no way be called members or parts of the same Church as long as they are visibly separated from Catholic unity. For groups of this kind lack that living authority established by God, which teaches men about matters of faith and morals especially, and guides them in all that pertains to eternal salvation.

Also these groups vary continually in their teachings, nor does this changeableness and instability ever cease. As everyone easily understands and plainly and openly acknowledges, this is directly opposed to the Church instituted by Christ the Lord, in which the truth must always remain immutable, never subject to change, just as the deposit handed over to the Church is to be guarded whole and entire.

What Pope Pius IX wrote concerning Protestants in 1868 is as valid today as it was then, but is certainly not stated unequivocally in the Decree on Ecumenism, even though it is not specifically contradicted.

The Protestant observer Dr. Oscar Cullmann considers that the decree contains a passage which is "the most revolutionary to be found not only in the *schema de oecumenismo* but in any of the schemata of the present Council".[43] The passage reads: "When comparing doctrines, they should remember that in Catholic teaching there exists an order or 'hierarchy' of truths, since they vary in their relationship to the foundation of the Christian faith".[44] Dr. McAfee Brown insisted that: "One must concur in Professor Cullmann's judgement and stress the importance of the concept in the *ecumenical revolution*"[45] (my emphasis). This phrase, a very effective time bomb, is right at the top of the hierarchy of ecumenical slogans, and is a standard text used by Protestants and some Catholic ecumenists for downplaying "stumbling blocks" in the path of reunion. Dr. McAfee Brown cited the dogma of the Assumption as a "stumbling block in ecumenical discussion" and would clearly like to see it well down on the scale of the "hierarchy of truths". He deplores Pope Pius XII's statement in his Bull on the Assumption that one who denies the dogma "has cut himself off entirely from the divine and Catholic faith".

It is worthwhile contrasting the passage cited by Dr. Cullmann from the Decree on Ecumenism with what Pope Pius XI taught in his encyclical *Mortalium Animos* on the Promotion of True Religious Unity.

> In matters of faith, it is not permitted to make a distinction between fundamental and so-called non-fundamental articles of faith, as if the first ought to be held by all, and the second the faithful are free to accept or not accept. The supernatural virtue of faith has, as its formal cause, the authority of God the Revealer, which suffers no such division. Therefore, as many as are of

> Christ give, for example, to the dogma of the Immaculate Conception the same faith they give to the mystery of the August Trinity, and they believe in the Incarnation of the Word no differently than they believe in the infallible teaching power of the Pope in the sense defined by the Vatican Ecumenical Council. That these truths have been solemnly sanctioned and defined by the Church at various times, some of them even quite recently, makes no difference to their certainty, nor to our obligation of believing them. Has not God revealed them all?

The Decree on Ecumenism itself informs us in the paragraph (11) prior to its hierarchy of truth time bomb, that: "Nothing is so foreign to the spirit of ecumenism as a false conciliatory approach which harms the purity of Catholic doctrine and obscures its assured genuine meaning".[46] The decree would have been far more unsatisfactory had not, as is mentioned above, Pope Paul intervened personally on 19 November 1964 and inserted nineteen changes into the text, much to the fury of the liberal Fathers and *periti*, and the Protestant observers. This was just one day before the vote was to be taken and made it too late for these changes to be debated. The decree states for example: "It is through Christ's Catholic Church alone, which is the all embracing means of salvation, that the fullness of the means of salvation can be obtained".[47] Dr. McAfee Brown commented:

> Dismay at this action was based on three considerations: (a) in the light of the conciliar affirmation of collegiality, the unilateral action of the Pope seemed particularly un-collegial, (b) if the Pope felt that changes were necessary they should have been introduced sooner so that they could have been subject to normal conciliar reflection, and (c) while most of the changes were merely

verbal, one at least was substantive and seemed to jeopardise the tone of the document as a whole.[48]

However strong his disapproval of the changes, Dr. McAfee Brown did not consider them to be too damaging; "The case of the Nineteen Interventions, while unfortunate, was not disastrous, and even the substantive change can be placed in a context which does not seriously impair the ecumenical significance of the document".[49] It is sad to note that there can be little doubt that the decree would have been passed the next day even without these interventions.

Father Raymond Dulac has analysed the Decree on the Renewal of the Religious Life, and he points out a number of ambiguous phrases which have been used as an excuse for destroying the entire basis of the religious life of some communities as intended by their founders.[50] Take what might seem the most trivial example, but one which has had results which every Catholic must have noticed, that of the religious habit. Paragraph 17 of the decree states that these should "meet the requirements of health and be suited to the circumstances of time and place as well as to the service required by those who wear them. Habits of men and women which do not correspond to these norms are to be changed". This all sounds reasonable enough, and it is hardly surprising that most Fathers passed it without a qualm. However, when read carefully it is immediately clear that the norms laid down in this time bomb are generalised enough to mean anything or nothing. It is no exaggeration to claim that some orders of women have become obsessed with the question of their habit; modification has followed modification until all too frequently they have done away with the habit altogether. It would be unfair to claim that the passage cited envisaged or encouraged the present deplorable state of affairs where so many nuns dress in a manner which varies from the ludicrous to the scandalous—but it certainly initiated the process which led to this. The phrase in question, to quote Archbishop Lefebvre, "now clearly admits all interpretations and has left all doors open".[51]

The Decree on the Ministry and Life of Priests has the following message according to a Protestant commentator, Dr. J. O. Nelson: "Come out of your solitary Masses, your prelatical doting upon rank or affluence, your privileged station at altar or confessional—and identify radiantly, humbly, with everyman"![52] A ridiculous interpretation?—perhaps. But this is precisely what thousands of Catholic priests have done, tens of thousands in the United States alone, to the extent of abandoning their vocations, marrying, and frequently leaving the Church completely.

The Constitution on the Sacred Liturgy is dealt with in detail in Chapter XVI. It will suffice to cite here the opinion of a Protestant commentator who is delighted with statements in the Constitution which are "bound to evoke the enthusiastic approval of anyone who believes that the Reformation was the work of the Holy Spirit".[53] No such comments were made when Pope Pius XII issued his encyclical *Mediator Dei*; no such comments were made when Pope Paul VI issued his encyclical on the Eucharist, *Mysterium Fidei*, in 1965. Indeed, in this encyclical Pope Paul not only used the traditional terminology, particularly that of Trent, but insisted upon the importance of not departing from it. He was singled out for particular censure precisely because of the contrast between the language of this encyclical and that of the Liturgy Constitution. Gregory Baum complains that Pope Paul teaches the doctrine of sacrifice and the Real Presence "in the context in which they emerged at the Council of Trent. Since Pope Paul's terminology is so different from the Constitution on the Liturgy, it is not easy to fit his encyclical harmoniously into the conciliar teaching of Vatican II".[54]

Archbishop Lefebvre has selected the Constitution on the Church in the Modern World (*Gaudium et Spes*) for particular mention in view of its equivocal nature.[55] This observation was confirmed by Dr. McAfee Brown. He found it a matter of very great encouragement that the document contains a "very important advance" in its teaching on marriage, "for it goes far beyond the traditional teaching that the procreation and education of children are the primary ends of marriage. Thanks to the intervention of such men as Cardinals Léger and Suenens, the document stresses the importance of conjugal love".[56] Monsignor Lefebvre saw the matter in a different light.

> Marriage was always traditionally defined by the first end of marriage, which was procreation, and the secondary end, which was conjugal love. Well, at the Council there was an expressed desire to change that definition and state that there was no longer a primary end, but that the two ends of procreational and conjugal love were equivalent. It was Cardinal Suenens who launched this attack on the very purpose of marriage, and I still remember how Cardinal Browne, Master General of the Dominicans, rose to cry "*Caveatis*! *Caveatis*! Beware! Beware"! He declared vehemently: "If we accept this definition we are running contrary to the whole tradition of the Church and we are about to pervert the meaning of marriage. We have no right to go against the traditional definitions of the Church".
>
> So great was the emotion aroused in the assembly that Cardinal Suenens was asked, I believe by the Holy Father, to make some slight alteration in the terms he had used, or even to change them altogether. That is only one example, but you can see how everything said on the question of marriage ties up with the false conception expressed by Cardinal Suenens, that conjugal love, now called quite simply and far more crudely "sexuality", is henceforth the end of marriage, not procreation

only. The result—in the name of "sexuality" all acts are permissible: contraception, birth control, the use of marriage with all that can hinder birth, and, ultimately, abortion. So it goes on.[57]

Commenting on Cardinal Browne's dramatic intervention, an American Father wrote in 1973: "We thought it amusing then; we might take it a little more seriously now".[58] It is important to note that Archbishop Lefebvre and Dr. McAfee Brown both detected the same possible interpretation of the document—although the latter approves while the former does not. As this chapter should make clear, Monsignor Lefebvre's case against the conciliar documents is strengthened considerably by the frequency with which his interpretations correspond with those of other commentators, sometimes at the opposite end of the theological spectrum.

One of the most serious omissions from the text of *Gaudium et Spes* is a specific condemnation of contraception. Catholics who have the determination and stamina to read the text of this verbose and vacuous document might well contend that it does contain a condemnation of contraception. The relevant passage reads: "...sons of the Church may not undertake methods of regulating procreation which are found blameworthy by the teaching authority of the Church in its unfolding of the divine law".[59] Dr. McAfee Brown complained that this passage is "deliberately ambiguous", but comforts fellow Protestants who might take a pessimistic view of the passage by explaining that "in spite of strong efforts to foreclose discussion of birth control, the Council deliberately left the matter open, and thus achieved at least a modest victory".[60]

There was a very close relationship between Protestant observers and the liberal *periti*, and when Dr. McAfee Brown used the word "deliberately" we can presume that he had good grounds for doing so. His interpretation of the text in question is identical with that of Charles Davis, an English *peritus* who has since apostatised and married. He writes:

> On the question of methods of birth control, the Council deliberately refrained from committing itself. Its carefully worded references to the subject do no more than state the obvious truth that unlawful methods, reprobated by the Church's teaching authority in interpreting divine law, are excluded. It does not determine what these are, nor does it touch the question of the precise authority of previous pronouncements. A footnote refers to *Casti Connubii* and to Pope Pius XII's address to midwives, but adds a reference to Pope Paul's allocution of 1964 and a statement that investigations of the matter are under way. There is thus no reinforcement of *Casti Connubii* and Pius XII's address. The Council leaves the matter alone, waiting for further clarification. Its decision to do so inevitably confirms that serious doubt exists on the subject within the Church.[61]

The story behind the insertion of the footnote referred to by Charles Davis (the famous footnote 14) reveals a great deal of the manner in which the conciliar texts were finalised. Pope Paul had been so disturbed at the ambivalence of the reference to birth control that he sent four special amendments to the commission intended to reinforce the traditional teaching. To add to the indignation of the liberals, the *periti* were asked to leave the room when the commission members were handed their copies. Among these amendments were to be a specific condemnation of contraception and the addition of a footnote referring to *Casti Connubii* and Pope Pius XII's allocution to midwives, which were to be cited as "the two most outstanding documents on this subject". The footnote was to include specific references to the pages in these documents condemning contraception. The machinations which took place to frustrate the Pope's intentions, amounting to outright defiance, are described in detail by Father Wiltgen and need not be repeated here.[62] Suffice to say, when the final revision of the schema was distributed to the Council Fathers on 3 December 1965, there was no specific reference to artificial contraceptives and the footnote did not contain the page references specified by the Pope. The commission, on its own initiative, had added a reference to Pope Paul's own 1964 allocution, cited by Charles Davis, referring to the fact that the question was under consideration. This allocution insisted that the traditional norms must be observed unless the Pope eventually modified them, but, as Charles Davis points out, the reference to the statement that investigations are under way "inevitably confirms that doubt exists on the subject within the Church".

Pope Paul gave way on the question of having a specific condemnation of artificial contraception within the text of *Gaudium et Spes,* but insisted that the page references he had specified should be included in the footnote. At the same time, he allowed the reference to his own 23 June 1964 allocution to remain as well. Thus, if the footnote is taken into consideration, the use of contraceptives is implicitly, even explicitly condemned—but this does not prevent Protestants and liberal Catholics from claiming with great satisfaction that the Pastoral Constitution *Gaudium et Spes* does not contain a specific condemnation of contraception—and this in a document purporting to deal with the Church in the Modern World where the question of contraception is one of the key factors which sets Catholics apart as a people peculiar to God, in the world but not of it. It will be shown in Chapter XIII that precisely the same state of affairs occurred in the section of this same constitution dealing with atheistic communism—or, rather, not dealing with it, for a specific condemnation of communism was excluded from the text by a process of calculated fraud.

Enough should have been written in this chapter to show how well justified was Archbishop Lefebvre's allegation that there are "time bombs" in the texts of Vatican II. This will be made even clearer as this book proceeds. The deficiencies of these documents do not simply consist in what Dr. McAfee Brown termed "deliberate ambiguity" but also in the tendency for truths unpalatable to Protestants to be played down or ignored altogether.

A final point which needs to be made is that some passages in the conciliar documents, particularly the Pastoral Constitution on the Church in the Modern World, are, to quote Dr. McAfee Brown once more, "too prolix, too general, and therefore sometimes disappointing".[63] Father Holloway insists, and the emphasis is his, that: *"The official decrees and documents* are beautiful, well suited as material for spiritual meditation and pastoral teaching". Readers will be able to form their own judgement. The documents are, as Father Bryan Houghton remarks, "there to be read by anyone with a sufficient supply of anti-soporifics".[64] There are, of course, passages which are not only orthodox but even inspiring, but there is also much which consists of little more than a long series of the most banal truisms imaginable. Cardinal Heenan remarked during one of the debates that: "It is more useful to dispense the sacraments than to write books on the Church, the People of God".[65]

It seems permissible to wonder whether some of the Fathers did not consider that calling them to Rome to promulgate such documents might not have been the most colossal waste of time, money, and energy in the history of the Church. Cardinal Heenan made the following comment with regard to Bishop Griffiths, Auxiliary of New York, "…one of the few scholars among the English-speaking bishops….He disagreed vehemently with some of the views expressed by German theologians and was convinced that they were bent on a course which might deliver the Church into the hands of the Lutherans". Bishop Griffiths had complained publicly "that the Council had been a waste of time. 'Lord', he quoted, 'we have laboured all night and have taken nothing'".[66]

Dr. Moorman, an Anglican observer, commented with regard to *Gaudium et Spes*, that some of it "is a bit pedestrian and banal":

> It hardly needed an assembly of 2,300 prelates from all over the world to tell us that "the industrial type of society is gradually being spread", or that "new and more efficient media of social communication are contributing to the knowledge of events"; and most people are already aware of the fact that "growing numbers of people are abandoning religion in practice". The whole of the first part, which attempts to describe the conditions in which modern man lives, inevitably falls a bit flat. It has all been said so many times before.[67]

It is worth noting that this constitution found room for page after page of similar prolix and general statements but no room for a specific condemnation of Communism or contraception within its actual text—and yet it professed to be concerned with the realities of the Church in the modern world!

The Decree on the Instruments of Social Communication has a similar sense of priorities: "Let efforts be expended to see that the noble and ancient art of the theatre, now widely popularised through the instruments of social communication, serve the cultural and moral development of audiences".[68] Xavier Rynne claims that some of the Fathers who voted for this decree had not even read it![69]

Time Bombs

Even in the most seemingly vacuous documents the *periti* have done their work well. The Decree on the Apostolate of the Laity is generally so turgid that few laymen would have the stamina to read through it. Even an enthusiastic Protestant commentator feels bound to remark that: "The paragraphs on the family and on young people seem less relevant to the realities of today's world than other parts of the document. I found myself saying 'yes, but how?' to many of the statements there".[70] Yet even this document contains its "time bombs". Paragraph 26, for example, gave the green light to the proliferation of councils and commissions which, from the parish to the international level, have enabled liberals to gain their stranglehold over the life of the Church. This process has been fully documented and analysed by Professor James Hitchcock in his book *The Decline and Fall of Radical Catholicism*:

> What is often called the "revolt of the laity" in the Church is in reality closer to a revolt of the experts, who use a democratic rhetoric to mask an elitist conception of religious reform. These experts have a constituency—a minority of educated laity in a few of the more advanced Western nations—who support them enthusiastically, look to them for leadership the bishops cannot provide, and sometimes urge them on to greater daring.[71]

And again: "Reformers have had for the most part not the slightest respect for the masses, and their formula for change has been entirely elitist, the imposing of a reform from above by an enlightened few".[72]

There is certainly no document which expresses the ethos of Vatican II more accurately than *Gaudium et Spes*. It is significant that it was composed in French and that the Fathers were given the French text with a Latin translation. Italian, English, German and Spanish versions were also provided, and this was the first time that the authors of a schema (draft document) had translated it into various languages for the convenience of the Fathers.[73] This schema, the celebrated (or notorious) Schema 13, was the draft schema for *Gaudium et Spes*. It was so-called because this was the number it acquired in the list of seventeen schemata to which the original seventy draft documents had been reduced (some accounts give the number as seventy-two).[74] It was described by Monsignor McVinney, Bishop of Providence (U.S.A.) as: "A doubtful compromise with everything which lies at the basis of the evils now affecting humanity".[75] Cardinal Heenan of Westminster, England, called the schema "unworthy of an ecumenical council of the Church".[76] Cardinal Ruffini deplored the image it evoked of the Church "on her knees, beseeching pardon for her faults".[77] Those who criticised Schema 13, and pointed out its incompatibility with previous authoritative papal teaching, were told that the ideas expressed in Schema 13 were the result of a long evolution. Quite true, agreed Monsignor Lefebvre: "The true sources of this schema can be traced back to the philosophers of the eighteenth century: Hobbes, Hume, Locke, Rousseau, then the liberal Catholicism of Lamennais which was condemned by Pope Leo XIII".[78] Henri Fesquet lavishes praise upon the schema, above all because it is centred upon man (*centré sur l'homme*)—this aspect alone is sufficient to mark its originality, he insists—and who would disagree with him?[79]

Cardinal Heenan has already been quoted in Chapter V to the effect that it was sometimes quite impossible for the Fathers to study all the amendments for which they were required to vote in one way or another. Henri Fesquet confirms that this was particularly true with Schema 13. "This situation", he wrote at the time,

> is greatly regretted by many Fathers who feel, not without reason, that they do not have sufficient time to give

serious consideration to a schema containing particularly complex material. It is certain that Schema 13 will suffer as a result, and that it would have been more logical (certain Fathers have no hesitation in saying "more conscientious") if the date for closing the Council had been determined on the basis of the time required to amend the schema rather than the reverse.[80]

Shortly before the conclusion of Vatican II, Douglas Woodruff expressed his views on the possible consequences of the Council:

> One of the few confident prophecies that can be made about the outcome of Vatican II is that there is going to be a great deal more theology, self-confident, often adventurous....There is more emphasis on Scripture, on the supremacy of conscience, on the invitation to all Christians to believe they have a part to play, minds to express, and contributions to make, because all the faithful are the chosen people of God. Then there will also be diversity of interpretations of the New Testament, by men self-confident that they alone are right, and that if the Church does not agree with them today she will be with them tomorrow, so why should they budge? The story of Protestant Christianity, basing itself on Scripture as the sole sufficient guide, and on the supremacy of conscience and of private judgement as formed by Scripture, has a tragic side, as a history of division and fragmentation and conflict, from which statistical researchers have extracted a total of over seventy thousand distinct Protestant communions.[81]

A "history of division and fragmentation and conflict"—this could be used to summarise the history of the Church since Vatican II. If a lay-editor was able to prophesy the consequences of the Council with such accuracy it is hard to understand why so few bishops were blessed with equal foresight, why, when Cardinal Browne called out his "*Caveatis*", most of them laughed. Few are laughing now. Writing with the benefit of hindsight in 1974, Cardinal Heenan accepted that: "The barque of Peter was ill-equipped to face a tornado. An unchanging Church does not know what to do when change sets in".[82] Commenting on the aftermath of the Council in the United States, he writes:

> The once docile American Church produced both clerical and lay rebels—among whom the most militant were the former clerics. Chastity and obedience were derided, priests and nuns forsook their vows, doctrines opposed to the fundamental teaching of the Catholic Church were taught by theologians who nevertheless refused to leave the Church. They were guided by a self-made magisterium. Priests and laymen without qualifications set up as theologians. Everyone except the Pope became infallible.[83]

But the Cardinal is nonetheless adamant that the Council itself, at least in its official documents, was in no way responsible for this all too accurate fulfillment of Douglas Woodruff's prophecy. Once again, readers must decide for themselves. If, for example, *Gaudium et Spes* had contained an explicit condemnation of contraception, and *Lumen Gentium* had kept the passage forbidding theologians to debate a matter upon which the Pope had pronounced, might this have taken some of the sting out of the attack on *Humanae Vitae*? Perhaps, perhaps not. The detailed study of the Liturgy Constitution which will be made in Chapter XVI will make it clear that the Cardinal has certainly been over-generous in absolving the conciliar documents *in toto* from any responsibility for the chaos in the post-conciliar Church.

"Events since the Council indicate that the bishops let loose far more than they expected", wrote Dr. McAfee Brown. He adds, with perfect accuracy, "the process of ecumenical escalation" has "been proceeding at a pace much more rapid than any could have calculated beforehand, and demands for radical change in the structures of contemporary Catholicism have become the order of the day....In addition, the Council documents themselves often implied more in the way of change than the Council Fathers were necessarily aware of when they voted".[84]

Read this last sentence once again and note that it comes from a Protestant with unimpeachable ecumenical credentials. It accords perfectly with what Cardinal Heenan testified concerning the Liturgy Constitution: "Subsequent changes were more radical than those intended by Pope John and the bishops who passed the decree on the liturgy. His sermon at the end of the first session indicates that Pope John did not know *what was being planned* by the liturgical experts" (my emphasis).

There were indeed, as Archbishop Lefebvre claimed, "time bombs" in the conciliar texts; time bombs planted there by the *periti* who, as the previous chapter showed, made no secret of the fact that they intended to detonate them after the Council. Detonate them they did, and the Church is still crumbling as the reverberations spread further and further afield. The fact that she has not collapsed completely is an impressive testimony to the fact that she is built upon a rock.

As a final testimony to the fact that the official documents of Vatican II are, in certain passages at least, compromise texts, it is possible to cite no less a witness than Hans Küng himself. It will be noted that he considers that an enlightened majority was forced to make do with compromise texts as a result of pressure from the Curia which "controlled the machinery of the Council". In an article printed in *The Times* on 28 August 1976 he conceded that:

> Moreover, it could and should be recognised that Monsignor Lefebvre is right in one respect. There is no doubt that post-conciliar development in a number of cases has gone beyond what was agreed at the Council, not only *de facto* but *de jure*, with the agreement of the Church leaders....Many Council documents were in fact compromises imposed on the majority by the conservative Curia which controlled the machinery of the Council....Compromises are liable to interpretation in different ways by different parties: a fact which has contributed substantially to the confusion and polarization in the post-conciliar Church.

In his *The Battle for the American Church* Monsignor George Kelly states: "The documents of the Council contain enough basic ambiguities to make the post-conciliar difficulties understandable".[85]

Notes

[1] ABS, p. 137.
[2] *Ibid.*, pp. 112.
[3] *Faith*, November 1975—Editorial. Subsequent citations from Father Holloway come from the same editorial.
[4] Abbott, p. 48.
[5] HG, p. 11.
[6] *Emendationes a Concilii Patribus scripto exhibitae super schema. Constitutionis Dogmaticae de Ecclesia,* Pars 1 (Vatican Press, 1963), pp. 43-44.
[7] JC, pp. 517-518.
[8] *The Times*, 13 December 1975.
[9] JC, p. 359.
[10] *Faith*, November 1973, p. 29.
[11] ABS, p. 82.
[12] CT, p. 397.
[13] ABS, p. 76.
[14] CC, pp. 61-62.
[15] RFT, p. 57.
[16] *Ibid.*, p. 95.
[17] CC, pp. 7-8.
[18] ABS, p. 107.
[19] JC, p. 339.
[20] CC, pp. 20-21.
[21] ABS, p. 108.

22 *The Tablet*, 4 May 1968, p. 441.
23 Abbott, p. 23.
24 *De Ecclesia*: the Constitution on the Church of Vatican Council II, with commentary by Gregory Baum, OSA (London, 1965), p. 24.
25 VO, p. 194.
26 Abbott, p. 374.
27 *Ibid.*, pp. 10-11.
28 *Ibid.*, p. 103.
29 *Ibid.*, p. 105.
30 ER, pp. 318-319.
31 Abbott, p. 98, footnote 3.
32 *Ibid.*
33 *Ibid.*, p. 367.
34 *Ibid.*, pp. 345-346.
35 *Ibid.*, p. 342.
36 ER, p. 197.
37 The word "Catholic" was inserted by order of Pope Paul.
38 The term *generale auxilium salutis* was taken from a letter of the Holy Office to Archbishop Richard J. Cushing, 8 August 1949, in which the position of Father Leonard Feeny concerning salvation outside the Church was rejected.
39 Abbott, p. 346.
40 ER, p. 197.
41 Abbott, pp. 358-359.
42 *Ibid.*, p. 369.
43 *The Ecumenical Review*, April 1965, p. 94.
44 Abbott, p. 354.
45 ER, p. 199.
46 Abbott, p. 354.
47 *Ibid.*, p. 346.
48 ER, p. 193.
49 *Ibid.*
50 *Itinéraires*, July 1971, p. 34.
51 ABS, pp. 112.
52 Abbott, p. 577.
53 *Ibid.*, p. 180.
54 *The Canadian Register*, 25 September 1965.
55 ABS, p. 84.
56 Abbott, p. 314.
57 ABS, pp. 107.
58 Archbishop R. J. Dwyer, *Twin Circle*, 26 October 1973, p. 11.
59 Abbott, p. 256.
60 *Ibid.*, p. 315.
61 *The Tablet*, 8 January 1966, p. 34.
62 RFT, pp. 267-272.
63 Abbott, p. 309.
64 *Christian Order*, June 1975, p. 358.
65 JC, p. 993.
66 CT, p. 376.
67 VO, p. 171.
68 Abbott, p. 328.
69 XR-II, pp. 254-256.
70 Abbott, p. 524.
71 DFRC, p. 48.
72 *Ibid.*, p. 83.
73 JC, p. 797.
74 XR-III, p. 115.
75 JC, p. 869.
76 RFT, p. 210.
77 JC, p. 868.
78 *Ibid.*, p. 857.
79 *Ibid.*, p. 798.
80 *Ibid.*, pp. 1054-1055.
81 *The Tablet*, 27 November 1965, p. 1319.
82 CT, p. 381.
83 *Ibid.*, p. 380.
84 ER, pp. 209-210.
85 Kelly, p. 20.

VII

The Prefabricators

It has already been shown that most bishops arrived at the Council without any clearly formulated views and policies and were thus ideally placed to be influenced by those who were quite definite about what they wanted. "If you had told me two years ago that I would be voting 'yes' for some of the things I have been voting for this session, I would have told you you were crazy", commented Bishop Joseph J. Mueller of Sioux City, Iowa.[1] Father Wiltgen has expressed his regret that all episcopal conferences did not work with the same intensity and purpose as the Rhine bishops and their supporters. "Had they done so they would not have found it necessary to accept the positions of the European Alliance with so little questioning. The Council would then have been less one-sided, and its achievements would truly have been the result of a world-wide theological effort".[2] Father Wiltgen is somewhat unrealistic here. The strategy of the Rhine Group was that of a definite party with a definite policy. The party expanded to become first the European and then the World Alliance—but there was the nucleus of a party and a definite policy to begin with. Without such a nucleus and without such a policy there was no hope of a viable alternative to the Rhine Group being formed. At a later stage the International Group of Fathers

(*Coetus Internationalis Patrum*), of which Archbishop Lefebvre was a leading member, began to offer sufficient opposition to make the Rhine Group anxious; but this did not happen until the third session when the control of the Rhine group was so absolute that it could not possibly be broken.[3] The fact is that most of the Fathers had come to the Council not as members of a party but simply as Catholic bishops. Why they had come to Rome, and what they were supposed to do there, was something they hoped to discover as the Council progressed. Father Raymond Dulac remarks that nine-tenths of the Fathers had certainly not known "of the existence of Monsignor Huyghe, Bishop of Arras, France, and that of Monsignor Vendargon, Bishop of Kuala Lumpur. Nonetheless they voted for them".[4]

But it was not simply the direct lobbying of the Rhine Group Fathers and *periti* which influenced the uncommitted Fathers. As subsequent chapters will make clear, the documents of the Second Vatican Council were influenced to varying degrees by the desire to conciliate Protestants and Communists, and the possibility that they were even influenced by more sinister forces cannot be excluded, as Chapter XIV will show. The greatest concern of many Fathers became that of coming to terms with "modern man", with the "spirit of the age", of entering into "a dialogue with the world". These are, of course, nebulous concepts to which it would be hard to attach any concrete meaning. To a very large extent they are the creations of the press, and in so far as they do have any meaning it is the meaning which the mass media impart to them. The mass media, the press in particular, played a key role in conjuring up the mood of the Council, the so-called "Spirit of Vatican II", the mood of euphoria in which so many of the bishops were happy to be told what the world expected from them and equally happy not to disappoint the world. "Many a bishop", Bishop Tracy wrote to his people in Baton Rouge, U.S.A., "revised the attitudes of a lifetime on certain reforms, once he saw the mood and spirit of the Council; hence the big votes which were all but unanimous on most points".⁵ This was not the first time that a press hostile to the traditional faith had tried to influence a general council. As Appendix III will show, an almost identical campaign to the one waged so effectively during the Second Vatican Council was waged without success during the First; and waged unsuccessfully due to the courageous and uncompromising stand of Pope Pius IX, whose pontificate was dedicated to fighting off all the forces which have emerged so triumphantly during and since Vatican II.

Father Louis Bouyer, who was certainly looked upon as a "progressive" before and during the Council, has remarked that: "I do not know whether, as we are told, the Council has freed us from the tyranny of the Roman Curia, but what is sure is that, willy-nilly, it has handed us over (after having first surrendered itself) to the dictatorship of the journalists, and particularly the most incompetent and irresponsible among them".⁶ When Father Bouyer states that the Council surrendered itself to the dictatorship of the journalists, he means, in effect, to the Rhine Group; for almost every influential journal and journalist supported the Rhine Group programme. Among the best known names are John Cogley of *Commonweal*; Robert Kaiser of *Time*; "Xavier Rynne" of the *New Yorker*; Michael Novak, who represented a number of American papers; Father Antoine Wegner of *La Croix*; and probably the most influential of all, Henri Fesquet of *Le Monde*. Most of the well-known journalists expanded their reports on the Council into books which appeared while it was still taking place, or shortly afterwards, thus extending and consolidating their own influence and that of the myth which they had created themselves, the myth which for most Catholics has become the real Council, the only Council that they have been allowed to know. The great exception to this list was Father Ralph M. Wiltgen of the Divine Word News Service whose book *The Rhine Flows into the Tiber* tells the story of "the unknown Council", the reality behind the myth. While his own sympathies tended to be with the progressives, he adhered to the highest possible journalistic standards and insisted on writing objective reports during the Council itself and in his book. Robert Kaiser concedes that "the reporters were almost all on the progressive side, probably because they instinctively realised that although Christianity was the same [sic], its message had to be adapted to the progress of history, while the motto of Cardinal Ottaviani, *'Semper Idem'*, carried to its logical conclusion, would put the Catholic press out of business tomorrow".[7]

Without any doubt, the most important and most influential thought-manipulating agency operating during and since the Council was the notorious IDO-C. It will not be discussed in any detail here as its activities from the Council to the present day are fully documented in what is probably the most famous of the *Approaches* supplements.[8] In December 1963, there came into existence a centre of information for Dutch bishops which published bulletins in Dutch. In due course, however, consequent on a demand from other groups, the centre began publishing information bulletins in French, German, Spanish, and Italian. This information centre, which from its inception bore the title DO-C (*Documentazione olandese del Concilio*), included non-Dutch specialists in religious information. Around the same period, in order to promote an exchange of information concerning the Council among progressive journalists, C.C.C.C. (*Centro di Coordinazione delle Communicazione sul Concilio*) came into being. At the end of the Council the work of this press bureau came to an end, for it had been conceived as a temporary establishment. However, with a view to maintaining such relations as had been established during the Council, the religious correspondents who composed it joined forces

The Prefabricators

with the Dutch agency and it was thus that IDO-C came into existence. It described itself as an international group with headquarters in Rome and a growing network of branches around the world. "Its specific function is to assemble and distribute documentation on the structural and theological effects of the continuing implementation of the decrees and the spirit of the Second Vatican Council. Among its subscribers were bishops; heads of diocesan commissions (liturgy, canon law reform, clerical-lay relations, etc.); professors of theology, Scripture, canon law, sociology, psychology, Church history, etc., and advanced students in Catholic, Protestant and Jewish seminaries; editors of Catholic, Protestant and Jewish newspapers; and editors of religious departments of big general newspapers". By 1971 it had evolved into what it is today "an independent, transconfessional and inter-disciplinary organization".

The extent of the IDO-C empire, the staggering number of journals which it controls or which act as its mouthpieces all over the world, and on both sides of the Iron Curtain, almost defies belief. Particularly important is its influence as a source of Catholic news for secular papers—it is no coincidence that almost every leading secular paper throughout the West presents the same items of religious news and with the same slant as the "establishment" Catholic press. The fact that the same news was presented, and even more important, *not* presented, is a fact which cannot be sufficiently stressed. As Hamish Fraser expressed it: "The power of modern media of communication to condition the human mind is never more manifest than when those in control decide that there shall be no communication".[9] Monsignor Rudolph G. Bandas of St. Paul, Minnesota, a Council *peritus* on two of its commissions, and one of the best theologians in the United States, did all in his power to counteract the Xavier Rynne, Robert Kaiser brand of reporting. He charged that "three-fourths of the information you get from the secular press is incorrect or completely false", and that "in the measure Catholic papers have copied the secular press they have contributed to the spread of misinformation".

The Catholic "establishment" in the United States is now very much a "progressive" establishment, and one dominated by IDO-C personnel. Writing in *The Critic*, a leading establishment journal, John Leo stated quite openly: "It is the Establishment that decides what Catholics will discuss, not just in Establishment journals, but after a time lag—in nearly all Catholic journals and discussion groups from coast to coast....The birth control discussion in the United States, for instance, was entirely an establishment production".[10]

In Chapter V reference was made to the journal *Concilium*, which has acted as the mouthpiece for the liberal *periti* since the Council, and it is worth repeating what was said in that chapter: "It is no exaggeration to claim that the IDO-C/*Concilium* establishment now constitutes a parallel magisterium which rivals that of the Pope as far as practical authority is concerned". Let those who doubt this read the *Approaches* dossier on IDO-C, which also reveals that among the journalists mentioned in this chapter who were listed by IDO-C as members of its international committee are John Cogley, Robert Kaiser, and Henri Fesquet. Fathers Baum and Laurentin, who doubled as journalists and *periti*, are also included on the list.

There has never been a Council in which slogans played so important a role as during Vatican II. The progressive establishment has now codified these slogans into a complete system of belief which its members clearly find more satisfying than Scripture and Tradition as the basis of their faith. The prime tenets of this new creed are to "read the signs of the times", to be "open", to "dialogue", to "cater for the needs of contemporary man", and above all to do everything in "the Spirit of Vatican II". It hardly needs adding that these slogans do not mean what they might appear to mean on a first reading. In fact, as with the "Newspeak" devised by George Orwell in his novel *Nineteen Eighty-Four*, some of these slogans mean precisely the opposite to what they might seems to convey. For example, to be "open" and to "dialogue" means, in practice, that wherever possible anyone who deviates from the party-line will be prevented from expressing his views in public, or at least in a manner which will enable a large section of the public to learn his views.

One of the key slogans, which was accepted as an article of faith from the very beginning of the Council, was the need for those in authority to respond to "public opinion". Monsignor Gerard Huyghe remarked after the first session that: "Formerly only theologians were interested in conciliar texts. Today bishops are faced with a public opinion which looks avidly to the texts coming out of the Council". He adds that this state of affairs has been brought about by the public press.[11] The manner in which the "public opinion" which the press claims to reflect, is often imposed upon the public by the press, is a fact of secular life. Father Bouyer stressed that "the *consensus fidelium* is something quite different from a public opinion which is manipulated and even prefabricated by a press which, even when it is not completely led off the track by its pursuit of the sensational, remains hardly or not at all capable of grasping the real import of the questions under consideration, or simply their true meaning".[12] Professor Hitchcock notes that:

> The radicals' most important weapon, however, has been publicity, and they quite early learned its great potential and how to exploit it....James Kavanaugh, a former priest who created a considerable sensation by his writings, was franker than most radicals in acknowledg-

ing what he was doing. "I'm working on the modern magisterium, public opinion", he wrote.[13]

Professor Hitchcock provides considerable documentation in *The Decline and Fall of Radical Catholicism* to show the contempt which progressives have for ordinary believers, who are described by the liberals in a series of documented quotations as "a herd" which is "straying apathetically behind" and is difficult to love. The ordinary believer is "a superstitious religious caterpillar". Father Gerard Sloyan, a prominent member of the catechetical establishment, applies to the Catholic laity the Duke of Wellington's celebrated remark about his own troops: "They may not scare the enemy, but by God they scare me".[14] Professor Hitchcock shows that the liberals' "formula for change has been entirely elitist, the imposing of reform from above by an enlightened few". He speaks of "their assumption that their own needs, their own sensibilities, their own insights have a priority and a superiority which the Church must recognise....When progressives speak of the Church's insensitivity to human needs and rigidity, they mean exclusively its insensitivity to their own needs...".[15] Once again, this theory of the duty of the Church to adapt to contemporary needs was put forward by the early Modernists. St. Pius X draws particular "attention to this whole theory of *necessities or needs*, for beyond all that we have seen, it is, as it were, the base and foundation of that famous method which they describe as historical".[16]

Xavier Rynne insists passionately that the Council had indeed responded to the needs of contemporary man by initiating a second Pentecost, and that those Catholics who attempted to resist what he termed a renewal were doomed to failure. He writes:

Though the Pentecostal nature of the Council has become more obvious than ever with the passing of each year, there are Catholics who deplore and resist the renewal and reform of the Church. They believe this to be a break with "tradition", by which they mean the practices of the nineteenth, eighteenth, and seventeenth centuries, when in reality the changes represent a return to the traditions of earlier centuries. As we state in the first chapter, no matter how much obstructionism there is, it is no longer possible for the Church to turn back the clock of renewal and reform. It can be impeded, and stalled, and perhaps even stopped momentarily, but a return to pre-conciliar and pre-Johannine thinking is no longer possible for the Church.[17]

As Appendix IX proves indubitably, far from initiating a renewal, Vatican II initiated what Louis Bouyer described accurately as the decomposition of Catholicism, a decomposition which has accelerated with each passing year. Rynne writes with complete contempt of any Council Father daring to dissent from the liberal agenda during the debate on the Constitution on Divine Revelation (*Dei Verbum*). They were engaged in

> a futile attempt to hold back the wheels of progress…revealing once more a pitiful lack of understanding of the momentous mystery involved in the Church's reception, explanation and preservation of the word of God…they have deliberately cut themselves off from the obvious inspiration of the Holy Spirit at the present juncture in the Church's development. Mistaking a stubborn allusion to outmoded formulas and a misconception of the spiritual nature of Christ's teaching as theological consistency, they use every means possible to thwart the mind of the

vast majority of the bishops who are giving witness to the mind of the Church now.[18]

In not one of his four books does Rynne display anything more than a superficial understanding of fundamental Catholic theology, and in some cases an embarrassing ignorance. He writes of the "obvious inspiration of the Holy Spirit", whereas inspiration ended with the death of the last apostle. The documents of Vatican II are by no means inspired, any more than were those of the Council of Trent or Vatican I. One presumes that he was not aware of the fact that "outmoded formulas" insisted on by the minority were the infallible and irreformable teaching of the Councils of Trent and Vatican I, which, thanks to the insistence of the minority Fathers and the intervention of Pope Paul VI, are clearly reflected in *Dei Verbum*. Rynne is indignant that "in his extreme anxiety to conciliate an unimportant minority, Pope Paul seemed to have forgotten that he might be doing less than justice to the majority".[19] By "unimportant", of course, Rynne means that they have the temerity to differ from his erroneous interpretation of divine revelation. An explanation of Catholic teaching on this fundamental dogma is provided in Chapter XI.

One of the most pressing of the alleged needs posited by the liberals concerned the liturgy, that "of accommodation to the manners and customs of peoples".[20] This "need" is given express recognition in the Liturgy Constitution of Vatican II![21] The elitist attitude which Professor Hitchcock rightly attributes to contemporary progressives is also remarked upon by St. Pius X in his encyclical *Pascendi Gregis*:

> It is pride which fills the Modernists with that self-assurance by which they consider themselves and pose as the rule for all. It is pride which puffs them up with the vainglory which allows them to regard themselves

as the sole possessors of knowledge, and makes them say, elated and inflated with presumption, *We are not as the rest of men*, and which, lest they should seem as other men, leads them to embrace and devise novelties even of the most absurd kind.²²

It hardly needs stating that the secular press has little sympathy for traditional Catholicism in any of its aspects, but where the reporting of Vatican II was concerned, Father Bouyer reserves particular censure for those so-called "Catholic" journalists who claimed "expert knowledge" but

> seemed tiresomely inclined to adopt the worst irregularities of their new craft by seeking out the sensational and even the scandalous when they were not imposing their own disreputable points of view with every means, including slander and blackmail. After that we need not complain if the professional journalists did not do much better.
> Since that time this phenomenon has only grown and become more complex. Most of the theologians who courted the "great" press contracted, with sometimes caricatural excesses, these glaring vices so cheerfully that it makes us wonder about the roots of their attachment to truth. When we see them today, in closed ranks, sending thundering condemnations of papal encyclicals to the press before even having had time to read them, in order to attempt to get ahead of, and if possible surpass the daring of the secular or non-Catholic commentators themselves, we can begin to appreciate the gravity of the evil.²³

Cardinal Heenan notes that among these "Catholic" reporters "was a surprising number of ex-seminarists. These men were regarded (and came to regard themselves) as qualified theologians and were responsible for interpreting the teaching of the Council to the world. They received most of their information from priests who had been brought to Rome by their bishops".[24]

The first task of the prefabricators was to fabricate a myth which would result in those being conditioned accepting certain basic assumptions. These would trigger off the required reflex when the correct stimulus was applied. Father Bouyer outlines this basic myth as follows:

> On the one hand there were the "bad guys", most of whom were Italians with the rare exception of an Irishman or a Spaniard. On the other side, the "good guys" were all non-Italians with one or two exceptions. One party included the Ottavianis, the Ruffinis, the Brownes, the Heenans, and the other the Frings, the Légers, the Suenens, and the Alfrinks, merely to mention the *porporati*. The first group was uniformly rascally, stupid and niggardly, while the second was equally beyond reproach, bright and noble. Such created mythology fittingly bolstered the slogans. On the one side you had tradition (identified as the most desperate obscurantism). While the other party bespoke complete newness in a noonday light. Authority was pictured as against freedom (and *vice versa*).[25]

St. Pius X had remarked on the Modernists' spirit of disobedience which "causes them to demand a compromise between authority and liberty".[26] Bishop Gordon Wheeler of Leeds, England, in a review of Robert Kaiser's *Inside the Council*, expresses himself in terms very similar to those of Father Bouyer:

> Like the Mounties from across the border he (Kaiser) always gets his man. And he got him—Cardinal Ottaviani and the Curia. As in the standard T.V. horse opera the cast is divided into "goodies" and "baddies". The former very very good and always rather larger than life, the latter the villains of the piece.[27]

To state that the progressive heroes were depicted as "larger than life" is a considerable understatement. Hamish Fraser noted that the progressive establishment has a particular talent for manufacturing synthetic reputations.[28] Some journalists were so caught up in the myth which they had created that they began to deify their heroes. Some examples of this kind of writing, reminiscent of the build-up given to the instant-stars of the recording world in pop-music journals, are provided in Appendix IV. A comparatively mild example can be seen in the "build-up" given by Michael Novak to Cardinal Suenens, Archbishop of Malines:

> Cardinal Suenens is a strong, direct, businesslike man. His influence at the Council seemed, for a time, second only to that of the Pope; so much so that there were those who, in the early stages of the session at least, were calling the Council "The First Council of Malines". On one occasion, when the Pope was visiting a church in Rome, Cardinal Suenens was seen taking the Pope by the arm, moving him here and there, introducing him; the Cardinal is the type of man who controls the situation in which he finds himself. His voice is emphatic and clear. His ideas are forcefully presented. He seems, *par excellence*, the type of the modern bishop: learned, active, capable, profound.[29]

Novak then goes on to cite in detail a long speech by Cardinal Suenens stressing the need for full scope to be given for the use of charismatic gifts which the Holy Spirit bestows upon so many members of the Church.

Hans Küng subscribes to the "goodies versus baddies" myth with a gusto equal to that of secular journalists. Even the progressive *Catholic Gazette*, published in England, carried a review by Father M. Gallon characterising Küng's book *The Changing Church* as not worthy of serious consideration. Father Gallon comments on Dr. Kung's enthusiasm for such words as "intrigue", "obstructionism", and "brute use of power" to describe the "baddies"—and yet he claims recognition as a serious theologian. The Curia "although certainly in good faith is unfortunately backward-looking, ghetto-bound and unecumenical, both traditionalist and nationalist in its thinking, which identifies itself with 'the Church' and would 'excommunicate' everyone who thinks otherwise".[30]

Xavier Rynne assures us that:

> Behind the scenes curial agents pursued their witch-hunt tactics in France, Germany, Spain, and even the United States, where several bishops were encouraged by the Apostolic Delegate to aid him in ferreting out "dangerous" theologians and journalists. Pressures were also put on official representatives of the Catholic press in America to whitewash the reputation of Cardinal Ottaviani, who now began to grant interviews.[31]

Monsignor Rudolph Bandas of St. Paul, Minnesota, said publicly on more than one occasion, that the possible good effects of the Council were being sabotaged by misinformation propagated by vast sections of both the secular and religious press. He expressed himself particularly bewildered and saddened by reports appearing in *Time*, *Newsweek*, and the *New Yorker*.[32] Father Bouyer wrote:

And it must be said, whatever respect we may have for our bishops and for the conscientiousness with which they wished to perform their task in the Council, many of them were ill-prepared to exercise their role amid the blasts of such a clamorous publicity, which was so often motivated by concerns that had very little in common with what they should have been. Under these circumstances, we ought not to be too surprised, especially during the last sessions of the Council, if many of the Fathers' interventions and reactions were much more 'conditioned' (doubtless without their realising it!) by a desire to please their new masters.[33]

A stage was reached, eventually, when some Fathers felt that more could be gained by a statement to the press than a speech in the Council hall. Archbishop T. D. Roberts, S.J., a very progressive English Father, told a gathering of reporters that: "I know that if I give my talk to the press many more of the bishops will see it and understand it than if I give it in the *aula*".[34]

Cardinal Heenan complained that although secrecy was supposed to be maintained regarding speeches made in the Council hall, and an oath had been taken to this effect, even during the first session this was often no more than a fiction, "the substance or, more often, the complete text, was available to enterprising journalists".[35] This illustrates the close co-operation which existed between the liberal Fathers, their *periti*, and the press. Twelve hours before the Council Fathers knew whom they had elected to the conciliar commissions the complete list had appeared in a secular paper![36] The French bishops considered *La Croix* an important part of their armoury, and in the second session its editor-in-chief doubled both as a *peritus* and a reporter. According to Robert Kaiser, *La Croix* "presented consistent, exhaustive reports, usually full of actual quotes from the Council floor.

Le Monde's reporter, Henri Fesquet, turned in three or four stories a week full of insight and penetration. It was obvious that many of the Fathers and theologians were using *La Croix* and *Le Monde* to get the word".[37] He claims that the *New Yorker* was "required reading" and that the bishops were eager to learn from its "mystery man, Xavier Rynne".[38] Kaiser was assured by a member of Cardinal Bea's Secretariat that the press "had a profound influence on the Fathers. It was, in fact, one of the factors which helped the Fathers to find their collegiality, their sense of universal responsibility for moving the barque of Peter".[39]

There was a great deal of informal contact between the liberal journalists, Fathers, and *periti*. Robert Kaiser and his wife gave regular Sunday evening buffet suppers at which leading representatives of all three groups attended. "These suppers were a small powerhouse of energy and conversation, one of the most successful institutions in Rome. Here Father Malachi Martin, S.J., the thin, wiry, Irish, Scripture scholar dashed from group to group with his rapid-fire questions and bits of information; Father Francis X. Murphy, C.Ss.R., smoked his pipe in his sly, observant way. A wide spectrum of the world's bishops appeared on alternate Sundays".[40] "No reporter knew more about the Council" than Robert Kaiser, according to Michael Novak in his absurdly titled book *The Open Church*. No one "had talked with more of its personalities, prominent or minor; had more sources of information to tap....In the English-speaking world, at least, perhaps no source was to have quite the catalytic effect as *Time* on opinion outside the Council and *even to an extent within it*".[41] (My emphasis.) It is worth noting how here, as elsewhere in the chapter, the same conclusions are reached by those with views at the opposite ends of the theological spectrum—Novak and Father Bouyer are both agreed regarding the influence of the press, but differ as to whether the influence was good or bad. Robert Kaiser is also in accord with Father Bouyer concerning the extent of press influence—but there is no doubt that he considers it to have been all to the good. "One wonders", he asks, "why there should be no 'outside influence' on a Council Father… Is the authority of the Church meant to dominate or serve? If it is to dominate, then there is no need for the bearers of that authority to listen. But if it is to serve, then those bearers of authority have to be attentive to the expressed needs of the world".[42] Kaiser assumes, of course, that the "expressed needs of the world" correspond with the esoteric preoccupations of his own elitist clique. He goes on to explain that some members of the Church are "very possibly full of the charismatic influence of the Holy Spirit", and that the only way in which the institutional Church—i.e. the bishops—can learn what the Spirit who "breathes where it wills" wishes them to learn from the fortunate possessors of these charisms "is through the instrumentality of the modern press".[43]

The theory that God teaches the bishops through the instrumentality of the liberal press is certainly novel; the depressing fact is that it was a theory which was accepted wholeheartedly by so many of the bishops who vied with each other in their "concern to please their new masters". According to Cardinal Suenens:

> Two thousand eight hundred bishops represented the faithful people at the Council, and it was the faithful people who dictated the nine thousand proposals. [It was] the people again who, present at the Council with the Holy Spirit, breathed on to the prepared schemata in order to direct them. The current of public opinion was blowing at all levels. The schema on the Church, for example, began with the People of God with baptism as the common bond, and not with the hierarchy. But in order to strengthen the awareness of the People of God

and for the Christian to assume his adult responsibilities in the Church of today, he needs daily enlightenment on events which have to be seen in the light of faith: the Catholic journalist, then, is the theologian of the present day.[44]

Our Lord, of course, began His Church with the hierarchy who then built up the People of God by teaching and baptising them; He also stated that the faithful were to listen to the apostles, and that in listening to them they were listening to Him. Cardinal Journet speaks of "the virtue of apostolicity, and that it is the proper (efficient) cause of the Church, as fire is the cause of heat".[45]

Now the bishops are reduced to the status of delegates of the faithful, whose mind is to be made known through the oracle of the public press! However, Father Alting von Geusau, Secretary General of IDO-C until 1972, claimed during the final session of the Council that: "Christ came to communicate with the people: every attempt to impede communication is a sin. Vatican II has shown the Church that she was the People of God before becoming an hierarchy".[46] The fact that the prime achievement of IDO-C has been to impede communication within the Church on a scale and with an efficiency unprecedented in her history would not, of course, have been considered as sinful. As any exponent of situation ethics could explain, the sinfulness of a particular act derives not from the act itself but from the circumstances surrounding it—in this case what matters is not that communication is impeded but who is impeding it.

As is made clear elsewhere in this chapter, there were only too many Council Fathers willing to manifest uncritical acceptance of the elevated role which the press claimed for itself and to offer homage to their new mentors. "Public opinion has influenced the Council", explained Cardinal Koenig, Archbishop of Vienna. He continues:

Public opinion has now taken over the role played by kings and princes in former times. The role of official representatives and ambassadors is now exercised by journalists....When a Catholic journalist has something to say he need not always wait for the permission of a bishop or information from Rome. He must alert those whom he considers need to be alerted; he must incite to action those whom he considers need to be incited. He must inform the world about the Church and the Church about the world. He can and he must open the mouth and the ears of the Church. He must not allow her to remain either deaf or mute.[47]

Monsignor Stourm, Archbishop of Sens and a member of the French Episcopal Committee of the Press for the Council, offered the following tribute: "I must thank you for your fidelity and your elevated standard of professional integrity. Your task is not easy. I know your difficulties. I congratulate you on your magnificent effort. Satisfaction with the quality of your work is expressed on every side. This is all most encouraging for us".[48]

Once a Father was prepared to accept that public opinion, the voice of the people, was the voice of God, and that the journalists of the establishment press were the inspired and authentic interpreters of this infallible magisterium, then life was made very simple for him. "It was all good fun", wrote Archbishop R. J. Dwyer. "And when the vote came around, like wise Sir Joseph Porter, K.C.B., 'We always voted at our party's call; we never thought of thinking for ourselves at all'. That way you can save yourself a whole world of trouble".[49]

The American Press, in particular, played a decisive role in obtaining overwhelming approval by the Council for Father John Courtney Murray's schema on religious liberty. In his book *American Participation in the Second Vatican Council*, Monsignor V. A. Yzermans wrote:

> During the ninth public session, on December 7, 1965, Pope Paul VI formally promulgated the Declaration on Religious Freedom after a final vote of 2308 Council Fathers approving and 70 disapproving. It was a delightful victory for the American hierarchy....The American press also played no small role in fostering a healthy public opinion in favour of the document. From beginning to end, the press followed this document more closely than any other conciliar statement. It was, time after time, through every session of the Council, a constantly recurring subject for discussion at the American Bishops' Press Panel.[50]

Perhaps the most poignant moment of the Council occurred during the debate on the Liturgy Constitution. It was an incident which epitomised the ethos of the Council; the true "Spirit of Vatican II"; the real nature of the new order which has taken effective control of the "renewed" Church. Respect for the aged and compassion for the infirm are two essential characteristics of any civilised—let alone Christian—society. Similarly, any civilised group of men looks with gratitude on those who have spent a lifetime of dedicated effort in its service. Common courtesy demands that any sincerely held and reasonably expressed view should be listened to with respect, no matter now unacceptable it might be. Cardinal Ottaviani was old and partly blind; no living Catholic had served the Church with more zeal and devotion; he held his views with the deepest sincerity and, however outdated they may appear to some Catholics today, they are what most of us professed until 1962.

During the debate upon the liturgy the Cardinal's poor eyesight compelled him to speak without a text; he spoke from the heart about a subject which moved him deeply:

> Are we seeking to stir up wonder, or perhaps scandal among the Christian people, by introducing changes in so venerable a rite, that has been approved for so many centuries and is now so familiar? The rite of Holy Mass should not be treated as if it were a piece of cloth to be refashioned according to the whim of each generation.

There was a ten minute time limit on speeches. The Cardinal exceeded it and a bell was rung. Engrossed in his speech he did not hear it and carried on. "At a signal from Cardinal Alfrink, a technician switched off the microphone. After confirming the fact by tapping the instrument, Cardinal Ottaviani stumbled back to his seat in humiliation. The most powerful Cardinal in the Curia had been silenced and the Council Fathers clapped with glee".[51]

The Council Fathers "clapped with glee"! And why not? Cardinal Ottaviani was a "bad guy" and Cardinal Alfrink was a "good guy"! Xavier Rynne comments that it "seems to have caused Ottaviani [sic] to feel insulted and to remain away for almost two weeks".[52] In other words, the "bad guys" are poor losers! What, it seems permissible to wonder, would have been the reaction of Xavier Rynne and the press in general had Cardinal Ottaviani ordered Cardinal Alfrink to be cut off in mid-speech? It is impossible not to wonder if, as the half-blind Cardinal stumbled back to his seat, one of the gleeful Fathers did not stop clapping for a moment to say: "Prophesy unto us, who is he that cut thee off"?

After recounting this incident with unconcealed delight, and without the slightest trace of pity, Robert Kaiser passes on a little joke which circulated afterwards and somehow "caught the spirit of the occasion. The very next morning, went the story, Ottaviani [sic] came out of his apartment and found no chauffeur. He quickly hailed a cab, told him [sic], 'To the Council', and the driver drove him to Trent".⁵³ Ironically enough, if a Catholic is looking for clear and reliable conciliar teaching he could do no better than go to Trent or Vatican I.

The close co-operation between the liberal *periti* and the liberal press is indicated by the swift action which followed the displeasure of Robert Kaiser, John Cogley, and Michael Novak with the schema for the communications document. They notified their displeasure to four *periti* (including Father J. Courtney Murray, S.J., and Father Bernard Häring) who managed to secure the signatures of twenty-five Fathers to a circular urging a *Non placet* (no) vote. A German bishop handed out this circular to the Fathers as they arrived for the vote. This was a violation of the rules of the Council, and when Archbishop Felici arrived and attempted to seize the circulars, a scuffle ensued and the papal gendarmes had to be summoned.⁵⁴ Archbishop Lefebvre has testified to the manner in which the world press, the "Catholic" press above all, gave total support to the liberalising forces within the Council. He made particular mention of the extent to which the key battle over collegiality was fought by the liberals with the aid of "the entire Communist, Protestant, and progressive press".⁵⁵

St. Pius X warned that no one knows how to make better use of the press than the Modernist. It is hard to believe that what he wrote on this subject in *Pascendi Gregis* was not directly related to the situation during and after Vatican II.

> There is little reason to wonder that the Modernists vent all their bitterness and hatred on Catholics who zealously fight the battles of the Church. There is no species of insult which they do not heap upon them, but

their usual course is to charge them with ignorance or obstinacy. When an adversary rises up against them with an erudition and force that renders him redoubtable, they seek to make a conspiracy of silence around him to nullify the effects of his attack. This policy towards Catholics is the more invidious in that they belaud with admiration which knows no bounds the writers who range themselves on their side, hailing their works, exuding novelty in every page, with a chorus of applause. For them the scholarship of a writer is in direct proportion to the recklessness of his attacks on antiquity, and of his efforts to undermine tradition and the ecclesiastical Magisterium. When one of their number falls under the condemnations of the Church the rest of them, to the disgust of good Catholics, gather round him, loudly and publicly applaud him, and hold him up in veneration as almost a martyr for truth. The young, excited and confused by all this clamour of praise and abuse, some afraid of being branded as ignorant, others ambitious to rank among the learned, and both classes goaded internally by curiosity and pride, not unfrequently surrender and give themselves up to Modernism.[56]

Notes

[1] OC, p. 327.
[2] RFT, pp. 79-80.
[3] *Ibid.*, p. 148.
[4] *Itinéraires*, July 1971, p. 39.
[5] OC, p. 335.
[6] DC, p. 3.
[7] IC, pp. 171-172.
[8] Dossier on IDO-C.
[9] *Ibid.*, p. 16
[10] *Ibid.*, p. 36.
[11] IC, p. 186.
[12] DC, pp. 3-4.
[13] DFRC, p. 37.
[14] *Ibid.*, pp. 82-83.
[15] *Ibid.*, pp. 83 & 85.
[16] PG, p. 33.
[17] XR-III, pp. xii-xiii.
[18] *Ibid.*, p. 36.
[19] *Ibid.*, p. 252.
[20] PG, p. 32,
[21] Liturgy Constitution, §§ 37-40. Abbott, pp. 141-152.

22. PG, p. 52.
23. DC, pp. 5-6.
24. CT, p. 340.
25. DC, p. 9.
26. PG, p. 52.
27. *Catholic Gazette*, September 1963, p. 266.
28. *Dossier on IDO-C*, p. 38.
29. OC, p. 148.
30. *Catholic Gazette*, August 1965, p. 239.
31. XR-II, p. 29.
32. IC, pp. 186-187.
33. DC, p. 4.
34. OC, p. 158.
35. CT, p. 341.
36. IC, p. 191.
37. *Ibid.*
38. *Ibid.*, p. 155.
39. *Ibid.*, pp. 235-236.
40. OC, p. 211.
41. *Ibid.*, pp. 13-14.
42. IC, pp. 196-197.
43. *Ibid.*, pp. 197-198.
44. *La Croix*, 6 April 1965.
45. C. Journet, *The Church of the Word Incarnate* (London: Sheed and Ward, 1954), p. 16.
46. JC, p. 1035.
47. *Ibid.*, p. 1036.
48. *Ibid.*, p. 697.
49. *Twin Circle*, 26 October 1963, p. 2.
50. V. Y. Yzermans, *American Participation in the Second Vatican Council* (New York, 1967), pp. 101-102.
51. RFT, pp. 28-29.
52. XR-1, p. 117.
53. IC, p. 136.
54. RFT, pp. 132-134.
55. ABS, pp. 45, 46.
56. PG, pp. 54-55.

VIII

The Background to Protestantism

It has been shown in earlier chapters that a good number of the Council Fathers and *periti* had succumbed to the disease of ecumania, a state of mind in which the prime criterion for explaining any aspect of Church teaching is not whether it is true but whether it is ecumenical. It has also been shown that those with this ecumenical obsession were sufficiently powerful to adapt some of the Council documents to this standpoint, sometimes by ambiguity but more often by a change of emphasis. The true Catholic position can usually be found by those who look hard enough, but sometimes phrased in such muted tones that Protestant commentators have been able to give a number of the documents a most enthusiastic welcome. The influence of Protestantism upon the Council will be examined in more detail in the next chapter and will also be made very apparent in Chapters X and XVII. But before doing so it will be useful to take a look at the nature of contemporary Protestantism. The first and most obvious point to make is that it is not really possible to make any generalised statements about the positive aspects of Protestantism, i.e., common beliefs and common practices. It is worth recalling a comment by Douglas Woodruff cited in Chapter VI, that the history of Protestantism is one of division, fragmentation, and conflict—a fragmentation into seventy thousand distinct communions. But the process does not stop even here—for within each Protestant denomination each individual is his own pope in the final analysis. I have shown in my book *Cranmer's Godly Order* that the heretical concept of justification and grace devised by the Protestant Reformers dispensed with the need for a divinely founded Church mediating the grace of God to man and able to teach with authority. An infallible Magisterium was replaced by an infallible book, the Bible. But even an infallible book needs an interpreter, and the inescapable logic of Protestantism is that no individual has the right to impose his interpretation on another. Father Bouyer related that: "The Princess of the Palatinate once described German Protestantism to Louis XIV with this formula: 'In our country, everyone makes up his own little religion'".[1] Father Bouyer does not hesitate to point out the irony inherent in the fact that since the Council, within the Catholic Church, "Every priest, or almost every priest, is at this point today. All the faithful have to say is *Amen*. They are still blessed when the pastor's or the assistant's religion does not change every Sunday, at the whim of his reading, the foolery he has seen others at, or his own pure fancy".

Another fact inherent in the nature of Protestantism is that if each believer is free to make his own reason the ultimate judge of truth, then Protestantism must inevitably move towards rationalism. This is a process which Cardinal Manning analysed with great perceptiveness in 1877:

> Every age has hitherto had its heresy. It may be said that the nineteenth century has no heresy, or rather that it has all heresies, because it is the century of unbelief. The intellect of man for three hundred years has broken loose from the faith, and the heresy of the day is a heresy against the order of even natural truth; it is *the assertion that reason is sufficient to itself*. We, as compared with the

The Background to Protestantism

men of the sixteenth century, have a great advantage. We see the whole intellectual movement, which then began, fully worked out to its legitimate conclusion. They saw only the first deviation from the path, which then was hardly appreciable. *The reason of man either is, or is not, sufficient to itself.* If it be, then rationalism is its perfection. If it be not sufficient to itself, then something higher than reason is needed. Or, in other words, *reason is either its own teacher, or it needs a teacher higher than itself.* The Christian world till the sixteenth century believed that the teacher of the reason of man is God...and that the reason of man is thereby related to Him as a disciple to a guide. The movement of the sixteenth century in its last analysis is the assertion that the reason of man is the critic and the measure of all truth to itself. The Reformation in all its diversities of national and personal character—German, Swiss, French, English, Scottish—is all one in its principle. *It consisted of an appeal from the living authority of the Church to the inspired Scriptures,* or to the Scriptures with the written records of Christianity, tested and interpreted by reason. All particular controversies against particular Catholic doctrines or practices were no more than accessories and accidents to the main debate. *The essence of the Reformation consisted in the rejection of the doctrinal authority of the Church.* The Reformers denied it to be divine and therefore unerring and certain.

The history of the Reformed religion in Germany abundantly proves the truth of this assertion. It has had three periods. The first was a period of dogmatic rigor. The Lutheran doctrine was imposed and believed as the word of God. Men believed the Lutheran religion as they had before believed the Catholic, less only the principle. They had believed Catholic doctrine to be the word of God; they now believed the Lutheran to be the word of God. They had believed the voice of the Church before;

they believed the voice of the Bible now. It belonged to no individual to say what is the voice of the Church. But it was left for each to say what is the voice of the Bible. This period could not last long. Its own incompleteness suggested doubts. The contentions and contradictions of the Reformers shook the authority of the Reformation. Men of consecutive minds then began to give up dogma, and to withdraw into a personal piety. The second period was one of pietism, with a diminishing definiteness of Christian doctrines. But pietism, unsustained by the positive objects of faith, could have no duration in itself. It is like the seed which, having no root, withers away. It soon passed into the third period, which was one of rationalism. Pietism hid its eyes from doctrines which it was tempted to doubt; but rationalism looked them steadily in the face, and searched beyond them into the reason, evidences, and authorities on which they rested. The search was soon over. It terminated in a book, and the book rested upon human history. Book by book the Holy Scriptures was tried by rationalistic criticism, and rejected until the whole Bible was banished to the realm of myths, and the Lutheran Reformation was ruined at its base. The rationalists of today in Germany are the legitimate sons of the Lutherans of three hundred years ago. [My emphasis.][2]

In his encyclical *Pascendi Gregis*, Pope St. Pius X warns "by how many roads Modernism leads to atheism. The error of Protestantism made the first step on this path; that of Modernism makes the second; atheism makes the next".[3] The epitomisation of the process described by the Cardinal and the Pope is found in the writing of such German biblical scholars as Bultmann. Cardinal Heenan wrote:

The Background to Protestantism

> Too many theologians have accepted Bultmannism as the only authentic revelation. This is surprising because Bultmann did not say anything essentially different from the theologians once called Modernists....Radicals used to be content to explain away mysteries and miracles. Bultmann explains away the whole gospel....In his view, the story of Christ is no more historical than the story of creation in Genesis is scientific. Incarnation, the virgin birth, and Trinity and, of course, the resurrection are all myths. It is as absurd to talk of God on earth as of God in heaven...God does not exist outside this world.[4]

Given the truth of the thesis which has been put forward in this chapter, it is quite clear that the ecumenical movement as it now exists is based on the completely false premise that organic unity with Protestants can be achieved by ecumenical negotiations. Such a belief is the most illusory form of utopianism imaginable. The often impressive structures of the major Protestant bodies are, in reality, no more than facades behind which there exists a series of ill-defined systems undergoing an inexorable process of mutation into rationalism.

The more those in authority attempt to bring the Church closer to Protestantism, the closer they are bringing it to religionless Christianity, to rationalism. Father John McKee has written a detailed and well-documented study of both the original and the contemporary Modernists in which he makes this very point:

> As today's imbalance springs from an inferiority-complex, from a desire to take on the colour of the surrounding society, it will not end with an advance towards conservative Protestant beliefs. Thanks to liberal Protestantism, the "stout Protestants" have lost a lot of weight. The society around us is humanist, and, that be-

ing so, the wilder ecumenism is not a swing towards our Protestant brethren but a leap through the paper-hoop of liberalism towards humanism; Modernism is disbelief, not sectarian Christianity.[5]

It is no coincidence that those countries in which the process of ecumenical compromise has the longest tradition, i.e. the countries of the Rhine, are those in which Catholicism has been most affected by rationalism. This tendency was already manifesting itself in Germany at the time of the First Vatican Council. It was above all in Munich, among Döllinger and his supporters, that the nineteenth-century liberals went into schism as a response to the definition of papal infallibility.
Cardinal Manning has explained the process by which the rationalistic trends found among German Lutherans began to infect their Catholic compatriots. He defines as the essence of German philosophy as it had then developed that:

> God is the world, and the world God; that all things are manifestations or emanations of God, and that God by necessity creates or manifests Himself for His own justification; that He cannot reveal Himself to men by outward revelation or through the senses; that all materials of reason are derived only through the external world; that religious belief and religious feeling are one and the same; that faith is founded in the feeling of the reality of the ideal; that nothing is to be believed, nor can be required of man to believe, which is not capable of demonstration. These propositions were actually before the minds of those who elaborated the first Constitution on Catholic Faith, for these and the like aberrations in philosophy had been spreading for generations through the German people. It is true that they were the offspring of Lutheranism, and existed formally in the

The Background to Protestantism

non-Catholic schools; but it is to be remembered that in the mixed universities the Catholic and Protestant populations were confounded together, and that the government appointed Protestant professors, at whose lectures Catholics attended. Infection cannot be circumscribed, nor diseases kept within a ring-fence. The same habits of mind are found to pervade men of the same nation, and among Catholic philosophers unsound theories had begun to appear. Pius IX, during his pontificate, had been compelled to condemn three or four philosophies which were being taught by Catholic professors.[6]

Cardinal Heenan remarked in 1972 upon the extent to which the disease of rationalism is now rampant within the Catholic Church:

> Theological controversy is no longer interdenominational. Orthodoxy and, if the word may still be used, heresy, have become transconfessional....There is a remarkable unanimity about the theological works which have appeared in recent years. Theologians seem to read mainly each other's books. Unlike academics in other fields they appear to spend little time in research....One does not need to be a prophet to realise that without a dramatic reversal of the present trend there will be no future for the Church in English-speaking countries.[7]

This, then, is what is at stake—the future of the Church not just in the English-speaking but in all the advanced Western countries. The Church has become, as Father Bryan Houghton wrote, the talking Church, and in the present ecumenical dialogue she is in the process of talking herself out of existence in the West.

Cardinal Heenan's warning was confirmed in the most startling, horrifying manner with the publication of the notorious Dutch Catechism (Common Catechism).[8] It was described by its publishers as "an epoch-making attempt to state with one voice the common basis of Christian belief". What it does do, in fact, is to remove the entire basis of any form of Christian belief—either Catholic or Protestant—by denying or casting doubt on fundamental doctrines of the faith. It was, of course, greeted with a chorus of adulation from both Catholic and Protestant liberals—a striking confirmation of Cardinal Heenan's remark that heresy and orthodoxy are now transconfessional. Monsignor Eugene Kevane, in his book *Creed and Catechetics*, saw the Dutch Catechism as being "heavily infected with the remnants of Modernism. The characteristics of its Neo-Modernistic catechetical approach, its ambiguities, its omissions and its outright doctrinal errors, live on in many...programs of religious education, and in teaching aids which implement them".[9]

Commenting on the Catechism in the *Homiletic and Pastoral Review* in an article entitled "Process Theology and the Crisis in Catechetics", Father Edwin C. Garvey wrote:

> The Declaration of the Papal Commission of Cardinals on the new Dutch Catechism, published in 1968, found it necessary to accuse this Catechism of brutal education by the omission of central truths of the Catholic faith. This commission pointed out that basic doctrines such as original sin, satisfaction and redemption by Christ, the nature of the Mass, the Real Presence, the Ten Commandments, the communion of saints, the angels and the devils, immortality of the soul, the nature of the Church, the role and prerogatives of Mary, were either completely neglected or were vaguely taught. Those familiar with religion textbooks presently used in America know that the same criticism can be validly made of many....At the present time the disease of Modernism has become so

pervasive and so virulent that, by comparison, as Maritain writes, the Modernism of Pius X's time was only a mild hay fever compared to the neo-modernist fever of today.

It was precisely to emphasise the elements being passed over in many modern educational systems, or being incorrectly taught, that Pope Paul VI issued his *Credo of the People of God*. Conservative Catholics and Protestants now have more in common with each other than with the liberals in their own communion. A Catholic is obviously much closer in belief to an evangelical Protestant who accepts the divinity of Christ, the virgin-birth, the resurrection, and the doctrine of the Trinity than with a nominally Catholic Modernist who accepts none of these doctrines. The point will soon be reached, it if has not been reached already, when the line of demarcation will be between those who believe in a personal, transcendent God and those who believe there is no God but the world.

Protestants who wish to hold fast to the basic Christian dogmas are alarmed at the manner in which Catholic ecumenists are now blundering towards rationalism with all the haste and enthusiasm of a horde of lemmings. Father Bouyer wrote:

> It is what is most jumbled, inorganic and amorphous about the rest of Christianity that they have suddenly and gleefully discovered. But even that does not satisfy them, and they want to flirt with every form of belief and especially non-belief. In other words, as one of the best contemporary ecumenists, a Protestant, observed with ironic sadness: "The greatest danger for ecumenism is that Catholics grow into enthusiasts for everything we have recognised as harmful, and abandon everything whose importance we have rediscovered".[10]

Once the position has been reached that there is no God, outside this world, i.e. that the world, that mankind itself, is God, then it is only logical that Christians should devote all their energies into building up an earthly paradise rather than saving men's souls for an illusory paradise in heaven. Christ said that the hatred of the world would be a distinguishing mark of His disciples; because they loved Him the world would hate them. This has proved to be true throughout the history of the Church—but with that hatred there has always been mingled respect. The abysmal state of contemporary Catholicism is made most manifest in the fact that it is not feared or hated but despised by the world. Progressive Catholics, lay and clerical, are falling over each other in their anxiety to bow down and worship the world, to worship the new deity they name Progress with a zeal they never displayed in the service of the Blessed Trinity. To quote Father Bouyer again:

> Catholics today endlessly drag themselves along on their bellies before the more or less cloven hoofs of all the golden calves with which progress teems. But what is really extraordinary is that while at their orisons, they do not hear the enormous burst of laughter gradually growing in the world at the spectacle presented by their maniacal servility. Actually, people stopped taking them seriously long ago. But what else would you want them to do at this sudden and unexpected crawling on all fours by people who turned their backs on you for generations, but hold their sides? Yet, there are sensitive people in the world, and more than Catholics imagine, who not only are not carried away by all this mouldy incense, taken away from God for the sole benefit of their nostrils, but who find the stench of this abject humility nauseating.[11]

The Background to Protestantism

Christians of all denominations are now devoting themselves to the construction of this earthly paradise with the zeal their predecessors displayed in propagating the Gospel, and in this endeavor they are happy to collaborate with any variety of Marxist. This is a phenomenon which will be examined in Chapter XI. This tendency to make the first priority of the Christian the building of the earthly paradise has made inroads into the Church in the nineteenth century, particularly in France. It will be examined in Chapter XV. It is the "horizontal" Christianity, which, Father Paul Crane explained, "sees this earth as the be-all and end-all of man, which believes in the temporal kingdom and sees man eventually as capable of attaining it in the shape of perfect earthly happiness, not only for himself, but for society as a whole, here on this earth".[12] The movement to build such a society is now given religious expression in the so-called "liberation theology", a theology which is dedicated not to liberating man from sin but from oppressive social structures. This "liberation theology" must be condemned because it is an aberration; God did not become Man to lead a revolution but to atone for sin and reconcile man with God. But there are clear implications regarding the manner in which men should behave towards each other inherent in His teaching, and in the fact that since Christ became our Brother His Father is also our Father. The fact that the present revolutionary and social reforming movement, which has developed in the Church since Vatican II, must be opposed does not, as Father Paul Crane insisted, imply "an addiction to the *status quo*" in South America or any other part of the world. This movement must be opposed because of its secularist and anti-Christian philosophy. Father Crane writes:

> There are many in the Church, far more radical in the field of social reform than they are, who share with the secularists an abhorrence for the establishment against

which they are in revolt, but who are opposed utterly to the secularist basis of the philosophy which sustains their anti-establishment and—often without realising it—anti-religious strivings.[13]

It hardly needs saying that this anti-Christian liberation theology is firmly established within the World Council of Churches or that the principal aim of many Catholic ecumenists is to drag the Church into this organization, an organization which it is no exaggeration to designate as the anti-Church. Those who are seriously interested in the direction Protestantism is taking at present need only examine the activities of the World Council of Churches. There is, of course, strong opposition to it among some Protestants, but this tends to be on an individual basis rather than as representatives of their particular denominations.[14]

Ecumenical dialogue with Protestant denominations is futile, because no hope of corporate reunion exists, and dangerous, because it induces those engaged in ecumenical discussion to minimise Catholic truth in the interests of spurious agreements—the notorious Agreed Statements provide proof enough of this.[15] Those engaged in trying to come to an agreement tend to make reaching the agreement their first priority, and this is an understandable attitude. They feel that if no agreement is reached they have failed, not realising that an agreement not based on truth is the real failure. The story of the ecumenical dialogue which the Council initiated has been one of continual concessions by the Catholic Church to Protestantism—without any reciprocation. Once again, the Agreed Statements provide obvious examples, but the most serious instance has been the modification of the Roman Mass to make it as acceptable as possible to those who reject Catholic teaching on sacrifice and transubstantiation. This will be made abundantly clear in the third book in this trilogy, *Pope Paul's New Mass*,

The Background to Protestantism

which will show how closely the post-conciliar reforms correspond with those of Cranmer, which were examined in the first book, *Cranmer's Godly Order*. The next two chapters in the present book will show that this preoccupation with conciliating Protestants is manifested in the phrasing of some of the Council documents themselves. At the same time, the ecumenical dialogue has opened a door through which the disease of rationalism, so rampant among Protestant denominations, has been able to enter and contaminate the Mystical Body itself—and consequently weaken its ability to combat the forces of revolution, which have never seemed closer to eclipsing the Church of Christ than they do at present.

It should be equally clear that ecumenical dialogue with Protestants is futile because the logic of their system means that, in the last resort, a Protestant leader can speak only for himself. They have no authority other than the Bible, which ultimately each believer is free to interpret according to the dictates of his own reason. It is true that some denominations, the Anglicans for example, profess to accept the historic creeds and *some* councils. But who is to say what any particular article of a creed means, and who is to say which councils are to be accepted? Archdeacon Pawley, an Anglican observer at Vatican II, admits himself that Anglicans are not even sure which councils they do recognise. "Anglican Churches have made no official ruling as to how many they recognise, and since they hold the three creeds (Apostles', Athanasian, and Nicene) as having authority they must presumably accept the general authority of the first four councils in which those creeds were defined".[16] One thing that Archdeacon Pawley has no hesitation in affirming is that Anglicans most certainly do not recognise Vatican II as a general council. "We say the Council cannot be considered an ecumenical council in succession to those of the undivided Church, but is a domestic conference of the Roman Catholic Church only".[17]

Anglicans, of course, still adhere to, and have no intention of abandoning, their "branch theory" of the Church, i.e. that the Church is now divided into different branches of which theirs is one, but one which is far more Catholic than the Church of Rome. To quote Archdeacon Pawley again: "The reformers were at great pains to continue in the Church of England both the faith and the ministerial structure of the One, Holy, Catholic and Apostolic Church. Far from having jettisoned the 'old faith', she has kept it intact; it is the Roman Catholic Church which had added innovations".[18] "The champions of the English reforms were put to death", writes the Archdeacon, "particularly Archbishop Cranmer, and Bishops Ridley, Latimer, and Hooper, who, if and when the Anglican Church takes up again the business of 'canonization', will certainly be honoured by the Church of England as martyrs for the faith".[19] There are ample quotations from their works in *Cranmer's Godly Order*; they were indeed willing to die for their beliefs, but as their own writings make clear, what they believed was not the faith of the One, Holy, Catholic, and Apostolic Church.

It would be very hard to find any particular doctrine and state that it represents Anglican belief. All that can be done is to state that it represents the beliefs of some Anglicans. Monsignor G. P. Dwyer, the Catholic Archbishop of Birmingham, England, during the Council, remarked in a speech during the debate on ecumenism:

> It is a great mistake to imagine that Catholic and non-Catholic Christians always or even usually are in agreement about fundamental doctrines. In fact, we are very far apart on many matters of faith and morals. For instance: you can never be sure that the non-Catholic with whom you are speaking, even if he is a bishop, believes

The Background to Protestantism

in the Virgin Birth of Christ or His bodily resurrection from the dead. What is more, even our separated brethren who are sound on these matters and really hold the doctrine of the true faith, are still unwilling to say that those who deny these fundamental doctrines are denying the Christian faith.[20]

The truth of this statement cannot be illustrated better than by quoting from a letter (in the possession of the author) sent by an Anglican bishop to a member of his diocese who had written to him asking him to explain exactly what the Church of England did teach about the Eucharist as different ministers had been giving him conflicting explanations. The bishop replied that it was quite impossible for him to answer this question, and continued:

> The doctrine of the Church of England on the Holy Communion has been expounded in four or five different ways. The truth of the matter is that the Church of England is not at all anxious to be too explicit, and in this great wisdom was shown. The Church of England has been satisfied to state first, that transubstantiation is not true, and secondly that Christ does give Himself as our spiritual food. Further than that there are no definitions. How can anybody define exactly the way in which Christ comes to His people in Holy Communion? Who knows and who has the right to dogmatise?

Monsignor Dwyer was equally correct in pointing out the importance of differences in moral teaching. The Anglican bishops are not opposed to abortion on principle, although some are opposed to it on demand. Their attitude to contraception is impossible to reconcile with the official Catholic position, although unofficially some Catholic bishops and even whole hierarchies have adopted the Anglican standpoint in practice, i.e. it is for each individual to make his own decision. Thus in morals, as in doctrine and liturgy, the practical effect of ecumenical dialogue is the Protestantisation of the Catholic Church. There is certainly a grim irony in the fact that the strictures passed upon Protestants by Monsignor Dwyer are now applicable to many Catholics. You can never be sure that the Catholic with whom you are speaking, even if he is a bishop, believes in the Virgin Birth of Christ, His bodily resurrection from the dead, let alone that contraception is intrinsically evil as taught by Pope Paul VI in *Humanae Vitae* (1968).

The only Catholic and practical form of ecumenism is to present the faith courteously and clearly to Protestants as individuals, doing everything possible to clear away misconceptions without compromising the truth. What the Church teaches is true, and it follows that where Protestants reject Catholic teaching they are rejecting the truth, however sincere they may be in their beliefs. No one is more injured by the policy of Catholic ecumenists in obscuring the truth to please Protestants than are Protestants themselves. If they are given the impression that one religion is as good as another they are unlikely to abandon their errors and accept the invitation made by Pope Pius XI in *Mortalium Animos*. Any form of ecumenism which does not base itself upon this invitation is a betrayal of the Catholic faith:

> Let these separated children return to the Apostolic See established in the city which the Princes of the Apostles, Peter and Paul, consecrated with their blood, to this See, "the root and matrix of the Catholic Church", not indeed with the idea or hope that "the Church of the living God, the pillar and ground of truth" will abandon the integrity of the faith and bear their errors, but to subject themselves to its teaching authority and rule.

The Background to Protestantism

The Decree on Ecumenism states:

> The manner and order in which Catholic belief is expressed should in no way become an obstacle to dialogue with our separated brethren. It is, of course, essential that doctrine be clearly presented in its entirety. Nothing is so foreign to the spirit of ecumenism as a false conciliatory approach which harms the purity of Catholic doctrine and obscures its assured genuine meaning.[21]

As this false conciliatory approach is now most certainly the guiding spirit of the present ecumenical dialogue, and this is a fact which can be demonstrated objectively, then those Catholics who resist are acting in accordance with the letter of the Council.

Notes

[1] DC, p. 31.
[2] TSVC, pp. 124-126.
[3] PG, p. 51.
[4] *Times Literary Supplement*, 22 December 1972.
[5] J. McKee, *The Enemy within the Gate* (Houston, Texas: Lumen Christi Press, 1974), p. 150.
[6] TSVC, pp. 127-128.
[7] *Op. cit.*, note 4.
[8] *The Common Catechism* (London, 1975).
[9] E. Kevane, *Creed and Catechetics* (Boston: St. Paul Editions, 1983), p. xvi.
[10] DC, p. 34.
[11] DC, pp. 40-41.
[12] *Christian Order*, December 1973, p. 736.
[13] *Ibid.*, February 1976, p. 91.
[14] B. Smith, *The Fraudulent Gospel* (London, 1977).
[15] M. Davies, *The Order of Melchisedech* (Roman Catholic Books, 1995), Chapter VI and Appendix VIII.
[16] AVCC, p. 38.
[17] *Ibid.*, p. 104.
[18] *Ibid.*, p. 22.
[19] *Ibid.*, p. 17.
[20] *The Tablet*, 7 December 1963, p. 1340.
[21] Abbott, p. 354.

IX

Protestant Pressures

The 450th anniversary of the Protestant Reformation was celebrated in Wittenberg on 31 October 1967. A number of Catholic representatives joined a thousand Protestant delegates from all over the world to pay tribute to Martin Luther. A personal representative of Cardinal Bea, from his Unity Secretariat, found it "difficult to hold a continuous conversation, so frequently must he shake another evangelical hand".[1] One of the Lutheran observers at the Second Vatican Council, Dr. K. E. Skydsgaard, "spoke of the way in which the Second Vatican Council seemed in many ways to have brought the Catholic Church very close to the Protestant Churches".[2] Mention has already been made of the extent to which this is clearly the opinion of the Protestants who provided commentaries for the conciliar documents in the Abbott edition. Similar expressions have been made elsewhere. Archdeacon Pawley, an Anglican observer, finds that "the 'dialogue' envisaged by the Decree on Ecumenism and encouraged by Pope Paul VI has exceeded the wildest hopes entertained for it".[3] He remarks, with great satisfaction, "The true picture of the Council was that it represented a powerful victory of the forces of renewal in the Church of Rome over the conservative immobilism of its central government".[4] Pastor Roger Schutz, the prior and founder of the Protestant community at Taizé, also an observer at Vatican II, stated that the Council had "exceeded our hopes".[5] Dr. Oscar Cullmann, the noted Swiss theologian, declared: "The hopes of Protestants for Vatican II have not only been fulfilled, but the Council's achievements have gone far beyond what was believed possible".[6]

A report in *The Tablet* in February 1966 included the following:

> The Council's statement on the Catholic Church's understanding of itself was an answer to Luther's basic concerns that was late in point of time but close as far as content was concerned, said the German Evangelical theologian Professor Peter Meinhold of Keil in Stuttgart last week. In the Second Vatican Council, with its fundamental explorations and practical reforms, he saw the honouring of Reformation demands in a way no one would have dared hope up till now. Comparing statements from the Council's Constitution on the Church with Luther's theology, he demonstrated that in their basic concerns the two were in surprising agreement over long passages. This showed the extent to which the Churches had overcome their past and come closer to each other without betraying themselves.[7]

This final sentence is inaccurate as it is the Catholic Church which has made a unilateral move towards the Protestant denominations. This movement still remains entirely one-sided and consists of what Protestant leaders consider as the Church of Rome "seeing the light" at last. Some Protestant spokesmen have been commendably honest in making their own position clear. Dr. Skydsgaard, who found it unbelievable a few years before Vatican II that the "Roman Church" would ever change, was full of praise for the Council during its second session but warned that it would be an illusion for Catholics to imagine that any number of Protestants "looked upon the Roman Catholic Church with 'nostalgia' or desired to 'return' pure and simple to the bosom of a Church which they still regarded as defective. The Churches must sit down and talk over their differences as 'equals' and as 'equals' again to be reunited".[8]

Professor George Lindbeck, of the Yale Divinity School, and Lutheran observer, was happy to note that "the Council marked the end of the Counter-Reformation". He expressed his satisfaction at "the rejection of the proposed schema on the sources of revelation as well as the results of the discussion on the liturgy".[9] Catholic traditionalists must concur, however regretfully, that the Council certainly did mark the end of the Counter-Reformation. The Counter-Reformation initiated what is possibly the greatest era of true renewal in the entire history of the Church. Every true renewal in Church history has a common characteristic, the emergence of great saints. Monsignor Philip Flanagan, former Rector of the Pontifical Scots College in Rome, pointed out in a sermon preached at an *Approaches* conference in 1972 that God sent an abundant crop of saints during the Counter-Reformation period:

> Church leaders like St. Pius V and Charles Borromeo, apostolic priests like Ignatius of Loyola and Francis Borgia and Philip Neri, mystics like Teresa of Avila and John of the Cross and Peter of Alcantara, theologians like Robert Bellarmine and Peter Canisius, young saints like Aloysius Gonzaga and Stanislaus Kostka and John Berchmans, missionaries like Francis Xavier and Francis of Solano, apostles of charity like Vincent de Paul and Peter Claver and John of God and many others engaged in a variety of good works and social reforms—education, care of the sick or the orphans, care of the slaves, preaching to the poor, care of prisoners and so on. One thing

all these saints had in common besides their love of God and of their neighbour was their devotion to the Church. For them it was *only* in and through the Church that they could find God and serve their neighbour.[10]

"Where are the songs of Spring? Aye, where are they?" asked Keats. Where, one might ask, are the fruits of Vatican II? Aye, where are they? There are, of course, those who would consider Protestant satisfaction with the Council to be one of its most evident and welcome fruits. Others among us would consider the fact that those who reject Catholic truth and find the teaching of the Council far more satisfactory than any previous presentation of the faith is a cause for serious concern. Whichever view is taken, more than sufficient evidence has already been presented in this book to prove that mainstream Protestants found the Council very much to their taste. Protestant satisfaction with Vatican II is hardly surprising in view of the extent to which they influenced its proceedings. That Protestant influence upon the Council would be considerable was made a certainty when the Secretariat for the Promotion of Christian Unity was established on 5 June 1960. It is now one of the most powerful forces in the Vatican. Its purpose was to establish relations with Christian bodies outside the unity of the Church and invite them to send representatives to the Council.[11] Dr. McAfee Brown emphasised that:

> It is significant that this secretariat was established independently of the Curia—the court of officials that helps the pope with the running of the Church—and that it thus had considerably greater freedom and maneuverability than would otherwise have been the case. It is also significant that, although originally established to work in conjunction with the Council, it was broadly hinted that the secretariat might remain as a permanent

structure of the Roman Catholic Church once the Council was over, a hint which has since become an established fact....

That the formation of the secretariat was not merely a hollow and formal gesture became clear when Pope John indicated those who were to serve within it. As head of the secretariat he appointed Augustin Cardinal Bea, S.J., a German Biblical scholar, who subsequently became one of the real leaders of the Council, and who made of the secretariat an exceedingly significant organ of ecumenical exchange as well as a very powerful force within the Council itself....For the task of actually running the secretariat the Pope chose Monsignor (now Cardinal) Jan Willebrands, a leading Dutch ecumenist with much experience in ecumenical affairs....As the Council got underway, the very existence of the secretariat, coupled with its independence of the Curia, proved important ecumenical boons, for most of the conciliar matters dealing with ecumenical affairs were included within the portfolio of the secretariat. Thus it was the secretariat that had the task of drafting the crucial schema "On Ecumenism"; it was the secretariat that provided the succession of texts for the statements on Religious Liberty and on the Jews; and it was the head of the secretariat, Cardinal Bea, who was appointed co-chairman (with Cardinal Ottaviani) of a special conciliar commission to write a new version of the ecumenically crucial document "On Revelation".[12]

Sufficient should have been written concerning this document in Chapter VI to indicate which of the co-chairmen was able to make his views predominate. The very presence of Protestant observers at the Council was bound to have an inhibiting effect upon the debates. No good-mannered host would wish to express opinions which might offend a guest in his house if he could help doing so. It is obvious that the presence of these Protestant observers with whom the Council Fathers mixed freely, and with whom many established friendly personal relations, must certainly have resulted in some Fathers minimising or even passing over in silence aspects of the Faith which might cause offence to their Protestant guests. The testimonies of some Council Fathers that this was definitely happening have already been cited in Chapter VI. Archbishop Lefebvre issued a warning about this tendency as early as March 1963.[13] In October 1964 he complained that: "Thus, on those points of specifically Catholic doctrine, one is forced to compose schemata which attenuate or even completely banish anything which could displease the Orthodox and, above all, the Protestants".[14] As is so often the case, Monsignor Lefebvre's judgement is confirmed by someone speaking from the opposite standpoint. Dr. Moorman, leader of the Anglican delegation, noted that the observers "were providing some kind of check on what was being said".

> Every bishop who has stood up to speak has known that, in the tribune of S. Longinus, was a group of intelligent and critical people, their pencils and biros poised to take down what he said and possibly use it in evidence against him and his colleagues on some future occasion....Members of the Council tended, therefore, to be very sensitive to what the representatives of those other communions were thinking, and did their best to avoid saying anything which was likely to cause offence. If some Father forgot himself and said things which were bound to cause a flutter in the observers' tribune, he was sometimes rebuked by some later speaker.[15]

Protestant influence did not consist only in this inhibiting effect upon what the Fathers said; they were sometimes able to have their own views put forward in the debates. Dr. Moorman revealed that "although the observers were not allowed to speak in the Council, their speeches were sometimes made for them by one or other of the Fathers".[16] The observers were able to "make their views known at special weekly meetings of the (Unity) Secretariat, and had personal contacts with the Council Fathers, *periti*, and other leading personalities in Rome".[17] Professor Oscar Cullmann, a Lutheran delegate, remarked after only six weeks: "I am more and more amazed every morning at the way we really form a part of the Council".[18]

Cardinal Bea testified to the extent of the contribution made by the observers in formulating the Decree on Ecumenism. At a reception organised by his Unity Secretariat he commented: "I do not hesitate to assert that they have contributed in a decisive way to bringing about this result".[19] Professor B. Mondin, of the Pontifical Propaganda College for the Missions, has testified that such observers as Dr. Cullmann made "a valid contribution" to drawing up the Council documents.[20] Dr. McAfee Brown wrote that:

> As the sessions of the Council unfolded, the role of the observers became more and more that of informal participants. The observers did not, of course, have either voice or vote, but as *rapport* and trust were established between the observers and the Council Fathers, there was an increasingly high rate of exchange of opinion. The Secretariat for the Promotion of Christian Unity arranged official weekly meetings of the observers and members of the Council, at which the observers were asked to comment frankly on the documents under discussion, and—particularly when the documents dealt with ecumenical issues—the opinions of the observers were taken with real seriousness by the leaders of the Council. Frequent changes in the wording or the tone of

the final documents can be traced to these briefing sessions.[21]

The very close relationship between the observers and the liberal *periti* was disclosed by Father Schillebeeckx when he remarked: "One is astonished to find oneself more in sympathy with the thinking of Christian, non-Catholic 'observers' than with the views of one's own brethren on the other side of the dividing line. The accusation of connivance with the Reformation is therefore not without foundation. What is, in fact, happening then?"[22] What indeed?

"We found ourselves meeting together at the beginning of a road whose end only God knows", commented Dr. Skydsgaard.[23] The situation which developed during Vatican II, and the inevitable consequences for the Church if the road taken during this council should be followed to its end, were foreseen and described by Pope Pius XII in *Humani Generis*. A policy of appeasement could certainly end in unity, he agreed, but added that: "The world may indeed be united, but only in a common ruin". In this same encyclical he spoke of a danger "all the more formidable because it is disguised under the cloak of good intentions". Pope Pius adds that some of those he is criticising are "inspired by motives praiseworthy in themselves"—and this is a point upon which it is worth laying some stress. It is legitimate to point out that the Catholic tradition of absolute fidelity to the truth, and its fearless and unambiguous proclamation, was compromised during the Council and has been even more seriously compromised since, to advance the cause of the spurious form of ecumenism so consistently condemned by Pope Pius XII and his predecessors. This policy is mistaken, and its consequences have been disastrous, and it is quite legitimate to point this out. But the cause of orthodoxy is not helped by speculating upon the motives of Catholic ecumenists. Some are certainly sincere

Protestant Pressures

and dedicated men whose motives are praiseworthy, and to attempt to label them all as participants in a sinister conspiracy not only weakens the traditionalist case but is an offence again justice. It is possible that some of the decisions of Vatican II were influenced by participants in a malicious conspiracy to destroy the Church—this possibility will be discussed in Chapter XIV—but nothing but harm can result from attempting to link any individual with such a conspiracy without producing conclusive evidence to substantiate such an allegation.

However sincere the motives behind this misguided policy of appeasement may be, its fruits are now available for all to see. Our Blessed Lord gave one task and one task only to His Church: this was to evangelise the world, to "Go forth and teach all nations". The most manifest result of the Council has been the replacement of evangelisation by dialogue. There is now little effort to convert anyone to Catholicism, be they pagans, members of some non-Christian monotheistic religions, Protestants, or even Marxists. At every level, from the Vatican to the smallest parish, there is an obsessive preoccupation among the progressive elite to dialogue with anyone about anything and for any length of time. The Council was the catalyst which enabled the bishops, in a state of euphoria, to drop the daunting task of evangelising the mission countries and re-evangelising the de-Christianised masses in some of their own countries—let alone presenting Catholicism as *the* viable and coherent alternative to Marxism. Missionary activity in some non-Christian countries is frowned upon now, in some circles at least. No prelate can speak upon the subject of the missions with greater authority than Archbishop Lefebvre, who had remarked:

> Today we are seeing many missionaries who have returned from the field refusing to go back. The idea is

drummed into them at all the sessions, all the meetings everywhere. Delegates from France have adjured them: "Beware especially of proselytising. You should realise that all the religions you may encounter have considerable value and that missionaries should therefore stick to the development of these countries with its resulting progress—social progress". No longer true evangelization and sanctification.[24]

There are, of course, endless tracts of print in the Council documents explaining how the world is to be evangelised—but on a practical level there is little sign of this being translated into action. In 1974 the bishops of the world held a synod devoted to the subject of evangelisation. Their meeting produced a plethora of words, but it is extremely unlikely that a single soul will be won from the kingdom of darkness to the kingdom of light as a result of their very tedious and very expensive deliberations. Much of what they said has been committed to print and distributed at every level throughout the Church so that the faithful can discuss the discussions of their bishops. After an analysis of the working-paper which the bishops of England and Wales were to use as the basis of their contribution to the synod, Father Paul Crane, S.J., remarked:

What amazed me, then, as I read and re-read my way through this official working paper was that its author—whoever he may be—appeared so utterly unaware of this essential fact: that the Church is so busy tearing herself to pieces, engaged in what the Holy Father himself has sorrowfully described as a process of "auto-destruction", as to make effective evangelisation a near impossibility; that her troubles are from within herself and that she must first get herself right, give herself back the truth before she can give it to others....What is this madness which causes those occupying responsible posts in the Church persistently to turn a blind eye to the disease which is gripping its vitals? Do they think you can get rid of an illness by ignoring its existence; that fatuous optimism is any kind of substitute for a cowardly unwillingness to face the truth, however unpleasant that may be?...evangelisation can no more be carried out in these circumstances than you can expect a sick man to get up from his bed and run a hundred yards in record time.[25]

The most obvious result of Vatican II is, as Father Bryan Houghton pointed out in the June 1975 issue of *Christian Order*, that the Catholic Church is now "the talking Church". Before the Council she devoted her efforts to the serious business of evangelisation, now she talks about it. To a very large extent her leaders have substituted ecumenism for evangelisation as their first priority, particularly in the Western countries. A vast new ecumenical bureaucracy has come into being. There are countless commissions, conferences, publications, and courses concerning ecumenism. Those who immerse themselves in it can make it a full-time occupation without the slightest difficulty. In contrast with the daunting task of evangelisation, especially among the de-Christianised masses who form the majority in most Western countries, the effort put into ecumenism is never without its immediate and tangible reward. Ecumenists claim, and some might even believe it, that no large scale progress can be made in the field of evangelisation because the divisions among Christians are such a source of scandal that the Gospel loses its credibility. The priority, they claim, must be unity and then Christians can really make an impact on society.

Where Catholics are concerned, as the previous chapter made clear, the progress in ecumenical dialogue is accompanied by the progressive dilution of Catholic truth. And, as this chapter also showed, the predominant trend in Protestantism is towards rationalism. If present trends continue, should unity ever be achieved, the message that the new pan-Christian Church would proclaim to the world would be little more than an echo of what the world is already saying. There would, in fact, be nothing to convert the world to as the world would have converted the Church. Ecumenists on the Catholic and Protestant sides are infected by an ostrich syndrome. Their endless talks take place with their heads buried deep in ecumenical sand, which is guaranteed to insulate them from the truth. Out in the real world the churches of all denominations are emptying; the more progress made by ecumenists the fewer the number of Christians offering worship to God each Sunday. But this causes ecumenists no concern. The justification for, and satisfaction in, ecumenical activity derives from the very fact that it is taking place. It is a self-perpetuating organism giving the impression of constant and escalating progress. One conference leads to another; national committees mutate into international committees; there is now an ecumenical jet-set with privileged members who meet each other in one exotic setting after another. This is particularly true of the Joint Catholic-Anglican International Committee responsible for the so-called Agreed Statements on the Eucharist and Ministry (*sic*). Cardinal Heenan wrote as early as 1966:

> There is almost a fraternity of international conference speakers who appear on both sides of the Atlantic at meetings of every theological complexion. There is no little danger that the multiplication of conferences will lead to a neglect of pastoral action. If too much time is spent on speculation, there will be too little spent in preaching the word of God. That, incidentally, is one of the dangers of ecumenism. We can become so engrossed

in discussing each other's theology that the flocks committed to our care, feeling unwanted, may begin to disperse.[26]

These were truly prophetic words—and as the ecumenical initiatives proliferate, the pace of the dispersal accelerates. No one is more reminiscent of the professional ecumenist than Hitler in the last days of the Third Reich, sitting in his bunker and issuing orders to non-existent armies, dreaming of new weapons which would bring him victory. Meanwhile his empire crumbled around him; the victory for which he hoped had long been an impossible dream. But Hitler could not face reality, he preferred to live out his illusion to the end. The professional ecumenist is equally unable to face up to the reality that what has become his one obsessive preoccupation has not only become irrelevant but a hindrance to the preaching of the Gospel—but those infected by ecumania show little if any interest in preaching the Gospel; ecumenical dialogue has become an end in itself for them. Ecumenism—ecumania, to give it a more accurate name—is truly the sickness of the Church today. Nothing is too precious or too sacred to be sacrificed in its interests—not even the traditional Roman liturgy, the most precious heritage of the Western Church, indeed, quite possibly the greatest treasure of our entire Western civilisation. But the traditional Mass was an obstacle to ecumenism—so the traditional Mass had to go. This will be the subject of the third book in this series.

What might appear to have been a digression on the subject of ecumenism is, in fact, very relevant to the theme of this chapter, Protestant influence upon Vatican II. No reasonable person could deny that the disease of ecumania is spreading throughout the entire organism of the Mystical Body as a direct result of the presence of Protestant observers at the Second Vatican Council—even though the symptoms were there long before, lying dormant, waiting for the right conditions to enable the virus to activate itself and then proliferate. The symptoms of the disease were accurately diagnosed in a series of papal documents from *Pascendi Gregis*, through *Mortalium Animos* to *Humani Generis*. Thus, though their influence on the course of the Council and the working of its documents was considerable, the impact of the Protestant observers was most manifest in the setting into motion of a movement which no group or individual within the Church seems willing or able to stop. "In ten short years the Council has taken on the dimensions of a world revolution", wrote Archdeacon Pawley in 1974.[27] He finds this a cause for particularly great rejoicing in view of the pessimism felt by Protestant ecumenists during the pontificate of Pope Pius XII. The dogma of the Assumption and the encyclical *Humani Generis* in particular had given rise to great despondency—particularly the teaching in *Humani Generis* that "the Mystical Body of Christ and the Roman Catholic Church were equal and co-terminous".[28] "The outlook for ecumenical understanding was black indeed".[29] But the Archdeacon is now delighted at detecting signs in the documents of Vatican II that the Mystical Body and the Roman Catholic Church are "no longer being considered as exactly identical".[30] This question, largely hinging on the use of the word "subsists", was discussed in Chapter VI.

An assertion by the Archdeacon which no reasonable person could deny is that the movement given such impetus by Vatican II "in its general trend is irreversible".[31] The most dramatic manifestation for the ordinary Catholic is one which has already been mentioned in this chapter, the Protestantisation of our liturgy. This, too, has won high praise from Archdeacon Pawley, who notes that it has, in many places, "outstripped the liturgy of Cranmer, in spite of the latter's four hundred years' start, in its modernity".[32] It is above all this new liturgy which he considers to have "changed relationships out of all recognition. For the revised Roman liturgy, so far from being a cause of dissension, now resembles the Anglican liturgy very closely. It has also demonstrated the value, under certain circumstances, of an authoritarian government. For instance of the pains and agonies of experiments, objections, counter-objections, and a multitude of parallel revisions existing at the same time, the new Roman liturgy came into existence simultaneously all over the world".[33] Similar sentiments have been expressed by spokesmen for a number of Protestant denominations, some far more evangelical in character than the Church of England. A detailed examination of the Protestant attitude to the new Mass, and its implications, must be left for the next book.

Archdeacon Pawley's remarks not only highlight the present abject state of the One, Holy, Roman, Catholic, and Apostolic Church but also provide an invaluable insight into the Anglican mentality. The Archdeacon is a typical Anglican minister, very sincere, full of good will, but quite capable of looking upon the Roman Mass as "a cause of dissension". When looked upon in their historical perspective his remarks are quite grotesque. In the sixteenth century those exercising effective control over the Church *in* England broke away from the Catholic Church, with which the English Church had always been in communion, and established the Church *of* England—an heretical and schismatic sect. They devised a new Communion Service to give liturgical expression to their heretical doctrines, and, as Father Fortescue explains, "broke away utterly from all historical liturgical evolution".[34] St. Pius V, in opposition to the heretical liturgies which had been devised wherever Protestants gained political power, codified the existing Roman rite, which dated back in all essentials to the time of St. Gregory the Great, and extended its use throughout the Latin Church. It has been celebrated throughout the length and breadth of the entire world, wherever priests of the Roman Rite have taken the Gospel. Yet to Archdeacon Pawley it is "a cause of dissension"—and a cause of dissension because it does not conform to the heresies of the Thirty-nine Articles! The spectacle of an Anglican minister reprimanding the universal Church for not bringing her liturgy into line with that of his sect could once have aroused no reaction but tolerant laughter among Catholics, but now they must weep, for those governing the Church today have gone a long way to removing this particular "cause of dissension", this obstacle to ecumenism, and have gone as far as they dare in bringing the Catholic liturgy into line with his, and received a pat on the back from the Archdeacon for doing so!

As is so often the case, Archbishop Lefebvre assessed the situation perfectly: "All these changes have but one justification, an aberrant, senseless ecumenism that will not attract a single Protestant to the Faith but will cause countless Catholics to lose it, and will instill total confusion in the minds of many more who will no longer know what is true and what is false".[35]

To avoid any possible misunderstanding, it must be made clear that nothing which has been written in this chapter, or in the whole book, for that matter, should be interpreted as being in opposition to true Catholic principles of ecumenism, which we all have a duty to implement. What is opposed here is the present ecumenical movement which has deviated from sound Catholic principles to embrace the false irenicism so consistently condemned by the popes. "It is dishonest to dissemble", wrote Cardinal Heenan, and he insisted that: "The ultimate object of ecumenism is reunion of all Christians under the Vicar of Christ".[36] Indeed, Catholics motivated by true feelings of charity towards their separated brethren will spare no effort to bring them back to their Father's house. It is the ecumenist who follows a policy of appeasement who is lacking in charity towards Protestants, for by giving the impression that one religion is as good as another he will encourage Protestants to remain outside the visible unity of the Church where they cannot be secure of their salvation. In his encyclical letter on the Mystical Body of Christ, Pope Pius XII issued an invitation to those outside the Church similar in tone and spirit to that issued by Pope Pius XI in *Mortalium Animos*, and cited at the conclusion of the previous chapter; it is an invitation which shows that there need be, and can be, no conflict between *Veritas* and *Caritas*, between the duty towards Truth demanded by the nature of Christ's divinely founded Church, and the duty of Charity towards those deprived of the grace of belonging to that Church.

> These, too, who do not belong to the visible structure of the Catholic Church, We committed at the beginning of Our Pontificate...to God's care and keeping, and We gave them the solemn assurance that, following the Good Shepherd's example, We desired nothing better than that they should "have life and have it more abundantly".... We invite them all, each and everyone, to yield their free consent to the inner stirrings of God's grace and strive to extricate themselves from a state in which they cannot be secure of their own eternal salvation; for though they may be related to the mystical Body of the Redeemer by some subconscious yearning and desire, yet they are deprived of those many great heavenly gifts and aids which can be enjoyed only in the Catholic Church. Let them enter Catholic unity, therefore, and joined with us in the one organism of the Body of Jesus Christ hasten together to the one Head in the fellowship of most glorious love. We cease not to pray for them to the Spirit of love and truth, and with open arms We await them, not as strangers, but as those who are coming to their own Father's house.

The full extent of the debacle of Vatican II lies in the fact that, as has already been indicated in this chapter, far from even thinking of entering Catholic unity, Protestant leaders are now confident that the Catholic Church is coming to accept the basic doctrines of the Reformation. Pastor G. Richard-Molard covered Vatican II for the French Protestant journal *Réforme*. While he regretted that a small number of Catholic bishops still confused truth itself with the teaching of the Catholic Church, he was generally optimistic. He affirmed that any Protestant present at the Council who might have felt tempted to modify any of the major axioms of the Reformation (*proclamations majeures*) would be "lacking in intelligence or deaf for failing to see or hear that for more than two years—and doubtlessly for even longer—so many believing Catholics, priests and laymen, had been probing the Scriptures, searching, praying, and suffering to arrive at this moment, and by other ways, at the point where they too accept these very same axioms". Pastor Richard-Molard, like Archdeacon Pawley, is confident that the process of renovation set in motion by the Council is more or less irreversible (*quasi irréversible*) and with consequences for the future which will be considerable.[37]

Notes

[1] *The Tablet*, 11 November 1967, p. 1173.
[2] *Ibid.*
[3] RCFC, p. 353.
[4] *Ibid.*, p. 351.
[5] *The Tablet*, 16 February 1963, p. 236.
[6] XR-IV, p. 256.
[7] *The Tablet*, 5 February 1966, p. 171.
[8] XR-II, p. 273.
[9] *The Tablet*, 16 February 1963, p. 177.
[10] Sermon preached at an *Approaches* conference, 4 November 1972.
[11] RFT, p. 120.
[12] ER, pp. 64-66.
[13] ABS, pp. 14-15.
[14] *Ibid.*, p. 76.
[15] VO, p. 26.
[16] *Ibid.*, p. 28.
[17] RFT, p. 123.

[18] *Ibid.*, p. 124.
[19] *The Tablet*, 31 October 1964.
[20] *L'Osservatore Romano* (English edition), 14 June 1973, p. 8.
[21] ER, pp. 66-67.
[22] *Catholic Gazette*, January 1964, p. 6.
[23] RFT, p. 124.
[24] ABS, p. 109.
[25] *Christian Order*, May 1974, p. 296 ff.
[26] *The Tablet*, 20 August 1966, p. 954.
[27] RCFC, p. 339.
[28] *Ibid.*, p. 313.
[29] *Ibid.*
[30] *Ibid.*, p. 343.
[31] *Ibid.*, p. 315.
[32] *Ibid.*, p. 349.
[33] *Ibid.*, p. 348.
[34] *The Mass* (London, 1976), p. 206.
[35] *World Trends*, May 1974.
[36] *Catholic Gazette*, May 1965.
[37] JC, pp. 510-513.

X

Mother of the Church

The influence exercised upon the Council by Protestants is well illustrated in relation to Our Lady. In justice to the Protestant observers it must be made clear that this stemmed not so much from any behind-the-scenes pressures which they may have exerted upon the liberal Fathers and *periti*, but from the fact that the principal preoccupation of so many of these liberals was "What will the Protestants think?" rather than, "In what way can we most fittingly honour the Mother of God and clarify her role in the economy of salvation?"

The question of the Council and Our Lady needs to be discussed under three main headings:
1. The separate schema.
2. The title "Mediatrix of All Graces".
3. The title "Mother of the Church".

The Rhine Group programme was quite definite. It was opposed to a separate schema being devoted to Our Lady, to the full title "Mediatrix of All Graces", and to the title "Mother of the Church".

1. The Separate Schema

During the preparatory work for the Council it had been intended to include any conciliar pronouncement on Our

Lady within the schema on the Church, but the Preparatory Commission eventually decided unanimously to devote a separate schema to the Blessed Virgin. After several changes of title the schema was eventually called "On the Blessed Virgin Mary, Mother of the Church".[1] Cardinal Ottaviani had hoped that the Council would discuss this short, six-page schema before the close of the first session. The happy result, he believed, would have been that "the Council Fathers, 'with the assistance of Our Lady, would then have concluded the first session in union and harmony'. But his plea had been ignored".[2] The fact that there was to be a separate schema devoted to Our Lady, and its contents, aroused the displeasure of Protestants and their Catholic sympathisers.

There had been legitimate differences of opinion among Catholic theologians before the Council, not on the fact that Mary had co-operated with Our Lord in the economy of our salvation, but on the nature and extent of that co-operation. An important school of thought, favoured by Pope Pius XII, had come to see Our Lady as co-operating in the acquisition of our salvation and wished to see the Magisterium define her as Co-Redemptrix and Mediatrix of All Graces. Another school favoured an approach emphasising her position as a member of the Church like ourselves, differing from us not in the essence but in the degree of her perfection. While the former view is incompatible with Protestantism, the latter has distinct ecumenical possibilities. The devotion of a separate schema to Our Lady would be seen by Protestants as favouring the former view; they would regard its inclusion within the schema on the Church as an important ecumenical concession. The rejection of the plan for a separate schema became the first priority for those Fathers and *periti* who considered the ecumenical aspect of the Council as its most important dimension.

Leading German Protestants had made it clear that Catholic teaching on Our Lady was a major impediment to reunion; that a separate schema on her, if approved, would erect a new wall of division; that if the Blessed Virgin was even mentioned it should be in the schema on the Church; and even that the Council should either keep silent on the subject or reprehend those guilty of excesses.³

The manner in which a single theologian could impose his views on the Council, provided he could gain the approval of the German bishops, has been mentioned in Chapter V. In the case of the separate schema this is exactly what Karl Rahner did. He claimed that if the schema was accepted as it stood "unimaginable harm would result from the ecumenical point of view—all the success achieved in the field of ecumenism through the Council and in connection with the Council will be rendered worthless by the retention of the schema as it stands".⁴ He asked the Rhine bishops to "declare openly" that they could not accept the schema as it stood.⁵ The Rhine Group forces were accordingly deployed and went into action as soon as the topic was raised during the second session. Cardinal Frings felt it would be "most fitting" to include everything pertaining to Our Lady in the schema on the Church as, among other things, "such action would do much to foster dialogue with the separated Christians".⁶

A Croatian *peritus*, Father Carolus Balic, was particularly active in combating the Rhine campaign, as were many bishops from the Latin countries. One of the Rhine arguments was that a separate schema would be taken as defining something new, but a Brazilian Servite bishop, Giocondo Grotti, pointed out that there were separate schemata on a good number of topics but no one claimed that anything new was being defined here:

> Does ecumenism consist in confessing or hiding the truth? Ought the Council to explain Catholic doctrine, or the doctrine of our separated brethren? Hiding the truth hurts both us and those separated from us. It hurts us because we appear as hypocrites. It hurts those separated from us because it makes them appear weak and capable of being offended by the truth. Let the schemata be separated. Let us profess our faith openly. Let us be the teachers we are in the Church by teaching with clarity, and not hiding what is true.[7]

When the vote came the Rhine Group won by a majority of only seventeen votes. Even Xavier Rynne accepts that "It would be difficult to describe it as a victory for the progressives".[8] (This had been a procedural matter and a fifty-one per-cent majority was sufficient.) The progressive *Catholic Gazette* has conceded that Our Lady was included in the schema on the Church "with the feelings of non-Catholics in mind" rather than "give her a separate schema to herself, as many devout Catholics wished them to do".[9]

An interesting insight into the progressive mind is the manner in which Xavier Rynne describes the campaign of the Rhine Group to do away with the separate schema. It is those who attempt to maintain the *status quo* who are made to appear contentious and their efforts are described as "an extraordinary and intensive propaganda barrage on behalf of a separate schema on the Blessed Virgin Mary".[10]

Among the most active supporters of the separate schema were the Council Fathers from the Eastern Rites. *The Tablet* reported that:

> When the Fathers arrived at St. Peter's (to vote) they found oriental bishops lobbying (and it was the day Mass was celebrated in the Ukrainian rite by the recently released Archbishop Slipyi), handing out mimeo-

graphed sheets with arguments why, out of reverence, Our Lady should get a separate schema to herself....It is ironical that the ecumenical movement, which wants to face both the Orthodox and the Protestants, finds these two groups of separated brethren taking opposite views on Marian devotions.[11]

Orthodox Christians do indeed have a great devotion to Our Lady and, in fact, use the term Mediatrix. The fact that the Fathers had been made aware of this caused great concern to the Theological Commission which circulated a document stating that although the Orthodox used the word they did not use it as a base for a theological system. The Irish Mariologist, Father Michael O'Carroll writes:

> The greatest theological system on our Lady's universal mediation is from an Orthodox theologian, Theophanes of Nicea (d. 1381). Theophanes is one of the Palamite theologians, named from the greatest of them, St. Gregory Paloamas (d. 1359). Gregory was himself quite explicit: "No divine gifts can reach either angels or men, save through her mediation". Theophanes set forth a closely argued exposition of Mary's universal mediation. For example: "It cannot happen that anyone of angels or men, can come otherwise, in any way whatsoever, to participation in the divine gifts flowing from what has been divinely assumed, from the Son of God, save through His mother...Mary is the dispenser and distributor of all the wondrous gifts of the divine Spirit".[12]

Protestant observers have made no secret of their satisfaction at the relegation of Our Lady to the schema on the Church. Dr. McAfee Brown considered it to be an "item of ecumenical importance".[13] He explains that: "In this way, the separate and independent extension of Marian theology was effectively checked".[14] Dr. Moorman, leader of the Anglican delegation, could not refrain from expressing his relief at the final outcome when he considers that: "A mere handful of votes (twenty-one in all) would have turned the thing the other way, with results which might have proved disastrous. Many of the observers wondered if this was a sign that the Holy Spirit was at work".[15]

2. The Blessed Virgin Mary—Mediatrix of All Graces

It was shown in Chapter III that most of the bishops who arrived in Rome for the Second Vatican Council were not really sure why they were there or what direction the Council would take. An Anglican observer, Archdeacon Pawley writes that:

> Even after its announcement there were those who spoke of it as a device for giving conciliar approval to one or two doctrines which the Pope had in mind. One English Roman Catholic bishop, who must be allowed to remain anonymous, wrote in his diocesan leaflet: "It is an open secret that the bishops are assembling with great hopes of new definitions to supplement the dogmas of the Catholic Faith already revealed. It is my personal hope that the Holy Father will see fit to crown our love of our glorious and Blessed Mother, Queen of Heaven and Ever Virgin, with the definition of the dogmas *Maria Mediatrix* and *Maria fons Gratiae*, which have ever been in the prayers and devotions of the faithful".[16]

The application of the title *Mediatrix* to Our Lady is by no means new and can be traced back to the Fathers of the Church. The title is attached to Mary in official Church documents—including papal bulls and encyclicals dating from *Ineffabilis* of Pope Pius IX (1854), and has also been introduced into the liturgy of the Church through the Feast of the Blessed Virgin Mary, Mediatrix of All Graces.[17] But the Protestant observers were not simply opposed to the devotion of a separate schema to Our Lady—they were far from pleased with what it contained. They did not wish simply that the original schema should be relegated to the schema on the Church but that it should be considerably modified. Dr. Moorman wrote:

> The schema produced in 1962 began well enough with a number of quotations from the Bible indicating Mary's place and her co-operation in the divine plan. But it began to arouse suspicions in the minds of some of the observers when it began to speak of her as "not only Mother of Jesus, the one and only divine Mediator and Redeemer, but also joined with him in carrying out the redemption of the human race". Suspicion grew when it went on to speak of her as "administrator and dispenser of heavenly graces", and finally as "mediatrix of all graces". Nor were they comforted by the appended note which pointed out that these were not new phrases or titles since each of them had appeared in some papal pronouncement, and that some of the expressions proposed by the "maximalists" had been deliberately omitted. As for the title of "co-redemptrix", the note goes on to say that although used by Pius X and Pius XI, it was left out of this schema so as not to offend the "separated brethren", though no attempt was made to disassociate the Council from this title or to throw any doubts upon its validity.[18]

At the Fulda Conference, Karl Rahner stated quite correctly that the acceptance of Our Lady as Mediatrix of all

Graces was not a dogma of the faith but simply a doctrine commonly held by Catholics.[19] However, such doctrines can eventually be defined as dogmas binding upon the faithful. A doctrine which is held universally, particularly when it is incorporated into the liturgy, may well be proclaimed as a dogma by the Pope—the dogmas of the Immaculate Conception and the Assumption of Our Lady provide obvious examples. In fairness to Father Rahner, it must be mentioned that his opposition to the inclusion of the title *Mediatrix* in the conciliar documents by no means indicates that he does not accept it himself. The relevant entry in his theological dictionary shows that he by no means rejects it.[20] However, in this matter the Rhine bishops were not as content to follow his advice as they had been in the matter of the separate schema. They were not opposed to retaining the title *Mediatrix* although they were against *Mediatrix of all Graces*.[21] In a written intervention, Cardinal Spellman asked whether such titles used by the supreme pontiffs could be passed over simply "because they would be rather difficult for Protestants to understand—the task of an Ecumenical Council is to teach the members of the Church, rather than those outside of it".[22]

A good number of bishops from the Latin countries supported the inclusion of the title *Mediatrix*, including eighty-two from Portugal whose spokesman feared that its omission "would generate scandal among the faithful, since the public was by this time aware that the matter had been discussed in the Council hall".[23] Liberal Cardinals, such as Léger, Döpfner, Bea, and Alfrink, led the opposition to its inclusion. Surprisingly enough, Cardinal Suenens differed from the Rhine Group on this matter and criticised the revised text for minimising the importance of Our Lady, "a tendency which today constitutes a real danger".[24] In fact, this intervention is not so surprising as Cardinal Suenens had been noted for his devotion to the Mother of God and had written a most excellent book on Mary before the Council.[25] "For this one brief moment", writes Father Wiltgen, "Cardinal Suenens had the courage to break away from the party line and speak out his own mind".[26]

Eventually, a typical conciliar compromise was reached. The liberals agreed not to oppose the inclusion of *Mediatrix* if the conservatives did not insist on the title Mother of the Church. The very idea of making compromises with regard to the honour due to Our Lady is distasteful—but at least this was a set-back for the extreme liberals, but not too severe a set-back as they had managed to restrict the title to the one word *Mediatrix* and had excluded the three words "of all graces" to which the Protestant observers took such exception.

3. Mother of the Church

The title of the schema on Our Lady which it had been decided should be added to the schema on the Church had been "On the Blessed Virgin Mary, Mother of the Church". Contrary to what had been promised in the debate, the text was not simply transferred but, to quote Archbishop Mingo of Monreale, Italy, had been "absolutely and radically mutilated".[27] Among these mutilations a Spanish bishop laid special stress on the change of title to: "On the Blessed Virgin Mary, Mother of God, in the Mystery of Christ and of the Church". He claimed that the "revised text had reduced the doctrine on the Blessed Virgin Mary to the absolute minimum; yet it had been stated in the Council hall at the time of the vote that 'by inserting the schema on the Virgin Mary into the schema on the Church, no such diminution was intended or would be carried out'".[28]

Cardinal Wyszynski on behalf of seventy Polish bishops asked the Pope to proclaim Our Lady "Mother of the

Church", as did eighty Spanish bishops who pointed out that the title corresponded to pontifical documents issued by Popes Benedict XIV, John XXIII, and Paul VI. They wished to have the title restored to the schema where it had probably been inserted on the instructions of Pope John himself, but had been removed by the liberal-dominated Theological Commission on its own authority during its "mutilation" of the separate schema. The members of this drafting commission misled the Council Fathers on a number of occasions, either through ignorance or deliberate deception. They stated in a document distributed to the bishops that Pope Pius XII had never used the word Mediatrix. Father O'Carroll informs us that:

> He did so many times. I quote his plenary affirmation: "The maternal office in 'Mediatrix' really began at the very moment of her consent to the Incarnation. It was manifested for the first time by the first sign of Christ's grace at Cana in Galilee; from that moment it spread rapidly down through the ages with the growth of the Church" (*Per Christi Matrem*, 15 May 1947). He also said: "For she (Mary) has been appointed Mediatrix of all the graces which look towards sanctification and is properly called Mother and Queen of the Catholic priesthood and apostolate" (*Sedes Sapientiae*, 31 May 1956).[29]

In the end, as part of the compromise to enable the title *Mediatrix* to remain, the new title was accepted, and those who had demanded the inclusion of the title Mother of the Church had to be content with the following passage in Article 53 of the Constitution on the Church: "Taught by the Holy Spirit, the Catholic Church honours her with filial affection and piety as a most beloved mother".[30] However, the matter did not end there. By this time, although the effective control of the Rhine Group over the machinery of the Council was almost absolute, organised opposition was beginning to emerge. In the third session this resulted in the emergence of several organised groups which, although never approaching the numerical strength of the Rhine Group's World Alliance, were able to alert many of the middle-of-the-road Fathers as to what was happening and thus secure the correction of some of the more glaring deficiencies in the schemata. The schemata were, of course, now drafted by the conciliar commissions which were, for practical purposes, Rhine Group commissions. The most effective of these "opposition" groups was the International Group of Fathers (*Coetus Internationalis Patrum*). Archbishop Marcel Lefebvre was a leading member of this group, of which much more will be written in the chapter on Communism. The International Group of Fathers collected signatures for a petition to the Pope begging him to proclaim Our Lady as Mother of the Church. Other petitions to the same effect had been received, notably one from all the bishops of Poland.[31]

On Wednesday, 18 November 1964, Pope Paul announced at a public audience: "We are happy to announce to you that we shall close this session of the Ecumenical Council—by joyfully bestowing upon Our Lady the title due to her, Mother of the Church". The liberals had suffered several other reverses during this week, and it has come to be known as "Black Week" in their mythology.[32]

On Saturday, 21 November, on the last day of the session, the Pope stated in his closing address that at his own desire, in response to the wishes of many Fathers and suggestions from various parts of the Catholic world, "for the glory of the Virgin Mary and for our own consolation, We proclaim the Most Holy Mary as Mother of the Church". This announcement was greeted by a standing ovation, and the Pope was interrupted by applause seven times during his address. He also announced his intention of sending a golden rose to Fatima to "entrust to the care of this Heavenly Mother the entire human family, with its problems and worries, with its lawful aspirations and ardent hopes". Father Wiltgen considers this to have been a partial reply to the petition from 510 heads of dioceses, archdioceses, and patriarchates from 76 countries, begging the Pope to consecrate the entire world to the Immaculate Heart of Mary as Our Lady of Fatima had requested. In the face of opposition from Cardinal Bea and the bishops of France and Germany, Pope Paul had felt unable to take this step.[33]

Conclusion

Pope Paul's action enraged the liberals. "The promulgation of the misleading title *Mater Ecclesiae* against the expressed will of the Council majority, which will arouse in non-Catholic Christendom great indignation, and grave doubts as to the genuinely ecumenical sympathies of the Pope", was Hans Küng's verdict![34]

Professor Oscar Cullmann, a Lutheran observer, stated in a press conference:

> We cannot pass over in silence the disappointment we experienced at seeing the title *"Mediatrix"* given to Mary....The fact that the text on Mary, after so much discussion as to where it should be placed, should have finally become the concluding chapter of the schema on the Church—a decision which was intended to weaken Mariology—has in reality made it even stronger, because everything stated about the Church culminates, so to speak, in this chapter.

He also complained that in the many ceremonies which took place honouring Mary during the Council, together with statements made about her by both Pope John and Pope

Paul, meant that "Mariology at this Council has in general been intensified to a degree which is not in keeping with the ecumenical tendencies of Protestantism...and with a return to the Bible. Our expectations in this connection have not been fulfilled".[35]

What emerges from these facts is that Our Lady seems to have succeeded in turning the tables on the liberals. The inclusion of the schema on her in the Constitution on the Church had an effect precisely the opposite to what was intended; her title *Mediatrix* was included; and the title Mother of the Church was bestowed upon her in a far more solemn and public manner than would have been the case if the liberals had not made such efforts to eliminate it from the text of the Constitution.

It might seem that what this chapter has shown is precisely the opposite of what it was intended to show, in other words, the extent of Protestant influence upon the Council. This is not the case. The fact that the result of this influence turned out differently than intended does not alter the fact that so many of the Fathers and their advisers were prepared to go to such lengths to play down or ignore aspects of the faith which they feared would be unpalatable to Protestants. A separate schema on Our Lady was rejected for ecumenical reasons; the title Mother of the Church was excluded for ecumenical reasons; the words "of all graces" were removed from the title *Mediatrix* for ecumenical reasons. Dr. Moorman wrote:

> In its final form it was greeted by all but the most Protestant of the observers as a just and unexceptional statement which could not reasonably be accused of raising new barriers among the people of God. Certain titles are attributed to the Virgin—Advocate, Supporter, Helper, Mediator—but the two expressions most likely to cause

offence ("co-redemptrix" and "mediatrix of all graces") were carefully avoided.[36]

Dr. Moorman also considered that the titles which are used are qualified sufficiently to safeguard them from misinterpretation.[37] Dr. McAfee Brown was pleased to note that the chapter on Mary is "deliberately couched in as biblical a framework as possible, replacing the string of papal quotations that had characterised the earlier draft, so that there might be an ecumenical meeting point with Protestants and Orthodox, both of whom affirm the authority of biblical but not papal statements".[38] What this observer fails to make clear is that the Orthodox do indeed accept the doctrine of Mediatrix even if not on the basis of papal statements.

Despite its deficiencies the chapter on Our Lady has emerged as a fine if far from perfect exposition of the role of Our Lady in the Church. Furthermore, in no sense whatsoever have the developments in Marian doctrine, which many of the faithful hoped would emerge from the Council, been precluded—although there is little hope of their emergence in the present climate. Father Milan Mikulich rightly pointed out that the chapter on Our Lady is "…a point of arrival and a point of departure in the relationship between Mary and the Church":

> It is a point of arrival because in this chapter the theologians and the bishops arrived at the point of establishing the clearer terms concerning the relationship between Mary and the Church. It is a point of departure because the Council clearly states that it does not "have in mind to give a complete doctrine on Mary, nor does it wish to decide those questions which the work of theologians has not yet fully clarified". Those opinions—continues the Council—"may be lawfully retained which are propounded in the Catholic schools concerning Her, who

occupies a place in the Church which is the highest after Christ and yet very close to us".[39]

One final point of interest is that far from the reduction in length which the liberals had hoped for when they secured a vote against the separate schema, the chapter in the Constitution on the Church proved to be one-third longer.[40]

The attitude towards Our Lady manifested by the liberals during the Council has come to be the hallmark of those engaged in contemporary ecumenism. As stated above: When Catholic doctrine is to be explained the prime criterion is not: "Is this what the Church teaches?" but "Will this offend Protestants?" As Cardinal Heenan wrote: "Some over-enthusiastic ecumenists would jettison all Marian dogma in the belief that this would please Protestants".[41] Apart from anything else, this does less than justice to Protestants themselves for, to quote Cardinal Heenan again: "Catholics do less than credit to non-Catholics by thinking that they expect us to be silent about the claims of the Church. Those of us on terms of the closest friendship with other Christians know that they never want us to disguise the Church's claims. They respect an honest statement of Catholic belief and despise those who paint a false picture".[42]

Notes

[1] *Orthodoxy of Catholic Doctrine*, edited by Father Milan Mikulich, Vol. 3, No. 1, January 1974, p. 8 ff.
[2] RFT, p. 56.
[3] *Ibid.*, p. 92.
[4] *Ibid.*, p. 91.
[5] *Ibid.*, p. 92.
[6] *Ibid.*, p. 93.
[7] *Ibid.*, p. 95.
[8] XR-II, p. 170.
[9] *Catholic Gazette*, March 1964, p. 71.
[10] XR-II, p. 166.
[11] *The Tablet*, 3 November 1963, p. 1169.
[12] *Contemporary Insights on a Fifth Marian Dogma* (Goleta, California: Queenship Publishing), p.139.

[13] ER, p. 178.
[14] *Ibid.*, p. 321.
[15] VO, pp. 73-74.
[16] RCFC, pp. 339-340.
[17] For a full exposition see *Fundamentals of Catholic Dogma*, L. Ott, Book III, Part 3, Chapter 3.
[18] VO, p. 72.
[19] RFT, p. 92.
[20] *Concise Theological Dictionary* (Herder, 1965), p. 282.
[21] RFT, p. 92.
[22] *Ibid.*, p. 94.
[23] RFT, p. 156.
[24] *Ibid.*
[25] *Mary the Mother of God* (Hawthorn Books, 1959).
[26] RFT, p. 156.
[27] *Ibid.*, p. 155.
[28] *Ibid.*
[29] *Contemporary Insights*, pp. 138-139.
[30] Abbott, p. 86.
[31] RFT, p. 240.
[32] *Ibid.*, p. 234.
[33] *Ibid.*, p. 241.
[34] *Catholic Gazette*, August 1965, p. 239.
[35] RFT, pp. 158-159.
[36] VO, p. 74.
[37] *Ibid.*
[38] ER, p. 321.
[39] *Op. cit.*, note 1, p. 12.
[40] RFT, p. 159.
[41] CT, p. 354.
[42] *Ibid.*, p. 343.

XI

The Dogmatic Constitution on Divine Revelation—*Dei Verbum*

"What's in a name?" asked Shakespeare, "that which we call a rose by any other name would smell as sweet". Shakespeare might have revised his opinion had he studied the documents of Vatican II. Take the Dogmatic Constitution on Divine Revelation, for example: a perfectly orthodox title for what seems to be a perfectly orthodox document (and, indeed, there is nothing specifically unorthodox in it). However, the original schema for this Constitution had been entitled *De Fontibus Revelationis* (On the Sources of Revelation). Dr. McAfee Brown points out that "the key word was *fontibus*, and the key point was its appearance in the plural. The document was a good example of the ethos of pre-conciliar preparations. It had been drafted by conservative theologians, who stated in it that Scripture and tradition were the sources of Christian revelation, truth being found partly in one, partly in the other".[1]

The "conservative theologians" responsible for this title had, in fact, simply quoted the relevant sub-heading (*De Fontibus Revelationis*) from the second chapter of the Constitution on the Catholic Faith of the First Vatican Council.[2] This Constitution then repeats the teaching of Trent:

> Furthermore, according to the faith of the Universal Church, declared by the holy Council of Trent, this supernatural revelation is "contained in written books and in the unwritten traditions that the apostles received from Christ Himself or that were handed on, as it were from hand to hand, from the apostles under the inspiration of the Holy Ghost, and so have come down to us".

Pope Pius XII wrote in *Humani Generis* that:

> A theologian must constantly be having recourse to the *fountains* of divine revelation. It is for him to show how and where the teaching given by the Living Voice of the Church is contained in Scripture *and in our sacred tradition*, "be it explicitly, or implicitly, to be found there". (Pius IX, *Inter gravissimas*, 28 October 1870, *Acta*, Vol. I, p. 260.) This *twofold spring* of doctrine divinely made known to us contains, in any case, treasures so varied and so rich that it must ever prove inexhaustible. That is why the study of these hallowed *sources* gives the sacred sciences a kind of perpetual youth [my emphasis].[3]

Pope Pius XI had asked in *Mortalium Animos* what sort of Christian covenant could be imagined with those entering into it continuing to hold contradictory opinions. One of the examples he gave was of the irreconcilable difference between "those who affirm that sacred tradition is a true source of divine revelation and those who deny it". Protestants insist that the Bible alone is the one authentic source of revelation and for this reason to refer to the sources, in the plural, would be unecumenical. As Cardinal Heenan explained:

> The debate on Revelation brought to light the extent of confusion regarding ecumenism. Although the de-

The Dogmatic Constitution *Dei Verbum*

bate was ostensibly and immediately about Scripture and tradition, the point of the underlying disagreement was ecumenical. Some of the Fathers were evidently determined that Catholic doctrine must be stated only in terms which were acceptable to Protestants. They did not, of course, put it this way even to themselves. They took their stand on the Reformers' contention that the Bible is the only authentic source of doctrine. (Scriptural texts are rightly quoted to support all Catholic dogmas, but it is taking a liberty with language to say that the Immaculate Conception and Assumption are biblical truths. Some over-enthusiastic ecumenists would jettison all Marian dogma in the quite mistaken belief that this would please Protestants.)[4]

The Dogmatic Constitution on Divine Revelation is considered by some commentators to be the supreme achievement of the Council, more important even than *Lumen Gentium*, the Dogmatic Constitution on the Church.[5] The relatively short document consists of a preface and six short chapters, the whole covering, without notes, about ten pages. It was one of the most hotly contested documents of the Council, and by far the greater part is devoted to sacred Scripture, particularly to the questions of inspiration and historicity. The treatment of sacred Scripture will not be examined in this chapter, which will deal exclusively with the attempt of the liberal and ecumenical majority of Fathers to undermine, or at least to minimise, the role of oral tradition as an authentic source of Revelation.

Revelation may be defined as the communication of some truth by God to a rational creature through means which are beyond the ordinary course of nature. The essence of revelation lies in the fact that it is the direct speech of God to man. The Decree *Lamentabili* (3 July 1907) declares that the dogmas which the Church proposes to us as revealed are "truths which have come down to us from heaven" (*veritates e coelo delapsae*) and not "an interpretation of religious facts which the human mind has acquired by its own strenuous efforts" (Proposition 22).

Protestants and Catholics both agree that there is only one source of revelation, God, who reveals Himself to His faithful people, but Protestants insist that this revelation is confined to the sacred Scriptures alone, while the Catholic Church teaches infallibly that God also reveals Himself through oral as well as written tradition. The Council of Trent teaches:

> The holy, ecumenical, and general Council of Trent, which has lawfully assembled in the Holy Spirit and is presided over by the same three legates of the Apostolic See, has always as its purpose to remove error and preserve in the Church the purity of the Gospel which was originally promised by the prophets in Sacred Scripture and first promulgated by the Son of God Himself, our Lord Jesus Christ. He in turn ordered His apostles to preach it to every creature (Matthew 28:19ff.; Mark 16:15) as the source of all saving truth and moral teaching. The Council is aware that this truth and teaching are contained in written books and unwritten traditions (*contineri in libris scriptis et sine scripto traditionibus*) that the apostles received from Christ Himself, or that were handed on, as it were, from hand to hand, from the apostles under the inspiration of the Holy Spirit, and so have come down to us.[6]

The First Vatican Council, while treating of revelation in the second chapter of the Dogmatic Constitution on the Catholic Faith, 24 April 1870, quoted the teaching of Trent on the two sources of revelation, Scripture and tradition.[7] There is evidently no contradiction between accepting that

The Dogmatic Constitution *Dei Verbum*

God is the sole source of revelation, but that He transmits it to us in two ways or sources. Protestants who insist that the Scriptures form the sole source of revelation would certainly find it hard to explain the fact that the initial preaching of the apostles was based solely on oral tradition. Our Lord left His Church with no written books and with nothing but oral tradition to guide it. St. Paul insists on the necessity of holding fast to the Christian tradition (1 Cor. 11:2; 2 Thess. 2:15). Even when the Scriptures of the New Testament were written, the early Christians were well aware that it was tradition which settles the canon of Scripture, and that therefore the authority of Scripture was based on tradition. The canon of Scripture, that is the divinely inspired books of the Old and New Testaments, was laid down definitively by the Council of Trent, which proclaimed:

> Moreover, if anyone does not accept these books as sacred and canonical in their entirety, with all their parts, according to the text usually read in the Catholic Church and as they are in the ancient Latin Vulgate, but knowingly and wilfully condemns the traditions previously mentioned, let him be anathema.[8]

The consensus of the earlier and later Church Fathers upholds the authority of oral tradition, providing, of course, that it is apostolic. Clement of Alexandria taught that doubtful questions should be decided by an appeal to the apostolic Churches, and considers that tradition would have been a sufficient guide even if the Church had been left without any Scriptures at all (*Canon of the Church*, I, 19). Origen, the great representative of the early Alexandrian Church, taught that where differences arose among Christians "let the ecclesiastical teaching handed down by order of succession from the apostles, and abiding till now in the churches, be observed; that only is to be believed the truth which in no way differs from ecclesiastical and apostolic tradition" (*De Princip.*, I, 2, PG, xi, 116). Gregory Nyssen writes: "It is enough for the demonstration of our position to have the tradition which comes to us from the Fathers transmitted as an inheritance by succession from the apostles through the saints that followed them" (*Contra Eunom*, iv, PG, xlv, 653). St. John Chrysostom teaches that the apostles did not hand all down by epistles, but much also without writing. He continues: "The one and the other are worthy of belief, so that we consider the tradition of the Church also worthy of belief. It is a tradition: ask no more" (In 2. Thess., Hom. iv § 14, PG, lxii, 488). St. Epiphanius writes: "We must also use tradition, since all cannot be got from the divine Scripture, wherefore the divine apostles handed down some things in writing, others in tradition (*Haer.* lxi, 6, PG, xli, 1048).

There is thus a radical difference between Catholic belief on the necessity of oral tradition as a source of revelation, and Protestant teaching that no doctrine can be an article of faith unless it can be deduced clearly without the aid of oral tradition from the sacred texts. This fundamental incompatibility between Catholic and Protestant teaching posed a great problem for those bishops and *periti* at Vatican II for whom the ecumenical dimension of the Council took precedence over all else. Tradition as a source of revelation is anathema to Protestants and an insurmountable obstacle to unity, but as it is an infallible teaching of the Church it cannot possibly be abandoned.

The preliminary schema drawn up by the Theological Commission and presented for discussion by Cardinal Ottaviani during the first session (14 November 1962) was entitled the *Sources of Revelation,* and had as the title of its first chapter "Two Sources of Revelation". It came under fierce attack from Father Schillebeeckx, and was one of the four preliminary schemata that he demanded successfully should be rewritten.[9] The schema was denounced by liberal

The Dogmatic Constitution *Dei Verbum*

theologians as too negative, too aggressive, too intolerant, too one-sided, altogether outmoded, and lacking a pastoral tone.[10] In other words, the preliminary schema was totally orthodox, totally faithful to tradition, and therefore totally unacceptable to Protestants and their Catholic allies.

The true motivation behind the animosity towards the schema was made clear by Bishop Emile De Smedt of Bruges, Belgium, on behalf of the Secretariat for Promoting Christian Unity:

> Numerous Council Fathers have shown a truly ecumenical preoccupation in their examination of the schema on the sources of revelation. All sincerely and positively desire that the schema should foster unity.... We who have received from the Holy Father the task of working in this council towards the happy establishment of dialogue with our non-Catholic brethren beg all of you, venerable Fathers, to hear what the Secretariat for Promoting Christian Unity thinks of the proposed schema. As we see it, the schema is lacking notably in the ecumenical spirit. It does not constitute an advance in dialogue with non-Catholics, but an obstacle. I would go even further and say that it causes harm.[11]

We should be grateful to Monsignor De Smedt for stating so frankly that he and his liberal colleagues most certainly did not agree with what Pope John XXIII in his opening speech to the Council had described as its greatest concern: "The greatest concern of the Ecumenical Council is this: that the sacred deposit of Christian doctrine should be guarded and taught more efficaciously".[12] And again:

> The Twenty-first Ecumenical Council, which will draw upon the effective and important wealth of juridical, liturgical, apostolic, and administrative experiences, wish-

es to transmit the doctrine, pure and integral, without any attenuation or distortion, which throughout twenty centuries, has become the patrimony of men. It is a patrimony not well received by all, but always a rich treasure available to men of good will.[13]

Pope John called for a "serene and tranquil adherence to all the teaching of the Church in its entirety and preciseness, as it still shines forth in the acts of the Council of Trent and the First Vatican Council".[14] No Catholic teaching shines forth more clearly in the acts of these two councils than that of the two sources of revelation. Pope John did indeed state that: "The substance of the ancient doctrine of the deposit of faith is one thing, and the way in which it is presented is another".[15] By no possible stretch of the imagination can this statement be interpreted as a mandate for modifying traditional teaching in the interests of ecumenism. As Newman's *Development of Christian Doctrine* makes clear, as the centuries pass, the presentation of fundamental doctrines is made ever more clear, but later developments are always faithful to their origin in tradition or the Scriptures.

Monsignor De Smedt's speech can be interpreted only as meaning that his greatest concern, and that of his secretariat, was that the sacred deposit of Christian doctrine must be adapted to meet the wishes of Protestants. How was this to be done? It was evident that there could be no formal rejection of the teaching of Trent or Vatican I on the two sources. The only viable tactic would be to emphasise the role of Scripture at the expense of oral tradition. The newly written schema was entitled the Dogmatic Constitution on Divine Revelation, all mention of "sources" in the plural having been suppressed. The original first chapter, "Two Sources of Revelation" was replaced by two chapters on revelation itself, and its transmission, in which no distinction was made between Scripture and Tradition. The International Group of Fathers and other bishops dedicated to the defence of tradition were determined that the traditional and infallible teaching on the two sources of revelation should be stated explicitly in this dogmatic constitution, and this resulted in one of the longest and most determined debates witnessed throughout the Council. The new text was ready for discussion during the second session of the Council in 1963, but was not presented then but underwent further discussion within the Commission responsible for drafting the schema. It was presented for discussion and voted on in the third session, 1964, and alterations were made by the Commission in response to the *modi* (amendments) presented by the Council Fathers. The struggle went on till the very last moments before the definitive text was approved by an almost unanimous vote, and was promulgated in the fourth session on 18 November 1965. Much to the chagrin of the ecumenical establishment the minority of traditional Fathers, despite a series of rejections of their amendments, eventually secured several specific affirmations of the fact that there are two sources of revelation, not least because, as on other occasions during the Council, Pope Paul intervened in the interests of orthodoxy. On 24 September 1965 he sent the following quotation from St. Augustine to the Theological (drafting) Commission: "There are many things which the entire Church holds, and they are therefore correctly believed to have been taught by the apostles even though they are not to be found in written form".[16]

Before the final version of the schema could be voted upon, the Pope decided to reconvene the Commission and propose changes to three disputed articles which, if adopted, would enable him "in all tranquillity" to give the requested approval for the promulgation of the document which involved "great responsibility for him toward the Church and toward his own conscience".[17] Two of these articles related to sacred Scripture and one, Article 9, to the status of oral tradition. The following sentence was added to Article 9: "Consequently, it is not from Sacred Scripture alone that the Church draws its certainty about everything which has been revealed". An almost identical amendment had been submitted earlier to the Commission by 111 Fathers but had been rejected.

The finalised version of Chapter II contains a number of clear affirmations of the place of oral tradition as an authentic source of divine revelation. These affirmations include the following. God "commissioned the apostles to preach to all men that Gospel which is the source of all saving truth and moral teaching". It continues:

> This commission was faithfully fulfilled by the apostles who, by their oral preaching, by example, and by ordinances, handed on what they had received from the lips of Christ, from living with Him, and from what He did, or what they had learned through the promptings of the Holy Spirit. The commission was fulfilled, too, by those apostles and apostolic men who under the same Holy Spirit committed the message of salvation to writing.
>
> But in order to keep the gospel forever whole and alive within the Church, the apostles left bishops as their successors, "handing over their own teaching role" to them. This sacred tradition, therefore, and sacred Scripture of both the Old and New Testament are like a mirror in which the pilgrim Church on earth looks at God, from whom she has received everything, until she is brought finally to see Him as He is, face to face (1 John 3:2).[18]

And again:

> Therefore the apostles, handing on what they themselves had received, warn the faithful to hold fast to the traditions which they have learned either by word of mouth

The Dogmatic Constitution *Dei Verbum*

or by letter (cf. 2 Thess. 2:15), and to fight in defence of the faith handed on once and for all (cf. Jude 3).[19]

And again, one of the last additions to the text made, as explained above, at the Pope's request:

> It is not from sacred Scripture alone that the Church draws her certainty about everything which has been revealed. Therefore both sacred tradition and sacred Scripture are to be accepted and venerated with the same sense of devotion and reverence.[20]

Despite the fact that the treatment given to oral tradition in *Dei Verbum* is greatly overshadowed by that given to sacred Scripture we must be grateful to the International Group of Fathers and to Pope Paul VI for ensuring that the doctrine of the two sources is stated specifically, and orthodoxy upheld.

Notes

[1] ER, p. 163.
[2] D, 1787.
[3] HG, pp. 11-12.
[4] CT, p. 354.
[5] C. Butler, *The Theology of Vatican II* (London: Darton, Longman, &Todd, 1967), p. 28.
[6] Denzinger, *Enchiridion Symbolorum, Editio* 31, No. 783.
[7] *Ibid.*, No. 1787.
[8] *Ibid.*, No. 784.
[9] RFT, p. 23.
[10] *Ibid.*, p. 46.
[11] *Ibid.*, pp. 49-50.
[12] Abbott, p. 713.
[13] *Ibid.*, p. 715.
[14] *Ibid.*
[15] *Ibid.*
[16] RFT, p. 179.
[17] *Ibid.*, p. 181.
[18] Abbott, p. 115.
[19] *Ibid.*, pp. 115-116.
[20] *Ibid.*, p. 117.

XII

The Status of the Documents

What is the precise legal authority of the documents of Vatican II? The Council itself was undoubtedly an authentic Ecumenical Council of the Catholic Church. It was convoked regularly and was at all times recognised by the reigning pontiff. Its documents were passed by a majority of the Council Fathers, and were validly promulgated by the Pope. As such they represent official Church teaching no matter how much we may deplore the manner in which their sometimes unsatisfactory final format was arrived at. But not all official teaching has the same status—it is not necessary to be a theologian to appreciate that there is a great difference between an infallible dogmatic definition of Trent, accompanied by an anathema upon those who refused to accept it, and the admonition of the Fathers of Vatican II that we should patronise cinemas "managed by upright Catholics and others".[1] The banality of the Pastoral Constitution on the Church in the Modern World (*Gaudium et Spes*) has been referred to several times in this book. "Some of it", commented Dr. Moorman, head of the Anglican delegation to the Council, "is to the experienced reader a bit pedestrian and banal":

It hardly needed an assembly of 2,300 prelates from all over the world to tell us that "the industrial type of society is gradually being spread", or that "new and more efficient media of social communication are contributing to the knowledge of events"; and most people are already aware of the fact that "growing numbers of people are abandoning religion in practice".[2]

As a general council teaching in conformity with the Pope, Vatican II was in a position to impose definitive teaching with the authority of the Extraordinary Magisterium, which would demand our absolute internal assent. *But it did not do so.* The Council deliberately refrained from imparting to any of its documents the infallible status of a definition of the Extraordinary Magisterium. The key word here is definition. Only binding definitions of general councils are infallible. The terms "infallible" and "protected from error" can be taken as equivalent. An infallible pronouncement is simply one that is protected from error. It does not in any way imply that the pronouncement is inspired. Inspiration ended with the death of the last apostle. Nor does it imply that the pronouncement is expressed in the clearest possible manner, or that the doctrine which it teaches could not be presented more clearly in some future pronouncement.

There are no definitions in this technical sense in the teaching of Vatican II except where it quotes already existing infallible papal or conciliar teaching. The Fathers of Vatican II could indeed have invested some of their teaching with infallible authority, but nothing can change the indisputable fact that they did not. Cardinal Manning points out that general councils had always been "convened to extinguish the chief heresy, or to correct the chief evil of the time".[3] Bishop Butler, certainly England's most liberal Council Father, makes the same point:

The Status of the Documents

Such councils normally define doctrines and promulgate laws. The first of them all, the first Council of Nicea, did both these things. It defined that the Son of God is of one substance with His Father; and it issued practical instructions which are today regarded as the first elements of Canon Law....Vatican II gave us no new dogmatic definitions, and on the whole it preferred to leave legislation to other organs of the Church.[4]

He also explains that not "all teachings emanating from a pope or an ecumenical council are infallible. There is no single proposition of Vatican II—except where it is citing a previous infallible definition—which is in itself infallible".[5] Monsignor Lefebvre wrote: "This council, then, is not a council like the others, and for that reason we have the right to judge it prudently and with some reservation".[6] Vatican II, was, to quote Cardinal Heenan, "unique" because: "It deliberately limited its own objectives. There were to be no specific definitions. Its purpose from the first was pastoral renewal within the Church and a fresh approach to those outside".[7] Where doctrine and moral teaching is contained in the documents, we are bound, as the note of the theological commission states, "to accept it and embrace it according to the mind of the Synod itself...". In most cases this presents no problem as the doctrinal and moral teaching is, as Bishop Graber wrote, perhaps overstating the case, usually stated orthodoxly and even classically.[8] Where the teaching is unsatisfactory it is more often through what is not said than what is actually contained in the text; for example, there is no explicit condemnation of Communism or contraception in *Gaudium et Spes*.

An orthodox Catholic cannot, of course, refuse to accept officially promulgated conciliar teaching simply because the documents containing it do not possess infallible status. This would be to follow the example of those who rejected

Humanae Vitae on the grounds that it was not an infallible pronouncement. Infallible or not, *Humanae Vitae* represents the official teaching of the Church, as do the conciliar documents. However, as was stated at the beginning of this chapter, not all official documents have the same status. The degree of assent we are bound to give to papal or conciliar pronouncements is governed by a number of factors. What is the subject of the pronouncement? Matters of faith and morals obviously take precedence—*Humanae Vitae* comes into this category. Does the pronouncement contain some new teaching, or is it a restatement of previous authoritative papal or conciliar teaching? *Humanae Vitae* clearly comes into the latter category. While on this topic, it is worth noting that a document which is not in itself infallible can contain infallible teaching. The fine exposition of papal authority in the Vatican II Constitution on the Church is infallible (even though the constitution itself does not possess infallible status) because its teaching on this particular point is a restatement of teaching already proclaimed as infallible by Vatican I. In similar manner, as regards the use of contraceptives as intrinsically evil, the key doctrine of *Humanae Vitae*, this is also infallible in virtue of the ordinary teaching Magisterium of the Church for:

> Although individual bishops do not enjoy the prerogative of infallibility, they can nevertheless proclaim Christ's doctrine infallibly. This is so, even when they are dispersed around the world, provided that while maintaining the bond of unity among themselves and with Peter's successor, and while teaching authentically on a matter of faith or morals, they concur in a single viewpoint as the one which must be held conclusively.[9]

There can be no doubt that the fact that contraception is intrinsically evil is a doctrine concerning morals which has been taught by all the bishops in communion with the Pope. This is a fact which cannot be changed even though there are now many bishops who dissent from the teaching themselves.

Another factor which is important in assessing the documents of Vatican II, which can also be illustrated by reference to *Humanae Vitae*, is that a distinction can be made between specific and binding doctrinal or moral teaching which a document contains and the arguments adduced in its favour. While Catholics are bound to accept that contraception is intrinsically sinful they are not bound to accept that the arguments which Pope Paul puts forward to prove this are the best available, or even that they are convincing. Similarly, some documents of Vatican II contain vague generalisations, observations, exhortations, and speculation on the likely outcome of a recommended course of action. In 1959 Cardinal Tardini prophesied: "From what we can foresee today, it is more than probable that the Council will have a character that is practical rather than dogmatic; pastoral, rather than ideological; and that it will provide norms, rather than definitions".[10] The late Father Gustave Weigel, S.J., remarked with regard to a document that did not meet with his approval that while it is the "official and authentic doctrine of the Church", it will not become the "irreformable and one-for-all-times doctrine of the Church".[11] The Decree on Ecumenism states that: "Therefore, if the influence of events or of the times has led to deficiencies in conduct, in Church discipline, or even *in the formulation of doctrine* (which must be carefully distinguished from the deposit of faith itself), these should be appropriately rectified at the proper moment".[12] This, of course, is one of the most obvious of the "time bombs" referred to by Archbishop Lefebvre, and has been used by progressive Catholics as an excuse for changing the deposit of faith itself, under the guise of changing its formulation, especially in the fields of ecumenism and catechetics. It is impossible not to note that the most obvious place to find deficient definitions of doctrine is in the documents of Vatican II!

In discussing the status of these documents it is as well to point out that they do not all possess the same authority—one must presume that a dogmatic constitution carries more weight than a declaration, for example, but, as Dr. McAfee Brown makes clear from a Protestant standpoint, no one seems quite sure as to the exact status conferred upon any particular document by its title:

> In those early days of the Council there was much discussion about the relative degree of binding authority between, say, a "constitution" and a "decree". It seemed fairly clear that a "constitution" was of higher authority, and it would be a wise rule of interpretation to say that the "constitution" *On the Church*, for example, was the context in which to understand the "decree" *On Ecumenism*, rather than vice versa. As it actually worked out, however, there seemed little reason by the end of the Council why *The Church in the World Today* should be a "constitution" (albeit a "pastoral constitution") while the document on *Missionary Activity* should be a "decree" or the statement on *Religious Freedom* a "declaration".[13]

For those who can read and understand, this very perceptive comment is an admirable evocation of the ethos of Vatican II.

What is quite certain is that, as Archbishop Lefebvre insisted, no one, whatever his rank, can compel us to accept an interpretation of moral or doctrinal teaching in a conciliar document which conflicts with the previous teaching of the Church. There can be a development of doctrine, but, as Newman pointed out, where a new formulation is not faithful to the idea from which it started it is an unfaithful development "more properly called a corruption".[14] Quoting Bellarmine, Cardinal Newman also reminds us that: "All Catholics and heretics agree in two things: first that it is possible for a pope, even as pope, and with his own assembly of councillors, or with a general council, to err in particular controversies of fact, which chiefly depend on human information and testimony".[15]

In a case where a conciliar statement is used to justify a breach with authentic Catholic doctrine or tradition then such an interpretation must be refused even if the document itself seems to favour such an interpretation. As has been pointed out, one weakness of these documents is that they do not always say all that they ought to say, thus leaving the way open for a modernistic interpretation. Such an interpretation must always be refuted by reference to a previous council or authoritative papal statement. In his opening speech Pope John insisted on the adherence of the Second Vatican Council to the teaching of the Church in its serenity and precision, as it still shines forth in the Acts of Trent and Vatican I, which makes it clear that every Catholic has not simply the right but the duty to refute any interpretation which conflicts with the teaching of these councils. Archbishop Lefebvre advises us to take our stand on the pre-Vatican II position, without fear of appearing to disobey the Church by holding to a tradition which is two thousand years old.

> What is the criterion to judge whether the ordinary Magisterium is infallible or not? It is fidelity to the whole of tradition. In the event of its not conforming to tradition we are not even bound to submit to the decrees of the Holy Father himself. The same applies to the Council. When it adheres to tradition it must be obeyed since it represents the ordinary Magisterium. But in the event of its introducing measures which are not in accord with

tradition there is a far greater freedom of choice. We should therefore have no fear of assessing facts today because we cannot allow ourselves to be swept along on the wave of Modernism which would put our faith at risk and turn us unwittingly into Protestants.[16]

Once again, Monsignor Lefebvre's words are echoed from the opposite end of the theological spectrum. Bishop Butler writes:

> It remains true that, as conscience may in a particular case oblige us to disobey our bishop, so it may be our duty in particular circumstances to dissent from our bishop's teaching. There have been many heretical bishops, and some heretical councils. There has even been a pope, Honorius, proclaimed as a heretic by an ecumenical council.[17]

In his classic study *The Church of the Word Incarnate*, Cardinal Journet distinguishes between "those organs by which the Magisterium *can*, when it acts *suprema intentione*, speak with absolute authority and irrevocably", and "the organs by which the Magisterium can speak only with a prudential authority and in a non-definitive way" (emphasis in the original). The three organs by which the Magisterium can teach infallibly if it so decides, by making it clear beyond any possible doubt that it is acting *suprema intentione*, are: "the sovereign pontiff teaching alone (Solemn Magisterium not communicable to the Roman congregations), the sovereign pontiff teaching conjointly with the bishops assembled in a general council (Solemn Magisterium), the Sovereign Pontiff teaching conjointly with the bishops dispersed throughout the world (Ordinary Magisterium)".[18] (Journet is using the term "Solemn Magisterium" as equivalent to "Extraordinary Magisterium".) The term *suprema intentione* can best be defined as signifying beyond any possible doubt the intention of binding the Universal Church finally and irrevocably to an internal assent. A detailed explanation of the requirements for an infallible definition will be provided below.

It is not within the scope of this chapter to examine in detail the manner in which teaching coming only with the authority of the Ordinary Magisterium can be regarded as infallible. This depends largely upon the frequency and solemnity with which a particular teaching has been repeated by the popes, and by the unanimity with which it has been accepted by the bishops dispersed throughout the world. The fact that contraception is intrinsically evil might well be regarded as having been taught infallibly by the Ordinary Magisterium. It has been proclaimed consistently and authoritatively by successive popes, and, until the aftermath of Vatican II, was received and taught by the bishops dispersed throughout the world in complete unanimity with the popes. Dissenters from *Humanae Vitae* point out correctly that the encyclical is not in itself an infallible pronouncement, as it pertains only to the Ordinary Magisterium, but they fail to explain that it fulfils all the conditions for a teaching on faith or morals taught infallibly by the Ordinary Magisterium.

The decision of the Fathers of Vatican II not to invest their teaching with infallible authority, not to teach *suprema intentione,* can be compared with the case of a driver taking out insurance for his automobile. He can, if he so wishes, opt for fully comprehensive insurance which will cover him even for accidents caused by his own negligence. If, however, he decides to save money by opting only for third party, fire, and theft, he could hardly expect to be reimbursed by his insurance company if he damaged his car by backing it into a lamp post.

Pope John's Council

Infallible or Non-Infallible?

The testimonies which follow should be more than adequate to convince any reasonable person that the documents of Vatican II do not pertain to the Extraordinary Magisterium, and are, therefore, not necessarily infallible, and therefore not divinely protected from error. It is not my purpose in this chapter to claim that they contain error, but simply to prove that they are not protected from such a possibility, and that any infallible teaching contained in them is a citation of previous infallible teaching of the Magisterium. The first testimony should, in itself, suffice to do this, as it is the testimony of the sovereign pontiff, Pope Paul VI. In his general audience of 12 January 1966, he explained:

> In view of the pastoral nature of the Council, it avoided any extraordinary statements of dogmas endowed with the note of infallibility, but it still provided its teaching with the authority of the Ordinary Magisterium, which must be accepted with docility according to the mind of the Council concerning the nature and aims of each document.

What could be more clear? Pope Paul states unequivocally that the documents of Vatican II do not pertain to the Extraordinary Magisterium, and that they are not endowed with the note of infallibility.

The next testimony could, short of being a statement of the sovereign pontiff, hardly be more authoritative. It is an explanation given by the Council's own Theological Commission, cited by the Secretary of the Council, Archbishop Pericle Felici, in a theological note appended to the Dogmatic Constitution on the Church:

> In view of conciliar practice and the pastoral purpose of the present Council, this sacred Synod defines mat-

The Status of the Documents

ters of faith and morals as binding on the Church only when the Synod itself openly declares so. Other matters which the sacred Synod proposes as the doctrine of the supreme teaching authority of the Church, each and every member of the faithful is obliged to accept and embrace according to the mind of the sacred Synod itself, which becomes known either from the subject matter or from the language employed, according to the norms of theological interpretation.[19]

Needless to say, as was made clear in the subsequent statement by Pope Paul VI, which has already been quoted, the Council did not invest any of its teaching with the note of infallibility. This was made very clear in a book by Bishop B. C. Butler, in which he explained that "not all teachings emanating from a pope or an ecumenical council are infallible. There is no single proposition of Vatican II—except where it is citing previous infallible definitions—which is in itself infallible".[20] The Bishop has made an important distinction here. The documents of Vatican II do contain infallible teaching, but this teaching is infallible because it had already been proclaimed as such, and not because it is contained in a document of Vatican II.

An article by Father E. Doronzo, O.M.I., which appeared in the 14 September 1972 edition of *L'Osservatore Romano*, made a distinction between infallible and non-infallible statements of the Extraordinary Magisterium. What Father Doronzo is evidently attempting to do here is to stress the fact that the two sources of the Extraordinary and Infallible Magisterium, the pope and a general council, are not infallible in all their pronouncements. He explains:

> The Extraordinary Magisterium consists in a formal, explicit, and solemn declaration of doctrine made only by the supreme authority, expressed by the formula or

mode of declaration; this Magisterium can be either infallible or non-infallible. Examples of the former are the definitions of the primacy and infallibility of the pope by the First Vatican Council, of the Immaculate Conception by Pope Pius IX, and of the Assumption by Pope Pius XII. Examples of the non-infallible Extraordinary Magisterium include the various documents of Vatican II and most of the great papal encyclicals from Leo XIII to Paul VI.

The fact that the Magisterium can indeed present teaching that cannot be said with certainty to be free from error was admitted candidly by the German bishops in a very important joint-pastoral in September 1967. Their concern was principally with what the attitude of the faithful should be to such teaching, the attitude of theologians in particular. That there can be magisterial teaching open to the possibility of error was taken for granted.

> Beyond her guardianship of the inner substance of the faith the Church has, even at risk of going sometimes into error, to formulate teachings which have a certain degree of authority, while yet, since they are not definitions of faith, they are sufficiently provisional to admit a possibility of error.[21]

In his article "Magisterium" in *A Catholic Dictionary of Theology*, Father Joseph Crehan, S.J., provides an interesting insight into the degree of assistance given by the Holy Spirit to the Magisterium when it is not promulgating infallible decrees: "If, as Molina held, human weakness is a limiting factor even in the work of an ecumenical council, so that we ultimately get only the decrees that we deserve, and not all that the Spirit might have given us, then much more reasonably is a place to be found for human weakness in the day-

The Status of the Documents

to-day working of the Magisterium".[22] Father Crehan also draws our attention to the fact that the Council accepted the fact that it had "put forth its teaching without infallible definitions" by concluding the decree on the Church "with *decernimus ac statuimus* (`We decree and establish')", and not with the word *definimus*. The same formula was used for all the sixteen promulgated documents of the Council, and, as has been explained, infallibility pertains only to definitions. As Bishop B. C. Butler remarked in respect to papal definitions, but with equal applicability to those of a general council: "Infallibility is involved only when the papal definition is propounded as binding the whole Church finally and forever".[23]

In a profound study intended to enhance the authority of the Ordinary Magisterium, Dom Paul Nau, O.S.B., cites a number of authors who reckon the duty of Catholics when confronted with a statement of the Ordinary Magisterium "to be that of inward assent, not as of faith, but as of prudence, the refusal of which could not escape the mark of temerity, unless the doctrine rejected was an actual novelty or involved a manifest discordance between the pontifical affirmation and the doctrine which had hitherto been taught".[24] Dom Paul, basing himself upon the encyclical *Humani Generis,* insists that this attitude of mere prudence cannot be made a general rule to be observed towards the Ordinary Magisterium, and he is undoubtedly correct. He warns, with equal correctness, that a pronouncement of the Magisterium "always has the right to claim the benefit of any doubt". He adds that *Humani Generis* reserves such an attitude to an isolated pronouncement having a bearing on a matter which is still in dispute: "In this event, if the sovereign pontiff does not mean to commit himself to pronouncing a conclusive judgement, such a judgement would not fulfil the conditions required for infallibility and consequently it could not call for faith, but only for a respectful and prudent obedience".[25]

A very pertinent comment on the possibility of a magisterial pronouncement being open to the possibility of error written by Dr. Germain Grisez appeared in the July 1984 *Homiletic and Pastoral Review:*

> Obviously, teachings which are proposed infallibly leave no room for dissent on the part of faithful Catholics. However, other teachings of the Ordinary Magisterium can be mistaken, even though they may require and demand religious submission of mind and will. Such teachings can deserve acceptance inasmuch as they are the Magisterium's current best judgement of what God's word requires of Christians. However, that judgement, on the leading edge of developing doctrine and in truly prudential matters, can be mistaken, and faithful Christians can be led by superior claims of faith itself to withhold their submission to it.[26]

Dom Paul Nau's insistence that the withholding of submission of inward assent to a pronouncement of the Ordinary Magisterium could only occur in the most exceptional circumstances is echoed by Dr. Ludwig Ott. He explains our duty towards the teaching of the Ordinary Magisterium as follows:

> The ordinary and usual form of papal teaching activity is not infallible. Further, the decisions of the Roman Congregations (Holy Office, Bible Commission) are not infallible. Nevertheless, normally they are to be accepted with an inner assent which is based on the high supernatural authority of the Holy See *(assensus internus supernaturalis, assensus religiosus)*. The so-called *silentium obsequiosum,* that is "reverent silence", does not generally suffice. By way of exception the obligation of inner agreement may cease if a competent expert, after a

renewed scientific investigation of all grounds, arrives with a positive conviction that the decision rests on an error.[27]

It is hard to imagine a more evident case of a document than *Dignitatis Humanae* to which the sovereign pontiff did not wish to commit himself to pronouncing a conclusive judgement. It would also be hard to imagine a document which, to a greater extent than *Dignitatis Humanae*, contained teaching that was "an actual novelty or involved a manifest discordance between the pontifical affirmation and the doctrine which had hitherto been taught". This is a point that is thoroughly examined in my book *The Second Vatican Council and Religious Liberty.*

It now remains to explain in detail the conditions necessary for a magisterial teaching to be classified as a definition of the Extraordinary Magisterium, but before doing so it is necessary to understand the precise meaning of infallibility.

What Is Infallibility?

God alone is absolutely infallible. The infallibility with which He endowed His Church has limits and conditions. Infallibility is concerned primarily with certainty rather than with truth. The dogma of the Immaculate Conception was as true before the Constitution *Ineffabilis Deus* of Pope Pius IX in 1854 as it was after the definition. The definition gave us certainty of the truth of the dogma. Infallibility is the impossibility of falling into error, and an infallible pronouncement is one that is incapable of error or deception. The Church is infallible in her office of teaching owing to the perpetual assistance of the Holy Ghost promised to her by Our Lord, when, either in the exercise of her Ordinary and Universal Magisterium, or by a solemn pronouncement of the supreme authority (Extraordinary Magisterium), she proposes, for the acceptance of the universal Church, truths of faith or morals that are either revealed in themselves or connected with revelation. (This chapter is concerned only with the Extraordinary Magisterium.) The supreme authority of the Church, her Extraordinary Magisterium, is exercised by the Roman pontiff when he speaks *ex cathedra*— that is, when by virtue of his supreme apostolic authority, he defines a doctrine regarding faith or morals to be held by the Universal Church. The definitions of a general council also constitute an exercise of the Extraordinary Magisterium and are infallible providing that they are ratified by the pope. But the pope does not require the ratification of a general council or of the bishops of the Church for his own definitions. *Pastor Aeternus*, the First Dogmatic Constitution on the Church of Christ of the First Vatican Council, teaches that "such definitions of the Roman Pontiff are irreformable of themselves, and not in virtue of the consent of the Church". *Pastor Aeternus* declared the extent of infallible teaching to be the same for the pope and the Church. The full text of the solemn definition of *Pastor Aeternus* follows, and what it states with regard to an *ex cathedra* definition of the pope applies equally to a doctrinal definition of a general council. The four conditions which are necessary for a papal or a conciliar definition to be considered infallible will be explained in detail after the definition.

The Solemn Definition

> Therefore, faithfully adhering to the tradition received from the beginning of the Christian faith for the glory of God our Saviour, the exaltation of the Catholic religion, and the salvation of Christian people, with the approv-

al of the sacred council, We teach and define that it is a dogma divinely revealed: that the Roman Pontiff, when he speaks *ex cathedra*, that is, when, in discharge of the office of pastor and teacher of all Christians, by virtue of his supreme Apostolic authority, he defines a doctrine regarding faith or morals to be held by the Universal Church, is, by the divine assistance promised to him in Blessed Peter, possessed of that infallibility with which the Divine Redeemer willed that His Church should be endowed in defining doctrine regarding faith and morals; and that, therefore, such definitions of the Roman Pontiff are of themselves, and not from the consent of the Church, irreformable.

Canon: But if anyone, which may God avert, presume to contradict this Our definition, let him be anathema.[28]

Infallible Definitions

The conditions for an infallible definition of the Extraordinary Magisterium are, therefore:

(1) It must be a definition of the supreme teaching authority in the Church, either the pope alone teaching *ex cathedra* in his official capacity as shepherd and pastor of all Christians; or the bishops of the world assembled together in union with the pope in an ecumenical council.[29]

(2) An infallible definition must concern a matter of faith or morals. The Revelation committed to the Church by Our Lord Jesus Christ, and which ended with the death of the last apostle, is the direct or primary object of infallibility. But the scope of infallibility is not confined to Revelation. There is an indirect or secondary object of infallibility. This comprises truths which, though not formally revealed, are so intimately connected with revealed truth that one could not be denied logically without denying the other. Teaching

which comes within the scope of the Church's secondary infallibility is known either as a theological conclusion or a dogmatic fact.[30]

(3) The decision must bind the Universal Church (*ab universa Ecclesia tenendam definit*). Decrees which bind only part of the Church are not definitions. It is not absolutely necessary that the decree should be directly sent or addressed to the entire Church. It is sufficient for the supreme authority to make clear its intention of binding the Universal Church. A pope could address the hierarchy of a single country, condemning a heresy prevalent within that country, but using terms which made it clear that the heresy, no matter where it manifested itself, was not compatible with the Catholic faith.[31]

(4) The intention of binding the Universal Church must be exteriorised, that is, made clear beyond any possible doubt. It must be manifest that the definition constitutes an explicit, final, and irrevocable judgement binding the entire Church to an irrevocable internal assent. No specific formula is essential to prove the final and irrevocable nature of the definition. All that is necessary is that it should be the manifest intention of the supreme authority to settle the matter for ever. This is because no believer who pays due attention to Christ's promises can refuse to assent with absolute and irrevocable certainty to a definition of the Extraordinary Magisterium. But before being bound to give such assent the believer has a right to be certain that the teaching in question is definitive (since only definitive teaching is infallible).*

---

* The imposition of a definition under pain of anathema (excommunication) is a common but not essential method of indicating that the supreme teaching authority has made a final decision. Two expressions universally accepted as certainly signifying a definitive decision are: *definimus* and *auctoritate apostolicae definimus*. Thus, in defining the Dogma of the Immaculate Conception, Pope Pius IX gave irrefutable proof of the definitive nature of the decree with the words: "By the

The Status of the Documents

The clear principle governing the interpretation of the authority of a teaching of the Magisterium is that given in the Code of Canon Law, i.e., where the Church's intention to bind definitively is not expressed clearly there is no right to speak of an infallible decree. But even here there is a final but vital restriction on the scope of infallible teaching. Where a document of the Magisterium contains a doctrine which is to be treated as definitive and infallible, it is only that part of the document containing the actual definition which is infallible. For example, the Bull *Ineffabilis Deus*, proclaiming the Immaculate Conception, is quite lengthy, but the strictly definitive and infallible portion is contained in the concluding sentences only, beginning with the words: "To the glory and honour of the holy and undivided Trinity...". In the documents of Trent and Vatican I, statements of Church teaching, which are sometimes very detailed, are summarised in brief "canons" imposing the essence of this teaching under pain of anathema. The reasons and arguments upon which a definition is based do not form part of the infallible definition itself, unless these reasons or arguments are expressly defined. The solemn definition of papal infallibility from *Pastor Aeternus*, cited above, is, in itself, an excellent example of an infallible definition of the Extraordinary Magisterium.[33]

However, it will be found that more often than not the abuses committed in the name of Vatican II have no specific justification in an official document. The Constitution on the Liturgy contains much sound doctrine, some important doctrinal points which could have received much clearer emphasis—why was the word "transubstantiation" not used?—and some guidelines for reform which, in cer-

---

authority of Our Lord Jesus Christ and of the Blessed Apostles Peter and Paul, and by Our own authority, We declare, pronounce, and define the doctrine ... to be revealed by God and, as such, to be firmly and immutably held by all the faithful".[32]

tain respects, have proved a blueprint for revolution. It does not contain one word to indicate that by 1973 it would be possible, in some countries, for standing communicants to receive the host in their hands from a girl in a mini-skirt, not as an aberration but in accordance with regulations laid down by the Vatican. But the fact that they have the approval of the Vatican does not in any way affect the fact that they are abuses. The atmosphere the Council generated (the "Spirit of Vatican II") and the documents it promulgated set in motion a process which has inevitably involved the Church in a process of self-destruction, as the statistics cited in Appendix IX prove beyond any possible doubt.

In many respects, the documents were a dead letter from the day they were promulgated, and there is no longer a great deal to gain from insisting that they mean one thing rather than another. What is needed is a clear restatement of authentic doctrine, and a reinstatement of traditional practices (particularly the Mass of St. Pius V), which could bring an end to the present chaos—even if it meant the departure of large numbers of those whose adherence to the Church is no more than nominal.

The bishops themselves have given the lead in the manner in which they expect the norms laid down by the Council to be followed—those which suit them they implement and those which do not they ignore. They were, for example, *ordered* by the Council to ensure that the faithful can say and sing in Latin those parts of the Mass which belong to them and to make Gregorian chant the norm for sung Mass. There is not a single Western country in which this order has not been blatantly disobeyed.

What, then, must our attitude be to the documents of Vatican II? It must, above all, be a Catholic attitude and as such must exclude such simplistic responses as a "rejection" or "refusal" of the Council—whatever such terms may mean. Pope John Paul II was in complete accord with Archbishop

The Status of the Documents

Lefebvre in agreeing that the Council must be interpreted in the light of Tradition. We must make it clear that we will not allow any interpretation of the Council to be used to browbeat us into changing a single article of our traditional Catholic faith, and that, far from regarding it as some sort of super-council, we regard it as the least of all the councils; that when seeking clear and definite guidance we will look back to its predecessors. On the other hand, where we can refer to the documents of Vatican II in order to defend the authentic faith or refute abuses committed in the name of the Council, we would be foolish not to do so. "It is still too soon to pass a final judgement on the Council", writes Bishop Graber,

> but the fateful thing about it is that such great events as these affect various levels, indeed take place on various levels. Certainly the texts were formulated orthodoxly, in places nothing short of classically, and it will be our task for a long time to come to arm ourselves with the words of the Council to fight against its being undermined, above all to combat the famous 'spirit' of the Council. But since the Council was aiming primarily at a pastoral orientation and hence refrained from making dogmatically binding statements or dissociating itself, as previous Church assemblies had done, from errors and false doctrines by means of clear anathemas, many questions took on an opalescent ambivalence which provided a certain amount of justification for those who speak of the spirit of the Council. Furthermore, as we have already seen, a series of concepts came to the fore—e.g., fellowship between clerics, ecumenism, religious freedom—which it was no doubt possible to justify but which, to varying degrees, also had a boomerang effect.[34]

The quotation from the Decree on Ecumenism, cited earlier in this chapter, is a typical example of a conciliar text with a boomerang effect. It is no doubt possible, as Bishop Graber writes, "to justify" its contention that there can be deficient formulations of doctrine which should be rectified—but the boomerang effect is that this text is being used to justify giving an unsatisfactory and unorthodox formulation to doctrines which had previously been formulated in a perfectly orthodox and perfectly satisfactory manner.

"This Council, then, is not a council like the others", wrote Monsignor Lefebvre, "and for that reason we have a right to judge it prudently and with some reservation. We have no right to say that the crisis through which we are going is wholly unrelated to the Council, that it is simply a misrepresentation of the Council".[35]

We should, then, accept the conciliar documents as official, though not always well formulated, Church teaching which must be studied with prudence and reserve and measured against, and interpreted in accordance with, the traditional teaching of the Church—particularly the Councils of Trent and Vatican I. Pope John himself provided us with a mandate for this in his opening speech when he insisted that his own Council concurs "with tranquil adherence to all the teaching of the Church in its entirety and preciseness, as it still shines forth in the Acts of the Council of Trent and the First Vatican Council".[36] To repeat a comment made by Cardinal Heenan, cited earlier in this book: "I often wonder what Pope John would have thought had he been able to foresee that his Council would provide an excuse for rejecting so much of the Catholic doctrine which he wholeheartedly accepted".[37] In an address to the bishops of Chile on 13 July 1988, Cardinal Joseph Ratzinger, Prefect of the Congregation for the Doctrine of the Faith, commented:

The Status of the Documents

The Second Vatican Council has not been treated as a part of the entire living Tradition of the Church, but as an end of Tradition, a new start from zero. The truth is that this particular Council defined no dogma at all, and deliberately chose to remain on a modest level, as a merely pastoral council; and yet many treat it as though it had made itself into a sort of superdogma which takes away the importance of all the rest. This idea is made stronger by things that are now happening. That which previously was considered most holy—the form in which the liturgy was handed down—suddenly appears as the most forbidden of all things, the one thing that can safely be prohibited. It is intolerable to criticise decisions which have been taken since the Council; on the other hand, if men make question of ancient rules, or even of the great truths of the faith—for instance, the corporal virginity of Mary, the bodily resurrection of Jesus, the immortality of the soul, etc.—nobody complains or only does so with the greatest moderation.

Notes

1. Abbott, p. 327.
2. VO, p. 171.
3. PP, 111, p. 35.
4. *The Tablet*, 2 March 1968, p. 199.
5. *Ibid.* 25 November 1967, p. 1220
6. ABS, p. 137.
7. CC, p. 7.
8. ACT, p. 66.
9. Abbott, p. 48.
10. RFT, p. 20.
11. Abbott, p. 334.
12. *Ibid.*, p. 350.
13. ER, p. 176.
14. DCD, Ch. 1. Sect. II, II.
15. *Ibid.*, Ch. II, Sect II, II.
16. ABS, p. 116.
17. *The Tablet*, 25 November 1967, p. 1220.
18. C. Journet, *The Church of the Word Incarnate* (London, 1955), pp. 349-350.
19. Abbott, p. 98.
20. B. C. Butler, *In the Light of the Council* (London, 1968), p. 55.
21. *A Catholic Dictionary of Theology*, Vol. III (London, 1971), p. 227.
22. *Ibid.*, p. 228.
23. *The Tablet*, 8 November 1975, p. 1078.

24. Dom Paul Nau, O.S.B., *The Ordinary Magisterium of the Church Theologically Considered* ("Approaches", n.d.), p. 26. [This essay has been reprinted in *Pope or Church?: Essays on the Infallibility of the Ordinary Magisterium* (Angelus Press, 1998).]
25. *Ibid.*
26. *Homiletic & Pastoral Review*, July 1984, p. 14.
27. L. Ott, *Fundamentals of Catholic Dogma* (Cork, 1966), p. 10.
28. *Papal Teachings "The Church"* (Boston: St. Paul Editions, 1962), p. 217.
29. CE, Vol. IV, p. 676.
30. Ott, *Fundamentals of Dogma*, p. 299. CE, Vol. IV, p. 676, col. 1; Vol. VII, p. 799, col. 1.
31. CE, Vol. IV, p. 676, col. 1. DTC, Vol. VIII, col. 1700.
32. DTC, Vol. VII, col. 1703.
33. CE, Vol. IV, p. 676 and Vol. VII, pp. 796 & 800. DTC, Vol. VII, cols. 1699-1703.
34. ACT, p. 66.
35. ABS, p. 137.
36. Abbott, p. 715.
37. *The Tablet*, 18 May 1968, p. 489.

XIII

Left Turn

Since the first edition of this book in 1977 the Communist empire in Europe has collapsed, and the former subject nations are now members of the European Common Market. There can be no doubt that this collapse was initiated by the visit of Pope John Paul II to Poland in June 1979. My first inclination was to remove this chapter from the new edition, but on reflection the influence of Russia upon Vatican II is of considerable importance in any comprehensive account of the Council, not least in regard to the way in which any condemnation of Communism was sidetracked in the most devious manner possible. My original chapter therefore follows with very few changes.

Communist influence upon the Council was certain to be considerable if only because of the presence of Russian Orthodox observers. It scarcely needs pointing out that they were present only because the Soviet government felt that this would further its policy of detente—and it is also unnecessary to lay stress on the fact that for the Russians at the time of the Council detente was simply a tactic to be used wherever it would help in their campaign for world domination. The changing relationship between the Vatican and the Kremlin since the death of Pope Pius XII had involved a great deal of give and take—but the giving had all been on the part of the Vatican and the taking on the part of the Kremlin.

Communists had never made a secret of the fact that they regarded "dialogue" as a weapon in their bid for power. Once power is achieved it is normally the sincere if naive dialoguer who is the first to be eliminated. Father Henri Chambre, S.J., has provided a very perceptive analysis of the Communist "outstretched hand" technique in his book *Christianity and Communism*. He explains how this policy was based upon Communists making common cause with Catholics in political and ideological campaigns during which the Communists refrain from overt attacks upon the Christian religion, but attempt to alienate the ordinary faithful from the hierarchy and the Vatican:

> The policy of the "outstretched hand" to Catholics with its corollary—a cleavage between the faithful and the hierarchy—ultimately implies the claim that in practice the Communist Party should be the arbiter and the guardian of the Christian faith and Christian attitudes of mind for those Christians who accept such a situation....
>
> From even a brief analysis of the Communist tactic in a country like France, where Communists are not in the majority—and the same situation is found elsewhere—one fact is evident, namely, that under the pretext of advocating certain social, economic and political claims, an effort is made to win increasingly large groups of Christians over to Communism, with all that this implies.
>
> To achieve this, Communism monopolises the great ideals of justice, brotherhood, and peace, and asks the Christian masses to work with it in order to make them realities. Communists believe that common action along Communist lines is the best means of winning the wavering masses over to its side. All the more so since

common action is always accompanied by Communist explanations of the situation which, little by little, will commend the justice of the Communist position to the man who is carried along by this action and, since he has no leisure, forgets to reflect upon all the suggestions that are made to him. Further, the Communist criticism of the real or imaginary weaknesses of the Church leads the Christian who listens to it without submitting it to serious examination—and this in many cases could not be undertaken—to doubt the mystery of the Church's holiness, which cannot be immediately identified with that of her members, clerical or lay. At the same time, Communism shakes a man's faith in the God-man Jesus Christ, and prepares the ground for the acceptance of the Marxist concept of religion as a product of human social activity caught up in and conditioned by given economic, social, and political factors.[1]

Another description of the manner in which Communists use dialogue can be found in an analysis of the Marxist-Vatican detente, published by the Institute for the Study of Conflict, which is certainly the most reputable and authoritative body in Britain concerned with the study of Communist subversion on a world-wide basis.[2] In the analysis, a principal contributor to the Jesuit journal *Civilta Cattolica* is quoted as follows: "Communist parties tend to use dialogue to expand their audience and make the conquest of power easier. The Christian-Marxist contradiction is insoluble, insofar as every solution implies that one or the other renounces part of its very essence". Commenting on this, the author of the analysis explains:

> This statement was simply a repetition of the fundamental reason why the Church has always condemned Marxism, namely because of its essentially atheistic char-

acter, which renders any reconciliation with Christianity impossible. The whole structure of *Das Kapital*, as of the *Communist Manifesto*, rests on the belief in philosophical materialism, which requires man to be an end in himself and the explanation of all things. The idea of God enters into it only as a contrast and as an example of the suspension of the intellect, and evasion of effort and the survival of a prehistoric mentality. Marxism and Christianity are like fire and water, and any mixture resulting from an encounter can only leave the one or the other unrecognizable. Notwithstanding the numerous experiments—invariably failures—this same dialogue is still being pursued both in the political and religious spheres which merge through the ecumenical movement.[3]

Communist tactics are essentially pragmatic. Their aim is to achieve power, and the means they use to win converts who will further this aim is a matter of indifference to them. All that matters is to find "those who will further its ends".[4] It is worth noting that the fundamental Marxist belief, that "man is an end in himself and the explanation of all things", is not simply an axiom held in common with the mainstream of European Masonry but has clearly become, implicitly or explicitly, the basis of contemporary Modernism in both its Catholic and Protestant varieties. As was made clear in Chapter VIII, the ecumenical movement, as it exists at present, is moving not towards Christian unity, but unity in Rationalism. When interviewed in September 1974, Cardinal Mindszenty explained how Communists and democrats do not use the word "co-existence" in the same sense.

> What does the word mean? To speak of co-existence between East and West is to speak of two different and unequal concepts. On the one side, the Communist side, you have an unswerving system which is disciplined

despite the fact that it is based on intrinsic falsehood. On the Western side, you have only a watered-down philosophy, and a lack of any effective unifying principle. It is a hopeless contrast. Ever since the Second World War, the West has gone on giving up political terrain step by step, merely to appease the aggressors and traducers.[5]

On the same theme, he explains in his memoirs that:

The history of Bolshevism, which already goes back more than half a century, shows that the Church simply cannot make any conciliatory gesture in the expectation that the regime will in return abandon its persecution of religion. That persecution follows from the essential nature and internal organization of its ideology. Not even the Russian Orthodox Church has managed to escape persecution. It was persecuted during the period of coexistence and the period of subjugation. The experiences with negotiations between Budapest and the Vatican prove the same point.[6]

A good number of nominally Catholic countries, particularly in Latin America and the Latin countries of Europe, seem ideally suited for a Communist takeover, and the weakening of Catholic opposition to this aim was clearly a top priority. Evidence of a more sympathetic attitude to Communism displayed by a general council would obviously be of the greatest possible value in achieving this aim—and the total absence of any formal condemnation of atheistic Communism by Vatican II must have been a success far beyond anything the men in the Kremlin could have hoped for. History may well record that the war in Vietnam provided the crucial test of the will of the Western countries to halt the Communist advance—and that the Communist triumph was achieved less by their military successes than by the undermining of the American resolution to stand by her allies by means of what can accurately be described as a North Vietnamese fifth column working not simply within the United States but throughout the West. No single group was more active in this fifth column that the clergy of the Western Church—not excepting even the American hierarchy. The Marxist Allende came to power in Chile largely as a result of Catholic support, and this is a tendency which is becoming more manifest not simply throughout Latin America but in Portugal, Spain, France, and above all Italy. This new policy of appeasement reached its nadir when Pope Paul VI deprived Cardinal Mindszenty of his titles of Archbishop of Esztergom and Primate of Hungary despite the fact that the Cardinal had only agreed to leave Hungary after a solemn promise by the Pope that this would not happen. Even after arriving in Rome he was assured by Pope Paul: "You are and remain Archbishop of Esztergom and Primate of Hungary. Continue working, and if you have any difficulties, always turn trustfully to us".[7] On exactly the twenty-fifth anniversary of his arrest by the Communists, Cardinal Mindszenty was informed that the Pope had deprived him of these titles. He refused to subscribe to the official story that he had resigned, which he was urged to do as an act of spurious loyalty, and issued a public correction: "Cardinal Mindszenty has not abdicated his office as archbishop nor his dignity as primate of Hungary. The decision was taken by the Holy See alone".[8]

Pope Pius XII had refused to yield one inch to Communist pressure at the time of the Cardinal's "trial" and imprisonment in 1949. "Can you imagine a successor of St. Peter who would bow to such demands?" he had asked a vast crowd present at a public audience. "No!" they roared back. Pope Pius continued: "The Pope, by divine promise is, even in his human weakness, invincible and unshakable, herald of truth and justice, and of the various principles governing the unity of the Church". What had been unimaginable in 1949 had become undeniable in 1974. What brought about this calamitous *volteface* in the Vatican attitude towards Communism? The process began under Pope John XXIII when, in *Pacem in Terris*, he made a distinction between *error* and the *one who errs*, and between *false philosophical teachings* and the *historical movements* to which they have given rise. It was claimed that although once defined the false teachings *always remain the same*, the movements to which they give rise are influenced by *historical situations* and are subject to changes of a profound nature. Thus the condemnation of Communism by earlier Popes could not necessarily be considered as applying to present day Communists in any particular country. Communism as such remained wrong, but Communists, either as individuals or as the party in a particular country, were not necessarily so. "Besides", states *Pacem in Terris*, "who can deny that those movements, in so far as they conform to the dictates of right reason and are interpreters of the lawful aspirations of the human person, contain elements that are positive and deserving of approval?"

The visit of Khrushchev's son-in-law to the Vatican, which had preceded *Pacem in Terris*, gave a spectacular start to what is now known as the Vatican's *ostpolitik*—and added a million votes to the Italian Communist Party in the 1963 election. "The subsequent history of this dialogue is inherent in this juxtaposition of cause and effect: each step which the Church of Rome took towards the Communists brought an electoral, tactical, or strategic victory to the enemy religion of Communism".[9]

The Vatican considered that persuading Russian Orthodox observers to attend the Council was a matter of the very highest priority. Monsignor Willebrands secured something of a diplomatic triumph when, after negotiations in Paris and Moscow, two Russian Orthodox observers arrived at the very last minute, contrary to everyone's expectations. According to the Soviet News Agency, *Novosti*, the Russian delegates expressed their satisfaction at the "unaffected friendship" of the Pope.[10] It needs to be stressed that the administration of the Orthodox Church is under state control. If observers came to the Council it was because the Soviet government considered that allowing this would advance its political ambitions and for no other reason. In his justly celebrated 1972 Lenten Letter to the Patriarch Pimen, head of the Russian Orthodox Church, Solzhenitsyn asked what one could say in favour of "a Church administration that is at the mercy of atheistic dictators appointed to control it by the Department for Religious Affairs".[11]

Peter Nichols, Rome correspondent of *The Times*, claimed that during Monsignor Willebrands' Moscow visit (27 September – 2 October 1962) assurances were given that the Council would not "breathe a spirit of anti- Communism".[12] Henri Fesquet also suggests that the presence of the Russian observers might be explained by the fact that the Kremlin had received the assurances it had hoped for (*apaisements souhaités*).[13] If Monsignor Willebrands did enter into any definite agreement with the Kremlin it means that he, and those whom he represented, had decided for the Council what attitude it would adopt *vis-à-vis* Communism; in other words, the Council Fathers had been deprived of their freedom of action. That this really was the case appears more than likely in view of the extraordinary measures taken to prevent the Council condemning Communism, an incident which will be dealt with fully in this chapter. It is only fair to point out that Monsignor Willebrands' claims that the only promise he made was "that the problem was treated positively in the Council programme".[14]

The presence of the Russian observers was not universally popular—particularly among the Fathers from the Ukrainian Church in exile who decided to make a public protest.

Left Turn

The Vatican Secretariat of State managed to prevent this, but news of the intended move was leaked to the press. On 23 November Monsignor Willebrands felt obliged to make a press statement to the effect that "the Russians were most welcome, and that there had been no dealings with the Soviet Government, and that their presence could not be interpreted as a political manouevre [sic]".[15]

According to Fesquet, the French bishops refused to anathematise errors from the start.[16] Nor was there a word condemning totalitarianism, sabotage, terrorism, or guerillas—and even persecuted Catholics in Communist states were mentioned only twice. No effort was spared to avoid incurring the displeasure of the Communist world.[17] Cardinal Alfrink said more than once that any new condemnation of Marxism or Communism was to be avoided.[18]

What is quite certain is that the Russians were delighted with the way the first session went.

> In an interview published by *Novosti*, the Soviet news agency, the two Russian Orthodox observers at the Council, Archpriest Vitali Borovoy and Archimandrite Vladimir Kotlyarov, praised the Council's favourable and auspicious beginning as shown by the appeal of the Council Fathers for peace and by Pope John's pronouncements. They said they had both been treated with every consideration in Rome and received by the Pope with "a real friendship". The "growing prestige of the Russian Orthodox Church in ecumenical relations and its contributions to the struggle for peace" had also been reflected by the special attention shown to them by the Council Fathers, the press and the Roman public generally, they observed.[19]

One of the more sophisticated Soviet papers, the *Literary Gazette*, sent a special correspondent, M. Mchedlov, to Rome to cover the Council. He expressed approval at the general trend of the first session: "So far the die-hard conservatives have failed to carry the day, have not succeeded in their endeavor to turn the Council into a tool of their reactionary propaganda". Pope John received warm approval. "One must pay tribute", wrote Mr. Mchedlov, "to the Pope, John XXIII, who has taken up a realistic position *vis-à-vis* some of the burning problems of the day. New tendencies have come to the fore in Vatican policy since the beginning of his pontificate. It is characteristic of the Pope's messages and encyclicals that they no longer contain any overt furious condemnations of Communism, any expression of unconditional support for N.A.T.O., any appeals to Western powers to pursue a 'hard' policy towards the socialist countries". But Mr. Mchedlov was far from satisfied. "There are quite a few Catholic leaders who are still unwilling to give up their anti-Soviet and anti-Communist dogmas. They are headed by Cardinal Ottaviani and his ilk".[20]

Cardinal Ottaviani had made his own views very clear in 1960 in a speech which was seen at the time as an explicit criticism of the projected visit of the Italian president to Russia and has since been interpreted as an implicit criticism of Pope John's new attitude to Communism:

> In the twentieth century it is still necessary to deplore genocide, mass deportations, slaughter like Katyn Wood and massacres like Budapest. But some still stretch out their hands to the new Antichrist and even race to see who can first shake hands with him and exchange sweet smiles. Can a Christian confronted by one who massacres Christians and insults God smile and flatter? Can a Christian opt for an alliance with those who prepare for the coming of Antichrist in countries still free? Can we consider any relaxation of East-West tensions when

the face of Christ is once more spat upon, crowned with thorns and slapped?[21]

There have been suggestions from the fringe of the traditionalist movement that Pope John had Communist sympathies. Such a suggestion is quite ludicrous to anyone in the least familiar with his life, particularly through his own writing such as *Journal of a Soul*. It is quite certain that Pope John's policy of replacing anathema by dialogue played into the hands of the Communists—but this no more indicates that he was sympathetic to Communism than does Neville Chamberlain's policy of appeasement to Hitler indicate that the British Prime Minister was pro-Nazi. History contains countless examples of political and religious leaders whose errors of judgement have been most costly to those for whom they were responsible.

On 15 November 1960, Pope John received birthday greetings from Khrushchev who called him "a man of peace".[22] It is hardly likely that anyone needs telling that to be praised by a Soviet leader as "a man of peace" is equivalent to being called "a man whose policies are helping the Soviet plan for world domination". Dietrich von Hildebrand has emphasised that:

> It belongs to the very nature of Communism to aim at making the whole world communistic, with Soviet Russia as the supreme ruler. Thus, whether one licks the feet of Soviet Russia or kicks her in the back has not the slightest influence on her definite plans. She will deal with any partner not according to his friendly or unfriendly behavior but according to the long range plans dictated by her ideology.[23]

Dr. von Hildebrand states quite correctly that current Vatican policy was based on a most disastrous illusion:

It is the illusion that Communism, especially in Soviet Russia, has developed into humanitarian socialism. One believes that Soviet Russia today is no longer the same as under Stalin, Lenin, and even Khrushchev. This illusion is dangerous because it has gained great currency in the Vatican and among many Cardinals and Archbishops. In reality no change whatsoever has taken place, neither in the political views of Soviet Russia nor in the theoretical nature of Marxist Communism. The assumed "evolution", which is illusory, is in reality a mere tactical one. It is largely determined by the attitude of weakening resistance in the non-communist world and, especially, of what was in former times the most consistent and radical enemy of communism, the Roman Catholic Church.[24]

It should be pointed out, for those who are not aware of the fact, that Professor von Hildebrand's record of opposition to the Nazi tyranny enables him to assess totalitarian regimes from the standpoint of practical experience.

Pope John did not, of course, live to see his illusions shattered. He was not alive to witness his more humane brand of Communists invading Czechoslovakia in 1968 with as little compunction as Hungary had been invaded in 1956. When it suits the Soviets to dialogue they dialogue; when it suits them to make war they make war. There were a good many bishops present during Vatican II who had no illusions about Communism and were determined to do all in their power to ensure that it was condemned. A report in *The Tablet* at the end of the second session revealed that Pope Paul was considering "a schema on Communism, which is the most active and formidable of the heresies of the twentieth century. Pope John took strong steps to prevent anti-Communist speeches which might have prevented the coming of Orthodox observers".[25] In his Pastoral Letter, *The Vatican Council*, Cardinal Manning quotes with approval the opinion of Cardinal Pallavicini that "to convoke a general council except when absolutely demanded by necessity, is to tempt God".[26] He explains that throughout the history of the Church: "Each several Council was convened to extinguish the chief heresy, or to correct the chief evil, of the time".[27] Communism is certainly the chief evil of our time, "the most active and formidable of the heresies of the twentieth century", as *The Tablet* expressed it. Archbishop Lefebvre is in no way exaggerating when he writes:

> The refusal of this pastoral Council to issue any official condemnation of Communism alone suffices to disgrace it for all time, when one thinks of the tens of millions of martyrs, of people having their personalities scientifically destroyed in the psychiatric hospitals, serving as guinea-pigs for all sorts of experiments.[28]

This absence of any specific condemnation of atheistic Communism from the documents of the Council demonstrates more clearly than any other single factor its almost total lack of relevance to the *real* world in the second half of the twentieth century. It is almost as if the British Cabinet had met to consider the problems facing Britain in 1940 and issued a communique in which the fact that we were at war with Hitler was not even mentioned. The manner in which a condemnation of atheistic Communism was excluded from the Constitution on the Church in the Modern World is the most revealing example of the extent to which progressives were prepared to go to achieve their ends.

There had been considerable pressure within the Council for explicit teaching on Communism as such. The Rhine-controlled commissions which prepared the texts referred only to "atheism". Cardinal Wyszynski, who had more to fear from speaking out against Communism than any of his liberal counterparts in the West, demanded that there should be a schema on Communism: "If there is one grave error threatening the entire world today, that is it". [29] Another bishop with ample experience of Communism in action, Archbishop Paul Yu Pin of Nanking, China, asked in the name of seventy Fathers for a chapter on Atheistic Communism to be added to the constitution. He insisted that the Council must not neglect to discuss one of the "greatest, most evident and most unfortunate of modern phenomena" particularly in order to meet the expectations of "those who groan under the yoke of Communism and are forced to endure indescribable sorrows unjustly".[30] During the second session two hundred Fathers from forty-six countries had demanded a clear refutation of the errors of Marxism.

The most active force working against the progressives by the time the fourth session had begun was the International Group of Fathers led by Archbishop Lefebvre, Archbishop Sigaud, and Bishop de Castro Mayer. They drew up a petition giving ten reasons why Communism should be condemned and warned that if the Council remained silent on Communism it would be "equivalent to disavowing all that has been said and done up till now". (The Church had condemned Communism on more than two hundred occasions.) The prophecy made by the International Group of Fathers proved to be only too accurate—at least in the practical sphere, and, as has been made clear, Marxism is concerned *only* with the practical sphere. These Fathers also warned that unless this omission was rectified "tomorrow the Council will be reproved—and justly so—for its silence on Communism, which will be taken as a sign of cowardice and conniving".[31] The International Group of Fathers received strong support, and 450 Fathers signed written interventions asking for Communism to be treated specifically in the schema, which was due for revision.

On 13 November 1965, the commission responsible for the schema of the Constitution on the Church in the Modern World distributed the revised version of the schema, which, contrary to the rules of the Council, contained no mention of the 450 interventions and no reference to Communism. Bishop Carli sent an official protest to the Council Presidency quoting the Rules of Procedure which stated that "all amendments must be printed and communicated to the Council Fathers so that they can decide by vote whether they wish to admit or reject each one". He quite correctly pointed out that if the commissions, and all the commissions were Rhine Group commissions, were to decide what the Council Fathers could and could not be allowed to vote on, then they rather than the Fathers, constituted the Council.[32]

Cardinal Tisserant had the responsibility of conducting an official investigation. The first excuse given by the commission was that the interventions had not been handed in within the prescribed time limit: "I can confirm the fact that the amendment on Communism did not reach either the members of the commission of us *periti* who are part of the commission", explained one *peritus*, who added: "There is no intrigue here of any sort...".[33] This placed the blame upon the International Group of Fathers for failing to deliver the interventions on time. However, such a move on the part of the Commission had been foreseen by Archbishop Lefebvre, who, together with Archbishop Sigaud, had delivered the interventions in person at noon on 9 October 1965, *within* the prescribed time limit.[34]

This put the blame squarely back upon the commission, and eventually Archbishop Garonne of Toulouse had to apologise and admit that the interventions on Communism had "indeed reached the offices of our commission within the proper time, but were not examined when they should have been, because unintentionally they had not been transmitted to the Commission members".[35]

Both Father Wiltgen and the celebrated French writer Bernard Fay specifically name Monsignor Achille Glorieux, of Lille, France, as the man directly responsible for holding back the interventions. He was not disciplined but was appointed as Nuncio to Cairo.[36] However, it was too late for the text of the schema to be changed in the Council Hall, but the Pope himself intervened and ordered the inclusion of the words "has already repudiated" together with a footnote in the relevant section (Article 21). The final version reads: "The Church has already repudiated and cannot cease repudiating, sorrowfully but as firmly as possible, those poisonous doctrines and actions which contradict reason and the common experience of humanity, and dethrone man from his native excellence". The footnote refers to papal encyclicals condemning Communism, and thus it could be argued that it is condemned in this Constitution, if only indirectly. But the fact that the Council abstained from "explicit condemnation of Communism has indicated what would be called on the political level 'an opening to the left'", concedes a footnote in the Abbott edition of the Documents.[37] In another footnote it states that: "Through unintentional oversight members of the drafting commission had not seen copies of identical suggestions by 334 Fathers of which 297 had been filed with the Council's secretariat in due time urging an 'explicit' condemnation of Marxist atheistic communism".[38] There had, of course, been 450 names, all handed in at the same time, but the Commission would only admit to receiving between 297 and 334—reports vary. Fortunately, Archbishop Sigaud had 435 of the names on record and he went to the archives to see which ones were missing. He was told that the documents were unavailable.[39] A member of the Commission admitted that this was by no means the only intervention which had been "sidetracked" in this way.[40]

In a very revealing comment the Abbott edition remarks: "The Commission judged that its references to atheism satisfied the wishes of the Council as a whole".[41] In other words, precisely what Bishop Carli had stated in his protest, that "the Commission members rather than the Council Fathers constitute the Council".

To put this matter in its proper perspective, imagine what a furor there would have been, what endless outbursts of shock, indignation, and holy wrath from the secular and religious press, had Cardinal Ottaviani deliberately prevented a properly filed amendment from being voted on; lied about it; been proved to be lying; admitted doing the same thing on other occasions; and stated that, though the Fathers had not been given the chance to express their opinion, what he had done had satisfied the Council as a whole! The liberal journals would still be devoting entire issues to the topic each year on the anniversary of the event, and no *peritus* would have been able to hold up his head in progressive circles without having written at least one book on the scandal.

Archbishop Lefebvre writes:

> I know these things through personal experience. If I tell you of them it is not to condemn the Council. It could have been a magnificent thing, but, as matters fell out, it must be admitted that nothing can justify some occurrences. "Yet", you will say, "the Council is inspired by the Holy Spirit". Not necessarily. A pastoral, non-dogmatic council is a form of teaching which does not, of itself, invoke infallibility.[42]

It would be blasphemous to consider the Holy Ghost responsible for men ordained to the priesthood using lies and trickery to prevent a general council of the Church from condemning the most active and formidable heresy of the age. Although we can be sure that the Holy Ghost will have prevented even this "pastoral" Council from teaching formal heresy, we do not need to believe that it has said all that needed to be said on any particular topic, or even that what it does say is phrased in the clearest or most prudent manner.

It also needs to be emphasised that what has been written here with regard to conciliar statements can apply equally to papal pronouncements. Dietrich von Hildebrand has pointed out the danger inherent in the attitude of many loyal Catholics who, as a reaction to the attacks upon papal authority made by "progressives", now accept practical decisions of the Pope

> in the same way as *ex cathedra* definitions, or encyclicals dealing with questions of faith or morals which are always in full harmony with the tradition of the Holy Church and her Magisterium. This loyalty is really false and unfounded. It places insoluble problems before the faithful in regard to the history of the Church. In the end this false loyalty can only endanger the Catholic faith.... Obviously a political decision or a disciplinary one is not a dogma. It may be wise and bring forth fruitful consequences. Or it may be unwise and result in great hardships for the Church and great sufferings for mankind. We must realise that the present-day illusion that Communism has become "humanitarian socialism" is an error that has worse consequences than all the combined political errors in the almost two-thousand-year history of the Church.[43]

Cardinal Manning made the same point with regard to papal authority when he wrote:

The Pontiff speaks *ex cathedra* when, and only when, he speaks as the Pastor and Doctor of all Christians. By this, all acts of the Pontiff as a private person, or as sovereign of a state, are excluded. In all these acts the Pontiff may be subject to error. In one and one only capacity is he exempt from error; that is, when as teacher of the whole Church he teaches the whole Church in things of faith and morals.[44]

Before concluding this chapter it needs to be pointed out that the Constitution on the Church in the Modern World calls specifically for "sincere and prudent" dialogue with atheists. The Council did not condemn Communism—it asked for dialogue. Can it therefore be absolved from responsibility for the fact that so many Catholics, lay and clerical, flung themselves into the arms of Marxists not just to dialogue but to join the revolution? Those who might wish to absolve the Council from any responsibility would do well to read the proceedings of the Eleventh Congress of the Italian Communist Party, which stated that:

The extraordinary "awakening" of the Council, which is rightly compared to the Estates General of 1789, has shown the whole world that the old politico-religious Bastille is shaken to its foundations. Thus a new situation has arisen which should be met with appropriate measures. A hitherto unforeseen possibility has emerged for us to draw nearer to our final victory by means of a suitable manoeuvre...the Council itself is providing us *gratis* with the best means of reaching the Catholic public....Never was the situation so favourable for us (*Mai la situazione ci e stata cosi favorevole...*).[45]

By the end of 1975, the Communists had made such good use of the new situation that the possibility of their taking

Pope John's Council

over the administration of Rome itself in the near future—and by perfectly legal means—seemed a distinct possibility. Pope Paul himself was clearly anxious, and in an allocution which will be cited in Chapter XV, he made it obvious that he was losing hope of any positive results being achieved from the dialogue with Communism. On 19 October 1975, Cardinal Poletti, the Pope's Vicar-General for Rome, made a speech to the senior clergy of the diocese which must obviously have had the approval of the Pope himself:

> In a few months—perhaps the responsibility is ours—the City of Rome may be irresponsibly handed over to the Marxist administration, with all the resultant consequences....Ours, however, is a fear not due to material interests and concerns, but only to the inevitable confrontation that will arise between the City of God, which is the Church, and the City without God, which will involve the spiritual fate of many faithful in Marxist materialism.
>
> No one can wipe out this reality—not even with superficial illusions. Communism is, today still—as it always has been and will be—Marxist materialism. Tactically it may seek other expressions of tolerance, but in its essence, its substance, it is, and will remain, materialistic and atheistic. Perhaps for reasons of expediency it will not put itself against God at once, but it will always wish to be a City without God. Here the faith and souls are at stake....
>
> In this connection and to avoid any ambiguity, against every tendentious affirmation, I wish to state, without any possibility of denial, that any surrender to Communism or Marxism will never meet with my consent.[46]

This is, of course, simply a reaffirmation of the traditional Catholic attitude towards Communism cited earlier in this chapter, abandoned for a policy of dialogue with the disastrous results of which Cardinal Poletti speaks. Rome was indeed taken over by a Marxist administration, and was still being ruled by a Marxist administration in 2004.

Because the Church is holy, as well as one and Catholic, she will always have members imbued with holiness of such heroic dimensions that they will bring her glory out of apparent defeat and prove that God still raises up His confessors during periods of the most abject surrender. Every English-speaking Catholic venerates the memory of Saint John Fisher, few could even name one of the compromising bishops who chose accommodation to the spirit of the times rather than martyrdom. In this sense the post-conciliar Church was not devoid of glory, and this glory was most manifest in the great confessors of Eastern Europe; they represented the true countenance of the post-conciliar Church, the Church that continues to live out the sufferings of her crucified Saviour, a Church which is undergoing her most recent agony throughout South Vietnam. Cardinal Wyszynski paid tribute to the great cardinal-confessors of Eastern Europe in a sermon delivered to a congregation of students in St. Anne's Church, Warsaw, on 9 April 1974. It is their heroism, both before and since the Council, that enables the true countenance of Catholicism to be discerned through what Cardinal Wyszynski, himself one of the greatest of these confessors, termed the "artificial mist of doubt and uncertainty" which has permeated the Church since Vatican II:

> Recently there died in Czechoslovakia a Cardinal Trochata. Almost the whole of his life as a bishop he spent in prisons and concentration camps. He was chased out of his diocese and sentenced to forced labor in a factory. When he entered the factory the workers knew that he did not come as a worker-priest to earn his living, but

that he was condemned to the factory. His only fault was that he was a bishop of Christ's Church. This he had to atone for with twenty years' imprisonment.

Cardinal Stepinac too was a prisoner and an exile. He was buried in his Cathedral at Zagreb. The flowers and candles round his grave remind us of resurrection and life. He was hounded from his episcopal see because he was a bishop who bore witness to Christ. This was a crime.

Far from his diocese died Cardinal Beran, the Archbishop of Prague, having been first of all a prisoner in Dachau and then a prisoner of the present day. His guilt consisted of being a bishop and confessing Christ. He died as a saint.

Cardinal Mindszenty, the primate of Hungary, too, was a prisoner and was removed from his See. For what reason? Was he a criminal? An enemy of his people and country? No, he was a bishop and bore witness to Christ.

And Cardinal Slipyi, Archbishop of Lemberg, he too shared for more than twenty years the fate of the exiles and captives. He is now living outside his diocese and away from his country. Why? Once more, why? The cowards never give an honest answer to this question.

This is the true post-conciliar Church. God Himself answered the question of what this Church should be like when He sent cardinals to the front who, for the sake of Christ, became confessors, captives, and martyrs.[47]

Notes

[1] *Christianity and Communism* (Hawthorn Books, 1960), pp. 37-38.

[2] *Conflict Studies* (Editor Brian Crozier) No. 45, "Marxism and the Church of Rome."

[3] *Ibid.*, pp. 11-12.

[4] *Ibid.*, p. 12.
[5] *Sunday Telegraph*, 15 September 1974.
[6] *Memoirs* (London: McMillan, 1974), p. 244.
[7] *Ibid.*, p. 329.
[8] *Ibid.*, p. 246.
[9] *Op. cit.*, note 2, p. 6.
[10] XR-I, p. 79.
[11] Cited in *Approaches* No. 35, October 1973, p. 3.
[12] *Politics of the Vatican* (London, 1968), p. 209.
[13] JC, p. 40.
[14] RFT, p. 122.
[15] XR-I, p. 80.
[16] JC, p. 42.
[17] *Op. cit.*, note 2, p. 7.
[18] JC, p. 682.
[19] *The Tablet*, 1 December 1982, p. 1169.
[20] *Ibid.*, 22 December 1962, p. 1169.
[21] IC, p. 44.
[22] *Ibid.*, p. 45.
[23] *Satan at Work*, p. 38.
[24] *Ibid.*, p. 35.
[25] *The Tablet*, 14 December 1963, p. 1348.
[26] PP, III, p. 24.
[27] PP, III, p. 35.
[28] *Letter to Friends and Benefactors*, No. 9.
[29] ABS, p. 136.
[30] RFT, p. 273.
[31] *Ibid.*, p. 274.
[32] *Ibid.*, p. 275.
[33] *Ibid.*
[34] *Ibid.*, p. 276.
[35] *Ibid.*, p. 277.
[36] *Op. cit.*, note 2, p. 8.
[37] Abbott, p. 401.
[38] *Ibid.*, p. 217.
[39] RFT, p. 277.
[40] *Ibid.*, p. 276.
[41] Abbott, p. 217.
[42] ABS, p. 136.
[43] *Satan at Work*, note 23, p. 45.
[44] PP, III, p. 58.
[45] ACT, pp. 64-65.
[46] *Diocesan Review of Rome*, September-October 1975. The complete text was printed in *The Wanderer*, 20 November 1975.
[47] *Christian Order*, February 1975, pp. 69-70.

XIV

Pernicious Adversaries

Vatican II, as an event, is directly responsible for the resurgence and current ascendancy of neo-modernism within the Church, not because there is any explicit heresy within its sixteen official documents, but because it brought the neo-modernists together, enabled them to obtain key positions within the conciliar commissions, and to minimise, as far as possible, the extent to which the official documents would impede their aims. By bringing them together the Council gave their movement the impetus and organisation which has led to the present situation where it is the Magisterium, and not the Modernists, which is on the defensive. The Modernists are, as St. Pius X warned us in *Pascendi Gregis*, "the most pernicious of all the adversaries of the Church" and they propagate "the poisonous doctrines" taught by her enemies "by arts entirely new and full of deceit" in a manner that is "to be most dreaded and deplored, in her very bosom...". Their aim is simple: "to destroy the vital energy of the Church, and, as far as in them lies, utterly subvert the very Kingdom of Christ".[1]

Examples have already been given of some of the sources of the pressure exerted upon the Fathers which contributed directly or indirectly to the Modernist ascendency within the Council—the press, Protestantism, and Communism.

All played their part in loosing upon the Church in the so-called "Spirit of Vatican II" what St. Pius X designated as the principal doctrine of Modernism—that of *evolution*. "To the laws of evolution everything is subject under penalty of death—dogma, Church worship, the books we revere as sacred, even faith itself".[2]

Now the very notion of evolution means that something is evolving and that there is a point to which it is evolving. St. Pius X revealed this in a prophetic sentence: "The error of Protestantism made the first step on this path; that of Modernism makes the second; Atheism makes the next".[3] "Atheism makes the next"—The Church on the road to atheism? That this is indeed the case is the thesis of a book by Dr. Rudolph Graber, consecrated Bishop of Regensburg by Pope John XXIII in 1962.[4] (The fact that this book has been written by a German bishop is, like the presence of theologians of irreproachable orthodoxy among the *periti*, a warning against making sweeping generalisations.) Bishop Graber was one of the outstanding theologians in the German episcopate, and his stature was such that the German government wished to honour him with its Order of Merit in 1974. He declined to receive any honour from a government which had approved anti-Christian abortion laws. His book provides one of the very rare instances to which the overworked adjective "sensational" could be applied with perfect accuracy. It has not created a sensation, which is not surprising as the liberal press utilises an effective technique of ignoring any work which could harm its cause. The liberal Catholic establishment never tires of demanding the free circulation of ideas within the Church, but means, of course, only those ideas which it considers acceptable.

It is probable that many traditionally minded Catholics would be inclined to dismiss what Bishop Graber has written as too incredible to merit serious consideration. Such Catholics should first consider that what the Bishop alleges has also been taught by popes and that to dismiss the case as incredible is precisely the reaction desired by the enemies of the Church the Bishop wishes to expose. Catholic liberals are particularly zealous in ridiculing the very idea that there could be organised groups of evil men working to destroy Christ's Church. It needs to be stated that the task of discrediting the conspiracy theory is made much easier by some of its proponents who carry it to ridiculous lengths, and make allegations which they are quite unable to substantiate, sometimes against named individuals.

However, given the existence of Satan, it would be incredible if such groups did not exist—and no one is more zealous than the Catholic liberal in ridiculing the idea that Satan does exist. The most consistent tactic of the liberal, and he uses it consistently because it is successful, is to portray those who oppose him as rather pathetic figures, men with closed minds, men who fear change, men who live in the past and cannot adjust themselves to contemporary developments and insights. "There is little reason to wonder", wrote St. Pius X in *Pascendi* "that the Modernists vent all their bitterness and hatred on Catholics who zealously fight the battles of the Church. There is no species of insult which they do not heap upon them, but their usual course is to charge them with ignorance or obstinacy".[5] Thus the French Catholic apologist for Freemasonry, A. Mellor, writes that Catholics who oppose a reconciliation with Freemasonry are

> those who refuse to change their habits of thought and by the sort of intellectuals rightly or wrongly known as integralists. The latter are sometimes very competent theologians. In the depth of their being they no doubt feel an anxiety which will not let them rest. Any idea which is in the least degree new, in their eyes, smacks of heresy, irenicism, or syncretism. The hierarchy are trai-

tors. The Pope himself is not immune from their criticisms.[6]

When the newly appointed Jesuit General, Father Pedro Arrupe, made a speech during the Council warning Catholics of the forces ranged against the Church he was ridiculed by progressive journalists. Robert Nowell, writing in *The Tablet*, commented: "But the call to battle was most clearly sounded by the new Jesuit General, Father Pedro Arrupe, in his maiden speech, which can have served only to encourage the lunatic fringe on the right while disappointing, if not actually scandalising, everyone else".[7] This is what Father Arrupe actually said:

> The contrast between what the Church possesses and what she succeeds in imparting to men has become very obvious in this modern world, which ignores God—when it does not try to destroy the very notion of the Divinity. This mentality and the cultural environment that nourishes it is atheistic, at least in practice. It is like the City of Man of St. Augustine; and it not only carries on the struggle against the City of God from outside the walls, but even crosses the ramparts and enters the very territory of the City of God, insidiously influencing the minds of believers (including even religious and priests) with its hidden poison, and producing its natural fruits in the Church: naturalism, distrust, rebellion....This new godless society operates in an extremely efficient manner, at least in its highest levels of leadership. It makes use of every possible means at its disposal, be they scientific, technical, social, or economic. It follows a perfectly mapped out strategy. It holds almost complete sway in international organizations, in financial circles, in the fields of mass communications: press, cinema, radio and television.[8]

Nothing could be in greater contrast than Father Arrupe's assessment of the world and the optimistic picture found in *Gaudium et Spes* (the Constitution on the Church in the Modern World). The "Naturalism" referred to by Father Arrupe was designated as the animating spirit of Freemasonry by Pope Leo XIII in his encyclical *Humanum Genus*, condemning Masonry.

> The fundamental doctrine of the Naturalists is that human nature and human reason must be in all things mistress and guide. This decided, they either ignore man's duties towards God or pervert them by vague and erroneous opinions. For they deny that anything has been revealed by God; they do not admit any religious dogma or any truth that cannot be understood by the human intelligence; they deny the existence of any teacher who ought to be believed by reason of the authority of his office. Since, however, it is the special and exclusive function of the Catholic Church to preserve from any trace of corruption and to set forth in their integrity the truths divinely entrusted to her keeping, including her own authority to teach them to the world, and the other heavenly aids to salvation, it is against the Church that the rage of the enemies of the supernatural and their most ferocious attacks are principally directed.[9]

In this encyclical the Pope speaks of the age-long war between the Kingdom of God and the Kingdom of Satan which he considers to have been aptly described by St. Augustine under the image of two cities—citing St. Augustine directly: "Two loves have formed two cities; the love of self reaching to contempt of God, an earthly city; the love of God, reaching to contempt of self, a heavenly one".[10] "In our day", writes Pope Leo,

> the partisans of evil seem to be drawing closer together and, as a body, appear to be animated with extraordinary energy, under the leadership and with the assistance of the widely diffused and strongly organised associations known as Freemasonry. No longer concealing their designs, they are now, with the greatest audacity, preparing to rise up against God Himself. They are planning the utter destruction of Holy Church publicly and openly, with the intention of completely despoiling the Christian Nations of the benefits procured for them by Jesus Christ, Our Saviour, if that were possible.[11]

Pope Leo insists that no matter how benign a particular branch or particular lodge of Freemasons may be, under no circumstances could Catholics ever become members.

> Let nobody be deceived by a false appearance of honesty. It may appear to some that Freemasons do not demand anything that is openly opposed to religion and good morals. Nevertheless, since the fundamental animating principle of Freemasonry is vicious and immoral, to ally oneself with Masons or help them in any way cannot be lawful.[12]

This prohibition was incorporated into the 1917 Code of Canon Law, which ruled that those who join a Masonic sect or other societies of the same sort, which plot against the Church or any legitimate civil authority, incur *ipso facto* an excommunication simply reserved to the Holy See (Canon 2335). Incredible as it may seem, this prohibition was modified in 1974 on the grounds that it only forbids Catholics to join Masonic associations which plot against the Church and that they may, therefore, join those that do not. The 1983 Code of Canon Law rules (Canon 1374): "A person who joins an association which plots against the Church is to be punished with a just penalty; one who promotes or takes office in such an association is to be punished with an interdict". It will be noted that the new code does not specify Freemasonry by name. The 1974 concession and the 1983 Code must both be understood in the light of the authoritative Declaration on Freemasonry of the Sacred Congregation for the Doctrine of the Faith of 26 November 1983:

> The Church's negative judgement in regard to Masonic associations remains unchanged since their principles have always been considered irreconcilable with the doctrine of the Church and therefore membership in them remains forbidden. The faithful who enrol in Masonic associations are in a state of grave sin and may not receive Holy Communion.

It is to be regretted that the penalty of excommunication has evidently been abandoned. Leaving aside the question of plots against the Church, those who are initiated into Freemasonry participate in quasi-religious rituals which are incompatible with a profession of Christian faith. Walter Hannah proves this conclusively in his book *Christian by Degrees*. In a foreword to this book, Dr. E. L. Mascall, a leading Anglican theologian, writes: "I have been amazed and shocked at the idea of a Christian, and above all a Christian priest, taking part in some of the ceremonies he describes".[13] Dr. Mascall is, of course, referring to the fact that large numbers of Anglican clergy, including bishops, are also Masons.

St. Pius X has been quoted as claiming that poisonous doctrines intended to destroy the Church are being propagated in her very bosom in a deceitful manner—and that this is all part of a process which will end in atheism. Bishop Graber's thesis is that the secret societies which have been plotting to destroy the Church for centuries (as we have been warned by some of the greatest of modern popes) have long abandoned a policy of open confrontation for one of infiltration, with the object of destroying the Church from within as part of an evolutionary process which will terminate in a politico-religious collectivist world state which they would control. Such a state would, for all practical purposes, be atheistic—what religion remained would be little more than a form of pantheistic syncretism. In the chapter on Communism it was shown how Marxists made no secret of their aims or the tactics they employed to achieve them. Nor do the secret societies.

Bishop Graber documents the manner in which the secret societies, basically Masonic (although it is arguable that the Masons themselves were and are being manipulated by far more sinister forces) were responsible for the French Revolution which, more than any other single factor, launched the concepts and movements which, if successful, will destroy the Judeo-Christian basis of Western civilization. Bishop Graber does not argue that the French Revolution was directly planned and controlled by the Masons, many of whom remained loyal to the Crown. "Freemasonry does not conduct revolutions: it prepares the way for them and continues them". [14]

It is important to emphasise the fact that, particularly in Britain and the U.S.A., most Masons are ordinary, law-abiding and often religious people—no more concerned with subverting society than the average Catholic. This is particularly true of those in the lower grades or degrees. Pope Leo XIII took pains to stress this in the interests of justice when he wrote in *Humanum Genus*:

> Our remarks do not apply to each of the individual members of the Masonic body. Amongst these there may be some and even many, who though they have incurred the guilt of having enrolled themselves in such an asso-

ciation, yet do not personally take a vicious part in the crimes perpetrated by the organization and are ignorant of the final purpose for which it is working.[15]

No revolution is spontaneous. "They are preceded by a subterranean phase" in which the seeds of revolt are sown; this is followed by a period "incubation" and then comes the "eruption".[16] Bishop Graber shows that since the Council the main ideas of the Revolution have been spreading openly within the Church:

> the liberty to rebel against power structures in the Church, the equality in the democratization introduced through the council system in the parishes, and the fraternity in the horizontal neighborliness in which the vertical aspect, God and transcendency as a whole, is left out of consideration. The extent to which the Second Vatican Council is associated with the French Revolution is clearly evident in remarks made at the Eleventh Congress of the Italian Communist Party in 1964.[17]

The poisoned seeds planted within the Church by the secret societies "first came to the surface in the Modernism which appeared at the beginning of the twentieth century but which was immediately kept from developing by the energetic steps taken by Pope St. Pius X".[18] Bishop Graber considers it horrifying, when the writings of the secret societies are examined, "to see that in them all the ideas already appear towards the end of the century which are testing the Church to breaking point in the post-conciliar period".[19] The ultimate aim of these societies is the integration of all financial and social forces under a world government in which: "Catholicism like all religions would consequently be absorbed into a universal syncretism....In its final stages the completely achieved synarchy would represent the anti-church". They aim to create "an anti-church or a 'new' church by undermining and changing the function of the old Church and of achieving this less by an attack from the outside than by what is nowadays called in the political sphere the 'march through institutions'".[20] Their ideas, without being specifically named, "are absorbed into the spiritual circulation of the Church through the process of evolution..." in order to "deprive the Church of its supernatural character, to amalgamate it with the world instead of letting them run side by side as separate confessions, and thus to pave the way for a standardised world religion in a centralised world state".[21] The Masons announce quite openly: "The goal is no longer the destruction of the Church but rather to make use of it by infiltrating it".[22] One of their spokesmen, a former canon and "an apostate of the worst kind",[23] prophesied that "the divine cult in the form directed by the liturgy, ceremonial, ritual and regulations of the Roman Church will shortly undergo a transformation at an ecumenical council which will restore it to the venerable simplicity of the golden age of the Apostles in accordance with the dictates of conscience and modern civilization".[24] (The first of the general norms laid down for liturgical reform by Vatican II was that: "The rites should be distinguished by a noble simplicity".)

The absolute conformity of the post-conciliar liturgical reform with this prediction made simple coincidence seem far too naive an explanation. In the third book of this trilogy, *Pope Paul's New Mass*, detailed documentation will be provided proving that Father, later Archbishop, Bugnini had more influence than any other individual in concocting and imposing the post-Vatican II liturgical revolution. It became obvious that evidence of exceptional gravity concerning Archbishop Bugnini must have been brought before the Pope when, to the dismay of the liberals, he was not only dismissed from his position as secretary to the Congregation for Divine Worship but the Congregation itself was dissolved and merged with the Congregation for the Sacraments. Liberals made no secret of the fact that they regarded this as a most retrogade step which could endanger the future of the Bugnini reform.[25] Suspicion was heightened when he was packed off to Iran as Pro-Nuncio and it came as no great surprise when, in April 1976, Tito Casini, Italy's leading Catholic writer, was able to make public the fact that: "The reform has been conducted by this Bugnini who has been unmasked at last; he is indeed what we have long suspected: a Freemason".[26] Archbishop Lefebvre commented, in May 1976, "Now, when we hear in Rome that he who was the heart and soul of the liturgical reform is a Freemason, we may think that he is not the only one. The veil covering the greatest deceit ever to have mystified the clergy and baffled the faithful, is doubtless beginning to be torn asunder".[27] A detailed examination of the case of Archbishop Bugnini will appear in *Pope Paul's New Mass*. I do not claim to be able to prove that the Archbishop was a Mason, something that he denied vehemently, but that documentation given to Pope Paul VI convinced the Pontiff that the Archbishop was a Mason, and prompted his immediate dismissal. The Archbishop himself admitted that this was the case, but insisted that the Pope had been deceived by those wishing to discredit his liturgical reform.[28]

Monsignor Lefebvre reminds us that Pope Pius IX ordered the documents of the *Alta Vendita* to be published in order to alert the faithful to the plans of the Masons to infiltrate the Vatican and destroy the Church from within. Interestingly enough, the documents of the *Alta Vendita*, highest lodge of the *Carbonari*, an Italian secret society, were later published in Dublin in 1885 by Monsignor George F. Dillon as a response to the exhortation of Pope Leo XIII to "tear away the mask from Freemasonry". When the Pope was presented with a copy of Monsignor Dillon's book he was so impressed that he ordered an Italian version to be completed and published at his own expense. The unmasking of Archbishop Bugnini proves that the warning it contains has never been more pertinent.[29]

The *Permanent Instruction of the Alta Vendita*, included as Chapter XVIII, contains the following: "Our final end is that of Voltaire and of the French Revolution, the destruction forever of Catholicism and even of the Christian idea which, if left standing on the ruins of Rome, would be the resuscitation of Christianity later on". They seek "a Pope according to our wants"—not necessarily a bad one, in fact, a good man would suit them better, but one whom they will be able to manipulate. "The Pope, whoever he may be, will never come to the secret societies. It is for the secret societies to come first to the Church, in the resolve to conquer the two". "The work which we have undertaken is not the work of a day, nor of a month, nor of a year. It may last many years, a century perhaps, but in our ranks the soldier dies and the fight continues". The hour of the *Alta Vendita* will have come when its agents "have, by the force of events, invaded all the functions":

> They will govern, administer and judge. They will form the council of the Sovereign. They will be called upon to choose the Pontiff who will reign; and that Pontiff, like the greater part of his contemporaries, will be necessarily imbued with the Italian and humanitarian principles which we are about to put into circulation.... Let the clergy march under your banner in the belief always that they march under the banner of the Apostolic Keys. You wish to cause the last vestige of tyranny and oppression to disappear? Lay your nets like Simon Barjona. Lay them in the depth of sacristies, seminaries, and convents, rather than in the depths of the sea, and if you will precipitate nothing you will give yourself a

draught of fishes more miraculous than his. The fisher of fishes will become a fisher of men. You will bring yourselves as friends around the Apostolic Chair. You will have fished up a Revolution in Tiara and Cope, marching with Cross and banner—a Revolution which needs only to be spurred on a little to put the four quarters of the world on fire.

Those who might feel that it is impossible to take such a document seriously should bear in mind that it was published on the instructions of the Sovereign Pontiff in the hope of preventing the plans of the *Alta Vendita* from reaching fulfilment. It should also be noted that they did not hope to place one of their number upon the papal throne but to secure the election of an idealistic pope inspired by humanitarian ideals whom they would be able to manipulate. The clergy would not resist orders coming to them from the Vatican, no matter how distressing, because they would consider that in obeying they were marching "under the banner of the Apostolic Keys". Archbishop Bugnini may have been banished to Iran and his congregation dissolved, but his new Mass remained, and even as late as May 1976, Pope Paul VI had made it quite clear that he was not willing to repudiate it and urged the faithful to accept it without resistance.[30]

The secret societies which planned to destroy the Church by "reforming" it from within, did not simply want a new Mass, as Bishop Graber makes clear. Everything is to be "new": there will be a "new religion", a "new dogma", a "new priesthood" in which the new priests will be called "progressists", the soutane will be abolished, and marriage introduced.[31] An appeal to sensualism is to be a key weapon: "Create hearts full of vice and you will no longer have any Catholics. This is the corruption on a large scale, which we have undertaken, the corruption of the people by the clergy and that of the clergy by us, the corruption which leads the way to our digging the Church's grave".[32] The prime aim must be to win over the young: "Leave the older and more mature generations aside: go to the youth and if possible to the children". Particular attention must be paid to seminary students and "within a few years this same young clergy will, thanks to the force of events, take over all functions...".[33] To what extent did the secret societies influence Vatican II? Bishop Graber clearly believes their influence to have been considerable without, of course, being able to produce explicit evidence. Even though, as will be shown below, the Council most certainly did not achieve all that some Masons had hoped, Bishop Graber is able to demonstrate that the present orientations in the Church correspond very closely with those at which the strategy of the secret societies had aimed. Should these orientations continue to develop unchecked in their present direction the end result would most certainly be the very goal aimed at by the secret societies. As the case of Archbishop Bugnini proves, it would be stretching coincidence a little too far to insist that the correspondence of what is happening now with what the secret societies have been aiming at is mere chance. And those who will not take the word of Dr. Graber that these were their intentions would do well to read *Humanum Genus*. What Bishop Graber does provide evidence of is the satisfaction expressed by some branches of Masonry at the state of the Church following the Council. An article in *L'Humanisme*, journal of the Grand Orient of France, stated quite openly in 1968:

> Among the pillars which collapsed most easily we note the Magisterium; the infallibility, which was held to be firmly established by the First Vatican Council and which had just had to face being stormed by married people on the occasion of the publication of the encycli-

cal *Humanae Vitae*; the Real Eucharistic Presence, which the Church was able to impose on the medieval masses and which will disappear with the increasing inter-communion and inter-celebration of Catholic priests and Protestant pastors; the hallowed character of the priest, which comes from the institution of the Sacrament of Ordination and which will be replaced by a decision for the priesthood for a trial-period; the differentiation between the direction-giving Church and the black-clad (lower) clergy, whereas from now on the directions will proceed from the base of the pyramid upwards as in any democracy.[34]

In a case of the kind put forward by Dr. Graber no one piece of evidence can be decisive. The strength of the case comes from the cumulative effect of his evidence—and the few brief examples cited here only hint at this. In the interests of objectivity it is important to make it clear that the documents of the Council are regarded as very far from totally satisfactory by some leading Masons. The satisfaction of Grand Orient Masonry at the state of the Church following the Council has just been illustrated. However, Jacques Mitterand, a former Grand Master of the French Grand Orient, finds much to displease him in the finalised documents. He has some good words to say about the progressive attitudes of Pope John and Pope Paul, a heartening contrast with the "reactionary" outlook of Pope Pius XII.[35] But he makes it very clear that he considered Cardinal Ottaviani to have been the arch-villain in the Vatican. This great Cardinal was singled out for particular and often venomous censure by Catholic progressives, Protestants, Communists, and Freemasons. There could certainly be no more impressive tribute to his orthodoxy as the hatred of the world is designated in the Gospels as the mark of a true Christian.

Pope John's Council

Mitterand shows by citations from the documents of Vatican II, the Declaration on Religious Freedom in particular, that the Council came nowhere near to meeting the demands of his particular brand of Masonry. He is particularly incensed at the statement in the declaration that: "The Church is, by the will of Christ, the teacher of the truth. It is her duty to give utterance to, and authoritatively to teach, that Truth which is Christ Himself, and also to declare and confirm by her authority those principles of the moral order which have their origin in human nature itself". Although this particular declaration is far from satisfactory, every Catholic owes a debt of gratitude to the small but dedicated group of Fathers who left no effort unspared to fight for the inclusion of traditional teaching and did all in their power to challenge and amend those sections of the original schema that did not conform with tradition. They achieved far less than they wished, but without their efforts the form that the declaration would have taken does not even bear thinking about.

Mitterand claims, with great indignation, that the particular passage which has just been cited represents the very worst form of triumphalism. He insists that the Church can never have stated in terms so categorical, so definite in their brutality, her imperious claim to impose her own dogmas and underlined the fact that she considers these dogmas to be the sole truth.[36] The chapter in his book entitled "Humanism, the Council and Freemasonry" not only provides a useful corrective to exaggerated claims that the Council surrendered to Naturalism but also proves that at least some powerful Masonic associations remain as bitterly anti-Catholic as ever, and also that their opposition to Catholicism is based on the essential nature of the Church which is incompatible with Masonry. Once again a qualification is necessary, and it is only fair to stress that there is constant and often bitter conflict among the different Masonic associations, particularly the virulently anti-religious Grand Orient variety, espoused by Mitterand, and the religiously orientated Grand Lodge variety found in England with branches throughout the world. There are, however, "schismatic" Grand Lodge branches very much in sympathy with the Grand Orient brand of Masonry. Perhaps the clearest manner of illustrating the nature of Masonry is to compare it with the variety of Protestant sects which, while not united among themselves, are all incompatible with and hostile to Catholicism.

There is a vast literature devoted to the subject of the secret societies. While it would be foolish to ignore the possibility of these societies having exercised an influence during the Council it would be equally foolish to exaggerate its extent. Some Catholics are too inclined to attribute all the ills of the Church to conspirators who have infiltrated her ranks, sometimes Marxist, sometimes Jewish, sometimes Masonic, sometimes a combination of all three. The great danger here is to begin with a theory and then find the facts to prove it while ignoring evidence that points in another direction. St. Pius X warned us that the Church is under attack from internal enemies determined to destroy her from within, but we would be foolish to presume that most or even many of the leading liberals are deliberately conspiring to destroy the Church. Indeed, were they doing so they would hardly make such a spectacle of themselves by making public attacks on Catholic doctrinal and moral teaching at every opportunity. This is not how conspirators behave, as the case of Archbishop Bugnini makes clear. My own experience of the leading Catholic liberals in England has convinced me that most of them are not sinister but silly, not men of intellect and cunning following a pre-arranged plan to destroy the Church, but truly pathetic individuals, men of shallow intellect and weak personality whose one ambition is to appear in line with modern thinking.

Given that there is an organised conspiracy within and against the Church, nothing could be more likely to serve its purposes than the practice of those who interpret every event in the light of an obsessive conspiracy theory and hence create a climate in which an important warning, such as that given by Father Arrupe, can be ridiculed simply for stating that a conspiracy exists. The value of Bishop Graber's book is that he does not overstate his case, and it is one which every Catholic concerned at the decomposition of the Church should study, reading it in conjunction with *Humanum Genus* and *Pascendi*. Pope Paul VI assures us that the present destruction of the Church is self-destruction; St. Pius X warned that this was the intention of the Modernists, whose aims and beliefs approximate so closely with what Dr. Graber has shown to be the strategy of the secret societies. Such men are, as St. Pius X writes,

> the most pernicious of all the adversaries of the Church for, as we have said, they put into operation their designs for her undoing, not from without but from within. Hence the danger is present almost in the very veins and heart of the Church, whose injury is the more certain from the very fact that their knowledge of her is more intimate. Moreover, they lay the axe not to the branches and the shoots, but to the very roots, that is to the faith and its deepest fibers. And once having struck at this root of immortality, they proceed to diffuse poison through the whole tree, so that there is no part of Catholic Truth which they leave untouched, none that they do not strive to corrupt.[37]

The state to which they have reduced the Roman liturgy, the greatest glory of the Church and of Western civilization, bears a heartrending testimony to the efficacy with which these pernicious adversaries do their work.

Footnote. On 8 October 1976, *Le Figaro* published a report stating that Archbishop Bugnini denies that he has ever had any Masonic connections, and in fairness to the Archbishop this denial must be considered when examining the claim that he is a Freemason, which is reported in this chapter and elsewhere in the book. In addition to the public accusation made by Tito Casini in April 1976, in a work sold in Catholic bookshops all over Italy (see Note 26), and not denied until six months later in October, I have made my own investigation and can vouch personally for the authenticity of the following facts. A priest placed what he claimed was documentary evidence proving that Monsignor Bugnini was a Mason into the hands of the Pope himself and warned that if drastic action was not taken he would be bound in conscience to make the facts public. The sequence of events described on pp. 266-68 then followed. I owe this account to a Roman priest of the highest integrity who obtained the facts at first hand from the priest who gave the evidence to the Pope, and I have yet to see any alternative coherent explanation. However, my case against the liturgical reform is not based in any way on Archbishop Bugnini having been a Mason, or even on the existence of a Masonic conspiracy, but solely upon the reform itself and its effects.

Notes

[1] *Pascendi Gregis* (London: Burns & Oates, 1907), pp. 3-4.
[2] *Ibid.*, p. 31.
[3] *Ibid.*, 51.
[4] ACT.
[5] *Pascendi*, pp. 54-55,
[6] Cited in: L. De Poncins, *Freemasonry & the Vatican*, p. 17.
[7] *The Tablet*, 2 October 1965, p. 1081.
[8] *The Tablet*, 30 October 1965, p. 1225.
[9] The full text of *Humanum Genus* is available in *The Kingship of Christ and Organised Naturalism*, by Father D. Fahey. Page numbers refer to this edition. p. 63.
[10] *Ibid.*, p. 56, quoting the *City of God*, Book XIV, Ch. 17.
[11] *Ibid.*

[12] *Ibid.*, p. 76.
[13] *Ibid.*, p. 76.
[14] ACT, p. 31.
[15] *Op. cit.*, note 9, p. 62.
[16] ACT, p. 31.
[17] *Ibid.*, p. 31.
[18] *Ibid.*, p. 32.
[19] *Ibid.*
[20] *Ibid.*, p. 33.
[21] *Ibid.*, pp. 33 & 37.
[22] *Ibid.*, p. 39.
[23] *Ibid.*, p. 34.
[24] *Ibid.*, p. 35.
[25] *The Tablet*, 30 August 1975, p. 828.
[26] *Nel Fumo di Satana* (Florence, 1976), p. 150: "...a conclusione di una Riforma—condotta da un Bugnini che si è infine scoperto per cio che si sospettava: masone".
[27] *Letter to Friends and Benefactors*, No. 10.
[28] Annibale Bugnini, *The Reform of the Liturgy* (Collegeville, Minnesota: The Liturgical Press, 1990), p. 91.
[29] *Grand Orient Freemasonry Unmasked* (London, 1965).
[30] Address to the Consistory of Cardinals, 24 May 1976.
[31] ACT, p. 36.
[32] *Ibid.*, p. 40.
[33] *Ibid.*
[34] *Ibid.*, p. 70.
[35] J. Mitterand, *La Politique des Francs-Maçons* (Paris, 1973), p. 167.
[36] *Ibid.*, pp. 179-180. The passage criticised by Mitterand is found in Abbott, p. 694.
[37] PG, pp. 4-5.

XV

The Enigma of Pope Paul

The Pope is the Vicar of Christ; he is "sweet Christ on earth"; he is our Holy Father; he is the visible head of the Church; to be a member of the Mystical Body of Christ it is essential to be in communion with His Vicar. As it is impossible for the branch to live which is not united to the stem, so to those who are culpably outside the Body of Christ, outside the Church which He has founded, there can be no salvation. But "to some that Church has not been made known, to others she has been made known, but inculpably they have not recognised her for what she is. In their case we may be sure that God will take account of their good faith, of their sincere desire to please God, and will make it so that they receive grace from the life-giving Head. He will take the will for the deed, and those who are in inculpable error will be united 'by desire', though not in fact, to the visible Church of Christ".[1]

As will be shown below, the privilege of infallibility is not a quality inherent in the person of the pontiff but an assistance attached to his office as Pope. Nonetheless, Catholics, and none more so than in the English-speaking world, have in recent centuries manifested an intense loyalty to the person of the Sovereign Pontiff—and understandably so. For Catholics living in predominantly Protestant countries, loyalty to the person of the pope and loyalty to the Church founded by Christ were seen as synonymous, and this attitude was reinforced in the past two centuries by a succession of pontiffs whose wisdom and personal sanctity have made it appear that among the privileges granted by Christ to His Vicar have been those of impeccability and inerrancy. But this is not the case, as Peter's denial of Christ makes clear, to cite only the first and the most obvious example.

The attacks both on papal authority and the person of Pope Paul VI by liberal Catholics, in an unholy alliance with the entire world secular establishment, following his encyclical *Humanae Vitae*, have reinforced the tendency among orthodox Catholics to make the unconditional acceptance and defence of any and every decision of the pope the prime characteristic of a good Catholic. Dietrich von Hildebrand, who was decorated by Pope John Paul II for his services to the Holy See, and was second to no one in his love of and loyalty to the Church, considered it necessary to point out how mistaken this attitude is, this concept of "loyalty towards the Holy Father which is nobly intended, but in which practical decisions of the pope are accepted in the same way as *ex cathedra* definitions, or encyclicals dealing with questions of faith and morals which are always in full harmony with the tradition of the Holy Church and her Magisterium".

> This loyalty is really false and unfounded. It places insoluble problems before the faithful in regard to the history of the Church. In the end this false loyalty can only endanger the true Catholic faith....Obviously a political decision or a disciplinary matter is not a dogma. It may be wise and bring forth fruitful consequences. Or it may be unwise and result in great hardships for the Church and great sufferings for mankind. We must realise that the present-day illusion that Communism has become

"humanitarian-socialism" is an error that has worse consequences than all the combined political errors in the almost two-thousand-year history of the Church.[2]

As Dr. von Hildebrand states, to look upon every decision of the pope as inspired by God and not subject to criticism "places insoluble problems before the faithful in regard to the history of the Church". Those who base their defence of the faith on the axiom that whatever the pope decides must be right would find themselves in a hopelessly indefensible position once they began to study the history of the papacy. They would have to maintain that St. Athanasius was orthodox until Pope Liberius confirmed his excommunication; that this excommunication made his views unorthodox; but that they became orthodox again when Liberius recanted. In other words, there are no standards of objective truth at all; an article of faith becomes true or untrue simply because of the current attitude of the reigning pontiff. Similarly, in the year 896 Pope Stephen VI had the corpse of his predecessor Formosus taken from his tomb, put on "trial", condemned, stripped of his vestments, and then thrown into the Tiber. The dead pope was declared deposed and all his acts annulled, including his ordinations—a somewhat strange act as Pope Stephen VI had been consecrated as a bishop by Formosus! In 897 Pope Theodore II recovered the body of Formosus, had it interred with suitable ceremony in St. Peter's, and declared his ordinations valid. However, Pope Sergius III (904-911) reversed this decision and declared the Formosan ordinations to be null and ordered those ordained by him to be re-ordained.[3]

Without going into the rights or wrongs of the background to this bizarre affair, it makes one thing quite clear—at least some of the popes involved must have been in *error*, and in error on an important matter of discipline. It hardly needs stressing that the validity or otherwise of the Formosan ordinations is quite unconnected with the original deposit of faith and, as Cardinal Manning explains, infallibility "is simply an assistance of the Spirit of Truth, by Whom Christianity was revealed, whereby the head of the Church is enabled to guard the original deposit of revelation, and faithfully declare it in all ages....Whatsoever, therefore, is not contained in this revelation cannot be a matter for divine faith".[4] Cardinal Manning also writes: "Some have thought that by the privilege of infallibility was intended a quality inherent in the person whereby, as an inspired man, he could at any time and on any subject declare the truth. Infallibility is not a quality inherent in any person, but an assistance attached to an office...".[5] He points out that the decree of the First Vatican Council does not teach that the *charisma* of infallibility given to Peter and his successors "is an abiding assistance present always, but only never absent in the discharge of their supreme office. And it further declares the ends for which this assistance is given—the one that the whole flock of Christ on earth may never be misled, the other that the unity of the Church may always be preserved".[6] The decree

> explains and defines what the Council of Florence meant by saying that the Roman pontiff is "the pastor and teacher of all Christians". The definition says that he is so when he speaks *ex cathedra,* and he speaks *ex cathedra* when he defines anything of faith and morals to be held by the Universal Church. The phrase *ex cathedra,* though long used in the theological schools, was for the first time here inserted in a decree of an ecumenical council. Its meaning is plain. "The Scribes and Pharisees sit in Moses' seat", *in cathedra Moysis;* they spoke in his place and with his authority. The *cathedra Petri* is the place and authority of Peter, but the place and the authority means the office. All other acts of the head of the Church outside

of his office are personal, and to them the promise is not attached. All acts, therefore, of the pontiff as a private person, or as a private theologian, or as a local bishop, or as sovereign of a state, and the like, are excluded. They are not acts of the primacy. The primacy is in exercise when the teaching of the Universal Church is the motive and the end, and then only when the matter of the teaching is of faith and morals. In such acts the promise made to Peter is fulfilled, and a divine assistance guides and guards the head of the Church from error. The definition declares that he is then possessed of the infallibility with which Our Saviour willed to endow His Church.[7]

This lengthy introduction to the present chapter may appear to state only the obvious and to be unnecessary. On the contrary, as so many Catholics, and the very best Catholics at that, would be genuinely scandalised at the least criticism of any decision of the pope, it has been essential to show that such a criticism can be justified. The idea that the pope cannot be criticised is a post-Reformation attitude that was certainly not shared by our pre-Reformation ancestors, who did not have the least compunction about making their views with regard to the current pontiff known openly and forcefully. "Let the pope have pity upon holy Church and govern himself before he thinks about distributing grace to others", wrote Langland in the fourteenth century. "And sithen he prayed the pope; haue pite on holicherche, And er he gyue any grace gouerne first hymselue".[8] It is not, therefore, necessary for a distressed but loyal Catholic to say: "This must be good because it is being done with the pope's permission", when he goes to a church where a beautiful altar has been destroyed and replaced by a table on which a priest celebrates a form of Mass from which almost every reference to sacrifice and the real presence has been deleted; during which the priest is officially allowed to improvise in places; and during which a woman distributes Holy Communion into the hands of standing communicants. No, such a Catholic is entitled to use his God-given reason and to say: "This is bad and the pope has done wrong in authorising it".

Integral Humanism

Some Catholics were so distressed at the harmful effects of policies and changes approved by the pope that they devised completely irrational explanations. Caught up in the erroneous notion that any policy approved by a pope must, *ipso facto*, be beneficial to the Church, and yet too honest to evade the fact that some of the policies of Paul VI were manifestly bad, they sought a solution to their dilemma by various theories designed to show that as these policies were clearly harmful it could not have been the pope who approved them. The Pope was thus said to have been drugged and manipulated by enemies of the Church who had infiltrated the Vatican; and another theory is that he had been kidnapped or murdered and replaced by an imposter who wore a rubber mask! Various photographic "evidence" to prove this was produced, contrasting, for example, photographs of the ears of the true Paul VI with those of the substitute. I was given many examples of this "evidence" to convince me that I should endorse the substitute pope theory in my writing.

Once it is accepted that a pope can follow mistaken policies the necessity for such flights of fantasy vanishes. Those who are familiar with the background of Paul VI, while distressed at certain of his attitudes and policies, will not be surprised by them; they will accept them as the sad but predictable result of the philosophy which so influenced him during his most formative years, the philosophy of Integral

The Enigma of Pope Paul

Humanism. Once the nature of this philosophy, and Pope Paul's attachment to it, is appreciated, the events of his pontificate can be examined and explained in their proper perspective.

Integral Humanism is a philosophy which had been gathering momentum since the French Revolution and which, implicitly at least, denied the right of the Church to intervene in the social order; in other words, it represents a denial of the social kingship of Jesus Christ. In an attempt to stem this process Pope Pius XI instituted the feast of Christ the King with his encyclical *Quas Primas* in 1925. Hamish Fraser has written an important study on the significance of this encyclical and the nature and history of Integral Humanism, together with its influence on Pope Paul VI.[9] Much of what follows here is based upon his study, to which full acknowledgement is given.

In *Quas Primas*, Pope Pius XI protested at the fact that "The empire of Christ over all nations was rejected. The right which the Church has from Christ Himself to teach mankind, to make laws, to govern peoples in all that pertains to their salvation, that right was denied". He insists that "not only private individuals but also rulers and princes are bound to give public honour to and obedience to Christ...for His kingly dignity demands that the state should take account of the commandments of God and of Christian principles, both in making laws and in administering justice, and also in providing for the young a sound moral education". But civil governments, in Catholic as well as non-Catholic countries, were insisting that while the Church was entitled to legislate for its own members it had no right to demand that the state should conform its legislation to the law of God. This principle had also come to be accepted, on a practical level at least, by an increasing number of Catholics, including national hierarchies. A striking exception was the magnificent campaign initiated by the German hierarchy which resulted in Hitler withdrawing his euthanasia law. A recent and contrary example was the scandalous refusal of the English and Welsh hierarchy to lead the faithful in an all-out campaign to fight the abortion legislation which had resulted in the murder of six million unborn children by 2004.

The denial, even if only implicit, of Christ's social kingship was but one manifestation of the gradual retreat from the position in which the City of God stood out against the City of Man, and claimed the right to rule, to the position in which the City of God came to terms with the City of Man and tried to influence it. In practical terms, this involved the acceptance not simply of the autonomy of the City of Man but of the subjugation to it of the City of God. The Church must take her place on equal terms with other religions and philosophies within a world which she had a duty not to command but to serve. Catholics would work with any and every other group to build a just and humane society; they would remain faithful to the teaching of the Church and would act as a leaven to society and in doing so attract others to the Church, at least so the theory went. This attitude was given concrete manifestation in a number of Catholic social philosophies and movements which flourished at the end of the nineteenth and the beginning of the twentieth century—and which were rightly condemned as they were based on an untenable thesis which invariably resulted in a rejection of the true nature of the Church, no matter how vigorously and how sincerely the proponents of these movements denied the charge. The philosophy of Integral Humanism is in the direct tradition of such condemned movements as those of Lamennais or Marc Sangnier and his Sillon movement. This is explained in Appendix VI.

Integral Humanism first saw the light of day in a series of six lectures which Jacques Maritain delivered at the University of Santander in August 1934. Maritain had been a man of the "Right" up to 1926, but after the suppression of

The Enigma of Pope Paul

Action Française, which he had supported, he moved to the opposite end of the political spectrum and identified himself with a group based upon the extreme left-wing review *Esprit*, founded and edited by Emmanuel Mounier. From 1932 onwards *Esprit* had advocated collaboration with unbelievers, a policy which Maritain first opposed but then endorsed. In Mounier's perspective, the Church could not hope to regain her former status except by becoming involved in the social and economic revolution. "The duty of the priest", he said, "is to contribute towards the building of a socialist world". Moreover, he considered the Marxist movement very close to Christianity. "There is an historical Communism whose greatness we acknowledge and to whose message we listen. Communism is the bearer of part of the kingdom of God".

Maritain was in sympathy with much of what Mounier was seeking to achieve. But by formulating Integral Humanism he gave the *Esprit* group what in effect was a veritable theology of the incarnation of Christianity through the acceptance of democratic and revolutionary values and temporal involvement in their support. In this perspective, the "Left" was regarded as a living historical force. It was on the side of the masses that truth was to be sought. This state in Maritain's evolution was reached with the publication of *Christianisme et Démocratie* in 1945.

One of the most illuminating appraisals of Maritain's Integral Humanism is to be found in Jules Meinvielle's *De Lammenais à Maritain*.[10] After showing that Integral Humanism expressed anew, and in "Christian" terms, the ideas of those who had long sought to reconcile the Church's doctrine with the mind of the world, Father Meinvielle points out that what was novel in Maritain's contribution was his Thomistic reputation and the undoubted philosophic brilliance which enabled him to defend theses, which had previously been advanced by the enemies of religion, without appearing directly to contradict the teaching of the Church.

"The way in which Maritain intended to conciliate the Church with the modern world was", writes Father Paul Crane:

> through love, the dynamic of the new society, which Maritain saw as a world civilization in which men would be reconciled with each other in a brotherhood of justice, love, and peace. Despite diversity of religious beliefs, to which they could remain faithful without detriment to the final goal, men could be drawn in conscience and impelled by love to seek unity in the democratic achievement of universal brotherhood.[11]

Similarly, H. Le Caron, writing in *Le Courrier de Rome*, explains:

> The Integral Humanism of Maritain...is a universal fraternity of men of good will belonging to different religions or none (including even those who reject the idea of the Creator). It is within this fraternity that the Church should exercise a leavening influence without imposing itself and without demanding that it be recognised as the one true Church. The cement of this fraternity is the virtue of doing good, and understanding grounded in respect for human dignity.[12]

The same writer also points out that:

> This idea of universal fraternity is neither original nor new. It was already advanced by the philosophers of the eighteenth century and by the Revolutionaries of 1789. It is also the fraternity beloved of Freemasonry, and even of the Marxists. What distinguished Maritain's

Integral Humanism is the role it allocated to the Church. Within this "Universal Fraternity" the Church is to be the "Inspiratrice" or "Big Sister". And it goes without saying that for the "Big Sister" to win the sympathy of her "Little Brother" she must be neither intransigent nor authoritarian. She must know how to make religion acceptable. And so that the truths of faith and morality may be acceptable, Christianity must be practical rather than dogmatic.

When Maritain's *Humanisme Intégral* first appeared in 1936 it was the subject of a most perceptive review by Louis Salleron. Professor Salleron exposed the defects in Maritain's system, its internal contradictions, and the inevitable result should its principles be pursued to their logical conclusion. The complete text of this review is available as Appendix VII.

Pope Paul VI and Integral Humanism

Integral Humanism provided precisely the philosophic and theological justification sought for by those who wished to conciliate the Church with the modern world— and it needs to be stressed that in most cases this desire was inspired by the sincere belief that it was in the best interests both of the Church and of the world. Maritain's book *Integral Humanism* made a tremendous impact upon Catholic intellectuals throughout Europe despite its conflict with the insistence of Pope Pius XI that the duty of a Catholic was not to reconcile the Church with the world, but to make the world accept Christian terms of reference and think with the mind of the Church. One young Italian priest who was particularly impressed with Maritain's book was Giovanni Battista Montini. He had been born in 1897. His father was a Catholic journalist, outstanding for his courageous opposition to liberalism. Giovanni Montini was a delicate child, and when he manifested a vocation to the priesthood he was allowed to study at home instead of training in a seminary. As a university chaplain in Rome, he showed great courage in leading his students in their defence of Catholic principles against the fascism of Mussolini. He was so impressed by Maritain's book that he translated it into Italian himself, and he remained a devoted admirer of the French philosopher until his death. By this time Maritain was aghast at the spectacle of the Church not just kneeling but grovelling at the feet of the world. Before his death he wrote *The Peasant of the Garonne*, a scathing indictment of the trends now predominating in the Church, trends which, ironically, derive in no small measure from his own teachings. Maritain, of course, had never accepted the logical implications of Integral Humanism, which, if taken to their conclusion, must result in a denial of the divine nature of the Church and of her founder—for if Christ is God and the Church speaks with His voice, then she has a right to demand, as Pope Pius XI insisted, "that not only private individuals but also rulers and princes are bound to give public honour and obedience to Christ".

"Pope Paul was indeed a disciple of Jacques Maritain", writes Hamish Fraser,

> so much so that when one reads a typically Pauline socio-political allocution, one might well be reading Maritain. But Pope Paul is also like Maritain in his refusal to accept the logical implications of Integral Humanism...For even if his social ideology is completely at variance with that of all his predecessors—and of this there is no doubt whatsoever—like Maritain, Pope Paul has the faith of Peter. It is this which explains why the Council prompted Maritain to write *The Peasant of the Garonne* and why

The Enigma of Pope Paul

Pope Paul found it necessary to write *Mysterium Fidei*, the *Credo of the People of God*, and *Humanae Vitae*.[13]

The apparent enigma of Pope Paul can thus be understood within the context of his acceptance of Integral Humanism and the nature of the assistance given to a pope in the exercise of the papal *office*, as explained by Cardinal Manning earlier in this chapter. When he taught the entire Church, *ex cathedra Petri*, he repeated and defended the traditional teaching. When he decided upon practical policies, ranging from his Ostpolitik to liturgical reform, the influence of Integral Humanism was only too apparent.

A prime characteristic of Integral Humanism is its essentially optimistic bias—its exponents would term this a "positive attitude". It is based on the assumption that all men are basically good at heart, seeking the truth, and willing to co-operate for the common good. A theme of Michael Novak's book *The Open Church* is an optimistic picture of an "open Church" and an "open society" co-operating together in "the unrestricted drive to understand, and the quest for insight.[14] He has no time for the image of the Church as the embattled City of God fighting off the assaults of a hostile world, or what the Americanists termed the "fortress Church".

Vatican II was concerned not with condemnation, but with dialogue. This was made clear by Paul VI in his address to the Council on its closing day, 7 December 1965:

> Yes, the Church of the Council has been concerned, not just with herself and with her relationship of union with God, but with man—man as he really is today: living man, man all wrapped up in himself, man who makes himself not only the centre of his every interest but dares to claim that he is the principle and explanation of all reality. Every perceptible element in man, every one of

the countless guises in which he appears, has, in a sense, been displayed in full view of the Council Fathers, who, in their turn, are mere men, and yet all of them are pastors and brothers whose position accordingly fills them with solicitude and love. Among these guises we may cite man as the tragic actor of his own plays; man as the superman of yesterday and today, ever frail, unreal, selfish, and savage; man unhappy with himself as he laughs and cries; man the versatile actor ready to perform any part; man the narrow devotee of nothing but scientific reality; man as he is, a creature who thinks and loves and toils and is always waiting for something, the "growing son" (Gen. 49:22); man sacred because of the innocence of his childhood, because of the mystery of his poverty, because of the dedication of his suffering; man as an individual and man in society; man who lives in the glories of the past and dreams of those of the future; man the sinner and man the saint; and so on.

Secular humanism, revealing itself in its horrible reality, anticlerical, has, in a certain sense, defied the Council. The religion of the God Who became man has met the religion (for such it is) of man who makes himself God. And what happened? Was there a clash, a battle, a condemnation? There could have been, but there was none. The old story of the Samaritan has been the model of the spirituality of the Council. A feeling of boundless sympathy has permeated the whole of it. The attention of our Council has been absorbed by the discovery of human needs (and these needs grow in proportion to the greatness which the son of the earth claims for himself). But we call upon those who term themselves modern humanists, and who have renounced the transcendent value of the highest realities, to give the Council credit at least for one quality and to recognise our own new type of humanism: we, too, in fact, we more than any others, honour mankind.

And what aspect of humanity has this august senate studied? What goal under divine inspiration did it set for itself? It also dwelt upon humanity's ever twofold facet, namely, man's wretchedness and his greatness, his profound weakness—which is undeniable and cannot be cured by himself—and the good that survives in him which is ever marked by a hidden beauty and an invincible serenity. But one must realise that this Council which exposed itself to human judgement, insisted very much more upon this pleasant side of man, rather than on his unpleasant one. Its attitude was very much and deliberately optimistic. A wave of affection and admiration flowed from the Council over the modern world of humanity. Errors were condemned, indeed, because charity demanded this no less than did truth, but for the persons themselves there was only warning, respect and love. Instead of depressing diagnoses, encouraging remedies; instead of direful prognostics, messages of trust issued from the Council to the present-day world. The modern world's values were not only respected but honoured, its efforts approved, its aspirations purified and blessed.

Hamish Fraser, who was second to none in his knowledge of the forces ranged against the Church, assessed correctly that the error and weakness of both Vatican II and Pope Paul VI lie in their failure to appreciate the threat to the Church from the various revolutionary forces at work in the world today.[15] Robert McAfee Brown, a Protestant observer at the Council, was invited to add a commentary to the Pastoral Constitution on the Church in the Modern World in the Abbott translation. He echoes Hamish Fraser's disquiet at the apparent failure of the Council—this constitution in particular—to appreciate the extent and hostility of the forces ranged against the Church in this world:

> The document minimises the degree to which the Gospel is also a scandal and a stumbling-block, by which men can be offended as well as uplifted. (At a number of the press conferences in Rome, one could detect a desire on the part of the defenders of the schema to explain controversial portions in such a way that they would not seem 'offensive'.) The making of common cause with others must not be achieved at the price of blunting the uniqueness and distinctiveness of the Christian message.[16]

The making "of common cause with others" is, of course, the basis of Integral Humanism. The fact that the Council reduced itself to the extent of deserving such a reproach from a Protestant minister must surely be one of those "signs of the times" for which we are exhorted to be on the lookout. Charles Davis, an English *peritus* who left the Church and married, has recounted the point at which the Council was steered into the crucial change of direction which was to commit it to the policy of dialogue and making common cause with the world, in place of the traditional policy of confrontation. As the first session drew to an end, he informs us, there was great anxiety (presumably among the liberals) at the lack of real progress, but all this was changed on 4 December 1962 when Cardinal Suenens made his notable intervention:

> The unifying theme for the Council's work should be the Church. But the theme demanded a double development. First, the Church *ad intra*—the Church turned inwards upon itself to gain a new self-awareness. Second, the Church *ad extra*—the Church moving outwards

to make known its response to the problems confronting the world today. Among the problems mentioned by the cardinal were the dignity of the human person, responsible parenthood, social justice, peace and war. As the light of the nations, the Church, he asserted, must enter into dialogue with the world. The next day Cardinal Montini declared his support for Cardinal Suenens's programme.[17]

Father D. A. Campion, S.J., in his commentary on *Gaudium et Spes* in the Abbott translation, described the "making of common cause with others" as "a tendency to accentuate the positive in a realistic appraisal of trends and movements at work today in the City of Man".[18] The question at issue is just how "realistic" this appraisal really is. *Gaudium et Spes* is pervaded by the notion that all men are basically men of good will, seeking the truth and anxious to do good. Far from the notion of a conflict between the City of God and the City of Man (as set forth, for example, in the opening paragraph of Pope Leo XIII's *Humanum Genus*), this constitution envisages a future in which the two cities work together for the common good of mankind:

> While rejecting atheism, root and branch, the Church sincerely professes that all men, believers and unbelievers alike, ought to work for the rightful betterment of this world in which we all live alike. Such an ideal cannot be realised, however, apart from sincere and prudent dialogue. Hence the Church protests against the distinction which some state authorities unjustly make between believer and unbelievers, thereby ignoring fundamental rights of the human person. The Church calls for the active liberty of believers to build up in this world God's temple too. She courteously invites atheists to examine the Gospel of Christ with an open mind.[19]

It is hardly being cynical to speculate on the amusement with which this courteous invitation would have been received, if it had ever been received, in the guardrooms of the Gulag Archipelago or the garrisons of Hungary and Czechoslovakia!

The constitution also states that: "The Church further recognises that worthy elements are found in today's social movements, especially an evolution towards unity, a process of wholesome socialization and of association in civic and economic realms".[20] And again, "Christians, on pilgrimage towards the heavenly city, should seek and savour the things which are above. This duty in no way decreases, but rather increases, the weight of their obligation to work with all men constructing a more human world".[21]

Father Paul Crane, S.J., has pointed out that "in essence, there are, in the last analysis, two ideologies in this world— that which sees heaven as man's goal, and that which sees the be-all and end-all of his existence as here on this earth".[22] He shows that since the French Revolution a line of truly realistic popes had spared no effort to fight an increasingly powerful movement within the Church which has been pressing her continually to devote her principal efforts towards building up the earthly kingdom in co-operation with the City of Man. While there are statements in *Gaudium et Spes* which insist that the heavenly kingdom is still the primary goal of the Church, it is beyond dispute that the document displays a pervasive and obsessive preoccupation with the earthly kingdom. If the amount of print devoted to the former and the latter is compared, the contrast is both startling and depressing. It is replete with the spirit of Integral Humanism and Sillonism.

Despite Dr. McAfee Brown's reservations concerning *Gaudium et Spes*, he is generally favourable and remarks: "The critic who is still unconvinced that the document ushers in a new era is invited to compare it with an earlier Catholic treatment of the same issues—the Syllabus of Errors—and see if he does not emerge from the comparison rejoicing".[23]

The final condemned proposition contained in the Syllabus is that: "The Roman pontiff can, and ought to, reconcile himself, and come to terms with progress, liberalism, and modern civilization". It is worth studying *Gaudium et Spes* specifically with a view to seeing how far it has gone towards achieving the very aims condemned in the Syllabus. Before doing so one will need, as Father Bryan Houghton warns, "a sufficient supply of antisoporifics".[24] Dr. Johnson is reputed to have said that *Paradise Lost* is a poem to be read and then put aside. Those who undertake the task of slogging their way through *Gaudium et Spes* are likely to put it aside long before it has been read.

It would not be unfair to claim that Pope Paul made his supreme attempt to reconcile himself with modern civilization during his visit to the United Nations in October 1965. In his address to the General Assembly Pope Paul offered, on behalf of the Catholic Church, a totally uncritical, even adulatory, endorsement of this organisation. It is not my purpose here to discuss the merits and faults of UNO. During his speech before the General Assembly on 5 October 1965, Pope Paul, speaking in French, informed the delegates that he came bearing "a message for all mankind". The first part of this message "was a solemn moral ratification of this august institution". The Pope claimed that "the peoples turn to the United Nations as their last hope for peace and concord (*l'ultime espoir de la concorde et de la paix*): we make bold to bring with us their tribute of honour and hope, as well as our own". The conclusion of his message was, he said, concerned with the future:

> It is wholly concerned with the future. The structure which you have built must never fall into ruins: it must be perfected and adapted to the exigencies which the

history of the world presents. You mark a stage in the development of humanity; henceforth it is impossible to draw back, you must advance....We are tempted to say that your distinguishing characteristic reflects to a certain extent in the temporal order what our Catholic Church wishes to be in the spiritual order; unique and universal. It is impossible to imagine anything higher on the natural plane in the ideological structure of humanity.[25]

Henri Fesquet interpreted this speech as nothing less than a public endorsement of the principles of Integral Humanism, as what he terms "The recognition of humanity come of age" (*reconnaissance d'une humanité adulte*). Fesquet writes:

> Paul VI is conscious of the fact that contemporary humanity no longer looks to the altar or to the Vatican for its stability but to secular structures. Paul VI at UNO constitutes a recognition of the fact that the temporal powers, having come of age, have earned their independence vis-à-vis the Church: that humanity is now sufficiently adult to construct a natural morality which is not centred explicitly upon religion. Humanity today neither is nor believes itself to be religious, but it has faith in itself. This faith, though wholly secular, was, in a way, baptised by Paul VI.[26]

It is interesting to note that the Abbé de Nantes interpreted the Pope's speech to UNO in very similar terms to Henri Fesquet, although it goes without saying that while Fesquet approved the Abbé did not. The latter went as far as condemning as blasphemous and absurd the suggestion that the UNO could by any stretch of the imagination be said to reflect in the temporal order the role of the Church in the spiritual realm. "If one can speak about a temporal

The Enigma of Pope Paul

extension of the Gospel", he wrote, "then this must refer to a civilization based on Christianity, as is found in the Catholic nations, where Christ is the centre and the social order is indeed an extension of the Church, a work of grace and faith—and not to that hotbed of Masonry, the United Nations".[27] As a statement of principle it is hard to imagine any possible grounds upon which the Abbé de Nantes could be refuted, although on a factual level he would find it hard to point out many nominally Catholic countries in which the social order could truly be said to be based upon Christ.

Having cited the Abbé de Nantes it is necessary to make some reference to his *Liber Accusationis in Paulum Sextum*. The very serious accusations which he made against Pope Paul VI, the tone in which he made them, and above all certain inescapable inferences which emerged from his case, certainly scandalised many traditionalist Catholics. The Abbé's *Liber* is, however, an historic document of considerable importance, and nothing will be gained by ignoring its existence. The only serious attempt to face up to the implications of the *Liber* which has appeared in English so far has been by Hamish Fraser.[28] It is a study which should be read in conjunction with the *Liber*. He does not dispute the factual basis of the Abbé's case. When the Abbé de Nantes claims that the Pope has said something or done something it will be found that he has said or done what the Abbé alleges. When the Abbé claims that these words and actions have harmed the Church, or conflict with the words and actions of Pope Paul's predecessors, it will generally be found that such judgements are correct. But the Abbé frequently weakens his case by putting it in language which is manifestly lacking in the filial respect towards the Sovereign Pontiff, which he professes and, above all, when he speculates upon the motives of Pope Paul. It is in the best Catholic tradition to interpret the motives even of those with whom we disagree in the best possible light. Only too often the Abbé followed a contrary policy, even to the point of suggesting that Pope Paul was maliciously attempting to destroy the Church, and that he could be Antichrist upon the papal throne.

Pope Paul VI and Communism

Hamish Fraser remarked that: "Although for the last decade Rome has been resolutely opposed to anti-Communism, this does not mean that the Holy Father is pro-Communist".[29] There is a very important distinction here; the fact that Pope Paul VI completely reversed the militantly anti-Communist policy of Pope Pius XII did not mean that he approved of Communism in any way. He believed, in accordance with his philosophy of Integral Humanism, that more would be gained by a dialogue and, where possible, co-operation, with Communism than by a policy of confrontation. In a speech made in the first year of his pontificate he warned that the "subversive and anti-religious character (of Communism) continues to be entirely unchanged".[30] But on a practical level, because he was not prepared to give an anti-Communist lead to Catholics, the benefit to Communism was as great as if he had, in fact, been pro-Communist. Communists could well reverse the biblical text and state that "He who is not against me is for me".

While Pope Paul was certainly not pro-Communist his political sympathies were certainly far more towards the left than those of Pope Pius XII. Monsignor Montini had been dismissed by Pope Pius from his position as Pro-Secretary of State and created Archbishop of Milan. The Archbishop of Milan is invariably a cardinal, but no cardinal's hat was bestowed upon Archbishop Montini. According to the biography of Pope Paul published by the English Catholic Truth Society, "There was speculation that he (Pope Pius) thought Monsignor Montini's political sympathies were too far to

The Enigma of Pope Paul

the left to make him suitable as pope".³¹ Bishop William Adrian wrote that Pope Pius XII had become "wary of the liberal social and political experiments urged upon him by Monsignor Montini".³²

Michael Novak remembered a speech made by Archbishop Montini of Milan during the Second World Congress of the Lay Apostolate held in Rome in 1957. One section which Novak found particularly impressive ran: "We shall love our time, our civilization, our technical science, our art, our sport, our world. We shall love striving to understand, to have compassion, to esteem, to serve, to suffer. We shall love with Christ's heart".³³ In an assessment of Archbishop Montini's term of office in Milan, based largely upon a biography by Monsignor J. G. Clancy, Novak comments:

> In Milan he was frequently indecisive. Having expressed a solid, perceptive comment he was likely to add: "Other bishops look at it differently; maybe I'm wrong". He seemed to be still afraid, and when he did move it was as likely to be in fits and starts, at random. Beautiful plans were laid, but accomplishments were not great. Little by little, his paper *L'Italia* moved from right to left. But as late as June, 1960, he addressed a letter to his priests warning them that the new "opening to the left" in Italian politics was unsafe, dangerous, and offered with "insufficient guarantees".³⁴

By 1961, *L'Italia* had "moved far enough left to invite stinging letters from more than two-score parish priests in the archdiocese, who therewith cancelled their subscriptions to their own diocesan newspaper".³⁵

When he made his opening speech to the second session of the Council, the empty places of some bishops living in Communist countries, who had been refused permission to attend the Council, made it impossible for the Pope not to

Pope John's Council

be aware that there had been no real change in the nature of Communism. He referred to this fact in very strong terms, even though he did not actually use the word "Communist".

> We ought to be realists, not hiding the savagery that from many areas reaches even into this universal Synod. Can we be blind and not notice that many seats in this assembly are vacant? Where are your brethren from nations in which the Church is opposed, and in what conditions does religion exist in these territories? At such a reminder our thoughts are grieved because of what we know and even more because of what we cannot know about our sacred Hierarchy, our religious men and women, our countless children subjected to fear, to persecutions, to privations, to oppression because of their loyalty to Christ and to the Church.[36]

Michael Novak was somewhat distressed by these remarks as Pope Paul "seemed to be departing from the peaceful, optimistic ways of Pope John".[37] What mattered for Novak is not to be realistic but to be optimistic. Unfortunately, and only too characteristically, while Pope Paul stated that we "ought to be realists", on a practical level he followed his policy of dialogue—even to the extent of sacrificing Cardinal Mindszenty to placate Russia's Hungarian puppets, an incident which is documented in Chapter XIII. By 1975 the Pope had become so alarmed at the advances made by Communism in Italy that he made the following speech:

> Christianity sometimes seems to be overwhelmed by the longing for, and by the power of, a more effective, impetuous and revolutionary form of idea with which modern social life is being promoted today: a form that is independent, in fact polemical with regard to the so-

cial life derived from the Gospel. Christ, according to this view, is beaten by Marx. The ideal human society, it is said in spite of us, cannot be the result of love but of struggle, violence, and the defeat of one class by another: this is allegedly the desirable goal. It is unnecessary for us to say any more now, when the contemporary historical scene offers us, even too plainly, the elements of judgement that are in question. We would have easy arguments to bring forward in the discussion in defence of the Gospel, inviting people to reflect how the system opposed to that which we profess, because it is Christian and because it is really human, presupposes a violation of the principle of real social life. This latter must be human for all and respectful of the deep prerogatives of man, his dignity, his freedom, his equality. The aforesaid system, on the contrary, is based on hatred and systematic struggle; it is based on collective selfishness as a remedy for the selfishness of the individual or of a group. It seems to ignore the complementary nature of free social functions and to repudiate, as a normal formula of social life, orderly participation in both economic and cultural and political processes. Basically it refuses united collaboration for a common, just prosperity. It therefore gradually disregards spiritual coefficients, necessary though they are for the life of a free, orderly community, and replaces them with rigid public norms, tending to be impersonal and conservative.[38]

Even in this speech there are disturbing phrases, despite its realistic admission that co-existence between Catholicism and Communism is not possible. The Pope's principal objection to Communism here is not that it cannot be reconciled with the Truth of the Gospel, but that Communists are not respecting the rules for peaceful co-existence and collaboration for the common good. As was made clear in

Chapter XIII, Communists have never made any secret of the fact that for them dialogue, co-existence, or common action with believers is simply a means to an end. Countless Catholic spokesmen, popes included, have also warned that this was so—and yet Pope Paul seemed genuinely astonished that this really was the case. As a result of his reversal of the anti-Communist policy of his predecessors, the Catholic Church, the only viable ideological bulwark against Communism, has been effectively neutralised. If Pope Paul had devoted the rest of his pontificate to an all-out political crusade against Communism there is little likelihood that it would have had much, if any, effect. And should the Communists ever achieve power in Italy, a very different kind of dialogue will follow, as Solzhenitsyn warned in an address given in New York on 9 July 1975:

> In the Soviet Union this dialogue was a simple matter: they used machine guns and revolvers. And today, in Portugal, unarmed Catholics are stoned by the Communists. This happens today. This is dialogue....And when the French and Italian Communists say that they are going to have a dialogue, let them only achieve power and we shall see what this dialogue will look like.
> When I travelled in Italy this past April I was amazed to see hammers and sickles painted on the doors of churches, insults to priests scrawled on the doors of their houses. In general, offensive Communist graffiti covers the walls of Italian cities. This is today, at a time before they have achieved power.
> This is today....Just let them reach power in Italy and we shall see what the dialogue will look like then.[39]

It must also be noted that there are a number of instances in which Pope Paul's policies in the international field have been far from neutral. His attitude to the Communist ag-

The Enigma of Pope Paul

gressors in Vietnam was, to put it mildly, hardly calculated to advance the causes of Christianity or freedom. Nor was his fierce attack upon the Spanish government for executing five terrorists who had been murdering policemen—making a total of eight executions in Spain in the previous fourteen years. The chorus of condemnation launched against Spain for these executions, in September 1975, made horrifyingly clear the extent to which all the Christian denominations are now furthering the interests of the Revolution on a practical level—however much they may still deplore it in principle. "In Europe you would have thought that Franco was executing five of Our Lord's twelve apostles for the sin of going about the world preaching faith, hope and charity", wrote William F. Buckley.[40] Although the Pope made a token condemnation of terrorism during his address to an hundred thousand pilgrims gathered in St. Peter's Square for the canonisation of a Spanish saint, most of his indignation was reserved for the Spanish government whose action was described as "a homicidal repression". He added that in "this sad hour we raise a special prayer to the Lord, the God of pity and of pardon, that He may welcome the souls of the poor dead men and comfort their saddened relatives".[41] I did not notice any reference to the souls of the poor dead policemen or of their saddened relatives in the Pope's speech.

This speech gave even greater cause for unease when his failure to condemn the never-ending series of Communist crimes against humanity is considered; not to mention some of the unspeakable acts of terrorism perpetrated by the so-called liberation movements in Africa.

Pope Paul VI died on 6 August 1978 and, not surprisingly, received fulsome tributes from conservative Catholics throughout the world, in some cases giving the impression that he was the greatest pope in history. In the United States *The Wanderer* published page after page of glowing tributes, one headline reading: "A Truly Great Pontificate". What was surprising was the fact that unlike any of his predecessors he received a public tribute from the Communist Party. It read:

> THE COMMUNISTS OF ROME
> AND OF ITS PROVINCE
> Express their sorrow and condolences
> For the death of
> PAUL VI
> Bishop of Rome
> And remembering him
> Not only for his passionate involvement
> and the great humanity
> With which he worked for peace
> and the progress of peoples,
> to improve dialogue,
> comprehension and possible accords
> between men of different beliefs and ideals
> but also for the constant attention
> which he revealed for the moral
> and material improvement of Rome.
>
> Roman Federation
> of the Italian Communist Party

The Yugoslav dictator, President Tito, paid a tribute to the Pope which was published in *Politika*, Belgrade's leading Communist daily. According to the London *Universe* (25 August 1978):

> In a special message President Tito spoke of Pope Paul as a convinced partisan of peace and understanding between different peoples. "Pope Paul", says President Tito, "undertook a continual combat for international

co-operation in equality and peace. His conception of a world without war in which problems of racial discrimination, famine and under-development...must be rapidly solved, was of considerable support to the efforts of the international community".

Any comment on this tribute would be superfluous.

Pope Paul VI and Modernism

As previous chapters have shown, the Pope most certainly intervened on the side of orthodoxy on many occasions during the Council. The fact that he did this even though his personal sympathies clearly lay with the liberals is yet another example of Christ acting through His Vicar in the manner explained by Cardinal Manning. Unfortunately, as has also been made clear in previous chapters, his interventions were not always as effective as they might have been due both to the determination of the hard-core liberals to get their way in the face of opposition and of his own lack of determination in enforcing the implementation of his own amendments. To quote just one more example, the Pope sent fourteen amendments (*modi*) to be incorporated in the document on bishops. The members of the commission concerned asked the Pope whether he was ordering them to incorporate his amendments or simply proposing that they should. He replied that it was a proposition—the commission then decided to accept only three of the amendments and reject the remaining eleven.[42]

Mention has also been made in other chapters of Pope Paul's totally orthodox encyclicals which earned him the hatred of the liberals. After the Council, particularly during his Wednesday allocutions, he made endless condemnations of neo-Modernism in its innumerable manifestations—but in practice took no effective measures to implement orthodoxy. Just as he warned against the "opening to the left", but allowed his own paper to turn into a left-wing organ, so he warned about false notions of original sin, the Virgin Birth, or the Resurrection, but allowed notorious modernists who were teaching the heresies he condemned to continue in office as approved teachers of Catholic doctrine. The case of Hans Küng was particularly notorious.

Pope Paul had the Dutch Catechism examined by a commission of cardinals who showed that it was quite incompatible with the Catholic faith, but instead of ordering its withdrawal, and having everyone connected with it removed from their official positions, he allowed it to be published with a supplement, which no one needed to read, correcting some of its most glaring deficiencies. He provided a masterly analysis of the reasons why Communion should be received in the mouth, made it clear that he wished this practice to be retained, but allowed any hierarchy that wished to introduce Communion in the hand. Cardinal Heenan wrote:

> The Pope may be badly advised and physically weak, but he contrives to make his voice clearly heard and more often than not he displays a deep anxiety. Constantly he returns to the theme of erroneous teaching of theology. Unfortunately, his condemnations are made in general terms. Since nobody knows what theologians are being condemned it is impossible for bishops to take any action.[43]

The one dramatic and alarming exception to this policy was Pope Paul's intervention in the campaign against Archbishop Lefebvre. To all appearances the Pope had given public support to the campaign initiated by the French hierarchy against a saintly prelate whose sole crime was that of being orthodox and founding a seminary which was a

The Enigma of Pope Paul

living reproach to the chaos not simply in the few remaining French seminaries but in the French Church as a whole. Finally, on this particular topic, it is impossible not to note that, at the time when Modernism was flourishing in the Church as never before, Pope Paul abolished the anti-Modernist oath and the Index of forbidden books.

Pope Paul VI and Protestantism

Pope Paul's attitude to Protestants was exactly what would have been expected from a proponent of Integral Humanism: Protestantism must not be condemned as error but seen as a subject for dialogue. Despite all the setbacks and trials which followed the Council, despite the fact that he had wept from time to time, that he had lamented the fact that the smoke of Satan had entered the Church, that the Church was undergoing a process of self-destruction, Pope Paul did not abandon his basically optimistic outlook—for optimism is the basis of Integral Humanism. During a general audience in July 1974 he remarked:

> We have certainly heard of the severity of the saints with regard to the evils of the world. The reading of ascetic books on the overall negative judgement of earthly corruption is still familiar to many. It is certain, however, that we are now living in a different spiritual atmosphere, invited as we are, especially by the recent Council, to an optimistic vision of the modern world, its values, and its achievements. We can look with love and sympathy at humanity studying, working, suffering and progressing; in fact we are ourselves invited to foster the civil development of our times, as citizens who wish to join in the common effort for better and more widespread prosperity for everyone. The now famous Constitution *Gaudium*

et Spes entirely confirms us in what may be called this new spiritual attitude.[44]

Hamish Fraser noted that the old tradition which the Pope claims has now been replaced by the vision of Vatican II is endorsed not simply in pre-conciliar ascetic books but in many passages of the New Testament. "If the world hates you, know yet that it hath hated me before you. If you had been of the world the world would love its own; but because you are not of the world but I have chosen you out of the world, therefore the world hateth you" (Jn. 15:18-19).[45]

Just as it would be wrong to suggest that the Pope was pro-Communist in any way, although his policies served the purposes of Communism, it would be equally wrong to suggest that his theological views are in any way tainted by the Protestant heresy. Should this be the case, in view of such encyclicals as *Mysterium Fidei* and *Humanae Vitae*, in view of his *Credo* and of the innumerable totally orthodox discourses which he delivered frequently, it would mean that he was deliberately using his position to deceive the faithful and destroy the Church. There is no need to resort to so improbable an hypothesis when his attitude to Protestantism is considered in the light of his optimistic Integral Humanism. While rejecting Protestantism on a theoretical level, on a practical level he was willing to dialogue and collaborate with Protestant sects and treat them as if they were on equal terms with the Catholic Church. The disastrous effects of false ecumenism have been fully discussed in earlier chapters, and it would be dishonest to try to gloss over the fact that the Pope, more than any single individual, must accept responsibility for this situation. When Dr. Ramsey visited Rome the Pope treated him as if he really were an archbishop rather than a member of a Protestant sect which, where its own ordinal has been relied upon, has neither priests nor bishops. The only valid orders in the Church of

The Enigma of Pope Paul

England are possessed by apostate Catholic priests or by those whose confidence in their own denomination is so low that they have had themselves ordained by bishops of the Old Catholic Church using the Old Catholic Ordinal. The argument that some Anglican ministers have valid orders because Old Catholic bishops have taken part in their ordination, or because they have been ordained by Anglican bishops with Old Catholic orders, is quite invalid if the Anglican Ordinal was used. As Pope Leo XIII makes clear in *Apostolicae Curae*, the intention of the Anglican ordination rite is defective and as such cannot be used validly even by a lawful minister with the correct intention.[46] Valid orders would not be conferred even if Catholic bishops used the Anglican Ordinal.

Thus in presenting Dr. Ramsey with his own episcopal ring, and inviting him to bless the crowds outside St. Peter's, the clear impression was given, not least to Dr. Ramsey, that he really was an archbishop and the Primate of all England, successor of St. Augustine. Unfortunately, the Pope had a definite predilection for such impulsive and rather extravagant gestures, kissing the feet of the Metropolitan Meliton at the end of 1975, for example. Doubtlessly, he considers them examples of fraternal charity without realising the harm they do to the integrity of the faith. More seriously, he has referred to the Church of England as a "sister Church"—a phrase which has been seized on joyfully not simply by Anglicans but by Catholic ecumenists.[47]

Now this phrase is quite indefensible. It is legitimate to refer to Protestants as separated brethren—every child who is baptised is baptised into the Catholic Church and remains a Catholic until, after reaching the age of reason, he freely accepts the heretical tenets of the denomination to which his parents belong. Such children then become at least material heretics and/or schismatics without, of course, being in the least blameworthy. But the phrase "sister Church" is quite another matter. An individual baptised Christian who accepts the teachings of a heretical sect is a brother who has separated himself—but it is not possible for a group of Christians to separate themselves from the unity of the one, true, and indivisible Church and claim that they then constitute a Church. Sisters are children of the same parent with equal status and equal rights—but the Catholic Church and the Church of England are not children of the same parent, branches of the one Church. There is only one Church, the Church founded by Christ upon Peter, and those who reject communion with Peter cannot claim to be members of the Church of Christ whose Vicar Peter was, and whose successor Pope Paul was. In order to confirm this I obtained the advice of Monsignor Philip Flanagan, former rector of the Scots' College in Rome and a very reputable theologian. He answered that:

> The words "sister Churches" can only be legitimately used with regard to the Patriarchates in communion with Rome, and with regard to dioceses of which bishops belong to the Catholic Church. Each diocese is regarded as a "Church". On our bishop's anniversary we pray for him as the Bishop of the Church of his diocese. To describe the Church of England as a "sister Church" is an illustration of the use of diplomatic language which obscures the hard realities of the situation, is self-defeating, and brings upon the Church a reputation for equivocation.

When Paul VI made this remark he was not, of course, speaking *ex cathedra Petri*, and so, as the explanation given by Cardinal Manning earlier in the chapter makes clear, was not protected from error. On 30 June 2000 the Congregation for the Doctrine of the Faith published a document condemning the use of the phrase "sister Church" with regard

The Enigma of Pope Paul

to the Anglican Communion and restricting its use with regard to the Orthodox Church to individual dioceses which can be described as sister churches of Catholic churches (that is to say, dioceses—see pages 406ff.). The CDF makes it clear that the Catholic Church and the Orthodox as such are not, and must not be described as, sister Churches. The relevant section of the text reads as follows:

> Rome, 30 June 2000
>
> Your Eminence (Your Excellency):
>
> In recent years, the attention of this Congregation has been directed to problems arising from the use of the phrase "sister Churches", an expression which appears in important documents of the Magisterium, but which has also been employed in other writings, and in the discussions connected with the dialogue between the Catholic Church and the Orthodox Churches. It is an expression that has become part of the common vocabulary to indicate the objective bond between the Church of Rome and Orthodox Churches.
>
> Unfortunately, in certain publications and in the writings of some theologians involved in ecumenical dialogue, it has recently become common to use this expression to indicate the Catholic Church on the one hand and the Orthodox Church on the other, leading people to think that in fact the one Church of Christ does not exist, but may be re-established through the reconciliation of the two sister Churches. In addition, the same expression has been applied improperly by some to the relationship between the Catholic Church on the one hand, and the Anglican Communion and non-Catholic ecclesial communities on the other. In this sense, a "theology of sister Churches" or an "ecclesiology of sister

Churches" is spoken of, characterised by ambiguity and discontinuity with respect to the correct original meaning of the expression as found in the documents of the Magisterium.[48]

It is interesting to speculate on whether Cardinal Ratzinger was aware of the fact that Pope Paul VI had used the expression which his congregation condemned.

Pope Paul's keen interest in Protestantism, the Church of England in particular, began long before his election to the papal throne. Archdeacon Pawley, an Anglican observer at Vatican II, reveals that while still working in the Secretariat of State in 1949, Monsignor Montini manifested considerable interest in Anglicanism. He was visited by the Rev. L. Prestige, an Anglican cleric, who recorded that Monsignor Montini was anxious for further contacts. "Considerable discussion ensued as to whether such contacts should be made in England alone, or on the continent".[49] The continent was decided upon, and this was a common feature of "ecumenical dialogues" between Catholics and Anglicans stretching back to the eighteenth century—well-documented in Archdeacon Pawley's book. These dialogues were undertaken by continental Catholics, usually French, over the heads of their counterparts in England and were normally characterised by an almost total ignorance of the true nature of Anglicanism by these continental Catholics. This tended to give rise to the raising of false hopes, frequent disillusion, and an unjust reputation accorded to the Catholic authorities in Britain of being bitterly anti-Anglican. Archdeacon Pawley explains that:

> The Roman Catholic hierarchy in England would have shown itself distinctly resentful of any relations with Rome that were not channelled through itself. There was therefore no alternative at that stage to the development

The Enigma of Pope Paul

of relations and contacts by surreptitious means. And this opportunity Bishop George Bell exploited actively through several decades.[50]

The true reason for the lack of enthusiasm for such dialogue among English Catholics was that they understood the Church of England. Many of them were converts and realised the pointlessness of the type of dialogue being undertaken, not to mention that it manifested a blatant disregard for the authoritatively expressed wishes of the popes. The key fact which Catholics living among Anglicans appreciated is that there is really no such thing as Anglicanism. There are as many versions of Anglicanism as there are Anglican ministers. It would be impossible to find a doctrine which one held and which another did not contradict. (Catholics cannot comment upon this with any smugness as this is now increasingly the case among our own clergy.) In a most realistic, though very unecumenical comment—since he was not a Christian he did not need to be ecumenical—George Bernard Shaw wrote: "The Anglican Church is bound by a set of hopelessly contradictory articles which, as one of its greatest men has observed, can be subscribed to only by fools, bigots, or liars....The other sects are all over the shop intellectually".[51]

Monsignor Montini added his name to the list of continental priests who undertook discussions with Anglicans. He was visited by the Anglican bishop George Bell in 1955, and, according to Bishop Bell, complained that "although the Holy Father had often urged collaboration between Catholics and the separated brethren, he had never indicated how this should be done...". Bishop Bell compared Monsignor Montini's attitude to that of "a curate being discreetly critical of his vicar".[52] In the following year:

Pope John's Council

> Archbishop Montini received at Milan a delegation (arranged by Bishop Bell) of four Anglican priests and a layman who stayed with him some ten days....The archbishop was clearly trying to build up for himself a picture of other Christians on the basis of what they said about themselves....Though the meetings were clandestine in the extreme, they were 'leaked' to a few people in England at least, where those who heard about them were glad to learn of a new type of ecumenical encounter *'ultra montes'*.[53]

Given the truth of the assessment of Pope Paul's "optimistic" vision of the world which has been made in this chapter, it is fair to assume that the picture he formed of Anglicanism must have been favourable in the extreme. Quite naturally, the impression he made upon the Anglican authorities was equally favourable, so much so that upon the death of Pope John he became their most favoured candidate.

> Of all the possible choices (and there might have been many who could have done considerable harm to the Council—to the extent of abrupt closure, which would have been canonical) Montini was the most favoured candidate from the Anglican point of view....The new Pope was familiar with Anglican ways and aspirations, had visited England, and was known to be more liberal in his attitudes than Pope John.[54]

Pope Paul also "had far more conception of the problems of Christian unity than Pope John ever had".[55]

During the first session of the Council, the Protestant observers felt that "this shy, quiet, thoughtful, intelligent little man was quite definitely 'on our side'".[56] Although Pope John was much loved by Protestants for his personal qualities, they felt that his theological outlook left a lot to be desired: "Pope John, either through mistaken judgement of individual men, or because of failure to appreciate the nature of the questions involved, appointed to the membership of the preparatory commissions lists of men who were largely of known conservative sympathies, unqualified to handle the widespread demands for reform".[57] Prominent among these conservatives was, of course, Archbishop Marcel Lefebvre.

Dr. McAfee Brown, like other Protestant observers, regretted the fact that Pope John had not included an expression of contrition for the Catholic part in the "sin of division" when he made his opening speech to the Council. Hans Küng had suggested such an act, but Pope John had not followed his advice. An important distinction must be made here. It would be dishonest to deny that at the time of the Reformation the life of the clergy in some parts of Europe, not least in Rome, was such that good and sincere Catholics felt bound to protest. St. Thomas More was an inveterate opponent of clerical corruption. Others, and not surprisingly, asked themselves whether what they belonged to could really be the Church of Christ. Had these men remained within the Church and worked for the reform of these abuses they would have merited the term "reformers". However, those who did break with the Church did so not because of scandal but because they had concocted new doctrine. They broke away from the Mystical Body and set up heretical and schismatic sects of their own. There is, therefore, no basis whatsoever for an apology by the Catholic Church for the sin of schism when this sin was entirely on the Protestant side. No Catholic, by definition, can ever be in schism or guilty of the sin of schism. Be that as it may, the Protestants required an apology and an apology was duly offered in Pope Paul's opening speech to the second session:

> If we are in any way to blame for that separation we humbly beg God's forgiveness. And we beg pardon too of our brethren who feel themselves to have been injured by us. For our part, we willingly forgive the injuries which the Catholic Church has suffered, and forget the grief endured during the long series of dissensions and separations.[58]

Dr. McAfee Brown considers this step to have been of "monumental" importance, a real "breakthrough", not so much because of its inclusion in this particular speech, but because it resulted in the implementation of a Protestant desire to see such an apology included in the Decree on Ecumenism. "As a result of the pope's statement, the document that had originally omitted a statement of Catholic responsibility for the sins of division was criticised precisely for the omission".[59] These criticisms resulted in the fact that "the promulgated document has three explicit references to Catholic responsibility for the sins of division".[60] The most important of these, for Dr. McAfee Brown, is the admission of deficiencies in the formulation of doctrine, which must be rectified at the proper moment. "This statement opens up a host of possibilities for reform for it means that Pope John's distinction between the 'sacred deposit' of faith and ways of expressing that faith, as well as the strictures of Pope Paul and Cardinal Léger against 'theological immobilism', have been given conciliar approval".[61]

Bishop Moorman recounts with some embarrassment that:

> A year later, at the British Council of Churches' conference at Nottingham, an attempt was made to send a similar message to Rome, thanking the Pope and the Council for what they had done, and reciprocating the charitable and forgiving words which had been spoken. I

The Enigma of Pope Paul

regret to say that this suggestion was turned down, with acclamation from some members of the assembly.[62]

In the same opening speech the Pope explained that the principle concern of the second session would be to explain the intimate nature of the Church in a manner which would "merit the attentive consideration of our separated brethren also, and which, as We ardently hope, may make the path towards common agreement easier".[63]

It would, of course, be unjust and untrue to suggest that all Pope Paul's actions were pleasing to Protestants—more than enough has been written in previous chapters to prove how completely false such a suggestion would be. His interventions to have certain documents improved in the interests of orthodoxy won him applause neither from the observers, the liberal Fathers, nor the *periti*. Dr. McAfee Brown has remarked on the complexity of the Pope's character and his apparently contradictory behaviour:

> During the Council it was difficult to assess Pope Paul. Was he a "progressive" going slowly, or a "conservative" going fast, or something entirely different? His opening allocution, as noted above, gave nothing but joy to the progressives. Yet at the end of the third session he seemed to many to have retreated almost in panic from the implications of conciliar reform and to have become either the captive of, or the leader of, the voice of conservatism. On the eve of the fourth session he issued an encyclical on the eucharist, *Mysterium Fidei*, that seemed to most interpreters to be at best a backward-looking document and at the worst a repudiation of many of the creative insights of the already promulgated Constitution on the Sacred Liturgy. And yet Pope Paul emerged at the end of the fourth session as pope of the Church that did in fact enact the major items of legislation that

its critics had been fearful it would not enact. The decree on religious freedom, to take only one example, is now a fact, and one of the reasons it is a fact and not a bitter, unfulfilled memory is that Pope Paul resisted conservative pressures exerted on him, to the very final hours of the Council, to scuttle the document.[64]

The encyclical *Mysterium Fidei* was, to quote Bishop Moorman, "disappointing to those who felt that the Council was really trying to break away from medieval scholasticism and Tridentine theology and speak to the modern world in language which it could understand".[65] Gregory Baum commented: "Since Pope Paul's terminology is so different from the Constitution on the Liturgy, it is not easy to fit his encyclical harmoniously into the conciliar teaching of Vatican II".[66] Pope Paul was known in Italy as the "Hamlet Pope"—and Dr. McAfee Brown notes that two distinct sides of his personality continued to manifest themselves after the Council:

> On such matters as the condemnation of the American presence in Vietnam, Pope Paul has been prophetic far beyond others within the Catholic hierarchy, as his encyclical *Christi Matri Rosarii* (1966) demonstrated. His important encyclical on world development, *Populorum Progressio* (1967), was advanced enough to be described by the *Wall Street Journal* as "warmed-over Marxism". Yet on internal ecclesiastical matters, Paul has evinced increasing concern and apprehension about new theological currents, liturgical experimentation, initiatives taken by national episcopal conferences, and so forth. His *Credo*, a statement of Catholic faith for today, issued just before the fourth assembly of the World Council of Churches at Uppsala in July 1968, was dismissed even by some Catholic commentators as no more than a bold step

The Enigma of Pope Paul

into the fourteenth century. But the crowning enigma, and possible tragedy, of his pontificate was the encyclical *Humanae Vitae*, issued on July 29, 1968, which denied to Catholic couples the right to use artificial means of birth control, reversing the clear trends visible at Vatican II and in the reports of three post-conciliar papal advisory commissions. The irony of this encyclical is that the intent of the encyclical was clearly to invoke papal authority to settle a vexing moral problem for Catholics, and yet the result of the encyclical was to place that papal authority in greater jeopardy than it has ever been before, since many thinking Catholics have found it impossible in conscience to follow the papal teaching.[67]

One act of the Pope which won particular praise from the observers was the joint service held in St. Paul's Without the Walls on 4 December 1965. This joint-service "was entirely the Pope's idea", writes Bishop Moorman. It went far beyond anything the observers had hoped for:

> Common prayer, or *communicatio in sacris*, has always been regarded as a distant goal; but, before the Council ended, we had joined in a great act of worship in which the observers had been invited to play their part....Nothing of this kind had ever happened before, and by no means all the Council Fathers approved of it. After all, if, for many years, you have been teaching the faithful that it is sinful to worship with schismatics, it is a bit disconcerting if the Holy Father invites you to do this very thing. There were, therefore, some empty seats in the church on this occasion. Cardinal Döpfner, Archbishop of Munich, told me afterwards that he had found this service the most impressive moment in the whole Council. He certainly looked as if he was enjoying *"Nun danket alle Gott"*.[68]

Bishop Moorman's touch of irony brings up a most important point. There can be no doubt that in a number of respects Pope Paul was permitting changes which were not a development but a reversal of the policies of his predecessors. Common worship was forbidden under pain of grave sin by Canon 1258, and the standard manuals of moral theology provided explanations of why this was so, explanations deriving from the very nature of Christ's Church. While it can be argued that this is essentially a matter of discipline it can hardly be denied that doctrine was involved. To allow Catholics to participate in the services of, or in joint services with, members of schismatic or heretical sects is equivalent, on a practical level at least, to accepting the erroneous formula that one religion is as good as another. Previous popes had warned that nothing but indifferentism could spring from *communicatio in sacris*, and events have proved them right. Once again it is a question of ignoring objective standards—for something which is gravely sinful one moment to become meritorious the next implies that the acceptance or rejection of the claims of Christ's Church is, in itself, a morally neutral matter. And *communicatio in sacris* is by no means an isolated instance. Archbishop Lefebvre has listed a series of very authoritative papal pronouncements on such topics as Liberalism, Masonry, and religious liberty which, he insists, are now being totally contradicted.[69] Henri Fesquet provides ample evidence to substantiate this claim.[70]

It would be wrong to pass over the fact that the Pope's sympathy for, and desire to conciliate, almost any group outside the Church, and any group such as charismatics on the theological left of the Church, was not matched by any similar expression of concern for Catholic traditionalists. There are those who argue that he was forced into policies he did not approve of by his immediate entourage and that such traditionalists as Archbishop Lefebvre were kept from him by the same people. But statements purporting to have come from the Pope himself have denied this, and, in any case, it is impossible to believe that he did not know of the suffering to souls and the harm to the purity of doctrine resulting from such changes as those in the liturgy, which have been made to conciliate Protestants—as the third book in this series will make clear. Not one word of sympathy for traditional Catholics nor one concession to their requests came from the Pope during the entire Holy Year of Reconciliation. It is a hard thing to say, but he showed more public concern for the fate of the five Spanish terrorists executed in September 1975 than he showed during the whole of his pontificate for millions of anguished traditionalists. And yet it is precisely these same traditionalists, the rejected children of the Holy Father, who would remain most faithful and most loyal to him. If a verdict is to be passed upon the acceptability of Pope Paul and his policies to Protestants, it can surely best be provided by Protestants themselves. They are the best judges of the extent to which their demands are being met.

Despite the conciliar interventions, despite *Mysterium Fidei*, the *Credo of the People of God*, despite *Humanae Vitae*, Archdeacon Pawley is able to pass a favourable verdict upon the changes which have taken place within the Catholic Church "since the Vatican Council—some directly as a consequence of it, some originating in other causes. First among such changes are those which have been initiated by the Pope himself, and they are so many and so extensive as to entitle Paul VI to be thought of as the greatest reformer of the Roman Catholic Church since Hildebrand (Gregory VII 1073-1085)".[71] It may well be true to state that Pope Paul VI enacted reforms on as great if not a greater scale than Pope Gregory VII—but there is a difference in the fruits of these reforms upon which it is hardly necessary to comment. It can hardly be denied that his policies and reforms, although not intended to do so, actually helped the enemies of the

Church. The tribute of the Communist Party of Rome on his death on 6 August 1978 has already been cited. A tribute from the World Council of Churches on 7 August 1978 included the following:

> We recall with special gratitude the visit of His Holiness to Geneva in 1969 and the keen interest he showed in all our activities...the foundation has been laid for a new and lasting communion among all Christian Churches. The openness towards other Churches so strongly desired by the Second Vatican Council and expressed in the Decree on Ecumenism has become an irreversible reality. Pope Paul VI constantly sought to promote and deepen the understanding among the Churches; this was evinced by his great enthusiasm for the establishment of a joint working group between the Roman Catholic Church and the World Council of Churches....Pope Paul VI understood his ministry as an instrument in the service of peace in the world and indefatigably recalled the duty of the Church and indeed of every member of the Church to contribute to overcoming the menace of war. He encouraged a more vigorous witness to justice for the poor and the oppressed. The encyclical *Populorum Progressio* found a strong echo in the hearts of all Christians concerned with the destructive forces of injustice....His pontificate will be remembered as the period in which many Roman Catholic Christians have discovered new perspectives of witness and action in the life of society.

Oscar Cullmann, the noted Swiss theologian, summed up the Protestant verdict on Vatican II as follows: "The hopes of Protestants for Vatican II have not only been fulfilled, but the Council's achievements have gone far beyond what was believed possible".[72]

The Enigma of Pope Paul

A Masonic Tribute

Perhaps the most scandalous of all the tributes paid to Paul VI appeared in the Italian Masonic journal *Rivista Massonica* (No. V, Vol. LXIX-XIII *della nuova seria*). It published a tribute to Pope Paul VI which included the following:

> For other people it [the death Paul VI] is the death of a pope, an event which is proverbially rare, but which still happens at a distance of years and decades. For us it is the death of him who has put an end to the condemnation of Clement XII and of his successors. For the first time in the history of modern Masonry, the head of the largest religion in the West dies not in a state of hostility towards Freemasons (*non in stato di ostilita coi Massoni*). And for the first time in history the Freemasons can pay homage to the sepulchre of a pope without ambiguity or contradiction.

A Church in Ruins

Professor Georg May, Professor of Canon Law at the University of Mainz, and one of Germany's most respected theologians, gave the following assessment of the pontificate of Pope Paul VI in a lecture given to Una Voce Germany and published in the 30 June 1980 issue of *The Remnant*. There can be no plausible case for disagreeing with professor May's assessment:

> The pontificate of Paul VI was, as a whole, and aside from a few decisions and deeds, disastrous for the Catholic Church. He brought about and saw to it that there advanced in the Church and succeeded to positions of power those forces which paralysed and undermined it.

In all of history I know of no pope in whose reign such an unheard-of collapse from purely internal causes was to be seen as under the pontificate of Montini. Paul VI left his successors a frightful legacy: a Church in ruins.

Notes

1. TCC, p. 71.
2. *Satan at Work*, p. 45.
3. *The Popes* (London, 1964), pp. 159-162.
4. TSVC, p. 180.
5. *Ibid.*, p. 179.
6. *Ibid.*, pp. 182-183.
7. *Ibid.*, pp. 186-187.
8. *Piers the Plowman*, Passus V, 1, 51.
9. *Approaches*, Numbers 47-48, February 1976.
10. Available only in French and Spanish from CLC, 49 rue des Renaudes, Paris, 75017.
11. *Christian Order*, December 1973, p. 743.
12. *Courrier de Rome*, 15 October 1975.
13. *Approaches*, Numbers 47-48, p. 9.
14. OC, p. 361.
15. *The Abbé de Nantes Investigated* (*Approaches* supplement), p. 16.
16. Abbott, p. 315.
17. *The Tablet*, 8 January 1966, p. 33.
18. Abbott, p. 185.
19. *Ibid.*, pp. 219-220.
20. *Ibid.*, pp. 241-242.
21. *Ibid.*, p. 262.
22. *Christian Order*, December 1973, p. 736.
23. Abbott, p. 310.
24. *Christian Order*, June 1975, p. 736.
25. JC, pp. 925-936
26. *Ibid.*, p. 961
27. *Liber Accusationis in Paulum Sextum*, p. 17.
28. *The Abbé de Nantes Investigated.*
29. *Approaches*, Numbers 47-48, p. 27.
30. *Ibid.*
31. *Pope Paul VI*, Douglas Woodruff (London: CTS, 1974), p. 4.
32. *How Did It Happen?*, p. 5.
33. OC, p. 32.
34. *Ibid.*, p. 33.
35. *Ibid.*
36. *Ibid.*, p. 84.
37. *Ibid.*
38. *L'Osservatore Romano* (English edition), 27 November 1975, p. 1.
39. *Approaches*, Numbers 47-48, p. 30.
40. *The Enquirer*, 8 October 1975.
41. *The Catholic Herald*, 3 October 1975.
42. JC, p. 921.
43. *The Tablet*, 18 May 1968, p. 488.
44. *L'Osservatore Romano*, 11 July 1974.
45. *The Abbé de Nantes Investigated.*
46. This point has been made very clear by Father de la Taille, S.J.

He explains that in the making or production (confection) of a sacrament, the ministerial intention is concerned only with the application of a form complete in itself to matter which is of itself sufficient. "One thing, however, the ministerial intention can never do: it can never confer on the form a signification which the form does not possess. In other words, should the signification of the form itself be in any way deficient, the intention of the minister will not supply this deficiency". *The Mystery of Faith*, Book II (London, 1950), pp. 455-456.
47 *The Tablet*, 14 February 1976, p. 153.
48 This document and other documents of the Congregation for the Doctrine of the Faith can be found on the Vatican Website under the heading Congregation for the Doctrine of the Faith, Doctrinal Documents.
49 RCFC, p. 322.
50 *Ibid.*, p. 320.
51 "Provocations" in *G. K.'s Weekly*, 21 March 1935.
52 RCFC, p. 327.
53 *Ibid.*, p. 327-328.
54 *Ibid.*, p. 347.
55 VO, p. 32.
56 *Ibid.*, p. 60.
57 RCFC, p. 337.
58 ER, p. 110.
59 *Ibid.*, p. 111.
60 *Ibid.*, p. 112.
61 *Ibid.*, p. 114.
62 VO, p. 69.
63 OC, p. 80.
64 ER, pp. 171-172.
65 VO, p. 157.
66 *Herder Correspondence*, 1965, p. 359.
67 ER, pp. 172-173.
68 VO, pp. 30-31.
69 *Letter to Friends and Benefactors*, No. 9.
70 JC, pp. 343, p. 477, 478, 485.
71 RCFC, p. 357.
72 XR-IV, p. 256.

XVI

Planting the Time Bombs

The story of how the first four preparatory schemata were thrown into the wastepaper basket for the crime of failing to please Father Schillebeeckx was told in Chapter V. In his critique of the preparatory schemata, circulated in the name of the Dutch hierarchy, there was praise only for the fifth schema—the one on the liturgy. This was described as "an admirable piece of work".[1] Charles Davis, an English *peritus* who has since married and left the Church, also found little to please him in the preparatory schemata. He explains that there was a widespread lack of confidence in the seventy preparatory schemata with a total of nearly three thousand pages. The only one he had a good word for was the one on the liturgy, "which fortunately was substantially satisfactory".[2] By an interesting coincidence, the schema which Fathers Schillebeeckx and Davis found so pleasing was substantially the work of Father Annibale Bugnini in a commission dominated by Rhine Group bishops and *periti* and, Father Wiltgen tells us, "as a result, they had succeeded in inserting their ideas in the schema and gaining approval for what they considered a very acceptable document".[3]

As a result of the election described in Chapter IV, the Rhine Group secured an immediate majority on the Conciliar Liturgical Commission.[4] Even the solitary Asian representative obtained his place through the patronage of the Rhine Group as he had received his formal liturgical training from two of its members.[5] In an introduction to the Liturgy Constitution in the Abbott edition, Father C. J. McNaspy, S.J., remarks: "Father A. Bugnini, who had been secretary to the commission set up by Pope Pius XII, was happily made secretary of the commission".[6] Father McNaspy did not mention the fact that before the Council opened, Father Bugnini was dismissed from this post by Pope John XXIII, an action this most tolerant of popes would not have taken without very good reason.[7]

Xavier Rynne, in the best liberal tradition, is full of praise for his fellow liberals:

> The "model" liturgy commission deserves all the credit possible for the commendable way in which it handled the details of steering the measure through. It was fortunate in having such vigorous progressives as Cardinal Lercaro and Archbishop Hallinan of Atlanta among its members, and in being ably supported by a large number of equally forward-looking experts including Father Frederick McManus of Catholic University, Washington, D.C., and Godfrey Diekmann of the Benedictine Abbey at Collegeville, Minnesota...the French liturgist Father Mortimort gave biblical credit to the six men who had insisted on the extensive reforms called for by the majority of Council Fathers and rejected by the standpatters in the commission, saying: "Three there are who give testimony in heaven: Bishops Hallinan, Jenny, and Martin; and three there are who give testimony on earth: Fathers Wagner, McManus, and Mortimort". Thus neatly distinguishing between the bishops who did the voting and the experts who prepared the texts (cf. 1 John 5:7-8).[8]

Archbishop Hallinan was equally fulsome in his praise of the commission of which he was a member. The *periti* assigned to it represented, he claimed, probably the finest minds in the world today in terms of research, hard work, zeal, experimentation, and—to make sure he had neglected no aspect of their manifold talents—of "everything else"! The entire commission "has been open, it has been free, and it has certainly consisted of a group of dedicated men". Open? Certainly; to views and policies acceptable to the Rhine Group. Free? Certainly; free to implement policies acceptable to the Rhine Group. Dedicated? Certainly; but dedicated to what? The Archbishop took particular pleasure in the fact that the work done by the Liturgical Commission "was a real step toward the *aggiornamento*. This naturally is a cause of confidence and satisfaction to us all".[9]

The type of reform aimed for by the liberals was explained during the debate by a German-born missionary-bishop named Duschak. He wished for an "ecumenical Mass" which should be stripped of what he termed "historical accretions". He wished for the rite, form, language and gestures to be accommodated to the modern age. The Mass should be said aloud, in the vernacular, and facing the people. Bishop Duschak admitted that none of these ideas originated with the people whom he served, but he was sure that if put into practice they would eventually accept them.[10] In a book written *before* the Council, Archdeacon Pawley, who was to be an Anglican observer, mentioned the type of change he would like to see and which, from hints which had been dropped, he thought quite likely to be implemented. These were:

> (1) a demand for great concessions in the use of the vernacular, even that the whole Mass may be said in it; (2) the introduction in some form and in some circumstances of concelebration, large numbers of priests gathered

at, say, a clerical conference, and able to enjoy together the benefits of a single Mass instead of having to celebrate separately; (3) the abolition of the introduction to the Mass, the *Judica me, Deus*, and the "Last Gospel"; and (4) Communion for the faithful in both kinds.[11]

It is worth repeating that this was written *before* the Council had assembled! It hardly needs pointing out how closely the suggestions made by Bishop Duschak and Archbishop Pawley coincide not simply with the liturgical policies of the Protestant Reformers, but with those enunciated by the Masonic spokesmen cited in Chapter XIV. They also accord very closely with the suggestions for liturgical reform proposed by the Jansenist Synod of Pistoia in 1786, and condemned by Pope Pius VI in the Bull *Auctorem Fidei* of 1794.[12] The demand for the liturgy to be adapted to different ages and different peoples is one of the Modernist propositions condemned by St. Pius X in *Pascendi Gregis*. He explains that the Modernist concept of the evolution of worship—and for the Modernist everything must be continually evolving—"consists in the need of accommodation to the manner and customs of peoples, as well as the need of availing itself of the value which certain acts have acquired by usage".[13] Dom Prosper Guéranger was possibly the greatest of all liturgists, and in his book *Liturgical Institutions*, which appeared in 1840, he described what he termed as the "anti-liturgical heresy", certain characteristics of which are common to all those who have tried to undermine the Catholic faith by liturgical change. The type of change suggested by Bishop Duschak, which has been implemented throughout the Roman rite since the Council, has a great deal in common with this "anti-liturgical heresy"—as will be made clear in a synopsis of the relevant chapter in Dom Guéranger's book which is provided as Appendix VIII.

The progressive case was argued in the debates by such cardinals as Frings, Döpfner, Lercaro, and, during the first session, Cardinal Montini. Any drastic changes in the structure or language of the Mass were opposed by such conservatives as Cardinals Ottaviani, Browne, Godfrey, Bacci, McIntyre, and Spellman, and such prelates as Archbishop Dante, Papal Master of Ceremonies, McQuaid, and Castro Mayer. Cardinal Godfrey, Cardinal Heenan's predecessor as Archbishop of Westminster, is deserving of special mention. He was far more conservative than Cardinal Heenan and not only made his views known but insisted on their being complied with. Had he not died in the winter following the first session but remained to supervise the implementation of the conciliar decrees he would certainly have interpreted them strictly according to the letter of the Council rather than its alleged "spirit". While, as this book has made clear, Cardinal Heenan was well able to analyse a situation and detect what was wrong, he tended to lack firmness in ensuring that it was put right. Cardinal Godfrey "viewed the Vatican Council with great misgiving, and when his auxiliary, Bishop Cashman, asked his leave to return to England, he told him to stay 'because I need your *non placets*' ("No" votes)".[14]

The question of Latin became a kind of shibboleth separating conservatives and liberals. Cardinal Spellman wanted the entire Mass as then celebrated in the Roman rite to be retained intact. Cardinal Godfrey wanted the importance given to Latin increased.[15] Cardinal Siri warned that it is dangerous to multiply rites as this left the door open to abuses and constituted a threat to unity. Even the liberal Cardinal Montini was opposed to those parts of the Mass pertaining to the priest in his capacity as celebrant (now known as the "presidential prayers") ever being said in the vernacular. "When it is a matter of the language used in public worship", he said, "think seriously before you decide that those parts of the liturgy which belong to the priest as such should be in any other language than that handed down to us by our forebears; for only thus will the unity of the Mystical Body at prayer and the accuracy of sacred formularies be maintained".[16] The Bishop of Leeds, in a broadcast over Vatican radio, urged "that no violent change be wantonly made which would cut the Catholic people off from the immense heritage bound up with the Roman liturgy. When you talk about the liturgy of the Mass, the actions, gestures, words, you are touching the most sensitive and vibrant nerve in the Catholic religion. We shall have to go very carefully if we do make changes. So much of our personal life is bound up with the Mass, and with the Mass as we know it".[17]

An argument upon which the liberals set great store, and which they have used frequently since the Council, is that as the Last Supper was a vernacular celebration the Mass should be the same. Liberal accounts of the Council give pre-eminence to a speech by Maximos IV Saigh, Patriarch of Antioch. "It was also in Aramaic that He (Christ) offered the first sacrifice of the Eucharist, in a language understood by all the people who heard Him".[18] For all their much vaunted Biblical scholarship it seems that there are at least some liberals who are unaware that a major part of the Paschal liturgy was celebrated in Hebrew, a language that was no more comprehensible to the ordinary Jew in the time of Our Lord than is Latin to a contemporary Frenchman. This is a fact which can be confirmed by referring to any competent exegete—not excluding Protestants.[19] Hebrew was also used extensively in the synagogue service—in point of fact Our Lord never attended a wholly vernacular service in His life: "...the Essene texts have shown us how much Hebrew was in use as a *lingua sacra*".[20] Hebrew is still used as a liturgical language in Jewish worship. It is also worth noting that, as He died, Our Lord was praying in a liturgical language— "*Eli, Eli, lamma sabacthani?*"—the first words of Psalm 21, "not a cry of despair but, on the contrary, a hymn of supreme confidence in God despite profound suffering".[21] As St. Matthew makes clear, some of the bystanders did not understand Him and thought that He was calling upon Elias (Matt. 44:47).

Xavier Rynne concedes that probably the majority of Western prelates thought that they were only authorising the vernacular for the catechetical or dialogue portion at the beginning of the Mass while the principal parts would remain in Latin.[22] Indeed, the Fathers were assured that this would be the case and it was on this understanding that many of them voted for the constitution. Father Clifford Howell, probably England's best known liberal liturgist, has gone as far as admitting that "it is known that the Council did not intend to include the presidential prayers within the meaning of the phrase *partes ad populum spectantes* (parts which pertain to the people)". It was for the "reading and prayers of the faithful and also, as local conditions may warrant, for those items of the liturgy which pertain to the people" that an optional concession allowing the use of the vernacular was granted in Article 54. The priest's (presidential) prayers were excluded from the terms of Article 54. "Those who drew up the constitution thought it wiser to make this exception as a concession to conservative opinion".[23] But, as the next chapter will make clear, the constitution did not explicitly state that the priest's prayers, including the Canon, could *not* be said in the vernacular. Cardinal Heenan testifies that when the Fathers voted for the constitution they did not foresee "that Latin would virtually disappear from Catholic churches".[24] He further states that in the debate on the liturgy the bishops were given the opportunity of discussing "only general principles. Subsequent changes were more radical than those intended by Pope John and the bishops who passed the decree on the liturgy. His sermon at the end of the first session shows that Pope John did not suspect what was being planned by the liturgical experts".[25]

Archbishop R. J. Dwyer, writing of the euphoric spirit of the Fathers on the day they voted in favour of the constitution by 2,147 votes to 4, comments with the sadness and wisdom of hindsight: "Who dreamed on that day that within a few years, far less than a decade, the Latin past of the Church would be all but expunged, that it would be reduced to a memory fading in the middle distance? The thought of it would have horrified us, but it seemed so far beyond the realm of the possible as to be ridiculous. So we laughed it off".[26]

Sufficient has now been written on this particular point to justify a claim that the Council Fathers were tricked on at least this one particular point and that, for example, the vernacular Canon constitutes a gross violation of their wishes. One prelate, who fulfilled important functions during the Council, has expressed himself very strongly on this matter: "I regret having voted in favour of the Council constitution in whose name (but in what a manner!) this heretical pseudo-reform has been carried out, a triumph of arrogance and ignorance. If it were possible, I would take back my vote, and attest before a magistrate that my assent had been obtained through trickery".[27]

Father Louis Bouyer, an outstanding figure in the preconciliar Liturgical Movement, claims that:

> In no other area is there a greater distance (and even formal opposition) between what the Council worked out and what we actually have....I now have the impression, and I am not alone, that those who took it upon themselves to apply (?) the Council's directives on this point have turned their backs deliberately on what Beauduin, Casel, and Pius Parsch had set out to do, and to which I had tried vainly to add some small contribution of my

own. I do not wish to vouch for the truth, or seem to, at any greater length of this denial and imposture. If any are still interested, they may read the books I wrote on the subject; there are only too many of these! Or better, they might read the books of the experts I have just mentioned, on whom they have been able to turn their backs.[28]

The late Monsignor Klaus Gamber was described by Cardinal Ratzinger as "the one scholar who, among the army of pseudo-liturgists, truly represents the liturgical thinking of the centre of the Church".[29] As regards the attitude the Council Fathers would have taken to the changes that have been foisted upon us in the name of Vatican II, he informs us in his book *The Reform of the Roman Liturgy* that: "One statement we can make with certainty is that the new *Ordo* of the Mass that has now emerged would not have been endorsed by the majority of the Council Fathers".[30]

The examples cited in Chapter VI should indicate the type of "trickery" used to induce all but four of the Council Fathers to cast their votes in favour of the Liturgy Constitution. Sufficient, well-concealed "time bombs" were inserted into the text to make possible precisely the type of ecumenical Mass advocated by Bishop Duschak, a type of Mass which would be more than warmly welcomed by Protestants. A selection of their comments will be provided in the third book in this series. The task of unearthing the time bombs themselves will be undertaken in the next chapter. At the same time, the constitution contains a wealth of orthodox writing and what appear to be sufficient safeguards to prevent any realisation of the fears of some Fathers that the type of reform which would emerge from the constitution would be the type of reform which did emerge.

The liberals were more than satisfied with their work. Where the reform of the liturgy was concerned, they had never believed they "would achieve so much".[31] A Benedictine liturgist explained that, far from being merely a new code of rubrics, the constitution called for "a reform of mind and mentality" and that it was based on "new theological perspectives".[32] Charles Davis had warned in 1960:

> Let no one, then, underestimate the significance and power of the liturgical movement. What is taking place is not the increasing popularity of a private hobby or interesting sideline, not a touching up of ritual anomalies, but a change, a renewal in the pastoral life of the Church. *And the concern is not with incidentals, but with the fundamentals of doctrine* [my emphasis].[33]

Xavier Rynne hailed the reform as one which furnishes "a realistic bridge for a dialogue with the Protestant Churches".[34] The Protestant liturgist Jaroslav Pelikan finds in it statements which "are bound to evoke the enthusiastic approval of anyone who believes that the Reformation was the work of the Holy Spirit....In fact, several of its fundamental principles represent the acceptance, however belatedly, of the liturgical programme set forth by the Reformers...."[35]

It was explained in Chapter V that the Rhine Group had pressed successfully for the establishment of post-conciliar commissions which would ensure that the progressive measures incorporated in the Council documents were not blocked by conservative forces in the Vatican after the Council. All that remained was to ensure that the liturgy was completely at their mercy by taking control of the post-conciliar Liturgy Commission. By this time, it was taken for granted that they would control any commission as a matter of course—and this one proved to be no exception. On 5 March 1964, *L'Osservatore Romano* announced the establishment of the Commission for the Implementation of the Constitution on the Liturgy, which became known as the *Consilium*, and was eventually to include six Protestant observers. The initial membership of forty-six, with Cardinal Lercaro presiding, consisted mainly of members of the conciliar commission which had drafted the constitution, with Father Annibale Bugnini, C.M., continuing in his role as Secretary.[36] Xavier Rynne takes great pleasure in noting that as its members "were generally known to be in favour of liturgical renewal, most liturgists were satisfied".[37]

In other words, the liberals had constructed the Liturgy Constitution as a weapon with which to initiate a revolution, and the Council Fathers then placed this weapon in the hands of the very men who had forged it. Archbishop R. J. Dwyer has observed, with the benefit of hindsight, that the great mistake of the Council Fathers was "to allow the implementation of the Constitution on the Sacred Liturgy to fall into the hands of men who were either unscrupulous or incompetent. This is the so-called Liturgical Establishment, a sacred cow which acts more like a white elephant as it tramples the shards of a shattered liturgy with ponderous abandon".[38] A greater mistake had, of course, been allowing the "time bombs" to be planted in the first place. The deficiencies in the Liturgy Constitution will appear only too obvious when they are examined in the next chapter, but it would be unfair to criticise the Council Fathers for failing to detect them at the time—after all, those who plant time bombs take every step to see that they are not detected and defused. The fact that only four Fathers voted against the constitution shows clearly that the very idea of its being used as it has been used "seemed so far beyond the realm of possibility as to be ridiculous". Pope John and the bishops did not, as Cardinal Heenan insists, "suspect what was being planned by the liturgical experts" and, to repeat a comment by Dr. McAfee Brown already cited in Chapter VI, "the Council documents often implied more in the way of change than the Council Fathers were necessarily aware of when they voted". As late as 1965, the post-conciliar liturgical commission was still assuring national hierarchies that permission for a vernacular Canon would never be granted to anyone in any country (*nunquam nulli*).[39] By 1975, with the introduction of three new Eucharistic Prayers for children and two for "reconciliation", permission had been granted not for one but for *nine* vernacular Canons! By, and well before, 1975, permission had also been given for any number of objectionable innovations which were not even mentioned during the debate on the Liturgy Constitution, nor even hinted at in it, and which would certainly have horrified most of the Council Fathers. The fact that Holy Communion can now be given to standing communicants in their hands by laywomen with the full approval of the Vatican provides an obvious example. But a detailed examination of the abuses which have accompanied the liturgical revolution must await the third book in this series. The present work is intended only to show how the ground was prepared for them.

The one ray of comfort as regards the Liturgy Constitution, and an indication that the Holy Ghost has not abandoned the Church, lies in the fact that "this promulgation would be disciplinary not doctrinal in character, and as a consequence would not involve the Church's infallibility".[40]

Notes

[1] RFT, p. 23.
[2] *The Tablet*, 8 January 1966, p. 33.
[3] RFT, p. 23.
[4] *Ibid.*, p. 18.
[5] *Ibid.*, p. 35.
[6] Abbott, p. 134.
[7] *Lo Specchio*, 29 June 1969.
[8] XR-II, pp. 304-305.
[9] RFT, p. 67.
[10] *Ibid.*, pp. 38-39.
[11] AVVC, p. 77.
[12] Denziger, 1531-1533.
[13] PG, p. 32.
[14] *The Tablet*, 21 February 1976, p. 184.
[15] XR-I, p. 101.
[16] *The Tablet*, 11 January 1964, pp. 35-36.

[17] *Ibid.*, 11 December 1962, p. 1167.
[18] XR-I, p. 103.
[19] J. Jeremias, *The Eucharistic Words of Jesus*, 3rd edition (SCM Press, 1966), pp. 85, 86, 196.
[20] *Ibid.*, p. 197.
[21] *Catholic Commentary on the Holy Scriptures* (London, 1953), p. 403, col. 1.
[22] XR-I, pp. 11-12.
[23] *The Tablet*, 13 June 1964, p. 660.
[24] *Ibid.*, 16 September 1972, p. 893.
[25] CT, p. 367.
[26] *Twin Circle*, 26 October 1973.
[27] Monsignor Dominico Celada, *Lo Specchio*, 29 July 1969.
[28] DC, p. 99.
[29] K. Gamber, *The Reform of the Roman Liturgy* (RRL), (Harrison, N.Y.,1993), p. xiii.
[30] *Ibid.*, p. 61.
[31] RFT, p. 138.
[32] XR-II, p. 329.
[33] *Liturgy and Doctrine* (London, 1960), p. 100.
[34] XR-II, p. 305.
[35] Abbott, pp. 180-181.
[36] RFT, p. 140.
[37] XR-II, p. 330-331.
[38] *The Tidings*, 9 July 1971.
[39] *The Tablet*, 20 March 1965, p. 333.
[40] XR-II, p. 297.

XVII

Unearthing the Time Bombs

It was shown in the previous chapter that too much blame should not be attached to the Council Fathers for failing to detect the time bombs which had been inserted in the Constitution on the Sacred Liturgy (which will be referred to from now on as CSL). In his authoritative book, *La Nouvelle Messe*, Louis Salleron remarks that far from seeing it as a means of initiating a revolution, the ordinary layman would have considered the CSL as the crowning achievement of the work of liturgical renewal which had been in progress for a hundred years.[1] Let there be no mistake, there was great need and great scope for liturgical renewal within the Roman rite, but a renewal within the correct sense of the term, using and developing the existing liturgy to its fullest potential. As was remarked in Chapter II, where, as in the case of Mesnil St. Loup this was done, the life of the Mystical Body became manifest; Catholicism was seen as it could be but rarely was.

It could be argued that the study of the CSL which is to be made here lacks balance as it says little about the admirable doctrinal teaching and pastoral counsel which the constitution contains, while stressing a few alleged deficiencies. The fact is that the liturgical revolution which has emerged from the constitution has been initiated precisely on the basis of the very few clauses discussed in this chapter. Those who gained control of the *Consilium* which implemented the CSL used these clauses in precisely the manner they had intended to use them when, as members of the conciliar Liturgical Commission, they had inserted them into the CSL. The constitution itself became a dead letter almost from the moment it was passed with such euphoria by the Council Fathers. It could have been used to initiate the type of true renewal initiated by Père Emmanuel in Mesnil St. Loup, a renewal faithful to the authentic liturgical principles endorsed by the popes and expounded in documents ranging from *Tra le Sollicitudini* of St. Pius X (1903) to the *Instructio de Musica Sacra et Sacra Liturgia* of Pope Pius XII (1958).[2] But discussing what might have been is the most fruitless of occupations—it is what actually happened that matters. "Are these Fathers planning a revolution?" demanded a horrified Cardinal Ottaviani during the debate on the liturgy.[3] Indeed they were, or at least the *periti* as whose mouthpieces they acted were. The extent to which this was the case has been made clear in earlier chapters, Chapter V in particular. The full extent of episcopal subservience to the *diktat* of the "experts" was made clear by Archbishop Lefebvre in a lecture he gave in Vienna in September 1975. He explains that the French Episcopal Conference "held meetings during which they were given the exact texts of the speeches they had to make. 'You, Bishop So-and-So, you will speak on such a subject, a certain theologian will write the text for you, and all you have to do is read it'".[4]

A revolution had indeed been planned—and it was to be initiated by the time bombs concealed in the CSL. It is with these liberal time bombs that this chapter is concerned, not with the orthodox padding used to conceal them. No Catholic can be too familiar with *Mediator Dei*.[5] It is, perhaps, the most perfect exposition of the nature of the liturgy which has ever been written. In this encyclical Pope Pius XII defines the liturgy as follows: "The sacred liturgy is the public worship which our Redeemer, the Head of the Church, offers to His heavenly Father and which the community of Christ's faithful pays to its Founder, and through Him to the Eternal Father; briefly, it is the whole public worship of the Mystical Body of Jesus Christ, Head and members". This definition requires us to bear in mind, when discussing the CSL and the reforms purporting to emanate from it, that:

1. The liturgy is primarily an act of worship offered to the eternal Father.

2. It is an action of Christ, *actio Christi*, something Christ does.

3. The members of the Mystical Body associate themselves with their Head in offering this worship.

These principles, of course, apply to the entire Divine Office and not simply to the Mass. Pope Pius explains that the essence of the Mass is found in the fact that it is an action of Christ, the extension of His priesthood "through the ages, since the sacred liturgy is nothing else but the exercise of that priestly office".

Our word liturgy is derived from the Greek *leitourgos*, which originally designated a man who performed a public service. In the fifth century B.C., a *leitourgos* in Athens fitted out a warship at his own expense, trained the crew and commanded it in battle. In Hebrews 8:1-6, Christ is referred to as the *Leitourgos* of holy things. The liturgy is *His* public religious work for *His* people, *His* ministry, *His* redeeming activity. It is above all *His* Sacrifice, the Sacrifice of the Cross, the same sacrifice that He offered on Calvary still offered by Him through the ministry of His priests. He is the principal offerer of the Sacrifice of the Mass, and to offer the Mass nothing is necessary but a priest, the bread, and the wine. There is no necessity whatsoever for a congregation; when defining the essence, the nature of the Mass, the presence of the faithful need not be taken into account; while it is obviously desirable it is not necessary. When the faithful are present they are able to join themselves in mind and heart with what Christ does in *His* liturgy. We offer Him and we offer ourselves with Him. (The fact that the faithful offer the sacrifice with and through the priest is stressed in *Mediator Dei*.) Needless to say, even when a priest offers Mass with only a server it is still a public act of worship made by the whole Church, for:

> Every time the priest re-enacts what the divine Redeemer did at the Last Supper, the sacrifice is really accomplished; and this sacrifice always and everywhere, necessarily and of its very nature, has a public and social character. For he who offers it acts in the name both of Christ and of the faithful, of whom the divine Redeemer is the Head, and he offers it to God for the Holy Catholic Church, and for the living and the dead.[6]

According to Robert Kaiser, the battle over the CSL was won by the liberals on 7 December 1962 when the preface and first chapter were approved with only eleven dissenting votes.

> To the Council's progressives, euphoric over other battles fought and won, this was a sweet message. True, they would have to vote on other chapters, but they would be mere formalities. "Within the preface and first chapter", a member of the Liturgical Commission told me, "are the seeds of all the other reforms". It was true also that the Pope would have to ratify the action. But no one thought he would attempt to veto what the Council had spent so long achieving.[7]

He did not!

Unearthing the Time Bombs

One of the first points made in the preface is that the Council intends to "nurture whatever can contribute to the unity of all who believe in Christ; and to strengthen those aspects of the Church which can help to summon all of mankind into her embrace". Those who drafted the constitution clearly envisage the liturgy as a means of promoting ecumenism. It follows from this that the traditional Roman Mass which emphasised precisely those aspects of our faith most unacceptable to Protestants must be considered as hampering ecumenism. However, the CSL gives the impression that there is no danger of any drastic change in any of the existing rites of Mass, among which the Roman rite was clearly paramount, as: "this most sacred Council declares that holy Mother Church holds *all* lawfully acknowledged rites to be of equal authority and dignity; that she wishes *to preserve them in the future* and to foster them in very way". (My emphasis.) These reassuring words are qualified by the additional desire of the Council that: "where necessary the rites be carefully and thoroughly revised in the light of sound tradition, and that they be given new vigour to meet the circumstances and needs of modern times" (Art. 4). How it was possible to preserve these rites while revising them to meet certain unspecified circumstances and needs of modern times is not explained. Nor is it explained how such a revision could be carried out in the light of sound tradition as it had been the sound (and invariable) tradition of the Roman rite never to undertake any drastic revision of its rites, a tradition of well over a thousand years' standing which had been breached only during the Protestant Reformation, when every heretical sect devised new rites to correspond with its new teachings. There had, of course, been liturgical development within the Roman rite, as in all rites, but it had been by the scarcely perceptible process described in Chapter IX of *Cranmer's Godly Order*. It is important to note that the predominant characteristic of this development was the addition of new prayers and gestures which manifested ever more clearly the mystery enshrined in the Mass. As is made clear in *Cranmer's Godly Order*, the Protestant Reformers removed prayers which made Catholic doctrine specific, under the guise of an alleged return to primitive simplicity. Pope Pius XII specifically condemned "certain attempts to reintroduce ancient rites and liturgies" on the grounds that they were primitive. He designated it as

> an attempt to revive the "archaeologism" to which the pseudo-Synod of Pistoia gave rise; it seeks also to reintroduce the pernicious errors which led to that Synod and resulted from it, and which the Church, in her capacity of watchful guardian of "the deposit of faith" entrusted to her by her divine Founder, has rightly condemned. It is a wicked movement, that tends to paralyse the sanctifying and salutary action by which the liturgy leads the children of adoption on the path to their heavenly Father.[8]

The liturgical principles of Pistoia have, of course, been imposed throughout the Roman rite as part of the conciliar reform, even though not specifically ordered by the Council—but, as this chapter will make very clear, the CSL provided the door through which they entered. It is worth pointing out that the "circumstances and needs of modern times", which Article 4 of the CSL claims that the liturgy must be adjusted to meet, have occurred with great regularity throughout history. It is within the nature of time to become more modern with the passing of each second, and if the Church had adapted the liturgy to keep up with the constant succession of modern times and new circumstances there would have never been any liturgical stability at all. If this need does exist it must always have existed, and it seems hard to believe that the Holy Ghost had not been

Unearthing the Time Bombs

guiding the Church until He revealed it to the Fathers of the Second Vatican Council. Papal teaching on the need to adapt the liturgy to keep pace with modern times is conspicuous only by its absence—and this is hardly surprising when this alleged "need" is examined in a dispassionate and rational manner. When do times become modern? What are the criteria by which modernity is assessed? When does one modernity cease and another modernity come into being?

The complete fallacy of this adaptation to modernity thesis was certainly not lost upon some of the Council Fathers. Bishop (later Cardinal) Dino Staffa pointed out the theological consequences of an "adapted liturgy" on 24 October 1962. He told 2,337 assembled Fathers:

> It is said that the Sacred Liturgy must be adapted to times and circumstances which have changed. Here also we ought to look at the consequences. For customs, even the very face of society, change fast and will change even faster. What seems agreeable to the wishes of the multitude today will appear incongruous after thirty or fifty years. We must conclude then that after thirty or fifty years all, or almost all of the liturgy would have to be changed again. This seems to be logical according to the premises, this seems logical to me, but hardly fitting (*decorum*) for the Sacred Liturgy, hardly useful for the dignity of the Church, hardly safe for the integrity and unity of the faith, hardly favouring the unity of discipline. While the world therefore tends to unity more and more every day, especially in its manner of working or living, are we of the Latin Church going to break the admirable liturgical unity and divide into nations, regions, and even provinces?[9]

The answer, of course, is that this is precisely what the Latin Church was going to do and did, with the consequences for the integrity and unity both of faith and discipline which Bishop Staffa had foreseen.

Articles 5 to 13, which deal with the nature of the liturgy, contain much admirable doctrinal teaching but also some which seems disturbingly lacking in precision. Christ's substantial presence in the Blessed Sacrament is referred to as if it is simply the highest (maximal) expression of His presence in the liturgy, a presence which is listed in a variety of manners such as the reading of Holy Scripture or the fact that two or three are gathered together in His name. He is present "especially under the Eucharistic species" (*Praesens...maxime sub speciebus eucharisticis*: Article 7). One fact which is made very clear in *Cranmer's Godly Order* is that all the Protestant Reformers agreed that Christ was present in the Eucharist; what they rejected was the dogma of His substantial presence. If there is one word which was, and is, anathema to Protestants it is the word "transubstantiation". Protestants will profess belief in Christ's "real presence", in His "eucharistic presence", in His "sacramental presence"—Lutherans even accept His "consubstantial presence"—but what they will not accept, what is anathema to them, is the one word "transubstantiation". It is, therefore, astonishing to find that this word does not appear anywhere within the text of the CSL. This is a scarcely credible break with the tradition of the Catholic and Roman Church in insisting on total and absolute precision when treating of the sacrament which is her greatest treasure, for it is nothing less than God incarnate Himself, whose Mystical Body the Church is.

The contrast between the traditional precision of the Church and the CSL can be made clear with just one example. Compared with the CSL the following would seem to be an extremely, perhaps an exceptionally, comprehensive definition of Christ's Eucharistic presence. "Christ is, after the consecration, truly, really, and substantially present under the appearances of bread and wine which has then ceased to exist, only the appearances remaining". Readers will be surprised to learn that this definition was condemned as "pernicious, derogatory to the expounding of Catholic truth (*perniciosa, derogans expositioni veritatis catholicae*)". This was, in fact, the definition put forward by the Jansenist Synod of Pistoia and was condemned by Pope Pius VI specifically for its calculated omission of the term "transubstantiation", which had been used by Trent in defining the manner of Christ's Eucharistic presence and in the solemn definition of profession of faith subscribed to by the Fathers of that Council (*quam velut articulum fidei Tridentinum Concilium definivit* [D 877, 884], *et quae in solemni fidei professione continetur*). The failure to utilise the word "transubstantiation" was condemned by Pope Pius VI "inasmuch as, through an unauthorised and suspicious omission of this kind, mention is omitted of an article relating to the faith, and also of a word consecrated by the Church to safeguard the profession of that article against heresy, and because it tends to result in its being forgotten as if it were merely a scholastic question".[10]

While discussing this particular point it is impossible not to note what could be described as the truly supernatural correspondence between what Pope Pius VI wrote in 1794 and what Pope Paul VI wrote in his encyclical *Mysterium Fidei* in 1965. Mention has been made in earlier chapters of the antipathy this encyclical aroused among both Protestants and liberal Catholics who did not hesitate to stigmatise it as incompatible with the "spirit" of Vatican II! Pope Paul condemns opinions relating to "Masses celebrated privately, to the dogma of transubstantiation and to eucharistic worship. They seem to think that although a doctrine has been defined once by the Church, it is open to anyone to ignore it or to give it an interpretation that whittles away the natural meaning of the words or the accepted sense of the concepts".[11] The Church teaches us, insists Pope Paul, that our Blessed Lord "becomes present in the sacrament precisely by a change of the bread's whole substance into His Body and the wine's whole substance into His Blood. This is clearly a remarkable and singular change, and the Catholic Church gives it the suitable and accurate name of transubstantiation".[12] Mention has already been made in this book of Pope John's claim in his opening speech to the Council that: "The substance of the ancient doctrine of the deposit of faith is one thing, and the way in which it is presented is another". Pope Paul states in *Mysterium Fidei*:

> This rule of speech has been introduced by the Church in the long run of centuries with the protection of the Holy Spirit. She has confirmed it with the authority of the councils. It has become more than once the token and standard of orthodox faith. It must be observed religiously. No one may presume to alter it at will, or on the pretext of new knowledge. For it would be intolerable if the dogmatic formulas, which ecumenical councils have employed in dealing with the mysteries of the most Holy Trinity, were to be accused of being badly attuned to the men of our day, and other formulas were rashly introduced to replace them. It is equally intolerable that anyone on his own initiative should want to modify the formulas with which the Council of Trent has proposed the Eucharistic Mystery for belief. These formulas, and others too, which the Church employs in proposing dogmas of faith, express concepts which are not tied to any specified cultural system. They are not restricted to any fixed development of the sciences nor to one or other of the theological schools.[13]

How it is possible to reconcile such statements not only with those of Pope Paul, the Pope of the Council, but Pope Paul who has been inflexible in imposing the spirit, the "orientations" of the Council, it is difficult to say. There is little that can be added to what was written in Chapter XV; let it suffice here to say that Peter has spoken through Paul.

Notwithstanding the deplorable absence of the term "transubstantiation" from the CSL, Articles 5 to 13 do contain much orthodox teaching, teaching which must have gone a long way towards prompting conservative Fathers to vote for the constitution and diverting attention from the time bombs in the text. The victory and triumph of Christ's death are again made present whenever the Mass is offered (Art. 6). The Mass is offered by Christ "the same one now offering through the ministry of priests, who formerly offered Himself on the cross" (Art. 7). "Rightly then is the liturgy considered as an exercise of the priestly office of Jesus Christ" (Art. 6). It is "the summit toward which all the activity of the Church is directed; at the same time it is the fountain from which all her power flows" (Art. 10).

In Article 11 there appears one of the key themes of the CSL. Pastors of souls are urged to ensure that "the faithful take part knowingly, actively, and fruitfully". Similar admonitions are included in *Mediator Dei*, but in this encyclical and in the CSL the Latin word which has been translated as "active" is *actuosus*. There is a Latin word *activus* which is defined in Lewis and Short's Latin Dictionary as active, practical, opposed to *contemplativus*. The same dictionary explains *actuosus* as implying activity with the accessory idea of zeal, subjective impulse. It is not easy to provide an exact English equivalent of *actuosus*, the word involves a sincere, intense perhaps, interior participation in the Mass—and it is always to this interior participation to which prime consideration must be given. The role of external gestures is to manifest this interior participation without which they are totally without value. These things should not only manifest but aid the interior participation which they symbolise. No gesture approved by the Church is without meaning and value—the striking of the breast during the *Confiteor*, making the sign of the cross on the forehead, lips, and heart at the Gospel, genuflecting at the *Incarnatus est* during the Creed and the *Verbum caro factus est* of the Last Gospel, kneeling for certain parts of the Mass, the Canon in particular, bowing in adoration at the elevations, joining in the chants and appropriate responses—all these are appropriate external manifestations of the internal participation which the faithful should rightly be taught to make knowingly and fruitfully. But Pope Pius XII points out that the importance of this external participation should not be exaggerated, and that every Catholic has the right to assist at Mass in the manner which he finds most helpful:

> People differ so widely in character, temperament and intelligence that it is impossible for them all to be affected in the same way by the same communal prayers, hymns, and sacred actions. Besides, spiritual needs and dispositions are not the same in all, nor do these remain unchanged in the same individual at different times. Are we therefore to say—as we should have to say if such an opinion were true—that all these Christians are unable to take part in the Eucharistic Sacrifice or to enjoy its benefits? Of course they can, and in ways which many find easier: for example, by devoutly meditating on the mysteries of Jesus Christ, or by performing other religious exercises and saying other prayers which, though different in form from the liturgical prayers, are by their nature in keeping with them.[14]

As Pope Pius explains at great length in *Mediator Dei*, what really matters is that the faithful should unite themselves with the priest at the altar in offering Christ and should offer themselves together with the divine Victim, with and through the great High Priest Himself. There is a clear change of emphasis between *Mediator Dei* and the CSL which states (Art. 14) that "in the restoration of the sacred liturgy, this full and active participation by all the people is the aim to be considered *before all else*: for it is the primary and indispensable source from which the faithful are to derive the true Christian spirit". (My emphasis.) As a footnote in the Abbott translation remarks with perfect accuracy: "This theme of awareness and active participation by the faithful is another basic theme of the constitution".[15] Now, interpreted in the sense given to the word *actuosus* in this chapter, this "basic theme" can be placed within the context of the liturgical movement given such impetus by St. Pius X and his successors. But as *actuosus* has been invariably translated by the word active, which is interpreted in its literal sense, the necessity of making, as Article 14 directs, full and active congregational participation the prime consideration in "the restoration and promotion of the sacred liturgy", has resulted in the congregation rather than the divine Victim becoming the focus of attention. On a practical level it is the coming together of the community which matters, not the reason they come together; and this is in harmony with the most obvious tendency within the post-conciliar Church—to replace the cult of God with the cult of man. This is, of course, in perfect conformity with the direction being taken by the present ecumenical movement, a point which was examined in Chapter VIII.

Once the logic of making the active participation of the congregation the prime consideration of the liturgy is accepted, there can be no restraint upon the self-appointed experts intent upon its total de-sacralisation. It is important to stress here that at no time during the reform have the wishes of the laity ever been taken into consideration. Just as in the Soviet Union the Communist Party "interprets the will of the people" so the "experts" interpret the wishes of the laity. When, as early as March 1964, members of the laity in England were making it quite clear that they neither liked nor wanted the liturgical changes being imposed upon them, one of England's most fervent apostles of liturgical innovation, Dom Gregory Murray, put them in their place in the clearest possible terms in a letter to *The Tablet*: "The plea that the laity as a body do not want liturgical change, whether in rite or in language, is, I submit, quite beside the point". He insists that it is "not a question of what people want; it is a question of what is good for them".[16]

Hence the demand that the full and active participation of the congregation "be considered *before all else*" is a time bomb of virtually unlimited destructive power placed in the hands of those invested with the power to implement in practice the details of a reform which the Council authorised but did not spell out in detail. Thus, although the Council says that "other things being equal" Gregorian chant should be given pride of place in liturgical services (Art. 116), the "experts" can and did argue that this was most certainly not a case of other things being equal as the use of Gregorian chant impeded the active participation of the people. The music of the people, popular music, pop music, is, say the "experts", clearly what is most pleasing to them and most likely to promote their active participation which, in obedience to the Council, must be considered above all else. This has led to the abomination of the "Folk Mass", which certainly has no more in common with genuine folk music than it does with plainchant. It also illustrates the ignorance of, and contempt for, the ordinary faithful manifested by these self-styled "experts". Because the housewife or the manual worker listens to pop music on a transistor to relieve the monotony of the day's routine, it does not follow that they are incapable of appreciating anything better, or that they wish to hear the same sort of music in church on Sunday. The same is equally true of young people; if the liturgy is reduced to the level of imitating what was being heard in the discotheques last year then the young will soon see little point in being present. Dietrich von Hildebrand has correctly defined the issue at stake as

> whether we better meet Christ in the Mass by soaring up to Him, or by dragging Him down into our own pedestrian, workaday world. The innovators would replace holy intimacy with Christ by an unbecoming familiarity. The new liturgy actually threatens to frustrate the confrontation with Christ, for it discourages reverence in the face of mystery, precludes awe, and all but extinguishes a sense of sacredness. What really matters, surely, is not whether the faithful feel at home at Mass, but whether they are drawn out of their ordinary lives into the world of Christ—whether their attitude is the response of ultimate reverence: whether they are imbued with the reality of Christ.[17]

It is worth noting that Professor von Hildebrand issued this warning against the clear direction which the liturgical reform was taking in 1966, a direction in which it was being steered by "experts" claiming that they knew the style of celebration which was necessary to ensure that the congregation could participate actively and this, they could point out, was what the Council had decreed must "be considered before all else".

The next time bomb is located in Article 21. It states that "the liturgy is made up of unchangeable elements divinely instituted and elements subject to change". This is perfectly correct—but it does not follow that because certain elements could be changed they ought to be changed. The entire liturgical tradition of the Roman rite contradicts such an assertion. "What we may call the 'archaisms' of the Missal", writes Dom Cabrol, "father" of the liturgical movement, "are the expressions of the faith of our fathers which it is our duty to watch over and hand on to posterity".[18] Similarly in their defence of the Bull *Apostolicae Curae*, the Catholic bishops of the Province of Westminster insisted that:

> In adhering rigidly to the rite handed down to us we can always feel secure....*And this sound method is that which the Catholic Church has always followed*...to *subtract* prayers and ceremonies in previous use, and even to remodel the existing rites in the most drastic manner, is a proposition for which we know of no historical foundation, and which appears to us absolutely incredible. Hence Cranmer in taking this unprecedented course acted, in our opinion, with the most inconceivable rashness.[19]

But the CSL takes a different view, so startling and unprecedented a break with tradition that it seems scarcely credible the Fathers voted for it. The CSL states that elements which are subject to change "not only may but ought to be changed with the passing of time if features have by chance crept in which are less harmonious with the intimate nature of the liturgy, or if existing elements have grown less functional". These norms are so vague that the scope for interpreting them is virtually limitless, and it must be kept in mind continually that those who drafted them would be the men with the power to interpret them. No indication is given of which aspects of the liturgy are referred to here; no indication is given of the meaning of "less functional" (how much less is "less"?), or whether "functional" refers to the original function or a new one which may have been acquired. All the Mass vestments could be abolished on the basis of this norm—they no longer fulfill their original function of standard dress in the early years of the Church. On the other hand they have now acquired an important symbolic function and could also be said to add to the dignity of the celebration.

Article 21 refers, of course, to the liturgy in general, but specific reference is made to the Mass in Article 50:

> The rite of the Mass is to be revised in such a way that the intrinsic nature and purpose of its several parts, as also the connection between them, can be more clearly manifested, and that devout and active participation by the faithful can be more easily accomplished.
>
> For this purpose the rites are to be simplified, while due care is taken to preserve their substance. Elements which, with the passage of time, came to be duplicated, or were added with but little advantage, are now to be discarded. Where opportunity allows or necessity demands, other elements which have suffered injury through the accidents of history are now to be restored to the earlier norm of the holy Fathers.

Those who have read *Cranmer's Godly Order* will be struck immediately by the fact the Cranmer himself could have written this passage as the basis for his own reform! There is not one point here which he did not claim to be implementing. Archdeacon Pawley has already been cited in Chapter IX as praising the manner in which the liturgical reform following Vatican II not only corresponds with but has even surpassed the reform of Cranmer. It will be shown in the third book of this series what a very close correspondence there is between the prayers which Cranmer felt had been added to the Mass "with little advantage" (almost invariably prayers which made Catholic teaching explicit) and those which the members of the *Consilium*, which implemented the norms of Vatican II (with the help of Protestant advisers), also decreed had been added "with little advantage" and must "be discarded".

Article 21, together with such Articles as 1, 23, 50, 62, and 88, provides a mandate for the supreme goal of the liturgical revolutionaries—that of a permanently evolving liturgy.[20] In September 1968 the bulletin of the Archbishopric of Paris, *Présence et Dialogue,* called for a permanent revolution in these words: "It is no longer possible, in a period when the world is developing so rapidly, to consider rites as definitively fixed once and for all. They need to be regularly revised". This is precisely the consequence which Bishop Staffa had warned would be inevitable, in the speech cited earlier in this chapter. Once the logic of Article 21 is accepted there can be no alternative to a permanently evolving liturgy. It was explained in Chapter V how the Council *periti* established the journal *Concilium,* which can be considered as their official mouthpiece. Writing in this journal in 1969, Father H. Rennings, Dean of Studies of the Liturgical Institute of Trier, writes:

> When the Constitution states that one of the aims is "to adapt more suitably to the needs of our own times those institutions which are subject to change" (Art. 1; see also Arts. 21, 23, 62, 88) it clearly expresses the dynamic elements in the Council's idea of the liturgy. The "needs of our time" can always be better understood and therefore demand other solutions; the needs of the next generation can again lead to other consequences for the way worship should operate and be fitted into the overall activity of the Church. The basic principle of the constitution may be summarised as applying the principle of a Church which is constantly in a state of reform (*Ecclesia semper reformanda*) to the liturgy which is always in the state of reform (*Liturgia semper reformanda*). And the implied renewal must not be understood as limited to eliminating possible abuses but as that always necessary renewal of a Church endowed with all the potential that must lead to fullness and pluriformity. It is a mistake to think of liturgical reform as an occasional spring

Unearthing the Time Bombs

clean that settles liturgical problems for another period of rest.[21]

This could hardly be more explicit. It is clear that Cardinal Heenan was not speaking entirely in jest when he remarked:

> There is a certain poetic justice in the humiliation of the Catholic Church at the hands of liturgical anarchists. Catholics used to laugh at Anglicans for being "high" or "low"....The old boast that the Mass is everywhere the same and that Catholics are happy whichever priest celebrates is no longer true. When on 7 December 1962 the bishops voted overwhelmingly (1,922 against 11) in favour of the first chapter of the Constitution on the Liturgy they did not realise that they were initiating a process which after the Council would cause confusion and bitterness throughout the Church.[22]

This concept of a permanently evolving liturgy is of crucial importance. St. Pius V's ideal of liturgical uniformity within the Roman rite was considered as a reasonable ideal by Father Adrian Fortescue, England's greatest liturgist.[23] But this ideal has now been cast aside to be replaced by one of "pluriformity" in which the liturgy must be kept in a state of constant flux. Is Father Rennings's desire for a *liturgia semper reformanda* a legitimate interpretation of the CSL? When he speaks of "the Council's idea of the liturgy" he means, of course, the idea of the commission which drafted the CSL and the commission *officially* charged with implementing it. In practice this comes to the same thing. The idea of the experts was certainly not the idea of the majority of the 1,922 bishops who cast their *placet* votes on 7 December 1962. They would certainly have been reassured by a stipulation contained in Article 23. In order to maintain "sound tradition" a careful investigation is to be made before implementing any changes. "This investigation should be theological, historical and pastoral". If this was not reassuring enough "there must be no innovations unless the good of the Church genuinely and certainly requires them; and care must be taken that any new forms should in some way grow organically from forms already existing".

It is an instructive exercise to go through the changes which have been made in the Mass step by step, beginning with the abolition of the *Judica me* and ending with the abolition of the Last Gospel, or even the Prayers for Russia, and trying to decide exactly why the good of the Church genuinely and certainly required that each particular change *must* be made. Has the good of the Church really been enhanced because the faithful have been forbidden to kneel at the *Incarnatus est* during the Creed? It would be equally enlightening to be told the exact process by which, for example, the new offertory prayers (based on a Jewish form of grace) grew from "forms already existing". The *Consilium* presumably interpreted this phrase as already existing in the liturgy of *any* religion. There is most bitter irony in another admonition contained in Article 23 which states that: "As far as possible, notable differences between the rites used in adjacent regions are to be carefully avoided". It is now hard to credit that some adjacent parishes belong to the same religion, so great is the contrast between their respective modes of celebrating Mass.

Another time bomb is contained in Article 33. "Although the sacred liturgy is above all things the worship of the divine Majesty, it likewise contains abundant instruction for the faithful". Take careful note of the "although". The essential nature of the liturgy as a solemn act of worship offered to the eternal Father seems to be safeguarded—but on a practical level little more is heard of "the worship of the divine Majesty" but a great deal about the "abundant instruction of the faithful". For the Protestant, it is the *written word* of the Bible which is of paramount importance in worship; it is to receive this written word in readings and preaching that they come together, and to respond by praising God in prayers and hymns. The Catholic assists at Mass primarily by adoring, offering, and then receiving the Incarnate Word Himself. Those wishing to change the Mass in the interests of ecumenical convergence have been able to utilise Article 33 to add considerable emphasis to the instructional part of the Mass, while prominence given to the sacrifice has been considerably diminished. Xavier Rynne notes with satisfaction that the CSL "establishes the function of the Word of God in liturgical worship, placing the emphasis on Scripture as understood by modern biblical theology, and thereby furnishing a realistic bridge for a dialogue with the Protestant Churches whose worship has always been biblically rather than sacramentally orientated".[24]

Article 34 states that the reformed liturgy must be "distinguished by a noble simplicity". There is, needless to say, no attempt to explain what "a noble simplicity" is. It must be "unencumbered by useless repetitions" without explaining when a repetition becomes useless. The very dreary repetitions which have been introduced in the Responsorial Psalm and the Bidding Prayers (Prayer of the Faithful) are presumably useful—although precisely what they are useful for must remain a mystery. Article 34 also insists that the new rites must "be within the people's powers of comprehension". What is meant here by the word "people"? University graduates, the illiterate, or those in the middle? Must anything that anyone cannot comprehend be excluded? The latitude this article gave the *Consilium* hardly needs elaborating.

Article 37 claims that "the Church has no wish to impose a rigid uniformity on matters which do not involve the faith or the good of the whole community". It explains that anything in the way of life of various races and peoples that "is not indissolubly bound up with superstition and error she studies with sympathy and, if possible, preserves intact. Sometimes in fact she admits such things into the liturgy itself, as long as they harmonise with its true and authentic spirit". In practical terms this has meant unrestricted pluriformity with one exception—and in this case the most rigid uniformity is very much *de rigueur*, a uniformity which is rigid in not admitting the Mass of St. Pius V into the liturgy. This would appear to be the one thing in the way of life of so many Catholic peoples that is so bound up "with superstition and error" that it cannot be admitted to the liturgy. This has certainly been the unanimous view of every Protestant sect—but some now take a very different view of the "reformed liturgy". The ultra-evangelical Church of the Confession of Augsburg, Alsace-Lorraine, issued a statement after the meeting of its Superior Consistory on 8 December 1973, permitting its members to receive Holy Communion in Catholic churches. "We attach great importance to the use of the new prayers with which we felt at home, and which have the advantage of giving a different interpretation to the theology of sacrifice that we were accustomed to attribute to Catholicism. These prayers invite us to recognise an evangelical theology of sacrifice".

The principle enunciated in Article 37 is expanded in Article 38 and constitutes a time bomb with a capacity for destruction almost equivalent to that of the principle of permanent liturgical evolution. "Provided that the substantial unity of the Roman rite is maintained, the revision of liturgical books should allow for legitimate variations and adaptations to different groups, regions, and peoples, especially in mission lands". (Excluding, of course, any group wishing to retain the Mass of St. Pius V.) The mention of mission lands here is highly significant as most Fathers would presume that this was where these adaptations would take place. However, the carefully worded text does not say "only" but "especially" in mission lands. True, the article states that "the substantial unity of the Roman rite" is to be maintained—but what "substantial unity" means is not indicated and it would be for the *Consilium* to decide, and for the members of the *Consilium* (like Humpty Dumpty) words mean whatever they want them to mean. Once this principle of adaptation has been accepted there is no part of the Mass which can be considered exempt from change; even the words of consecration have been altered to bring them very close to the formula adopted by Cranmer in his reform.[25]

But Article 38 by no means concludes the subject of adaptation. Without giving the least idea of what is meant by "legitimate variations and adaptations", the CSL goes on in Article 40 to state that in "some places and circumstances, however, an even more radical adaptation of the liturgy is needed". Without explaining what is meant by a "radical adaptation" the need for "an even more radical adaptation" is postulated! More radical than what? Once this bomb has exploded its effects cannot be controlled. The Council Fathers, like Count Frankenstein, had given life to a creature which had a will of its own and over which they had no power. As early as 1965, Cardinal Lercaro, head (or figurehead) of the *Consilium*, felt it necessary to send a letter to the bishops of the world begging them to stem the tide of unauthorised radical adaptations which endangered what he considered to be the sound official reform. He may have honestly failed to appreciate that these unofficial adaptations were simply the logical extension of the official radical adaptations enshrined in the articles of the CSL which have been discussed in this chapter. The *Consilium* was, he assured them, engaged on "general reform of the liturgy which went right to its very foundations". Such a reform "could not be completed in one day". The new norms had been "conceived with a certain elasticity, which could permit adaptation, and in consequence great pastoral efficacy. That did not mean that every priest was free to devise whatever rites suited him". He did not wish "the sense of fraternity, of a family assembled" which had already made progress and needed to make even more, to stifle the "sense of hierarchy in the Church". Somehow or other the bishops needed to "put the brakes on arbitrary experiments, to this uncontrolled variety, and even the danger that the laity would...lament and murmur as did the sons of Israel against Moses and Aaron". He did not, of course, wish to imply that "unity consisted in stifling or eliminating variety"—he could hardly imply this as the CSL had called for variety, and his own *Consilium* was already interpreting this call with a liberality far beyond anything the majority of Fathers would have dreamed possible. However, Cardinal Lercaro insisted that this variety should not be allowed to degenerate "into incoherence". He begged for patience, urging the bishops to bring an end to the

> personal, premature, and noxious experiments, which God does not bless and which, in consequence, cannot result in lasting fruits; on the contrary, they injure the piety of the faithful and the renewal which has been so devoutly undertaken. They also prejudice our own efforts, for they are general, arbitrary initiatives, which finish by casting an unfavourable light on the work carried out with circumspection, a sense of responsibility, prudence and a true understanding of pastoral needs.[26]

Note that these startling admissions were made in 1965, and even by then the principle of a continually evolving, radically adapting, and legitimately varied liturgy was raging unrestrained throughout the Latin Church. Once again there is a striking similarity with Cranmer's reform or, in this instance, the situation immediately prior to the introduction of the 1549 Prayer Book. Numerous attacks upon traditional Eucharistic teaching were published which the authorities reproved but took no effective steps to suppress; the Council issued orders restraining innovations in the liturgy while letting it be known that such innovations were not unpleasing to them; the king, like Cardinal Lercaro, even found it necessary to issue a proclamation urging radical reformers "to stay and quiet themselves with this our direction—and not enterprise to run afore and so by their rashness to become the greatest hinderers" of change.[27]

The *Consilium*, as did the Council of King Edward VI, took little or no action against the "unofficial" innovators—indeed, how could it have done so? The official and unofficial innovators were on the same wavelength, in the same camp, pursuing the same course as the official innovators. There was no disagreement on principle; there was no dispute that there should be continual evolution, adaptation, and variety. The division on a matter of principle lay between the official and unofficial innovators on the one hand, and on the other the traditionalists who wished to retain the traditional unity of the Roman rite.

Cardinal Lercaro's letter did nothing to halt the spread of "arbitrary initiatives". Rome adopted the tactic of bringing unofficial innovations to an end by making them official. Communion was given in the hand unofficially—let it be given in the hand officially! Communion was distributed by laymen—then appoint laymen as extraordinary ministers of Holy Communion. Those who considered that the essence of the Mass lies in its being a common meal began, not without logic, to receive Communion at more than one Mass on the same day—then let a long list of occasions when this was permitted be published. Priests began using extempore prayers—then let provision for extempore prayer be made within the official reform. New "Canons" were composed, so let three new "Canons" be provided—new "Canons" still went on being composed, so add another five. This is a process which will be documented fully in the next book in this series. But it can be noted even here that the logic of this policy could not possibly be lost upon the unofficial innovators—let them introduce and spread their liturgical fantasies and the Vatican would eventually legalise them, and even if it did not, the possibility of action being taken against them was remote in the extreme, particularly after the introduction of the new Mass in 1969. After that date there were traditionalist priests who continued saying or reverted to the Mass of St. Pius V—and hounding them from their parishes provided those in the Vatican and national hierarchies with a penchant for repression ample scope to indulge it. Furthermore, Cardinal Lercaro's profession of "circumspection, a sense of responsibility, prudence, and a true understanding of pastoral needs", takes on a very hollow ring now that the fruits of his official reform are available for anyone to see.

The time bombs inserted in the CSL have been exploded with a destructive power far beyond what the revolutionaries who planted them there could have dared to hope for. Their reverberations will continue to spread while there is anything left to which the name "official" can be attached. Father Bugnini was rewarded for his part in the reform with an archbishop's mitre. He claimed in 1974, and who could dispute his claim, that: "The liturgical reform is a major conquest [sic] of the Catholic Church, and it has ecumenical dimensions since the other Churches and Christian denominations see in it not only something to be admired in itself, but equally as a sign of further progress to come".[28] As is always the case, every concession to revolutionaries is followed by new and more radical demands. It might have been imagined that by 1971 there had been enough variety and legitimate adaptation to suit everyone—far from it! Writing in *Concilium* (the journal should not be confused with the commission, *Consilium*, which is spelled with an "s"), Father Andrew Greeley, while deploring the "occasional madness" of the "underground" liturgy, considers it to be "a creation of those who want in their liturgical experience more of what liturgical symbolism was originally intended to convey—that is, intimate and intense friendship". (Contrast this with the explanation of the nature of the liturgy given earlier in this chapter.) Among the examples of "occasional madness" cited by Father Greeley are the "marijuana Mass, Mass with crackers and whiskey used as the elements for consecration, 'Teenage' Masses with Coca Cola and hot dog buns". However, the basic position of the participants in underground Masses is, claims Father Greeley, "unanswerable". He claims that "the underground is a judgement on us for our failure to understand the implications of the symbolism of the Eucharist as a family meal. If we do not provide a family meal for an increasing number of Catholics, then they will provide one for themselves".[29]

As a final example of a time bomb in the text of the CSL—it would become tedious to enumerate them all—the point must be made that while stating that the regulation of the liturgy is a responsibility reserved to the Apostolic See (Article 22), local ecclesiastical authorities are positively encouraged to propose any 'adaptations' they deem necessary (Article 40). They are reminded of the limitations of their powers of initiative, but the possibility of these powers being extended is more than implicit (Articles 22 and 36). This has resulted in the hierarchies of such countries as France and Holland making themselves, for practical purposes, the sole arbiters of what they will or will not allow—which, again upon a practical level, means that they will allow anything but the Mass of St. Pius V. The Indian bishops have even introduced their own Canon!

One apparently insurmountable obstacle to the revolution which the time bombs in the CSL were intended to initiate was the use of Latin in the liturgy. While the Latin language remained the norm there could, in fact, be no revolution. The Latin language has been, as Dom Guéranger makes clear in Appendix VIII, a principal target of the liturgical heretics:

> Hatred for the Latin language is inborn in the heart of all the enemies of Rome. They recognise it as the bond of Catholics throughout the universe, as the arsenal of orthodoxy against all the subtleties of the sectarian spirit.... We must admit it is a masterblow of Protestantism to have declared war on the sacred language. If it should ever succeed in destroying it, it would be well on the way to victory.

Prophetic words indeed!

Earlier chapters have already included a number of quotations by Council Fathers which make it clear that the virtual abolition of the Latin language from the Roman rite was not only not intended by the Council Fathers but the possibility of this happening would not have been taken seriously by them had anyone suggested it could happen as a result of the CSL. In this respect at least it could seem that they had made their intentions explicit. Article 36 states:

> 1. Particular law remaining in force, the use of the Latin language is to be preserved in the Latin rites.
> 2. But [and what an important "but" this is!] since the use of the mother tongue, whether in the Mass, the administration of the sacraments, or other parts of the liturgy, may frequently be of great advantage to the people, the limits of its employment may be extended. This extension will apply in the first place to the readings and

directives, and to some of the prayers and chants, according to the regulations on this matter to be laid down separately in subsequent chapters.

3. It is for the competent territorial authority mentioned in Article 22, 2, to decide whether, and to what extent, the vernacular language is to be used according to these norms; their decrees are to be approved, that is confirmed, by the Apostolic See. And, whenever the procedure seems to be called for, this authority is to consult with bishops of neighbouring regions employing the same language.

Other conditions are also laid down, but the key points are contained here. Another factor militating in favour of the continued use of Latin has been pointed out by Louis Salleron. Not only does Article 36 state specifically that Latin is to be retained in the Latin rite (*in Ritibus latinis servetur*: the jussive subjunctive *servetur* denotes a command), but it can also be said to denote this in a negative manner. For had the three paragraphs which have been cited intended that the vernacular should become the norm, writes Professor Salleron, "the construction of the text would have been reversed. We would have read something like this: 'The use of vernacular languages will be introduced into the Latin rite…', and any exceptions or reservations in favour of the Latin language would then have been listed".[30]

This observation is reinforced by the instruction in Article 36, 3, stating that the competent territorial authority can decide whether and to what extent the vernacular is to be used in accordance with the norms laid down. The use of the word "whether" makes it quite clear that the vernacular need never be used at all. Similarly, Article 116 states that:

> The Church acknowledges Gregorian chant as proper to the Roman liturgy: therefore, other things being equal,

it should be given pride of place in liturgical services. But other kinds of sacred music, especially polyphony, are by no means excluded from liturgical celebrations, so long as they accord with the spirit of the liturgical action, as laid down in Article 30.

A good deal more could be written on this topic—but to little purpose. Perhaps Latin, Gregorian chant, and polyphony have all but vanished from the generality of churches because they were considered as obstacles to the active participation of the people, which the CSL had decreed should take priority over all else. The fact that even in 1965 the *Consilium* itself was still maintaining that permission for a vernacular Canon would never be granted to anyone, as was shown to be the case in Chapter XVI, indicates that the liturgical revolution had made even more rapid conquests than liberals had dared to hope during and immediately after the Council. One of France's best known progressive liturgists has admitted: "Nothing in the Constitution on the Liturgy gave us any reason to suppose that, four or five years later, a single document would make it possible to bring in the Canon in modern languages".[31] Within ten years, as had already been noted, there were also eight additional "official Canons" in modern languages!

The effects of the reform are now manifest for everyone to see—and the most evident of these effects has been a decline in Mass attendance which has increased in extent the more radical the reforms have been. It fell from 41 per cent of the population in France in 1964 to 14 per cent in 1975.[32] It would certainly be impossible to prove that every Catholic who has ceased attending Mass has done so because he dislikes the liturgical reforms. Progressive liturgists claim that many Catholics don't go because they would actually like the reforms to be more radical! What any sociologist could certainly have pointed out is that to completely disrupt the established customs of any community in so drastic and abrupt a manner, particularly a community which had always made stability so important a characteristic, must certainly loosen the bonds which hold its members together. This is a subject which is dealt with fully in Chapter IX of *Cranmer's Godly Order*. Pastorally, the reform has been a fiasco, a disaster even. What sort of success can be attributed to pastoral measures which are followed by a large proportion of the flock they are intended to help leaving the sheepfold for new pastures? All this has been done in the interests of a spurious form of ecumenism which has not brought true religious unity as much as one step nearer. "All these changes have but one justification", remarks Monsignor Lefebvre, "an aberrant senseless ecumenism that will not attract a single Protestant to the Faith but will cause countless Catholics to lose it, and will instill total confusion into the minds of many more who will no longer know what is true and what is false".[33] The complete accuracy of Monsignor Lefebvre's assessment of the nature and effects of the reform will be made very clear in the third book of this series, *Pope Paul's New Mass*. It will suffice here to quote from an article written by a young and outspoken Italian prelate, Monsignor Domenico Celada. His remarks appeared in the Italian journal *Lo Specchio* on 16 May 1969. Since that day the situation he describes has changed only for the worse:

> The gradual destruction of the liturgy is a sad fact already well known. Within less than five years, the thousand-year-old structure of divine worship which throughout the centuries has been known as the *Opus Dei* has been dismantled. The beginning was the abolition of Latin, perpetrated in a fraudulent manner. The Council had in fact clearly laid down that "The use of the Latin language is to be preserved", while permitting the use of the vernacular *in certain places, in certain cases,*

and *in certain parts of the rite*. By contrast, and in defiance of the authority of the Council, Latin has been suppressed practically *everywhere, at all times*, and in *all parts of the rite*. The Church's language has been abandoned, even at international liturgical functions. The universality of the Church is today claimed to be stressed by the use, on such occasions, of as many different languages as possible. The result is that—unless these are used simultaneously—all those parts of the rite which are not in one's own language become incomprehensible. It is Pentecost in reverse: while at Jerusalem the people *"ex omni natione, quae sub caelo est"* understood the words of the apostles, who were speaking but one language, so today, when all the different languages are spoken, nobody can understand anything. Instead of Pentecost, we should rather speak of Babel.

We have seen, during these past years, the abolition of those sublime gestures of devotion and piety such as signs of the cross, kissing of the altar which symbolises Christ, genuflections, etc., gestures which the secretary of the congregation responsible for liturgical reform, Father Annibale Bugnini, has dared publicly to describe as "anachronisms" and "wearisome externals". Instead, a puerile form of rite has been imposed, noisy, uncouth and extremely boring. And hypocritically, no notice has been taken of the disturbance and disgust of the faithful....Resounding success has been claimed for it because a proportion of the faithful has been trained to repeat mechanically a succession of phrases which through repetition have already lost their effect. We have witnessed with horror the introduction into our churches of hideous parodies of the sacred texts, of tunes and instruments more suited to the tavern. And the instigator and persistent advocate of these so-called "youth Masses" is none other than Father Annibale Bugnini. It is here recalled that he insisted on continuing the "yea, yea Masses" in Rome, and got his way despite the protest of Rome's Vicar General, Cardinal Dell'Acqua. During the pontificate of John XXIII, Bugnini had been expelled from the Lateran University where he was a teacher of liturgy precisely because he held such ideas—only to become, later, secretary of the congregation dealing with liturgical reform.

The background to Archbishop Bugnini's dismissal has already been examined in Chapter XIV. It would be impossible to place too much stress upon the fact that Archbishop Bugnini was the moving spirit behind the entire liturgical reform—a point which, with surprising lack of discretion, *L'Osservatore Romano* emphasised when it attempted to camouflage the reason for his abrupt dismissal by lavishing praise upon him. Monsignor Bugnini was, the Vatican journal explained, the co-ordinator and animator who had "directed" the work of the commissions.[34] It also needs to be stressed that the liturgical reform was not concerned solely with the Mass but extended to all the sacraments, not hesitating to interfere with their very matter and form in some instances. The wholesale and drastic nature of this reform constitutes a breach with tradition unprecedented in the history of the Church—and the fact that the co-ordinator and animator who directed it was a Freemason might rightly give every faithful Catholic cause for alarm. While this book (and this series) is concerned principally with the Mass, the next volume will devote some space to changes made in the rites of some of the other sacraments. The modifications made in the rite of Ordination are, if anything, even more serious than those made in the Mass. Pope Paul himself had to intervene and personally correct the very serious deficiencies in the new Order of Baptism for Infants which had been promulgated with his approval in

1969.³⁵ This provides another demonstration of the fact that papally approved texts are not, and should not be, exempt from criticism—particularly when they involve changes in traditional rites. Had the Pope not been made aware of the serious disquiet aroused by the New Order of Baptism for Infants he might not have re-examined it and made the important revisions which he promulgated in 1973.

Finally, some comfort at least can be taken from the fact that Archbishop Bugnini's Masonic associations were discovered in time to prevent him fully implementing the fourth and final stage of his revolution. He had divided this revolution into four stages—firstly, the transition from Latin to the vernacular; secondly, the reform of the liturgical books; thirdly, the translation of the liturgical books; and fourthly, as he explained in his journal *Notitiae*, "the adaptation or 'incarnation' of the Roman form of the liturgy into the usages and mentalities of each individual Church, is now beginning and will be pursued with ever increasing care and preparation".³⁶

Archbishop Bugnini made this boast in 1974, and in some countries, India in particular, the fourth stage was already well advanced when he was dismissed in 1975. Only time will reveal whether it has been possible to contain or even reverse this process of adaptation—and the extent to which the desire to reverse it exists in the Vatican.

Notes

1. *La Nouvelle Messe* (Paris, 1970), p. 17.
2. *The Liturgy,* Papal Teachings series (St. Paul Editions, 1962).
3. XR-1, p. 116.
4. *Approaches*, February 1976, Ecône Supplement, p. 21.
5. This encyclical is easily available on the Internet.
6. *Mediator Dei*, para. 88.
7. IC, 222.
8. *Mediator Dei*, paras. 65-69.
9. IC, p. 130.
10. Denziger, 1529.
11. *Mysterium Fidei*, para. 10.
12. *Ibid.*, para. 46.
13. *Ibid.*, para. 24.
14. *Mediator Dei*, para. 115.

15 Abbott, p. 143.
16 *The Tablet*, 14 March 1964, p. 303.
17 *Triumph*, October 1966.
18 Introduction to the Cabrol edition of the Roman Missal.
19 The Cardinal Archbishop and Bishops of the Province of Westminster, *A Vindication of the Bull "Apostolicae Curae"* (London, 1898), p. 42.
20 A detailed study of this point is available in the *Approaches* Supplement, *Report from Occupied Rome*.
21 *Consilium*, February 1969, p. 64.
22 CT, p. 367.
23 A. Fortescue, *The Mass* (London, 1917), p. 208.
24 XR-II, p. 305.
25 CGO, Appendix 3.
26 *Notitiae* (official journal of the *Concilium*), Nos. 9-10, Sept.-Oct. 1965, p. 257, ff.
27 CGO, Chapter XI.
28 *Notitiae*, No. 92, April 1974, p. 126.
29 *Concilium*, February 1971, p. 66.
30 Salleron, pp. 19-20.
31 *Nouvelles Instructions pour la Réforme Liturgique* (Paris, 1967), pp. 12-13.
32 *La Croix*, 29 June 1975.
33 *World Trends*, May 1974.
34 *L'Osservatore Romano*, 20 July 1975.
35 *Notitiae*, No. 85, July-August, 1973, pp. 268-272.
36 *Op. cit.*, note 28.

XVIII

Counting the Cost

Despite the efforts of the press, at no time did the Second Vatican Council capture the imagination of the ordinary Catholic. For the man in the pew, "the Council" is little more than a word which is used by the man in the pulpit to justify liturgical change. If he wonders why his children no longer learn anything about their faith at school, this is also the result of "the Council"; if he asks why nuns keep changing their habits, or have abandoned their habit altogether, the answer is "the Council". But it would be very hard to find a man in the pew who could name, let alone had read, a single Council document. The alleged enthusiasm which the Council has evoked among ordinary Catholics is simply an instance of liberal Catholics, clerical and lay, projecting their own preoccupations upon the laity at large and presuming that whatever they happen to want at a given moment must naturally be the ardent desire of the whole Church.

The apathy of the ordinary laymen to "the Council", in England at least, was illustrated dramatically at a "Welcome Home" rally organised for the English and Welsh bishops in January 1966. The liberals who had organised the rally somewhat rashly presumed that only the vast expanse of London's Albert Hall would suffice to cope with the multitudes that would come flocking not simply to welcome home their bishops but give public witness to their enthusiasm for "the Council". Even the Albert Hall, they presumed, could not possibly accommodate the anticipated throng and so (in those pre-Women's Lib days) admittance was restricted to men only. To the embarrassment of the organisers, so few men turned up that those who were up in the balcony were requested to come down and sit in the stalls.[1]

This is a graphic illustration of the apathy which has since marked the attitude of ordinary Catholics towards "The Council". Even those who number themselves among the intelligentsia and profess familiarity with and support for the teaching of the Council would often find themselves hard put to demonstrate any first-hand knowledge of the official documents. To give just a single example, one Terence Wynn, a Catholic journalist who was editor of *The Universe*, had no hesitation in stating in the Catholic press that Mass should be celebrated facing the people "because the bishops of the world meeting at the Vatican Council considered it a necessary liturgical change so that the laity could become more involved in the offering".[2] This makes it clear that the man who was editor of Britain's largest Catholic paper had not even glanced through the Liturgy Constitution; had he done so he would be well aware that it does not even mention Mass facing the people, let alone insist upon it as a necessary change. Nonetheless, Terence Wynn, like so many others of his ilk, had no hesitation in delivering pompous admonitions to Catholics who, unlike him, actually have read the Council documents and are able to offer informed criticisms of reforms purporting to be enacted in their name. Similarly, in his editorial of 21 May 1976, Wynn informed his readers who might criticise the introduction of Communion in the hand by the English and Welsh hierarchy that this "is still an accepted way of receiving the Sacrament in Eastern Catholic and Orthodox rites". This, of course, is the most utter nonsense imaginable and a typical

Counting the Cost

illustration of the intellectual standards to be expected from liberal propagandists.

The cost of the Council in material terms has been calculated and put on record. The Holy See alone spent about £3,430,000, which does not, of course, include the huge sums dispensed by national hierarchies. The two coffee bars alone cost several hundred million lire, and it is estimated that half-a-million cups of coffee were drunk. During the course of the Council 234 Council Fathers died—12 cardinals, 68 archbishops, 148 bishops, 3 prefects apostolic, and 3 superiors of religious orders.[3] On a more positive note, some very attractive commemorative stamps were issued by the Vatican Post Office.

But where the life of the Church is concerned it will never be possible to estimate the cost of the Council. It has probably made itself most manifest where the most precious and most essential characteristic of the Church is concerned— her unity. During his General Audience of 31 March 1976, Pope Paul himself lamented

> the infractions, the temptations, the paralysis, which have been manifested within the Church, with regard to the principle of unity, even after the Council....The fine flourishing associations that used to group organically the ranks of the People of God (even in a form which always left room for improvement), have broken up to a large extent....The ecclesial community par excellence, the parish, has also been subject in many places to a slackening of its usual ties, often so beautiful and in conformity with the Catholic spirit. The people of God no longer feels itself "one heart and one soul" (Acts 4:52) as were the believers of the first generation...an excessive and often incorrect application of "pluralism" has shattered, in various fields of ecclesial life and Catholic activity, that exemplarity, the harmony, that collabora-

tion, and therefore that efficiency, which the presence of the Church in the world is justified in expecting from her children.

Catholic organisations have broken up, parish life has slackened, Catholics are no longer of "one heart and one soul", harmony and collaboration within the Church have been shattered—and it is the Pope himself who tells us this! Not least among the factors which have contributed to the disintegration of unity within the Latin Rite has been the application of the principle of "pluralism" in the liturgy to the extent that the Mass, which enshrines the Sacrament of Unity, differs in its form of celebration not simply from country to country but from parish to parish—and each stage of this process has received the formal approval of the Pope. If any attempt is to be made to assess the cost of the Council in spiritual terms then all that can be done is to adapt the words of Tacitus and state: "When they create a wilderness they call it a renewal".[4]

Notes

[1] *The Tablet*, 22 January 1976, p. 110.

[2] *Catholic Herald*, 26 February 1971.

[3] *The Tablet*, 18 December 1966, pp. 1428-1429.

[4] *"Ubi solitudinem faciunt, pacem appellant."* Tacitus, *Agricola*, 30.

Appendix I

The General Councils of the Church

A. Ancient Church

1. Nicea I	325
2. Constantinople I	381
3. Ephesus	431
4. Chalcedon	451
5. Constantinople II	553
6. Constantinople III	680-1
7. Nicea II	787
8. Constantinople IV	869-70

B. Medieval Church

9. Lateran I	1123
10. Lateran II	1139
11. Lateran III	1179
12. Lateran IV	1215
13. Lyons I	1245
14. Lyons II	1274
15. Vienna	1311-12
16. Constance	1414-18

17.	Basle-Ferrara-Florence	1431-32
18.	Lateran V	1512-17

C. Modern Church

19.	Trent	1545-63
20.	Vatican I	1869-70
21.	Vatican II	1962-65

There is some discrepancy in the numbering given to general councils by different authorities. This list is given in Volume II of *A Catholic Dictionary of Theology* (London, 1967). In Addis & Arnold's *Catholic Dictionary*, Ferrara-Florence is separated from Basle and given the number "18". The numbering in the quotation given from Cardinal Manning in Chapter I does not correspond exactly with the numbering in *A Catholic Dictionary of Theology*. The appropriate entry ("Councils, General, How many?") in this authoritative work of reference provides a lengthy explanation of the problems involved in drafting a list of general councils.

Appendix II

Chronology of the Council

The events referred to in this book are not dealt with in chronological order, and this list will help readers to set them in their correct sequence.

1959 25 January: Pope John announces his intention of convoking a general council to the College of Cardinals.

1960 5 June: Pope John establishes the preparatory commissions and secretariats.

1961 25 December: Pope John convokes the Council with his Apostolic Constitution *Humanae Salutis*.

1962 20 July: Non-Catholic denominations are invited to send observers.

11 October: The Council opens.

13 October: The Rhine Group initiates its blitzkrieg by overthrowing the established election procedure during the first general congregation.

16 October: Second general congregation—voting for the conciliar commissions in accordance with the procedure demanded by the Rhine Group.

19 October: The Secretariat for Promoting Christian Unity granted status equivalent to that of a conciliar commission—it is independent of the Curia.

20 October: Third general congregation—results of the elections to the commissions are announced.

13 November: Announcement by Cardinal Cicognani, Secretary of State, that Pope John had decided to insert the name of St. Joseph into the Canon of the Mass with effect from 8 December 1962.

7 December: Preface and first chapter of the Liturgy Constitution passed with only eleven *non placet* (no) votes.

8 December: Solemn closing of the first session.

1963   3 June: Death of Pope John XXIII.

21 June: Election of Pope Paul VI.

29 September: Solemn opening of the second session.

29 October: Vote to include Our Lady in the schema on the Church.

29 November: Announcement that the Liturgy Constitution and Communications Decree are dis-

ciplinary and not doctrinal and do not involve the Church's infallibility.

4 December: Close of the second session and promulgation of the Liturgy Constitution.

1964   14 September: Solemn opening of the third session.

21 November: Close of the third session. Pope Paul proclaims Our Lady to be Mother of the Church.

1965   14 September: The fourth session opens.

4 October: Pope Paul goes to New York to address the United Nations.

4 December: Ecumenical service in St. Paul's Without the Walls.

7 December: Pastoral Constitution on the Church in the Modern World is promulgated.

8 December: Solemn closure of the Council.

Appendix III

The Press and the First Vatican Council

Thanks to Cardinal Manning, it is possible to draw up a comparison of what can only be described as the unholy parallel between the role played by the press during the First and Second Vatican Councils. This parallel is so close that it can only be concluded that the animating force behind the two campaigns was the same. According to Cardinal Manning:

> A belief had also spread itself that the Council would explain away the doctrines of Trent, or give them some new or laxer meaning, or throw open some questions supposed to be closed, or come to a compromise or transaction with other religious systems; or at least that it would accommodate the dogmatic stiffness of its traditions to modern thought and modern theology. It is strange that any one should have forgotten that every general council from Nicea to Trent, which has touched on the faith, has made new definitions, and that every new definition is a new dogma, and closes what was before open, and ties up more strictly the doctrines of faith. This belief, however, excited an expectation, mixed with hopes, that Rome by becoming comprehensive might be-

come approachable, or by becoming inconsistent might become powerless over the reason and will of men.[1]

Comment is hardly necessary on the extent to which these expectations were fulfilled as a result of Vatican II! The principal objective of the press campaign during Vatican I was to prevent the definition of papal infallibility.[2] This was, of course, the aim of all the powerful anti-Catholic forces throughout the world, forces which largely controlled the press even in nominally Catholic countries. Masonic influence has always been particularly strong where the press is concerned—when the objectives of Masonry are considered, this is hardly surprising. Once it became known that there were some bishops opposed to the proposed definition, a press campaign was launched in their favour. The situation here was the opposite of that at Vatican II—during Vatican I it was those in the minority who were the "goodies" and those in the majority who were the "baddies". Once the existence of this "international opposition" (the extent of which was greatly exaggerated) became known, then:

> In a moment, all the world rose up to meet them. Governments, politicians, newspapers, schismatical, heretical, infidel, Jewish, revolutionary, as with one unerring instinct, united in extolling and setting forth the virtue, learning, science, eloquence, nobleness, heroism of this "international opposition". With an iteration truly Homeric, certain epithets were perpetually linked to certain names. All who were against Rome were written up; all who were for Rome were written down.[3]

Cardinal Manning explains that:

> By a wonderful disposition of things, for the good, no doubt, of the human race, and above all of the Church

itself, the Council was divided into a majority and a minority: and by an even more beneficent and admirable provision, it was so ordered that the theology, philosophy, science, culture, intellectual power, logical acumen, eloquence, candour, nobleness of mind, independence of spirit, courage, and elevation of character in the Council, were all to be found in the minority. The majority was naturally a Dead Sea of superstition, narrowness, shallowness, ignorance, prejudice; without theology, philosophy, science, or eloquence; gathered from "old Catholic countries"; bigoted, tyrannical, deaf to reason; with a herd of "Curial and Italian Prelates", and mere "Vicars Apostolic". The Cardinal Presidents were men of imperious and overbearing character, who by violent ringing of bells and intemperate interruptions cut short the calm and inexorable logic of the minority. But the conduct of the majority was still more overbearing. By violent outcries, menacing gestures, and clamorous manifestations round the tribune, they drowned the thrilling eloquence of the minority, and compelled unanswerable orators to descend.[4]

Cardinal Manning went to great lengths to demythologise the false picture of the Council built up by the press. All its allegations, whether generalised or particular, are thoroughly examined and totally refuted—but as with Vatican II, it is myth which has remained the reality in the popular imagination. Vatican I even had its equivalent of Xavier Rynne, the "mystery man" of Vatican II whose pseudonym may have covered a collective identity.[5] Vatican I had its pseudonymous "Janus" whose efforts to destroy the authority of the Pope and the Council was "an elaborate attempt of many hands"—the "Janus", whose effort to destroy the authority of the Pope, was translated into several languages.[6]

Cardinal Manning made it a particular duty during the eight months in which he was a "close and constant witness of the procedure and acts of the Council, to keep pace with the histories and representations made by the press in Italy, Germany, France, and England". In answer to an enquiry from England as to what was to be believed concerning the Council he replied: "Read carefully the correspondence from Rome published in England, believe the reverse, and you will not be far from the truth".[7] He noted the manner in which the press campaign designed to undermine the Council had clearly been pre-arranged and was carefully co-ordinated.[8] "A league of newspapers, fed from a common centre, diffused hope and confidence in all countries, that the science and enlightenment of the minority would save the Catholic Church from the immoderate pretensions of Rome, and the superstitious ignorance of the universal episcopate".[9]

The circularisation of bishops during Vatican II also had its counterpart in Vatican I. "An anonymous document was received by the bishops which appeared simultaneously in French, English, German, Italian, and Spanish, elaborately arguing against the opportuneness of defining the infallibility of the Roman pontiff".[10] Cardinal Manning also remarks on how difficult such a press campaign made it for the Council to give its entire attention to the discussion of the important matters on its agenda—a problem which was magnified many times over for the Fathers of Vatican II.

> It is obvious that for the treatment of such matters as were before the Vatican Council a complete independence and tranquillity of mind were necessary—a thing impossible under the relentless assaults of hostile governments and an ubiquitous press, with the perpetual harassing of half-informed friends and the incessant misrepresentations of enemies.[11]

The secrecy of the Council was also violated, just as during Vatican II. The enemies of the Church

> were in intimate and constant communication with those who were in opposition in the Council. Many of them obtained every schema as it was distributed to the bishops. It is to be remembered that this fact proves the violation of the secret imposed on all who were within the Council, and in those who had sworn to its observance it involved perjury.[12]

The campaign against the Council failed, of course. It failed because the Pope did not weaken. He met error with condemnation and replied to demands to modify or adapt Catholic truth to the spirit of the age by restating it with the firmness and clarity of Trent—and despite the prophecies of her enemies that the declaration of papal infallibility would mark the death blow of the Church, she emerged stronger and more vigorous than ever. This, of course, evoked the full fury of the City of Man. The hatred of the world for the Church was made manifest, and at the same time manifested the divine nature of the Catholic Church; for the hatred of the world was designated by Christ Himself as one of the marks of His Mystical Body, which must not only preach Christ crucified, but will live out the mystery of His crucifixion and resurrection until He comes again in glory. Had Christ been prepared to enter into dialogue with His enemies, had He been prepared to adapt, to make concessions, then He could have escaped crucifixion—but of what value would the Incarnation have been? Pope Pius IX followed the example of Christ whose Vicar he was and:

> As the highest point attracts the storm, so the chief violence fell upon the head of the Vicar of Jesus Christ. On this I shall say nothing. Posterity will know Pius

the Ninth; and the world already knows him now too well to remember except with sorrow and disgust, the language of his enemies. "If they have called the master of the house Beelzebub, how much more them of his household?" No one has this privilege above the Vicar of the Master; and it is a great joy and a distinct source of strength and confidence to all of the household to share this sign, which never fails to mark those who are on His side against the world.[13]

Notes

[1] PP, III, p. 15.
[2] Ibid., p. 16.
[3] Ibid.
[4] Ibid., pp. 10-11.
[5] Newsweek, 12 August 1963, p. 77.
[6] TSVC, p. 67.
[7] PP, III, p. 2.
[8] Ibid., p. 15; TSVC, pp. 68 & 151.
[9] PP, III, p. 17.
[10] TSVC, p. 70.
[11] Ibid., p. 81.
[12] Ibid., p. 145.
[13] PP, III, p. 10.

Appendix IV

Liberal Mythology

It is something of an understatement to say that for the journalists who fabricated the conciliar myth, the "goodies" were merely very good. In Appendix III Cardinal Manning is quoted as remarking on the manner during Vatican I in which "all theology, philosophy, science, culture, intellectual power, logical acumen, eloquence, candour, nobleness of mind, independence of spirit, and elevation of character in the Council" were the prerogative of those Fathers of whom the press approved. Had the Cardinal made a similar study of Vatican II he would not have needed to change a word of this assessment. Some of the journalists became caught up in their own myth to the extent of practically divinising their heroes. Thus, in an eighteen-line description of Cardinal Bea, Robert Kaiser cannot conceal his adulation:

> The Cardinal has rounded blue eyes, observant, penetrating, flickering with sudden, deep intelligence...a thin, slight, stoop-shouldered frame, bowed but not weighted beneath the burden of thought, and giving the impression of a mind encased in a tenement of clay, bespoke the fire ready to be kindled, the suppleness of restraint, the measured discretion to accept the real, the reserved power to attempt the possible, the air of intellectual do-

minion and practical conviction that the draught of life's potion given to him was to be tasted to subtlest fineness, distilled and distinguished as a fine oblation to the Father of all things.[1]

Many readers will understandably refuse to believe that this, and the quotations which follow, can possibly be genuine; that such writing could have been put forward as serious journalism for which the writers expected and received payment. Those who take the trouble to obtain the books from which they were extracted will find that these really are samples of the writing of men before whom the American bishops bowed down to offer them homage as profound thinkers and representatives of informed lay opinion.

When Hans Küng spoke in America: "The tension in the hall was electric", writes Michael Novak. "In his clear, forceful voice, his blond hair shining in the lights, Father Küng brought the careful, strong theology of Europe to American audiences caught up in the enthusiasm of Pope John's *aggiornamento*".[2] Novak reports that Dr. Küng spoke to audiences up to eight thousand, and when he remarks that they were "caught up in the enthusiasm of Pope John's *aggiornamento*" this can be translated as meaning that they were reacting as Küng told them to react in response to what the press told them *aggiornamento* meant. This was only the initial stage of the Küng cult which the prefabricators were working on. Few of his works had been translated into English at that time, but the readers of liberal journals were told that he was a great theologian and profound thinker, and they responded with the conditioned reflex of adulation. Küng was the man to hear and the man to quote, so they duly heard him, and quoted him. Basically, there was not a great deal to choose between the "promotion" of Hans Küng to middle-class Catholic audiences and that of the Beatles to the teenage market, which was taking place at the same time. During the course of the Council Cardinal Antoniutti forbade seminarists to be present at conferences given by such *periti* as Hans Küng, and gave as his reason precisely the fact that those without an adequate theological foundation would be liable to idolise those who could appear to them as daring and brilliant theologians.

> It has happened frequently during both the first and second session that a conciliar expert, attached to some doubtful and difficult doctrinal thesis, has made his theory public in the lecture hall of a Roman college in the presence of students who looked upon the lecturer as an idol. The results cannot differ from those which occur in the realm of politics when a demagogue addresses the crowd.[3]

Robert Kaiser most certainly puts Cardinal Suenens in the same class as Cardinal Bea. "The Belgian Cardinal", he writes, "was an impressive figure, tall, lean, graying at the temples, his eyes flashing out of deep eye sockets. Though one of the youngest and newest cardinals, he already had a reputation as a towering intellectual, and the Fathers listened intently".[4] Needless to say, to have a reputation as a "towering intellectual" simply means that Mr. Kaiser and his friends state that this is the case! Kaiser then goes on to describe a speech by the Cardinal. "Many were stirred by his words—and those stirred included Pope John". One can only conclude that his knowledge of this fact indicates that Mr. Kaiser himself must have been blessed with some rare charismatic gift as the Pope was in his apartment at the time; nonetheless, even his most secret thoughts were known to the intrepid correspondent of *Time* who, according to Michael Novak, "had more sources of information to tap" than any other reporter at the Council. "In his private apartment," writes Kaiser, "John XXIII sat watching on closed circuit television, and he too, was stirred. 'At last, the Fathers are beginning to understand what this Council is for', he said".[5]

Any Father who expresses sentiments acceptable to Kaiser is rewarded with almost superhuman qualities. Bishop De Smedt makes a speech in favour of ecumenism and while doing so rolls "his eyes over the assembly with the pinpointing magnetism of the born orator".[6] He expounds the virtues of ecumenism with "obviously inspired words".[7]

Like all enthusiasts, Catholic liberals take themselves very seriously. Michael Novak reports on a long discussion which took place between some American journalist and two of the lay auditors charged with presenting lay opinion at the Council:

> The group met in a large sitting room, and seated themselves on soft divans and chairs. A maid dressed in a pink dress with a tiny white apron wheeled in a cart with espresso coffee, cigarettes, and cigars. The two auditors were eager to learn about the attitudes of laymen in the United States; the Americans tried their best to explain the position of the American Church, its coming out of the ghetto, the desire among the more highly educated Catholics to enter secular organisations and associations rather than Catholic ones....As the evening wore on, the maid brought in a tray of scotch, ice cubes, and water. In a mood of relaxation...they couldn't help reflecting on the creativity of this age in the Church's history. Here were six men trying to think what the future of the world in which they lived would be like....On one point they all agreed: they wanted to leave as many doors open as possible. Not enough thought had gone into the position of the layman in the world to make it easy, as yet, to see just who the layman is or what he can do....John Cogley, with his unassuming smile and diffident way, began to

talk more and more as the evening progressed. At one point he remarked that he did not like the word, the layman's "role". He liked to think of everything the layman did as sacramental, "even", he said, looking around the room in which the men sat, "even talking in this room, carrying on this conversation here tonight, I think that it's a holy thing, a good thing".[8]

Any comment on this utter drivel would be superfluous beyond wondering what the maid would have thought had she been invited to take part in the discussion, and what relevance the vacuous clichés of these self-appointed spokesmen for the laity would have had to the faith which she learned from her catechism. But now men like this have largely had their way; Vatican II has changed the Church into one vast discussion group, as Father Bryan Houghton has remarked. And what of those like the maid?—those who bring the whisky and cigars to those who sit on soft divans for "sacramental discussions". They are drifting away from the Church in their millions because they had imagined that religion was all to do with God; with worshipping Him, trying to obey Him, repenting when they did not, and trying again. If they want a discussion they can go to an espresso bar for it.

In contrast with the progressives, who are good, tolerant and brilliant, the "curialists" are not simply bad but brainless. "The bishops were learning, too, about the intellectual bankruptcy of the curialists in Rome. When they held conferences with integralist theologians, they found them a defensive lot, inclined to rely not on reasoned argument but on wild charges".[9] It must be presumed that Kaiser also used his charismatic gifts to discover these facts. In contrast with the curialists, theologians such as Hans Küng are "theologians on the march, men well equipped with the ideas that dovetailed neatly into the needs of pastors around the world".[10]

Pope Pius XII was no more than "a small town aristocrat" who wrote "rivers of words" but "was simply not listened to with understanding by a Church composed of intelligent beings". Kaiser is even able to reveal that the majority of laymen and not even all the bishops to whom the encyclicals of Pope Pius were addressed bothered to read them.[11] He makes special mention of the encyclical *Humani Generis*, which, he assures us, could not have survived the climate of Vatican II—and in this respect he is certainly correct, but this is a condemnation of the Council and not of the encyclical. "To this Council", he writes, "*Humani Generis* would have been too juridical, too scholastic, too authoritarian, too negative, too narrow, too pessimistic, destructive of theological progress, not ecumenical, not biblical, not patristic".[12]

The declaration of papal infallibility by Vatican I is described as "a heedlessly divisive act, and a demonstration of the futility of formalism in the face of the nineteenth-century revolt against authority".[13] Father Antoine Wegner of *La Croix*, whose influence upon the French bishops has already been referred to, makes the following comment with regard to Archbishop Carli of Segni: "He had often been heard in the first session. His pathetic voice will again often be heard, and his specious arguments in favour of the primacy and against the collegiality of the bishops".[14]

The crime of Bishop Carli was, of course, to hold different views from those of Father Wegner. Similarly, Henri Fesquet never has the slightest doubt that his grasp of theology is more profound than any bishops who had the temerity to depart from the prefabricated consensus which most Fathers had been conditioned to accept. Throughout his verbose and expensive book, *Le Journal du Concile* (over 1,100 pages, the epitomisation of the "Spirit of Vatican II"), there is more than the implicit presumption that to deviate by even a hair's breadth from the rigid party line which he adopts denotes intellectual bankruptcy and theological ignorance. He writes:

> For these bishops, and for those who think like them, it appears quite obvious that Catholicism is the only true religion and that the idea of being a Protestant or a Marxist is quite unthinkable. Such attitudes have horrified many who have heard them expressed, but they are indicative of an attitude still widely held in certain countries with a largely Catholic population. They reveal a scarcely credible narrowness of outlook and a total disregard for the elementary sense of respect for one's neighbour. This sectarianism is totally incompatible with justice and *a fortiori* the charity demanded by the Gospel.[15]

It would be hard to improve upon the last two sentences as a description of the establishment of which Monsieur Fesquet is so prominent a member.

Those with first hand experience of the Roman Curia and its officials take a very different view to that of the liberal journalists. Members of the Roman Curia, writes Cardinal Heenan, opposed the Council not because they were terrified lest

> power should pass from their hands. They were dedicated men, and those dedicated to a cause are not usually self-centred. Cardinals in the Curia, mostly wise old men, foresaw that the Council would cause an upheaval in the Church. The Pope, as every hierarchy received by him during the first session knows, thought of the Council as a glorified Synod of Rome. Would it be necessary, he asked us all, to have a second session and would the second session be the last?[16]

Pope John's Council

Dom Peter Flood, O.S.B., who, at the time of the Council, was certainly one of England's most distinguished Catholic scholars, spent a good deal of time working with the Curia in Rome before the Council. In a letter to *The Tablet*, he insisted that to talk of a need to reform the Curia was quite unjust. "I have indeed learnt", he wrote, "to have a very deep respect for the untiring and, in this world unrewarding, work of most curial officials and for their endless patience even under unjust suspicion and calumny. One can only hope that whatever reorganisation may come to pass will be recognised as such, and not as a reflection, in an adverse sense, on hardworking priests".[17]

It is for the reader to make his choice between the two pictures of the Curia. In fairness to Michael Novak, it must be noted that he did make an effort to balance his criticism of Cardinal Ottaviani and the Curia with a tribute to what he had the honesty to recognise as their obvious sincerity.

> There is no doubt, for example, that men like Cardinal Ottaviani, the son of a baker from Trastevere and a long and faithful servant of the Church, are personally admirable men, and attractive personalities. Many in Rome know the good that Cardinal Ottaviani does for the orphans near the Vatican and in other pious causes. His orphans call him "Father" not "Cardinal", and show genuine love and affection for him. Moreover, Cardinal Ottaviani's friends are many and devoted; they find him the most witty, urbane, gentle and sensitive of men. The same might be said of many other members of the Roman Curia; it is a mistake to picture them as villains, scoundrels, or willfully dishonest pursuers of their own power.[18]

This generous tribute indicates, once again, how wrong it would be to over-generalise or take too simplistic an attitude to any aspect of the Council, even the liberal journalists. Like most liberals, they are sad rather than sinister, men who think that what matters in life is to be "with it" rather than be right, although they may well believe in all sincerity that whatever transient "it" they happen to be "with" at a particular moment is the right thing with which to be.

Perhaps the most perfect evocation of the mentality of the establishment journalist is provided in a report by Henri Fesquet of some remarks emanating from M. Turowicz, a Polish member of IDO-C's international committee. Turowicz belongs to ZNAK, a Catholic group attached to the Communist-dominated National Unity Front in Poland. ZNAK was permitted to function because it suited the purposes of Communism to let it do so. Turowicz was allowed to say what he wished to say because it suited the purposes of Communism to let him do so. Any comment on his remarks would clearly be superfluous. Henri Fesquet writes:

> M. Turowicz, a Polish journalist from Cracow, has underlined the disadvantages of the reporting of religious news from too apologetic a standpoint, which underestimates the maturity of the Christian people and which, under the pretext of not scandalising the weak, does not dare to tell the whole truth. He insisted upon the principle by which the journalist, and no one else, judges what he can or cannot say.[19]

As a sad and very significant conclusion to this appendix, it can be noted that John Cogley, who was mentioned on page 398, had not only apostatised before his death in March 1976, but was actually studying for the ministry of the Protestant Episcopalian Church. The reasons which prompted him to apostatise are set out in his book *A Canterbury Pilgrim*, which was published in the same year.[20] As a reporter for the journal *Commonweal*, no one had been more influential than Cogley in moulding the opinion of American Catholics as to what they should think of the Council and its reforms. His prestige was such that he gave lectures to entire hierarchies who came dutifully to sit at his feet to be instructed on the nature of their authority and the manner in which they should exercise it.[21] Cogley was also a member of the International Committee of IDOC, together with Robert Kaiser, Henri Fesquet, Turowicz, and Gregory Baum.[22] In 1978, Baum married a former nun in Montreal without having received any dispensation from Rome releasing him from his priestly obligations and religious vows (he was a member of the Augustinian Order).[23] And as for Hans Küng, the most revered figure in the Liberal Pantheon, in December 1979, he was deprived of the right to teach as a Catholic theologian, to the outrage of Yves Congar and the other directors of the *Concilium*.[24]

Notes

[1] IC, pp. 34-35.
[2] OC, p. 15.
[3] JC, p. 676.
[4] IC, pp. 217-218.
[5] *Ibid.*, pp. 218.
[6] *Ibid.*, 166.
[7] *Ibid.*, p. 168.
[8] OC, pp. 15, 6-7.
[9] IC, p. 139.
[10] *Ibid.*
[11] *Ibid.*, p. 38.
[12] *Ibid.*, p. 209.
[13] *Ibid.*, p. 202.
[14] *The Tablet*, 8 August 1964, p. 752.
[15] IC, p. 492.
[16] CC, p. 2.
[17] *The Tablet*, 3 July 1965, p. 752.
[18] OC, p. 234.
[19] IC, p. 1035.
[20] *The Cincinnati Enquirer*, 22 December 1976.
[21] OC, pp. 154-155.
[22] "Dossier on IDOC", *Approaches*, 10-11, 1968.
[23] *The Pilot*, 24 February 1978.
[24] *The Catholic Herald*, 11 January 1980.

Appendix V

The Declaration *Dominus Jesus* Regarding the Term *Subsistit*

The following passage is extracted from the Declaration on the unicity and salvific universality of Jesus Christ and the Church *Dominus Iesus* (*Declaratio de Iesu Christi atque Ecclesiae unicitate et universalitate salvifica*), published by the Congregation for the Doctrine of the Faith on 6 August 2000. The full text is available on the Vatican Web site, "Documents of a Doctrinal Nature".

In connection with the unicity and universality of the salvific mediation of Jesus Christ, the unicity of the Church founded by Him must be firmly believed as a truth of Catholic faith. Just as there is one Christ, so there exists a single body of Christ, a single Bride of Christ: "a single Catholic and apostolic Church". Furthermore, the promises of the Lord that He would not abandon His Church (cf. Mt. 16:18; 28:20) and that He would guide her by His Spirit (cf. Jn. 16:13) mean, according to Catholic faith, that the unicity and the unity of the Church—like everything that belongs to the Church's integrity—will never be lacking.

The Catholic faithful are required to profess that there is an historical continuity—rooted in the apostolic succession—between the Church founded by Christ and the Catholic Church: "This is the single Church of Christ... which our Saviour, after His resurrection, entrusted to Peter's pastoral care (cf. Jn. 21:17), commissioning him and the other Apostles to extend and rule her (cf. Mt. 28:18ff.), erected for all ages as 'the pillar and mainstay of the truth' (I Tim. 3:15). This Church, constituted and organised as a society in the present world, subsists in [*subsistit in*] the Catholic Church, governed by the Successor of Peter and by the Bishops in communion with him". With the expression *subsistit in*, the Second Vatican Council sought to harmonise two doctrinal statements: on the one hand, that the Church of Christ, despite the divisions which exist among Christians, continues to exist fully only in the Catholic Church, and on the other hand, that "outside of her structure, many elements can be found of sanctification and truth", that is, in those Churches and ecclesial communities which are not yet in full communion with the Catholic Church. The interpretation of those who would derive from the formula *subsistit in* the thesis that the one Church of Christ could subsist also in non-Catholic Churches and ecclesial communities is therefore contrary to the authentic meaning of *Lumen gentium*. "The Council instead chose the word *subsistit* precisely to clarify that there exists only one 'subsistence' of the true Church, while outside her visible structure there only exist *elementa Ecclesiae*, which—being elements of that same Church—tend and lead toward the Catholic Church". But with respect to these, it needs to be stated that "they derive their efficacy from the very fullness of grace and truth entrusted to the Catholic Church".

Therefore, there exists a single Church of Christ, which subsists in the Catholic Church, governed by the Successor of Peter and by the bishops in communion with him. The Churches which, while not existing in perfect communion with the Catholic Church, remain united to her by means of the closest bonds, that is, by apostolic succession and a valid Eucharist, are true particular Churches (see below). Therefore, the Church of Christ is present and operative also in these Churches, even though they lack full communion with the Catholic Church, since they do not accept the Catholic doctrine of the Primacy, which, according to the will of God, the Bishop of Rome objectively has and exercises over the entire Church.

On the other hand, the ecclesial communities which have not preserved the valid episcopate and the genuine and integral substance of the Eucharistic mystery, are not Churches in the proper sense; however, those who are baptised in these communities are, by baptism, incorporated in Christ and thus are in a certain communion, albeit imperfect, with the Church. Baptism in fact tends *per se* toward the full development of life in Christ, through the integral profession of faith, the Eucharist, and full communion in the Church.

The Christian faithful are therefore not permitted to imagine that the Church of Christ is nothing more than a collection—divided, yet in some way one, of Churches and ecclesial communities; nor are they free to hold that today the Church of Christ nowhere really exists, and must be considered only as a goal which all Churches and ecclesial communities must strive to reach. In fact, "the elements of this already-given Church exist, joined together in their fullness in the Catholic Church and, without this fullness, in the other communities". "Therefore, these separated Churches and communities as such, though we believe they suffer from defects, have by no means been deprived of significance and importance in the mystery of salvation. For the spirit of Christ has not refrained from using them as means of salvation which derive their efficacy from the very fullness of grace and truth entrusted to the Catholic Church".

Commentary

Some traditional Catholics have questioned the possibility as to how there can be true churches not in communion with the pope or that "outside of her structure, many elements can be found of sanctification and truth". As was explained above, a distinction must be made between the universal Catholic Church and particular churches which are dioceses. One thus has the church of New York, the church of Milan, the church of Paris, the church of Madrid. These churches are, of course, in full communion with the Pope. The term Church is also used for the Catholic Eastern Churches which are also composed of individual dioceses (churches). But what of churches, dioceses, that have breached their unity with the Holy See? Do they cease to be particular churches? By no means. As was explained earlier, on 8 September 1868, in his Apostolic Letter *Arcano Divinae Providentiae*, Pope Pius IX wrote to all the bishops of the Churches of the Oriental Rite not in communion with Rome, inviting them to the Vatican to take part in the First Vatican Council on the same basis as Latin Rite bishops. There is thus no doubt whatsoever that the dioceses of the Eastern Orthodox Churches constitute true particular churches despite being schismatic.

And what of the claim that "outside of her [the Church's] structure, many elements can be found of sanctification and truth"? It hardly needs to be stated that this is evidently true in the case of the Eastern Orthodox Churches which have seven valid sacraments. Every valid sacrament is a sacrament of the Catholic Church even if celebrated outside

The Declaration *Dominus Jesus* Re: the Term *Subsistit*

her visible communion. Thus every baptism is a Catholic baptism, even in the most anti-Catholic Protestant denominations. Children baptised outside the visible unity of the Church remain Catholics until they have reached the age of reason and adhere to the heretical tenets of their sect, but as, almost invariably, they do so in good faith as a result of invincible ignorance, their heresy is only material and they incur no guilt.

Great anger was evinced among Anglicans and other Protestant denominations when the Congregation for the Doctrine of the Faith designated them as "ecclesial communities" rather than "Churches" on the grounds that ecclesial communities which have not preserved the valid episcopate and the genuine and integral substance of the Eucharistic mystery are not Churches in the proper sense; however, those who are baptised in these communities are, by baptism, incorporated in Christ and thus are in a certain communion, albeit imperfect, with the Church. Anglicans, of course, insist that they possess valid orders and a valid Eucharist. *Dominus Jesus* states with regard to these ecclesial communities:

> The Council instead chose the word *subsistit* precisely to clarify that there exists only one "subsistence" of the true Church, while outside her visible structure there only exist *elementa Ecclesiae*, which—being elements of that same Church—tend and lead toward the Catholic Church.

To accept that elements of the Church do exist outside the visible unity of the Church one needs only to examine the life of Cardinal Newman. In my biography of this giant of the Catholic Church, it can be seen clearly that even as an Anglican almost all his teaching was in perfect conformity with that of the true Church, and that his *Parochial and*

Plain Sermons may well be the most profound exposition of the Christian religion since the time of the Fathers.[1] It is unlikely that any Catholic scholar of his time had a knowledge of patristic theology that equalled that of Newman in his Anglican days. As my book shows, it was his study of the Fathers that eventually brought him into the Church. It is indeed these elements of the Church in Protestant denominations that led, and still lead, so many of their members into the true Church.

CARDINAL NEWMAN (1801-1890), On Baptism of Desire

One of the most remarkable instances of what I am insisting on is found in a dogma, which no Catholic can ever think of disputing, viz., that "Out of the Church, and out of the faith, is no salvation". Not to go to Scripture, it is the doctrine of St. Ignatius, St. Irenaeus, St. Cyprian in the first three centuries, as of St. Augustine and his contemporaries in the fourth and fifth. It can never be other than an elementary truth of Christianity; and the present pope has proclaimed it as all popes, doctors, and bishops before him. But that truth has two aspects, according as the force of the negative falls upon the "Church" or upon the "salvation". The main sense is, that there is no other communion or so-called Church, but the Catholic, in which are stored the promises, the sacraments, and other means of salvation; the other and derived sense is, that no one can be saved who is not in that one and only Church. But it does not follow, because there is no Church but one, which has the Evangelical gifts and privileges to bestow, that therefore no one can be saved without the intervention of that one Church. Anglicans quite understand this distinction; for, on the one hand, their Article says, "They are to be had accursed (*anathema-*

tizandi) that presume to say, that every man shall be saved *by* (in) the law or sect which he professeth, so that he be diligent to frame his life according to that law and the light of nature"; while on the other hand they speak of and hold the doctrine of the "uncovenanted mercies of God". The latter doctrine in its Catholic form is the doctrine of invincible ignorance—or, that it is possible to belong to the soul of the Church without belonging to the body; and, at the end of eighteen hundred years, it has been formally and authoritatively put forward by the present pope (the first pope, I suppose, who has done so), on the very same occasion on which he has repeated the fundamental principle of exclusive salvation itself. It is to the purpose here to quote his words, they occur in the course of his encyclical, addressed to the bishops of Italy, under the date of 10 August 1863.

> We and you know, that those who lie under invincible ignorance as regards our most Holy Religion, and who, diligently observing the natural law and its precepts which are engraven by God on the hearts of all, and prepared to obey God, lead a good and upright life, are able, by the operation of the power of divine light and grace, to obtain eternal life.

Who would at first sight gather from the wording of so forcible a universal, that an exception to its operation, such as this, so distinct, and, for what we know, so very wide, was consistent with holding it?

Footnote 7 reads:

> The Pope speaks more forcibly still in an earlier Allocution. After mentioning invincible ignorance he adds: "*Quis tantum sibi arroget, ut hujusmodi ignorantiae designare limites queat, juxta populorum, regionum, ingeniorum, aliarumque rerum tam multarum rationem et varietatem?*" "Who

claims for himself so much so that he can delineate the limits of ignorance of this kind according to the scheme and variety of peoples, regions, characters and so many other things?" 9 December, 1854.

CARDINAL MANNING (1808-1892), On the Workings of the Holy Spirit in the Church of England[2]

A LETTER TO THE REVEREND E. B. PUSEY, D.D.

The English people as a body are baptised, and therefore elevated to the order of supernatural grace. Every infant, and also every adult baptised having the necessary dispositions, is thereby placed in a state of justification; and, if they die without committing any mortal sin, would certainly be saved.They are also, in the sight of the Church, Catholics. St. Augustine says, *"Ecclesia etiam inter eos qui foris sunt per baptismum generat suos"*. A mortal sin of any kind, including *prava voluntas electio*, the perverse election of the will by which in riper years such persons chose for themselves, notwithstanding sufficient light, heresy instead of the true faith, and schism instead of the unity of the Church, would indeed deprive them of their state of grace. But before such act of self-privation all such people are regarded by the Catholic Church as in the way of eternal life. With perfect confidence of faith, we extend the shelter of this truth over the millions of infants and young children who every year pass to their Heavenly Father. We extend it also in hope to many more who grow up in their baptismal grace. Catholic missionaries in this country have often assured me of a fact, attested also by my own experience, that they have received into the Church persons grown to adult life, in whom their baptismal grace was still preserved. How can we, then, be supposed to regard such persons as no better than heathens? To ascribe the good lives of such persons to the power of nature would be Pelagianism. To deny their goodness would be Jansenism. And with such a consciousness, how could anyone regard his past spiritual life in the Church of England as a mockery? I have no deeper conviction than that the grace of the Holy Spirit was with me from my earliest consciousness. Though at the time, perhaps, I knew it not as I know it now, yet I can clearly perceive the order and chain of grace by which God mercifully led me onward from childhood to the age of twenty years. From that time the interior workings of His light and grace which continued through all my life, till the hour when that light and grace had its perfect work, to which all its operations had been converging, in submission to the fullness of truth, and of the Spirit in the Church of God, is a reality as profoundly, certain, intimate, and sensible to me now as that live. Never have I by the lightest word breathed a doubt of this fact in the Divine order of grace. Never have I allowed anyone who has come to me for guidance or instruction to harbour a doubt of the past workings of grace in them. It would be not only a sin of ingratitude, but a sin against truth. The working of the Holy Spirit in individual souls is, as I have said, as old as the fall of man, and as wide as the human race. It is not we who ever breathe or harbour a doubt of this. It is rather they who accuse us of it. Because, to believe such an error possible in others, shows how little consciousness there must be of the true doctrine of grace in themselves. And such, I am forced to add, is my belief, because I know by experience how inadequately I understood the doctrine of grace until I learned it of the Catholic Church. And I trace the same inadequate conception of the workings of grace in almost every Anglican writer I know, not excepting even those who are nearest to the truth.

But, further, our theologians teach, not only that the state of baptismal innocence exists, and may be preserved out of the Church, but that they who in good faith are out of it, if they shall correspond with the grace they have already received, will receive an increase or augmentation of grace.[3] I do not for a moment doubt that there are to be found among the English people individuals who practise in a high degree the four cardinal virtues, and in no small degree, though with the limits and blemishes inseparable from their state, the three theological virtues of Faith,[4] Hope, and Charity infused into them in their baptism. I do not think, my dear friend, in all that I have said or written in the last fourteen years, that you can find a word implying so much as a doubt of these workings of the Holy Spirit among all the baptised who are separated from the Catholic Church.

I will go further still. The doctrine, *"extra ecclesiam nulla salus"* is to be interpreted both by dogmatic and by moral theology. As a dogma, theologians teach that many belong to the Church who are out of its visible unity;[5] as a moral truth that to be out of the Church is no personal sin except to those who sin in being out of it. That is, they will be lost, not because they are *geographically* out of it, but because they are *culpably* out of it. And they who are culpably out of it are those who know—or might, and therefore ought to know—that it is their duty to submit to it. The Church teaches that men may be inculpably out of its pale. Now they are inculpably out of it who are, and have always been, either physically or morally unable to see their obligation to submit to it. And they only are culpably out of it who are both physically and morally able to know that it is God's will they should submit to the Church; and either knowing it will not obey that knowledge, or, not knowing it, are culpable for that ignorance. I will say, then, that we hopefully apply this benign law of our Divine Master as far as possible to the English people. First, it is applicable in the letter to the whole multitude of those baptised persons who are under the age of reason. Secondly, to all who are in good faith, of whatsoever age they be: such as a great many of the poor and unlettered, to whom it is often physically, and very often morally, impossible to judge which is the true revelation or the true Church of God. I say physically, because in these three hundred years the Catholic Church has been so swept off the face of England that nine or ten generations of men have lived and died without the Faith being so much as proposed to them, or the Church ever visible to them; and I say morally, because the great majority of the poor, from lifelong prejudice, are often incapable of judging in questions so removed from the primary truths of conscience and Christianity. Of such simple persons it may be said that *infantibus aequiparantur*, they are to be classed morally with infants. Again, to these may be added the unlearned in all classes, among whom many have no contact with the Catholic Church, or with Catholic books. Under this head will come a great number of wives and daughters, whose freedom of religious inquiry and religious thought is unjustly limited or suspended by the authority of parents and husbands. Add, lastly, the large class who have been studiously brought up, with all the dominant authority of the English tradition of three hundred years, to believe sincerely, and without a doubt, that the Catholic Church is corrupt, has changed the doctrines of the Faith, and that the author of the Reformation is the Spirit of holiness and truth. It may seem incredible to some that such an illusion exists. But it is credible to me, because for nearly forty years of my life I was fully possessed by this erroneous belief. To all such persons it is morally difficult in no small degree to discover the falsehood of this illusion. All the better parts of their nature are engaged in its support: dutifulness, self-mistrust, submission, respect for others older, better, more learned than themselves, all combine to form a false conscience, and the duty to refuse to hear anything against "the religion of their fathers", "the Church of their baptism", or to read anything which could unsettle them. Such people are told that it is their duty to extinguish a doubt against the Church of England, as they would extinguish a temptation against their virtue. A conscience so subdued and held in subjection exercises true virtues upon a false object, and renders to a human authority the submissive trust which is due only to the Divine voice of the Church of God.

Still further, I believe that the people of England were not all guilty of the first acts of heresy and schism by which they were separated from true Catholic unity and faith. They were robbed of it. In many places they rose in arms for it. The children, the poor, the unlearned at that time, were certainly innocent: much more the next generation. They were born into a state of privation. They knew no better. No choice was before them. They made no perverse act of the will in remaining where they were born. Every successive generation was still less culpable, in proportion as they were born into a greater privation, and under the dominion of a tradition of error already grown strong. For three centuries they have been born further and further out of the truth, and their culpability is perpetually diminishing; and as they were passively borne onward in the course of the English separation, the moral responsibility for the past is proportionately less.

The Divine law is peremptory: "To him who knoweth to do good, and doth it not, to him it is sin".[6] Every Divine truth, as it shines in upon us, lays its obligation on our conscience to believe and to obey it. When the Divine authority of the Church manifests itself to our intellect, it lays its jurisdiction upon our conscience to submit to it. To refuse is an act of infidelity, and the least act of infidelity in its measure expels faith; one mortal act of it will expel the habit of faith altogether.[7] Every such act of infidelity grieves the Holy Ghost by a direct opposition to His Divine voice speaking through the Church; the habit of such opposition is one of the six sins against the Holy Ghost defined as "impugning the known truth". Nothing that I have said above modifies the absolute and vital necessity of submitting to the Catholic Church as the only way of salvation to those who know it, by the revelation of God, to be such. But I must not attempt now to treat of this point.

Nevertheless, for the reasons above given, we make the largest allowance for all who are in invincible ignorance; always supposing that there is a preparation of heart to embrace the truth when they see it, at any cost; a desire to know it; and a faithful use of the means of knowing it, such a study, docility, prayer, and the like. But I do not now enter into the case of the educated or the learned, or of those who have liberty of mind and means of inquiry. I cannot class them under the above enumeration of those who are inculpably out of the truth. I leave them, therefore, to the only judge of all men.

Lastly, I will not here attempt to estimate how far all I have said is being modified by the liberation and expansion of the Catholic Church in England during the last thirty years. It is certain that the restoration of the Catholic Hierarchy with the universal tumult which published it to the whole world, still more by its steady, widespread, and penetrating action throughout England, is taking away every year the plea of invincible ignorance.

It is certain, however, that to those who, being invincibly ignorant, faithfully co-operate with the grace they have received, an augmentation of grace is given; and this at once places the English people, so far as they come within the limits of these conditions, in a state of supernatural grace, even though they be out of the visible unity of the Church. I do not now enter into the question of the state of those who fall from baptismal grace by mortal sin, or of the great difficulty and uncertainty of their restoration. This would lead me too far; and it lies beyond the limits of this Letter.

It must not, however, be forgotten for a moment that this applies to the whole English people, of all forms of Christianity, or, as it is called, of all denominations. What I have said does not recognise the grace *of* the Church of England as such. The working of grace in the Church of England is a truth we joyfully hold and always teach. But we as joyfully recognise the working of the Holy Spirit among Dissenters of every kind. Indeed, I must say that I am far more able to assure myself of the invincible ignorance of Dissenters as a mass than of Anglicans as a mass. They are far more deprived of what survived of Catholic truth; far more distant from the idea of a Church; far more traditionally opposed to it by the prejudice of education; I must add, for the most part, far more simple in their belief in the person and passion our Divine Lord. Their piety is more like the personal service of disciples to a personal Master than the Anglican piety, which has always been more dim and distant from this central light of souls.

CARDINAL FRANCIS BOURNE (1861-1935) Archbishop of Westminster—Preface to *Mortalium Animos* (1928)

If Christ has actually given a clear definite revelation of truth about God and His revelation to His creatures, and has promised that revelation shall continue to the end of the world, and be safeguarded against error, it follows that every creature who becomes convinced of the reality of that revelation is bound to accept it. If God the Creator speaks, the creature is bound to listen and to believe what He utters. Hence the axiom "Outside the Church there is no salvation". But, as it is equally true that without the deliberate act of the will there can be neither fault nor sin, so evidently this axiom applies only to those who are outside the Church knowingly, deliberately, and wilfully.

The Declaration *Dominus Jesus* Re: the Term *Subsistit*

And this is the doctrine of the Catholic Church on this often misunderstood and misrepresented aphorism. There are the covenanted and uncovenanted dealings of God with His creatures, and no creature is outside His fatherly care. There are millions—even at this day the vast majority of mankind—who are still unreached or unaffected by the message of Christianity in any shape or form. There are large numbers who are persuaded that the old covenant still prevails and are perfectly sincere and conscientious in their observance of the Jewish law. And there are millions who accept some fashion of Christian teaching who have never adverted to the idea of Unity as I have described it, and have no thought that they are obliged in conscience to accept the teaching and to submit to the authority of the Catholic Church. All such, whether separated wholly from the acceptance of Christ and His teaching, or accepting that teaching only to the extent in which they have perceived it, will be judged on their own merits. They are bound to accept and follow God's teaching so far as their reason rightly used shall lead them. They must obey the dictates of the moral law which their conscience imposes upon them. They must regret before God, and endeavour to undo, the faults and sins that they commit against their reason and their conscience. And they are bound at all cost to enter within the Unity of the Church so soon as they realise that that obligation is incumbent upon them.

When or how such a realisation may come to them no one can say. To what extent they may attain it is the secret of God. But this is certain, that no man of really good will is ever rejected by his Maker, and that to every soul is offered real opportunity of salvation. None can be lost, whether within or without the visible unity of the Church, except by his own deliberate fault.

Pope John's Council

CTS Pamphlet: CATHOLIC ANSWERS by Catholic Evidence Guild Speakers, published 1956

THE SALVATION OF NON-CATHOLICS

Although the Catholic Church, in her unique life, has reached wonderfully far in time and space, it cannot be said that she has taught all men in all ages. Yet the principle—"Outside the Church there is no salvation"—is fully accepted by Catholics. What becomes of those millions of people, separated from her by the period or place in which they live, or by lack of knowledge or any other circumstance beyond their control?

To become sons of God by grace, and to know Him intimately in heaven, men need Baptism, for it is the re-birth into His family. Now Baptism is very simple and remarkably universal. Anyone having the right intention and a little water can perform it, and anyone can receive it. This means of course that vast numbers of people outside the visible unity of the Church receive the life of grace through her first sacrament. Should they keep it securely through life, they will quite certainly see God in heaven.

Yet even this wide embrace leaves untouched great numbers of men and women who have never heard of Christian Baptism or who have missed its significance. In considering their position we must remind ourselves that Christ is the true light enlightening every man coming into the world. We know little of the subtle way in which He works upon the minds of those who do not know Him. But it is certain that the man who welcomes His approach and admits Him, even implicitly, would certainly seek Baptism if he realised that it was divinely intended for him. And where the obstacle is lack of knowledge or anything else beyond his power to remedy, Catholics believe that Christ brings the happy effects of Baptism to him, and he receives what is known as

The Declaration *Dominus Jesus* Re: the Term *Subsistit*

the Baptism of Desire. Here we have a door which is closed to no man.

But what of later falls from grace? The Catholic relies upon the Sacrament of Penance (Confession) to deal with his failures after Baptism. But many have missed, through no fault of their own, the enormous consolation of hearing a human voice declare, with authority, that their sins are forgiven. But even this loss does not mean that no mercy can reach them. It is a fact that sincere sorrow for sin, into which the love of God enters, really does restore the sinner. Where the sin is of a mortal nature, this sorrow needs to be based upon the pure love of God in Himself. It is certain that God is utterly aware of the half-lights and shadows of the pagan mind. Infinite mercy, dealing with it, can make the fullest allowances, and give and nurture all the fundamental faith and quality of contrition necessary to effect a perfect union with Himself.

In the light of all this, how can it be maintained that outside the Church there is no salvation? The reply is twofold:—

(i) Where Christ acts, the Church moves in Him, for He is its Head.

(ii) His action upon the individual soul tends always to draw it to the Church as to its sheepfold. A man is saved in so far as he is a Catholic, i.e., according to the truth and the grace that is in him; not in despite of the Church, but to the extent of his living relationship with her.

— Walter Jewell

Notes

[1] Michael Davies, *Lead Kindly Light* (Long Prairie, Minn.: Neumann Press, 2001).

[2] H. E. Manning, *The Workings of the Holy Spirit in the Church of England* (London: Burns & Oates, 1890), pp. 13-23.

³ Suarez, *De Div. Gratia*, lib. iv. c. xi.; Ripalda, *De Ente Supernaturali*, lib. i. disp. xx. sect. xii. et seq.; S. Alphonsi *Theol. Moral.*, lib. I. tract. I. 5, 6.

⁴ De Lugo, *De Virtute Divinae Fidei*, disp. xvii. sect. iv. v.; Viva, *Cursus Theol.* p. iv. disp. iv. quaest. iii. 7.

⁵ See Perrons, *Prefect. Theolog.* pars I. c. ii. I, 2 : "*Omnes et soli justi pertinent ad Ecclesiae animam. "Ad Christi Ecclesiae corpus secant fideles omnes tam justi quam peccatores*". St. Augustine expresses these two propositions in six words: "*Multae oves foris, multi lupi intus*". S. Aug., tom. iii. pars ii. p. 600.

⁶ James 4:17.

⁷ De Lugo, *De Divinae Fidei* disp. xvii. sect. iv. 53 et seq.

Appendix VI

Sillonism

Just as it is difficult to believe that St. Pius X did not compose *Pascendi Gregis* with the post-Vatican II situation in mind, so it seems hard to credit the fact that his encyclical on the Sillon was not addressed specifically towards the attitude to the world which has infected so many "socially aware" Catholics since the Council, and which was foreshadowed in the Constitution *Gaudium et Spes*. The word *"sillon"* is the French for "furrow", and it was under this title that a group of early Christian Democrats grouped themselves at the end of the nineteenth century. A principal error of the Sillonists was to put forward a concept of democracy which could not be reconciled with the teaching of a long line of popes stretching back as far as Pope Pius VI. Sillonism had more in common with the Masonic concept of democracy than the teaching of the popes. Basically, this false concept maintains that the authority to govern is delegated by the people to those holding authority—in other words, authority is vested in the people. Taken to its logical conclusion, such a concept leaves room neither for the social kingship of Christ nor for the right and duty of the Church to insist that states must conform their laws to the law of God. Pope Leo XIII went right to the heart of this error when he stated:

"Authority cannot be delegated by the people because, in the first place, it does not rest with the people".

All authority is, of course, vested in God, who delegates it to those who rule. There can be a variety of ways in which those who govern are invested with their authority. The Church is equally prepared to accept a monarchy or a government chosen by free elections, as in the Western democracies; what the Church is not prepared to accept is that elected representatives receive their authority from the people rather than from God and have the right to ignore the law of God in the "name of the people". However, the parallel between Sillonism and certain characteristics of the post-conciliar Church which will be emphasised in this appendix is not so much concerned with the technicalities of concepts of democracy which cannot be reconciled with Catholic teaching, but with the Sillonist attitude to the world. It will be seen that, as is the case with so many Catholics today, and with *Gaudium et Spes*, it is an utopian attitude in which Catholics are encouraged to co-operate with men of any beliefs or none in building up an earthly paradise based on the ideals of Liberty, Equality, and Fraternity—and in the construction of this earthly paradise Catholicism is only to be considered as on equal terms with other religions and philosophies.

St. Pius X opens his encyclical on the Sillon with words which, as is customary, have been taken as its title—*Our Apostolic Mandate*. This great saint has a concept of his apostolic mandate which is imbued with the most authentic sense of Catholic tradition. St. Pius X did not believe that his apostolic mandate required that he should dialogue with the world, explain Catholic teaching in terms which the world will find acceptable, or accept creeds and philosophies intrinsically imbued with falsehood as being on an equal basis with the Church of Christ. He wrote:

Sillonism

Our apostolic mandate requires of Us that We watch over the purity of the Faith and the integrity of Catholic discipline. It requires of Us that We protect the faithful from evil and error; especially so when evil and error are presented in dynamic language which, concealing vague notions and ambiguous expressions with emotional and high-sounding words, is likely to set ablaze the hearts of men in pursuit of ideals which, while attractive, are none the less nefarious. Such were not so long ago the doctrines of the so called philosophers of the eighteenth century, the doctrines of the Revolution and Liberalism which have been so often condemned; such are even today the theories of the Sillon which, under the glowing appearance of generosity, are all too often wanting in clarity, logic and truth.

Pope St. Pius X had no hesitation in praising the sincerity and idealism of the Sillonists—and this is an example which some Catholic traditionalists could learn from in their criticisms of "progressives". It is most certainly not the intention of this book to suggest that there is anything like a monopoly of virtue in the traditionalist wing of the Church—and among the faults to which some traditionalists are prone is that of imputing unworthy motives to their opponents. While it is legitimate to criticise the views of progressives, the policies they follow, and the effects of those policies, it is for God alone to judge their motives. St. Pius X writes: "For we love, indeed, the valiant young people who fight under the Sillon's banner, and We deem them worthy of praise and admiration in many respects. We love their leaders, whom we are pleased to acknowledge as noble souls on a level above vulgar passions, and inspired with the noblest form of enthusiasm in their quest for goodness". The Pope also praises the manner in which, initially, "the Sillon did raise among the workers the standard of Jesus Christ, the symbol of salvation for peoples and nations. Nourishing its social action at the fountain of divine grace, it did impose a respect for religion upon the least willing groups, accustoming the ignorant and impious to hearing the word of God".

But the Pope then points out that perceptive observers began to note alarming trends within the movement:

> Its leaders were young, full of enthusiasm and self-confidence. But they were not adequately equipped with historical knowledge, sound philosophy, and solid theology to tackle without danger the difficult social problems in which their work and their inclinations were involving them. They were not sufficiently equipped to be on their guard against the penetration of liberal and Protestant concepts on doctrine and obedience….The truth is that the Sillonist leaders are self-confessed and irrepressible idealists…they have a particular conception of human dignity, freedom, justice and brotherhood; and, in an attempt to justify their social dreams, they put forward the Gospel, but interpreted in their own way; and, what is even more serious, they call to witness Christ, but a diminished and distorted Christ….No, Venerable Brethren, We must repeat with the utmost energy in these times of social and intellectual anarchy, when everyone takes it upon himself to teach as a teacher and lawmaker—the City cannot be built otherwise than as God has built it; society cannot be set up unless the Church lays the foundations and supervises the work; no, civilisation is not something yet to be found, nor is the New City to be built on hazy notions; it has been in existence and still is: it is Christian civilisation, it is the Catholic City. It has only to be set up and restored continually against the unremitting attacks of insane dreamers, rebels, and miscreants. OMNIA INSTAURARE IN CHRISTO (To organise all things in Christ).

The Pope is particularly critical of the Sillonist notion of fraternity,

> which they found on the love of common interest or, beyond all philosophies and religions, on the mere notion of humanity, thus embracing with an equal love and tolerance all human beings and their miseries, whether these are intellectual, moral, or physical and temporal But Catholic doctrine tells us that the prime duty of charity does not lie in the toleration of false ideas, however sincere they may be, nor in theoretical or practical indifference towards the errors and vices in which we see our brethren plunged, but in the zeal for their intellectual and moral improvement as well as for their material well-being.

St. Pius X addressed this encyclical to the French bishops as the Sillon was a specifically French movement. He expresses his confidence that these bishops will share his indignation that:

> Distrust of the Church, their Mother, is being instilled into the minds of Catholic youth; they are being taught that after nineteen centuries She has not been able to build up in this world a society on true foundations; She has not understood the social notions of authority, liberty, equality, fraternity and human dignity....What are we to say except that there are two different men in the Sillonist; the individual, who is a Catholic, and the Sillonist, the man of action, who is neutral.

St. Pius X condemns as quite unacceptable the "ecumenical" dimension of the Sillon:

Here we have, founded by Catholics, an interdenominational association that is to work for the reform of civilisation, an undertaking which is above all religious in character; for there is no true civilisation without a moral civilisation, and no true moral civilisation without the true religion: it is a proven truth, an historical fact.... What are we to think of this appeal to all the heterodox, and to all the unbelievers, to prove the excellence of their convictions in the social sphere in a sort of apologetic contest? Has not this contest lasted for nineteen centuries in conditions less dangerous for the faith of Catholics? And was it not all to the credit of the Catholic Church? What are we to think of this respect for all errors, and of this strange invitation made by a Catholic to all the dissidents to strengthen their convictions through study so that they may have more and more abundant sources of fresh forces? What are we to think of an association in which all religions and even free thought may express themselves openly and in complete freedom? For the Sillonists who, in public lectures and elsewhere, proudly proclaim their personal faith, certainly do not intend to silence others nor do they intend to prevent a Protestant from asserting his Protestantism, and the sceptic from affirming his scepticism. Finally, what are we to think of a Catholic who, on entering his study group, leaves his Catholicism outside the door so as not to alarm his comrades...? The beneficiary of this cosmopolitan social action can only be a democracy which will be neither Catholic, nor Protestant, nor Jewish. It will be a religion...more universal than the Catholic Church, uniting all men to become brothers and comrades at last in the "Kingdom of God".

The Pope then expresses his deep sadness that an organisation which had "afforded such promising expectations" had been

> harnessed in its course by the modern enemies of the Church, and is now no more than a miserable affluent of the great movement of apostasy being organised in every country for the establishment of a One-World Church which shall have neither dogmas, nor hierarchy, neither discipline for the mind, nor curb for the passions, and which, under the pretext of freedom and human dignity, would bring back to the world (if such a Church could overcome) the reign of legalised cunning and force, and the oppression of the weak, and of all who toil and suffer.

Any comment on this passage would be superfluous beyond the earnest suggestion that every reader of this book should obtain the encyclical and study it carefully.[1]

Notes

[1] *Our Apostolic Mandate* is available from the Angelus Press. It is essential reading.

Appendix VII

Salleron on Maritain

When Maritain's book *Humanisme Intégral* first appeared it was reviewed by Louis Salleron in the *Revue Hebdomadaire* of 22 August 1936. This is certainly one of the most perceptive analyses of the deficiencies of Integral Humanism which has ever appeared, and it is even more remarkable for the fact that it was not written with the benefit of hindsight, but at the time when Maritain was at the height of his reputation. In contrast with Professor Salleron, many Catholic intellectuals not only failed to see that Integral Humanism was a system replete with the serious inconsistencies and self-contradictions exposed by him, but looked upon it as a blue-print for Catholic action in the temporal order which could prove to be the salvation of the Church in the twentieth century. As was mentioned in Chapter XV, Father G. B. Montini was so enthusiastic about *Humanisme Intégral* that he translated it into Italian.

In view of its exceptional relevance to the present situation in the Church, *L'Ordre Français* reprinted Professor Salleron's review in its issue of December 1973. The introduction it provided to the review is also included in this appendix, and the fact that it was written in 1973 should be noted when reading the comments on the situation in Chile. Professor Salleron has most kindly given his permission for a translation of his review to be included as an appendix to *Pope John's Council*. The review was translated by Geoffrey Lawman who also made his own translation of the extracts from *Humanisme Intégral* cited by Professor Salleron. For the convenience of readers who possess the official English translation, or who might obtain it from their libraries, I have included the page numbers on which these quotations can be found in the translation made by M. R. Adamson and published in London in 1938 under the title *True Humanism*. These page numbers will be found in brackets after those provided in the notes to the review which, of course, refer to the original French edition. Finally, this review does not make easy reading not least because, as Professor Salleron remarks, the style in which Maritain expresses himself is not always "as clear as it might be". The review needs to be studied rather than read, and to be studied carefully during the course of several readings. Careful note must be taken of Professor Salleron's remark that there are "many excellent things to be found in *Humanisme Intégral*". It would be surprising to find any Catholic who could read it without deepening his knowledge of theology, the history of the Church, and authentic Catholic social teaching. The book does, in fact, contain so much that is excellent that without the insights of such authorities on Catholic social teaching as Louis Salleron or Hamish Fraser the ordinary reader might well have overlooked its defects. And even where these deficiencies occur, Maritain's philosophic brilliance enables him, as Father Meinvielle is quoted as stating in Chapter XV, "to defend theses which had previously been advanced by the enemies of religion without appearing directly to contradict the teaching of the Church".

INTEGRAL HUMANISM
M. Jacques Maritain, Christian Marxist

In a recent article in *Carrefour*,[1] Louis Salleron reminded us, most opportunely, of some lines Jacques Maritain had written in his *Peasant of the Garonne*:

> I only know one example of an authentic "Christian revolution", and that is the one that President Eduardo Frei is trying to carry out in Chile at the moment, and it is by no means certain that it is going to succeed. (It is true too that among those of my contemporaries still alive as I write these lines, I can only see three revolutionaries worthy of the name: Eduardo Frei in Chile, Saul Alinski in America, and myself in France, light-weight though I am alongside the others, since my vocation as a philosopher has completely clouded any talents I may have had as an agitator.)

At a moment when events in Chile have taken the turn we all know of, and in view of the undeniable fact that it was the Catholics who put the Marxist Allende in power, it is interesting to note that Maritain has recognised Frei as a disciple of his. "Today", writes Louis Salleron, "the Christian intending to undertake Christian political action thinks that the Gospel message must be received as a political message, and this inevitably leads him to think that it is a revolutionary message. This is the very opposite of Catholicism, and indeed of Christianity". Louis Salleron does not hesitate to hold Jacques Maritain as principally responsible for this confusion.

In the *Revue Hebdomadaire* of 22 August 1936, Louis Salleron analysed Jacques Maritain's book *Humanisme Intégral*, which had just been published and which created a great stir at the time. It is interesting to note that this article of Louis Salleron, which we reproduce below *in extenso* appeared just a few weeks after the establishment of the Popular Front in France.

Nada, Nada, Nada, Nada
(St. John of the Cross)

"A Civil Guard, a big man with a bullet in his stomach, ceaselessly hiccups this word: 'Nothing, nothing, nothing...'" (Louis-Delaprée, reporting the Spanish Civil War in *Paris-Soir*, 28 July 1936).

It is not easy to talk about Monsieur Maritain.

On the purely contingent political and social problems of man's "here and now" he has taken up some very advanced positions, and yet his central concern has always been with what is eternal in philosophy and contemplation. This last has conferred on him an almost sacrosanct status, so that one hesitates to criticise him in the same way as one would any others of his contemporaries. Even when he initiates arguments in fields where we have a right to join in and take issue with him, he inspires us with a strange awe. However often he repeats that he is not involving the authority of Aquinas in such arguments, we still cannot help feeling a sort of unease; we are afraid of infringing some orthodoxy that is far above our heads and our understanding, or else we feel we may be attacking him unfairly in the name of such an orthodoxy. It is a most uncomfortable feeling.

So let it be understood quite clearly here that we leave it to others better qualified, or more presumptuous than ourselves to find fault with M. Maritain in the lofty spheres of theology or Thomism. It is on the rudimentary level of the most primary "degrees of knowing" that we take our stand in these observations suggested by a reading of his *Humanisme Intégral*.[2]

As a Christian before all else, M. Maritain is obsessed

by an *idée fixe*, the dechristianisation of the common people. His most heartfelt desire and aspiration is to see the masses restored to the communion of Christ.

This central concern inspires and determines every step in his thinking and all the progressive stances he takes up on temporal questions. We say this openly, so as to make it quite clear that however outspokenly we may criticise M. Maritain, we shall never be attacking the intention behind his work, a noble and moving intention which cannot help but gain the support of believers and the respect of non-believers. But, whether Christian or not, we remain free to criticise the theses and hypotheses in the political and social field that he is led to form in his pursuit of that intention. And, believe me, in this field we shall certainly not be the only ones to disagree with him.

The very title Maritain gives to his book reveals the full extent of his hope...and, in our eyes, the magnitude of his error or of his temptation. Integral Humanism for him is nothing other than Christian humanism, a humanism which recognises "that God is the centre for man", which presupposes "the Christian concept of man sinning and redeemed, and the Christian concept of grace and freedom."[3] In short, Integral Humanism is God-centred, whereas traditional humanism was man-centred.

"The fundamental defect of anthropocentric humanism", writes M. Maritain, "was that it was man-centred, not that it was a humanism".[4]

But it is surely obvious to everyone that humanism is by definition man-centred! The adjective is quite superfluous, a pure tautology, only possible through the linguistic trick of using a Greek root that repeats the meaning of the noun of Latin origin. The words themselves prove M. Maritain wrong, just as he proves history wrong. For it is indeed true that humanism—the thing and the word—arose as recently as the sixteenth century as a counterblast to the prevailing theocentrism, and ever since then has reappeared with each of the revolutions that have set man up against God by making man himself a god. When so many intellectuals declare that they support Communism in the name of humanism, the paradox is only an apparent one. Although absurd from all other points of view, their position is a valid one from the religious point of view. Communism gives them back a "soul"; it restores their "fertility", as Malraux says.

M. Maritain is aware of this, and he does not contradict it. (All his chapter entitled "The Tragedy of Humanism" is first rate.) But the conclusion he draws from this is that a total reversal of the terms is not merely possible but essential. He wants to replace pure atheism by a pure Christianity, to offer God to the man without God. Humanism is not to be abolished but transfigured, and this concept may well be called Integral Humanism.

"We believe", he writes, "that what we call Integral Humanism is capable of saving and fostering, within a fundamentally new synthesis, all the truths affirmed or glimpsed by socialist humanism, by uniting them in an organic and vital way to many other truths".[5]

In pure logic this is true. But it would be just as true to say "integral egoism", "integral hedonism", "integral communism": Since evil exists only as privation of being, any "integralised" evil becomes a good, becomes indeed the good. Any error becomes truth if one projects whatever truth it contains onto the absolute plane.

This applies too when one considers morality. The sinner seeks some immediate and temporary good. One could say, to a sinner who commits the seven deadly sins seventy times a day: "Go and ask God, and you will obtain straight away what you are so vainly pursuing". But that is no reason for calling sanctity "integral sin".

Of course, Maritain could reply that "sin" signifies evil as such, and that "integral sin" is nothing but evil at its maximum, whereas "integral humanism" signifies the maximalisation of whatever good is contained in the mixture of good and evil we call humanism. I do not disagree. All I am trying to do is to show how dangerous his use of language is; it is a verbal trick that does not help to resolve any of our problems, since it leads just as validly in two opposite directions. Unfortunately the danger implicit in M. Maritain's handling of words affects his philosophical (or apostolic) arguments too. He is tossing the coin for heads or tails, and there is no certainty that heads...the side with the cross on it...will come face upward.

Does M. Maritain have a doctrine of freedom? He says he does, but the underlying reason for his present social and political views is an historical determinism. This determinism does not attempt to conceal itself, and crops up on page after page of his argumentation.

M. Maritain divides the past into "historic ages", "ages of civilisation". He is entitled to do this; it is moreover a convenient way of explaining history. But his determinism becomes most clearly marked when he is discussing the present and future. M. Maritain claims, in fact, to be able to distinguish all those elements of the present that are of necessity for the future. In other words, he claims to know what the essential nature (he calls this the "historic climate") of the society of the future will be.

Setting as his objective the working out of "the concrete historical ideal" of a new Christendom, he writes: "What do we mean by 'concrete historical ideal'? It is an image projected into the future, signifying the particular, specific type of civilisation towards which a certain historical period is tending.

"When Thomas More, Fénelon, Saint-Simon or Fourier drew up their Utopias, what they were building was purely an *'ens rationis'*, a mental construct deriving its being entirely from their own reason, isolated from anything having real existence at a particular period and date, having no relationship to any particular historical climate; a construct expressing an absolute maximum of social and political perfection and whose structure it is possible to describe in every little imaginary detail, since it is a fictitious model, offered to our minds as a substitute for reality.

"By contrast, what we call a concrete historical ideal is not a pure creation of thought, but an ideal essence, one that is capable of attainment (with greater or less difficulty, more or less perfection, but that is another question; concerning only the process of realisation, and not the finished product), an essence that is capable of existence, calling into being an existence appropriate to a given historical climate, and then responding to a relative maximum (relative, that is, to that historical climate) of social and political perfection, and displaying—precisely because it implies an order capable of concrete existence—only those lines of force and adumbrations of a future reality whose final shape must be determined later".[6]

The style of the passage is not as clear as it might be, but the thought is crystal-clear, to the point where it immediately suggests a name to our mind, that of Marx.

It is not M. Maritain's habit to avoid dangerous encounters. And so he speaks of Marx. He blames him for having reduced man's freedom "to the mere spontaneity of a vital force",[7] and for "not having brought out clearly the notion of virtuality (potentiality)".[8] He also blames those who criticise Marxist Hegelianism and historical materialism and yet often accept the Marxist "way of posing the question".[9] The fact remains, that if we put his speculative posture on one side, he looks to us terribly Marxist himself, in a practical sense. Not Marxist in his conclusions, of course, but in his dialectic. What is more, he observes, very rightly, that "Marxism is only able to reject the concept of an ideal at the price of a contradiction (and, in fact, its propaganda evades neither the concept nor the term 'Communist ideal'). It expressly claims to be a philosophy of action, an action destined to transform the world, and how can man act on the world unless he sets himself a goal determined not solely by economic and social progress but also by his own choice and his own loves? A goal which includes not only the movement of objective reality, but also man's own creative freedom controlling and directing that movement? Such is precisely what I mean by concrete historical ideal".[10]

Between Marxism and the philosophico-social position of M. Maritain there are two theoretical differences: a doctrinal difference—M. Maritain believes in freedom, and Marx denies it; and a difference of purpose—M. Maritain pursues Integral Humanism while the Marxists are content with humanism pure and simple. But there is one very important similarity: M. Maritain is in agreement with the Marxists on how to interpret contemporary history and what direction its transformation will take. He is so much in agreement with them that his whole activity is nothing but a race, not a race to get there first (for the victory of Communism is presumed to be inevitable), but a race to arrive in time to effect an immediate transformation of defeat and error into triumph and truth in that new Christendom that he is working to bring about. He is in a sense in a hurry to arrive at that definitive simplification of the data of the problem. "The place is ready", he writes, "for a new absolutism, and this time a materialist one (whether open or disguised), more hostile than ever to Christianity....Thus the apparently most logical of historical positions reappears, and the old battles of the Christian faith against the despotism of the powers of the flesh".[11]

Readers might perhaps like us to give some evidence of this agreement we note between M. Maritain and the Marxists on the interpretation of contemporary history. We shall do so, but briefly: treated in full the subject would require many pages.

It is quite clear that when M. Maritain says that politics must "estimate the amount of energy available for historical realisation and the coefficient of futurity present in the good and evil aspects" of passing events; an agreement about the present implying a partial agreement about the future. It cannot be disputed that an agreement on the present is already in force.

M. Maritain considers, indeed, that the "proletariat" has made an historical advance by gaining a certain awareness of itself, which is both "an awareness of its offended and humiliated human dignity and an awareness of its historic mission".[12] But this awareness implies, in his eyes, a consequence: "If the proletariat asks to be treated as an adult, it follows that it is not to be aided, bettered or saved by another social class. It is to the working class itself, and to its historic upward climb, that the chief part in the next phase of evolution falls".[13] And he adds, "...since man is at the same time flesh and spirit, since any great enterprise in temporal history has its material, biological and sociological bases into which even man's animality and the whole wealth of his subrational being are incorporated and exalted, it is normal that in the transformation of a regime such as capitalism, it should be the working class that provides this sociological basis, and in this sense one can speak of its historic mission, and one can consider that the destiny of mankind depends largely today on what action it takes".[14]

All this is clear enough, but we are still in the field of generalisations. What follows, is, by contrast, quite concrete. Trying to foresee what form future political organisations "temporally and politically determined and specifically Christian in inspiration" could take, M. Maritain examines the position they would find themselves in at the present moment.

We feel it advisable to quote the passage in full.

"Their concrete situation (and hence their practical attitude) towards the Communist forces and those forces which, for lack of a more suitable generic name, we shall call 'fascist' (Italian fascism representing the first form under which certain basically common but very variously specified energies have manifested themselves in history) will in our view be determined primarily by the following dominant ideas or factual conditions: on the one hand the various sorts of fascism are all, by virtue of their original bent and their glorification of the state, in opposition to the historical ideal in which such political organisations should see their specificatory purpose, and opposed to the existential base itself, and to that very primordial necessity itself which they (the organisations) would recognise—by 'existential base' I mean the movement that bears history towards a substantial mutation in which the 'Fourth Estate'[15] will (whether under a good or a bad banner still depends a good deal on man's will) come into possession of property, real freedom and a real share in the direction of politics and the economy; and by 'primordial necessity' I understand the historic necessity to 'reintegrate the masses' into a civilisation Christian in its spirit. On the other hand, Communism does indeed recognise the existential base we have spoken of, but falsifies the notion because of its erroneous philosophy of man and society, and consequently distorts the direction to be given to its evolution. Where our new (Christian) political organisms would proclaim the overriding need to reintegrate the masses into a civilisation Christian in spirit, Communism declares the necessity of integrating them into a civilisation atheist in spirit; where our organisms would admit the need for a large measure of economic collectivisation so as to allow the individual to lead a supra-collective life, Communism intends a total collectivising of the economy in such a way that the whole life of the human being is thus collectivised.

"In this way, the goal and very *raison d'être* of the whole movement are perverted in the case of Communism, the historic basis (and the goal) are rejected in the case of fascism".[16]

This passage is all-important, for it clearly shows that although M. Maritain rejects both the various fascisms and Communism, he at least grants a certificate of orthodoxy to Communism as far as the "historical base" is concerned. That is all we wanted to prove.

Other texts are no less characteristic.

"Communism", writes M. Maritain, "appears as an erroneous system which both stimulates and distorts an historical process, positively given[17] in existence: the process of historical 'birth and decay' by virtue of which a new civilisation...will be established outside the shattered framework of bourgeois civilisation. By contrast, the different types of 'fascism' arose right from the beginning as defensive reflexes, both against this existential process and against Communism itself".[18]

I have given enough quotations to make my point. Once one has read them, one will not be surprised that

M. Maritain considers that "fascist and racist totalitarian regimes cannot grasp the movement of history in its most basic aspect"[19] and that these regimes appear to him as "historical fatalities that in reality make Communism or other historical disasters of equal magnitude all the more likely, since, although in their reaction against Communism they score immediate short-term successes that strike the imagination, they are incapable of rising above Communism and discovering the truly human form that the movement of history calls for. This discovery will only be made by an effort of the spirit and of human freedom overcoming the determinism of the material forces of progress".[20]

Such postulates seem dangerous to us, for they constitute in fact a net contribution to the cause of Communism.

Please do not accuse us of unfairly selective quotation. We know—and we have said so—that M. Maritain is too learned, too prudent and too sincere ever to fail to draw attention to doctrinal errors. He does not preach heresy, he does not preach Marxism, nor does he preach revolution. His reservation is always there, as a footnote or in a parenthetical clause. But we have a duty to look beyond these details. He has an accent, a slant, and it is his slant, his emphasis that we are focussing on and underlining here. The whole of M. Maritain's dialectic is purely Marxist and all his "socio-temporal" likes and preferences are directed towards Communism because it is only the latter that possesses an historical meaning and an historical mission. M. Maritain reprobates Communism, but he opens the way to it and fosters its realisation by the fact that he considers it to be the necessary end-product of the errors of the past, and to be the medium moreover for the transmission of a host of social truths which Christianity has the responsibility of bringing to full fruition. We defy any honest reader to challenge our interpretation.

Likewise, we do not think M. Maritain will accuse us of misinterpreting or distorting his thinking. In fact we think that, if an opportunity presented itself, he would confirm the attitude he has taken up as regards the present age, and would even contribute new justifications for his views. It seems likely that there is only one subject on which he would agree to a debate, and that would be the "historical basis" of his position. "Show me first of all that it is wrong", he would say.

But we should not agree to a debate on such a subject; its starting-point seems to us full of error. For although it is true that our acts follow us and that the present determines the future, it is impossible for us to know what these historical "lines of force" to which M. Maritain attaches such importance really are. And even if we did know them in the form in which they appear in our days, we could not imagine under what new form they would appear tomorrow; not only does the human will exist with its amazing capacity for creating history, but even if we remain on the plane of that social alchemy and its determinism that exercises such a strong effect on M. Maritain's mind, there are surprises...in fact we find nothing but surprises. Our imagination is so bound up in the superficial appearances of the moment that it soon grows exhausted by the effort of trying to invent the future. It is true that once the future has in its turn become the past, we manage to relate it to the earlier past with faultless logic. But our imagination had been incapable of conceiving it. It then had just been one of a great number of possibilities and, nine times out of ten, just the very one we had not foreseen.

Does this mean that man is powerless as regards the future? Certainly not. But the future does not belong to him, and the only hold he has on it is through his will and through his knowledge of laws and causes.

Let us take a good look at what separates us here from M. Maritain (once again we are speaking of his manifest tendencies, not of his doctrine). We say that the intelligence can know the immutable, that is to say the necessary relationships that exist between man's nature and the nature of things at each moment in history. This knowledge implies positive solutions in order that order, justice and peace may reign, all those elements, in short, of the common good of society, in which the Christian is as interested as the non-believer. Taking this knowledge as its starting point, the will of man then acts to impose his solutions. This seems to us a good translation of the admirable phrase of Canovas de Castillo when he said that one must make possible whatever is necessary. One must first of all make it possible, and then do it.

M. Maritain, on the other hand, starts (from a practical viewpoint) from a knowledge of progress, and goes on to infer its future development; and in order to modify this future he appeals less to our will than to our freedom, which he conceives as the spiritual directing element of a mysterious collective biology. For Maritain, the necessary is not so much what is (substantially and in a permanent manner) as what is becoming; and if he wanted to plagiarise Canovas de Castillo, he would willingly say, I think, that one must Christianise what is necessary. Hence the formulas one finds on every page of *Humanisme Intégral*, according to which one must "act upon history"[21] (why indeed not?), one must "devote all one's energy to constantly increasing the sum of goodness and justice in the bank account of history", and "not act as if, in order to separate the cockle from the wheat, we had to close the bank account and thus halt the very movement itself of that historical existence in which we are living", etc.[22]

At bottom, all M. Maritain's error arises from the fact that his immense generosity is badly ordered. We mean by this that its natural order or plane is that of thought, and that he wrongly transposes it onto the order or plane of action. By so doing he even vitiates his thought. He was made to know and explain, and nowadays he thinks less clearly and his explanations are all awry, thanks to his desire to direct a movement. Since he hasn't the slightest vocation for leading men or controlling events, he ends by bowing down and yielding to the allegedly irreversible trends of history, his hope and intention being to steer these by sheer force of spirit. Here he is doubly mistaken, since these inevitable trends do not exist, and also because spirit alone is powerless. If some new Joan of Arc should (purely as an hypothesis) arise and declare that "when it comes to exchanging hard knocks, we shall see which side God is on", no doubt M. Maritain would send her back to her parents after explaining to her that such bloodthirsty delight in fighting was no longer appropriate to the "historical climate" into which we are now entering. And yet our new Joan of Arc (once again as a pure hypothesis) could answer him just as the first Joan did to the doctors of Poitiers: "Sire, God has a book in which no clerk has ever read, however perfect he may be in clerkly learning".[23]

We need go no further. Our objection to M. Maritain's ideas is sufficiently clear without our saying any more.

Our criticism does not, in any case, prevent us from appreciating the many excellent things to be found in *Humanisme Intégral*; even less does it prevent us from paying homage to M. Maritain's many fine books of pure philosophy, which we have always read with great pleasure.

But M. Maritain must not try to turn himself into a social or political philosopher; he is quite unfitted for such a role, and is indeed positively dangerous.

Indignation, say the diplomats, is not a constructive state of mind in which to approach political affairs. Neither is the spirit of *"todo y nada"*.[24]

— Louis Salleron

Notes

[1] 18 October 1973, "Chile and Christian Politics".
[2] Published by Editions Montaigne, one volume.
[3] *Humanisme Intégral*, p. 35 (19).
[4] Ibid., p. 35 (19).
[5] Ibid., p. 98 (81).
[6] Ibid., p. 140, (121-122).
[7] Ibid., p. 141 (123).
[8] Ibid., p. 142 (124).
[9] Ibid., p. 155 (136).
[10] Ibid., pp. 143-144 (125).
[11] Ibid., pp. 172-173. Cf. also p. 258 (153-154).
[12] Ibid., p. 246 (225).
[13] Ibid., pp. 250 (229).
[14] Ibid., pp. 251-252 (230).
[15] M. Maritain means here the proletariat, not the press, often called the Fourth estate in English (translator's note).
[16] *Humanisme Intégral*, pp. 290-291 (268-269).
[17] In the philosophical sense (translator's note).
[18] *Humanisme Intégral*, p. 295 ((272-273).
[19] Ibid., p. 297 (275). In no sense should it be thought that Professor Salleron is expressing any sympathy with fascist or racist regimes. He is using this particular quotation to emphasise the fact that Maritain sees the advent of some form of Communism as inevitable, i.e. because in this instance Maritain is criticising these regimes for failing to accept that this is so ("the movement of history in its most basic aspect"). (Note by Michael Davies.)
[20] *Humanisme Intégral*, p. 300. It is surely worthwhile to emphasise the extent to which the vocabulary and, in a sense, the very curve or graph of all the arguments we have just quoted from M. Maritain, are impregnated with Marxism (277).
[21] *Humanisme Intégral*, p. 15 (xvi).
[22] Ibid., p. 236. The words *history, historic movement, historic forces, progress, energies, lines of force*, etc., recur constantly in M. Maritain's writing (215-216).
[23] One feels entitled to ask what "line of force" in the destiny of

France could be apparent to a Thomist philosopher in the year of grace 1429.

[24] I.e. "all and nothing".

Appendix VIII

The Anti-liturgical Heresy

The following paragraphs are taken from Dom Guéranger's *Liturgical Institutions*, Vol. I, Chapter IV, first published in 1840. The correspondence of the "anti-liturgical heresy" with the account of the Protestant Reformation in *Cranmer's Godly Order* is only to be expected. What many Catholics will find disturbing is the correspondence of some of the principles of this "heresy" with those enshrined in the Liturgy Constitution which was examined in Chapter XVI, and with the new Mass which the post-conciliar Liturgy Commission (*Consilium*) produced with the help of its Protestant advisers.

THE ANTI-LITURGICAL HERESY

To give an idea of the ravages of the anti-liturgical sect, it seems to us necessary to survey what the pretended reformers of Christianity have been doing for three centuries, and to present an integral picture of their deeds and their doctrine of "purifying" divine worship. Nothing could be more instructive or more proper to help one realise the causes of the rapid propagation of Protestantism. We shall see diabolical wisdom at work, striking skillful blows, and leading infallibly to vast consequences.

The first characteristic of the anti-liturgical heresy is hatred of Tradition as found in the formulas used in divine worship....Every sectarian who wishes to introduce a new doctrine finds himself, unfailingly, face to face with the liturgy, which is tradition at its strongest and best, and he cannot rest until he has silenced this voice, until he has torn up these pages which recall the faith of past centuries. As a matter of fact, how could Lutheranism, Calvinism, Anglicanism establish themselves and maintain their influence over the masses? All they had to do was substitute new books and new formulas, and their work was done. There was nothing that still bothered the new teachers; they could just go on preaching as they wished: the faith of the people was henceforth without defence....

The second principle of the anti-liturgical sect—to substitute for the formulas of the ecclesiastical teachings, readings from Holy Scripture....Since many centuries we know that the preference given by all heretics to Holy Scripture, over Church definitions, has no other reason than to facilitate making the word of God say all that they want it to say and manipulating it at will....

The third principle of the heretics concerning the reform of the liturgy is, having eliminated the ecclesiastical formulas and proclaimed the absolute necessity of making use only of the words of Scripture in divine worship, and having seen that Holy Scripture does not always yield itself to all their purposes as they would like, their third principle, we say, is to fabricate and introduce various formulas filled with perfidy, by which the people are more surely ensnared in errors and thus the whole structure of the impious reform will become consolidated for the coming centuries...all the sectarians without excep-

The Anti-liturgical Heresy

tion begin with the vindication of the rights of antiquity. They want to cut Christianity off from all that the errors and passions of man have mixed in, from whatever is "false" and "unworthy of God". All they want is the primitive, and they pretend to go back to the cradle of Christian institutions. To this end, they prune, they efface, they cut away; everything falls under their blows, and while one is waiting to see the original purity of the divine cult reappear, one finds oneself encumbered with new formulas dating only from the night before, and which are incontestably human, since the one who created them is still alive....Since the liturgical reform is being undertaken by the sectarians with the same goal as the reform of dogma, of which it is the consequence... they found themselves led to cut away in the liturgy all the ceremonies, all the formulas which express mysteries....No more sacramentals, blessings, images, relics of saints, processions, pilgrimages, etc. No more altar, only a table; no more sacrifice as in every religion, but only a meal....

Since the liturgical reform had for one of its principal aims the abolition of actions and formulas of mystical signification, it is a logical consequence that its authors had to vindicate the use of the vernacular in divine worship. This in the eyes of the sectarians is a most important item. Cult is no secret matter. The people, they say, must understand what they sing. Hatred for the Latin language is inborn in the heart of all the enemies of Rome. They recognise it as the bond of Catholics throughout the universe, as the arsenal of orthodoxy against all the subtleties of the sectarian spirit. They consider it the most efficient weapon of the papacy. The spirit of rebellion which drives them to confide the universal prayer to the idiom of each people, of each province, of each century, has for the rest produced its fruits, and the reformed themselves constantly perceive that the Catholic people, in spite of their Latin prayers, relish better and accomplish with more zeal the duties of cult than the Protestant people. At every hour of the day divine worship takes place in Catholic churches. The faithful Catholic who assists leaves his mother tongue at the door. Apart from the sermons, he hears nothing but mysterious words which, even so, are not heard in the most solemn moment of the Canon of the Mass. Nevertheless, this mystery charms him in such a way that he is not jealous of the lot of the Protestant, even though the latter doesn't hear a single sound without perceiving its meaning....We must admit it is a master blow of Protestantism to have declared war on the sacred language. If it should ever succeed in destroying it, it would be well on the way to victory. Exposed to profane gaze, like a virgin who has been violated, from that moment on the liturgy has lost much of its sacred character, and very soon people find that it is not worthwhile putting aside one's work or pleasure in order to go and listen to what is being said in the way one speaks in the marketplace.

In taking away from the liturgy the mystery which humbles reason, Protestantism took care not to forget the practical consequence, that is to say, liberation from the fatigue and burden of the body imposed by the rules of the papist liturgy. First of all, no more fasting, no more abstinence, no more genuflections in prayer.... Such are the principal maxims of the anti-liturgical sect. We certainly did not exaggerate in any way. All we did was to reveal the hundred times professed doctrines of the writings of Luther, Calvin, the one hundred signers of Magdeburg, of Hospinien, Kemnitz, etc. These books are easy to consult. That is to say that what comes out of them is under the eyes of all the world. We thought it useful to throw light on the principal features of sectari-

anism. It is always profitable to know error....It is now up to the Catholic logician to draw the conclusions.
— Dom Guéranger, *Liturgical Institutions*, 1840

The extent to which various features of the "anti-liturgical heresy" described by Dom Guéranger, and the consequences which he claims follow inevitably, have become part of the practical reform which, officially or unofficially, has followed the Council, varies not only from country to country but from parish to parish. While the Council did not order any of the liturgical abuses which now so distress faithful Catholics, it opened the door to them, as Chapter XVI made clear. It is impossible not to note the detail in which the anti-liturgical heresy is being repeated—the only days of fasting and abstinence which remain in the Roman Rite are Ash Wednesday and Good Friday!

Appendix IX

The Fruits of Vatican II

Cardinal Paul Poupard, President of the Pontifical Council for Culture, stated bluntly in January 2000: "The dechristianisation of Europe is a reality".[1] Cardinal Daneels of Brussels, Belgium, stated in an interview with the London *Catholic Times*, on 12 May 2000, that the Church in Europe is facing extinction. He lamented the vocations crisis in the West and remarked that: "Without priests the sacramental life of the Church will disappear. We will become a Protestant Church without sacraments. We will be another type of Church, not Catholic".[2] During the Synod of European Bishops in October 1999, Archbishop Fernando Sebastián Aguilar of Pamplona, gave the following gloomy but realistic assessment of Spanish Catholicism:

> For forty or fifty years, Spanish society has moved far away from the Church and the explicit acknowledgement of the treasures of the Kingdom of God. Cultural and spiritual secularisation has affected many members of the Church. The result of this has been the weakening of the faith and divine revelation, the theoretical and practical questioning of Christian moral teaching, the massive abandonment of attending Sunday Mass, the non-acceptance of the Magisterium of the Church in

those points that do not coincide with the trends of the dominant culture. The cultural convictions on which social life is based are undermined and are more atheistic than Christian.

The situation in Spain is parallelled throughout Europe and the entire First World, not least in English-speaking countries. This is particularly true where the teaching given in Catholic educational institutions at every level is concerned. The catechetical bureaucracies set up by the hierarchies threw out the traditional catechism and replaced it with an endless series of new texts. Having taught in Catholic schools throughout the thirty years following the Council, I can testify that these texts soon reached the point where they could hardly be termed even vestigially Catholic. New methods of teaching the Catholic religion were replaced by a requirement to teach a new religion that was not Catholic. Parents, priests, and teachers who protested were treated as Neanderthals. Countless protests were made to Rome, but they were ignored. Vatican policy has been to uphold the authority of the diocesan bishop, even if he is using that authority to destroy the faith. In 1977 a very good friend of mine, the late Canon George Telford, resigned from his position as Vice-Chairman of the Department of Catechetics for England and Wales because, he assured me, there was not one bishop in the country who was even interested in ensuring that children in Catholic schools were taught the Catholic faith. In his letter of resignation he stated bluntly: "Modern catechetics is theologically corrupt and spiritually bankrupt. Its structures and innovations are irrelevant and unmeaningful for the Catholic Faith, and can achieve nothing but its gradual dilution".[3]

The Australian Catholic monthly *AD 2000*, in its January 2003 issue, reported a speech made by Professor Denis McLaughlin, of the Australian Catholic University (ACU), to the National Conference of Australian Secondary School Principals in October 2002. His audience would certainly not have been pleased with what he had to say. His speech reported the findings of a survey that he had conducted into the beliefs, values and practices of Catholic student teachers. The survey found that most student teachers did not accept Church teaching in such areas as abortion, contraception, the Eucharist and women's ordination, and on these there were no significant differences between first year and final year students. This kind of thinking, according to Professor McLaughlin, is also to be found among practising Catholic school teachers, indicating that the downward spiral of belief and practice in the general Catholic population shows no sign of levelling out:

> The cult of individualism and subjectivism, so prevalent in modern Western culture, has also had its impact on religious education. This has led to the present widespread ignorance of the basics of the faith and their intellectual and historical underpinnings, making an already difficult situation for any religious faith commitment close to impossible. It is no wonder so many Catholics have made their peace with secularism and materialism under a thin veneer of cultural Catholicity. Their views on "gay" rights, divorce, abortion or women priests are indistinguishable from those of the rest of the population.

The professor's own ACU research confirms findings from other sources such as the Catholic Church Life Survey and Brother Marcellin Flynn: "Data obtained by ACU researchers in Sydney found that 97 per cent of young Catholics abandoned the practice of their faith within twelve months of completing high school….In other words, despite up to thirteen years of religious education, most young Catholics reject the very foundations of the Faith".

Pope John's Council

The descriptions by Canon Telford and Professor McLaughlin of the abysmal state of religious teaching in Britain and Australia are equally applicable to the United States. The stage has been reached where, if parents wish their children to know the Faith, they must teach it to them themselves, a task which, in fact, is their primary duty. In doing so it is imperative that they are completely sure of the doctrines that they teach, and a great service for concerned parents was provided by TAN Books in 2002 when it reprinted what is probably the best compendium of the faith on a popular level available in English: *This Is the Faith* by Canon Francis Ripley, who had worked very closely with Canon Telford in his unsuccessful campaign to have the Catholic Faith taught in Catholic schools. This is certainly a book which should be in every Catholic home.[4]

Statistics relating to England and Wales and the United States are appended to demonstrate that what we are witnessing is not a new Pentecost but a disastrous and terminal decline. These statistics are paralleled in every country of what is known as the First World. It is true that there has been an increase in the overall number of seminarians and ordinations since Vatican II, but this increase has taken place primarily in Third World areas such as Africa and Asia and, when examined carefully, cannot be attributed to the influence of the Council but to sociological factors which will not be examined in this book, which is concerned only with the First World. I will give just one example derived from a visit to an Indian seminary. It was completely full and could have been filled three or four times over, but in India ordination gives a man a certain social status and a guaranteed income, coming largely from abroad, which enables him to give financial support to his family. The doctrinal formation given in the seminary was of very dubious orthodoxy. I asked the Rector, who wore no priestly attire, if the seminarians studied St. Thomas Aquinas, and he burst out laughing. The walls of his office were decorated with pictures of scantily clad American female country singers. I asked why this was, and he replied that it enabled the seminarians to relate to him.

The Incredible Shrinking Church in England and Wales

The most evident characteristic of the Catholic Church in England and Wales is that it is shrinking at an incredible rate into what must be termed a state of terminal decline. The official Catholic Directory documents a steady increase in every important aspect of Catholic life until the mid-1960's, then the decline sets in. The figures for marriages and baptisms are not simply alarming but disastrous. In 1944 there were 30,946 marriages, by 1964 the figure had risen to 45,592, and in 1999 had plunged to 13,814—well under half the figure for 1944. The figures for baptisms for the same years are 71,604; 137,673; and 63,158. With fewer children born to Catholic couples each year the number of marriages must inevitably continue to decline, with even fewer children born—and so on. Nor can it be presumed that even half the children who are baptised will be practising their faith by the time they reach their teens. An examination of the figures of a typical diocese indicates that less than half the children who are baptised are confirmed, and a report in *The Universe* as long ago as 1990 gave an estimate of only 11 per cent of young Catholics practising their faith when they leave high school.

Apart from marriages and baptisms, Mass attendance is the most accurate guide to the vitality of the Catholic community. The figure has plunged from 2,114,219 in 1966 to 1,041,728 in 1999 and is still falling at a rate of about 32,000 a year.

In 1944, 178 priests were ordained; in 1964, 230; and in 1999, only 43, and in the same year 121 priests died.

In 1985, twenty years after the Second Vatican Council, bishops from all over the world assembled in Rome to assess the impact of the Council. This gave them the opportunity to accept that their implementation of it had been disastrous, and that drastic measures must be taken to give the faith a viable future in First World countries. Cardinal Basil Hume of Westminster insisted, on behalf of the bishops of England and Wales, that there must be no turning back from the policies they had adopted to implement the Council. A report in *The Universe* of 13 December 1985 informed us that the Synod had adopted Cardinal Hume's position without a single dissenting voice. The final sentence of this report must be described as ironically prophetic: "In the meantime the People of God have a firm mandate to further Exodus along the route mapped out by the Second Vatican Council". Change the upper case "E" of Exodus to a lower case "e", exodus, and this is precisely what has happened, and the exodus will continue until Catholicism in England and Wales vanishes into oblivion within thirty years, if not sooner. The Second Spring predicted by Cardinal Newman will end in the bleakest of winters.

The Incredible Shrinking Church in the United States

In March 2003 there was published in St. Louis what is certainly the most important statistical survey of the Church in the United States since Vatican II: *Index of Leading Catholic Indicators: The Church Since Vatican II*, by Kenneth C. Jones.[5] It provides meticulously documented statistics on every aspect of Catholic life subject to statistical verification, and is illustrated with graphs which depict in a dramatic visual manner the catastrophic collapse of Catholic life in

The Fruits of Vatican II

the United States since the Council. With the publication of this book no rational person could disagree with Father Louis Bouyer that: "Unless we are blind, we must even state bluntly that what we see looks less like the hoped-for regeneration of Catholicism than its accelerated decomposition".[6] Mr. Jones has given me his permission to quote from the introduction to his book, but before doing so I must quote from a report in the 23 March edition of the London *Universe*. Under the headline: *En Suite Monastery*, it reports: "A former Irish Carmelite monastery is expected to be turned into a country-club style hotel after its sale to a property developer. The Carmelite order had shut their house in Castle Martyr, Cork, last year after seventy-three years because of the downfall in vocations". This is but one of thousands of similar examples of the actual as opposed to the fantasy fruits of Vatican II. On page 100 of Mr. Jones's book there is a graph revealing that the number of Carmelite seminarians in the United States has decreased from 545 in 1965 to 46 in 2000, a decline of 92 per cent. This figure seems positively healthy when compared with the graph relating to the La Salette Fathers on page 99, which reveals a decline in the number of seminarians for the same period from 552 to just 1. Figures and graphs for every major religious order are set out in the book, and it would be hard to disagree with Mr. Jones's comment that: "The religious orders will soon be virtually non-existent in the United States". In the introduction to his book he writes:

> When Pope John XXIII opened the Second Vatican Council in 1962, the Catholic Church in America was in the midst of an unprecedented period of growth. Bishops were ordaining record numbers of priests and building scores of seminaries to handle the surge in vocations. Young women by the thousands gave up lives of comfort for the austerity of the convent. These nuns taught

millions of students in the huge system of parochial and private schools.

The ranks of Catholics swelled as parents brought in their babies for baptism and adult converts flocked to the Church. Lines outside the confessionals were long, and by some estimates three quarters of the faithful went to Mass every Sunday. Given this favourable state of affairs, some Catholics wondered at the time whether an ecumenical council was opportune—don't rock the boat, they said.

The Holy Father chided these people in his opening speech to the Council: "We feel we must disagree with those prophets of gloom, who are always forecasting disaster, as though the end of the world were at hand". Forty years later the end has not arrived. But we are now facing the disaster.

Even some in the Vatican have recognised it. Cardinal Joseph Ratzinger, Prefect of the Congregation for the Doctrine of the Faith, said: "Certainly the results [of Vatican II] seem cruelly opposed to the expectations of everyone, beginning with those of Pope John XXIII and then of Pope Paul VI"....

Since Cardinal Ratzinger made these remarks in 1984, the crisis in the Church has accelerated. In every area that is statistically verifiable—for example, the number of priests, seminarians, priestless parishes, nuns, Mass attendance, converts and annulments—the "process of decadence" is apparent.

I have gathered these statistics in *The Index of Leading Catholic Indicators* because the magnitude of the emergency is unknown to many. Beyond a vague understanding of a "vocations crisis", both the faithful and the general public have no idea how bad things have been since the close of the Second Vatican Council in 1965. Here are some of the stark facts.

The Fruits of Vatican II

- **Priests.** After skyrocketing from about 27,000 in 1930 to 58,000 in 1965, the number of priests in the United States dropped to 45,000 in 2002. By 2020, there will be about 31,000 priests—and only 15,000 will be under the age of 70. Right now there are more priests aged 80 to 84 than there are age 30 to 34.
- **Ordinations.** In 1965 there were 1,575 ordinations to the priesthood, in 2002 there were 450, a decline of 350 per cent. Taking into account ordinations, deaths and departures, in 1965 there was a net gain of 725 priests. In 1998, there was a net loss of 810.
- **Priestless parishes.** About one per cent of parishes, 549, were without a resident priest in 1965. In 2002 there were 2,928 priestless parishes, about 15 per cent of U.S. parishes. By 2020, a quarter of all parishes, 4,656, will have no priest.
- **Seminarians.** Between 1965 and 2002, the number of seminarians dropped from 49,000 to 4,700—a 90 per cent decrease. Without any students, seminaries across the country have been sold or shuttered. There were 596 seminaries in 1965, and only 200 in 2002.
- **Sisters.** 180,000 Sisters were the backbone of the Catholic education and health systems in 1965. In 2002, there were 75,000 Sisters, with an average age of 68. By 2020, the number of Sisters will drop to 40,000—and of these, only 21,000 will be aged 70 or under. In 1965, 104,000 Sisters were teaching, while in 2002 there were only 8,200 teachers.
- **Brothers.** The number of professed Brothers decreased from about 12,000 in 1965 to 5,700 in 2002, with a further drop to 3,100 in 2020.
- **Religious Orders.** The religious orders will soon be virtually non-existent in the United States.

For example, in 1965 there were 5,277 Jesuit priests and 3,559 seminarians; in 2000 there were 3,172 priests and 38 seminarians. There were 2,534 O.F.M. Franciscan priests and 2,251 seminarians in 1965; in 2000 there were 1,492 priests and 60 seminarians. There were 2,434 Christian Brothers in 1965 and 912 seminarians; in 2000 there were 959 Brothers and 7 seminarians. There were 1,148 Redemptorist priests in 1965 and 1,128 seminarians; in 2000 there were 349 priests and 24 seminarians. Every major religious order in the United States mirrors these statistics.

- **High Schools.** Between 1965 and 2002 the number of diocesan high schools fell from 1,566 to 786. At the same time the number of students dropped from almost 700,000 to 386,000.
- **Parochial Grade Schools.** There were 10,503 parochial grade schools in 1965 and 6,623 in 2002. The number of students went from 4.5 million to 1.9 million.
- **Sacramental Life.** In 1965 there were 1.3 million infant baptisms; in 2002 there were 1 million. (In the same period the number of Catholics in the United States rose from 45 million to 65 million.) In 1965 there were 126,000 adult baptisms—converts; in 2002 there were 80,000. In 1965 there were 352,000 Catholic marriages; in 2002 there were 256,000. In 1965 there were 338 annulments; in 2002 there were 50,000.
- **Mass attendance.** A 1958 Gallup poll reported that 74 per cent of Catholics went to Sunday Mass. A 1994 University of Notre Dame study found that the attendance rate was 26.6 per cent. A more recent study by Fordham University professor James Lothian concluded that 65 per cent of Catholics went

to Sunday Mass in 1965, while the rate dropped to 25 per cent in 2000.

The decline in Mass attendance highlights another significant fact: fewer and fewer people who call themselves Catholic actually follow Church rules or accept Church doctrine. For example, a 1999 poll by the *National Catholic Reporter* shows that 77 per cent believe a person can be a good Catholic without going to Mass every Sunday, 65 per cent believe good Catholics can divorce and remarry, and 53 per cent believe Catholics can have abortions and remain in good standing. Only 10 per cent of lay religion teachers accept Church teaching on artificial birth control, according to a 2000 University of Notre Dame poll. And a *New York Times*/CBS poll revealed that 70 per cent of Catholics age eighteen to forty-four believe the Eucharist is merely a "symbolic reminder" of Jesus.

Given these alarming statistics and surveys, one wonders why the American bishops ignore the profound crisis that threatens the very existence of the Church in America. After all, there can be no Church without priests, no Church without a laity that has children and practises the Catholic faith.

Yet at their annual conferences, the bishops gather to issue weighty statements about nuclear weapons and the economy. Then they return home to "consolidate" parishes and close down schools.

As Cardinal Ratzinger said, the post-Vatican II period "has definitely been unfavourable for the Catholic Church". This Index of Leading Catholic Indicators is an attempt to chronicle the continuing crisis, in the hope that a compilation of the grim statistics—in a clear, objective, easy to understand manner—will spur action before it is too late.

— Kenneth C. Jones, January 2003

Pope John's Council

Mr. Jones is, I fear, far too optimistic in hoping that the statistics in his book, "will spur action before it is too late". In the Conciliar Church today there is one, and just one, absolute, and this is, to repeat the words of Pope John Paul II, that the little seed planted by Pope John XXIII has become "a tree which has spread its majestic and mighty branches over the vineyard of the Lord", and that "It has given us many fruits in these thirty-five years of life, and it will give us many more in the years to come". I cannot imagine any bishop in the world, no matter how orthodox in his personal belief, no matter how generous to traditional Catholics in authorising the Missal of St. Pius V, who would have the courage to dissent from the insistence of Cardinal Basil Hume that there must be no turning back from the policies they had adopted to implement the Council. While, as Mr. Jones has proved, we are witnessing not the renewal but the "accelerated decomposition of Catholicism", our bishops, beginning with the Bishop of Rome, insist that we are basking in the fruits of a new Pentecost. One cannot help recollecting how, in the years following the Russian Revolution, the enforced collectivisation of the land had brought Russia to the edge of starvation, and week after week, month after month, year after year, official bulletins assured the Russian people that never before in the history of their country had they enjoyed so high a standard of living.

In *Liturgical Time Bombs* I have alleged no more than was alleged by Cardinal Ratzinger when he wrote: "I am convinced that the crisis in the Church that we are experiencing is to a large extent due to the disintegration of the liturgy...". In his address to the bishops of Chile on July 13, 1988, the Cardinal explained:

> The Second Vatican Council has not been treated as a part of the entire living Tradition of the Church, but as an end of Tradition, a new start from zero. The truth is that

this particular council defined no dogma at all, and deliberately chose to remain on a modest level, as a merely pastoral council; and yet many treat it as though it had made itself into a sort of superdogma which takes away the importance of all the rest. This idea is made stronger by things that are now happening. That which previously was considered most holy—the form in which the liturgy was handed down—suddenly appears as the most forbidden of all things, the one thing that can safely be prohibited.

Every Catholic devoted to the Traditional Latin Mass must pray each day for our Holy Father, and pray that he will remove every restriction from the celebration of the rite of Mass which Cardinal Newman stated (in *Loss and Gain*) that he could attend forever and not be tired, and which Father Faber described as "the most beautiful thing this side of heaven".

Notes

[1] *Le Spectacle du Monde*, January 2000.
[2] *Catholic Times*, 12 May 2000.
[3] *Christian Order*, April 1977, p. 205.
[4] Canon Francis Ripley, *This Is the Faith* (TAN Books edition, 2002).
[5] Available from Angelus Press.
[6] DC, p. 1.

Bibliography

Some of the books referred to in the notes have been abbreviated as follows.

Abbott   Abbott, Walter M., S.J., editor. *The Documents of Vatican II.* London, 1967.

ABS   Lefebvre, Archbishop Marcel. *A Bishop Speaks,* 2nd edition. Angelus Press, 2007.

ACT   Graber, Monsignor R. *Athanasius and the Church of Our Times.* London, 1974.

AER   *The American Ecclesiastical Review.*

AVVC   Pawley, B. C. *An Anglican View of the Vatican Council.* New York, 1962.

BAC   Kelly, Monsignor George. *The Battle for the American Church.* New York: Doubleday, 1979.

CC   Heenan, Cardinal J. *Council and Clergy.* London, 1966.

CE   *Catholic Encyclopedia.* New York, 1913.

CGO   Davies, Michael. *Cranmer's Godly Order.* Roman Catholic Books, 1995.

CT   Heenan, Cardinal J. *A Crown of Thorns*. London, 1974.

D   Denzinger, H. *Enchiridion Symbolorum*, 31st edition.

DC   Bouyer, L. *The Decomposition of Catholicism*. London, 1970.

DCD   Newman, J. H. *The Development of Christian Doctrine*. London, 1878.

DFRC   Hitchcock, J. *The Decline and Fall of Radical Catholicism*. New York, 1972.

ER   McAfee Brown, R. *The Ecumenical Revolution*. New York, 1969.

HG   Pius XII. *Humani Generis*. London: Catholic Truth Society, 1966.

IC   Kaiser, R. *Inside the Council*. London, 1963.

JC   Fesquet, H. *Le Journal du Concile*. H. Morel, 1966.

OC   Novak, M. *The Open Church*. London, 1964.

PG   St. Pius X. *Pascendi Gregis*.

PP   Manning, Cardinal H. *"Petri Privilegium": Three Pastoral Letters to the Clergy of the Diocese*. London, 1871. Each of the three pastoral letters has separate page numbering and the particular letter referred to is indicated by Roman numerals.

Bibliography

RCFC   Pawley, Bernard and Margaret. *Rome and Canterbury through Four Centuries.* London, 1974.

RFT   Wiltgen, R. *The Rhine Flows into the Tiber.* New York, 1967.

TCC   Smith, G. *The Teaching of the Catholic Church.* London, 1956.

TIC   Pelotte, D. E. *John Courtney Murray: Theologian in Conflict.* New York, 1975.

TSVC   Manning, Cardinal H. *The True Story of the Vatican Council.* London, 1877.

UEP   Lefebvre, Archbishop Marcel. *Un Évêque Parle.* Paris, 1974.

VO   Moorman, J. *Vatican Observed.* London, 1967.

XR-I   Rynne, X. *Letters from Vatican City.* New York, 1963.

XR-II ———. *The Second Session.* London, 1964.

XR-III ———. *The Third Session.* London, 1965.

XR-IV ———. *The Fourth Session.* London, 1966.

Index

adaptation principle, in Liturgy Constitution, 361-366
Adrian, Bp. William, 63-64, 299
Agreed Statements on Eucharist and Ministry, 154-155, 172
Aguilar, Abp. Fernando Sebastián, 453-454
Alfrink, Bernard Cardinal, 139
Allende, Salvador, 238
Alta Vendita documents, 267-269
American Participation in the Second Vatican Council (Yzermans), 138
Anglican Church, 155-158, 175-176, 308-314
anti-liturgical heresy, 447-451
anti-Modernist oath, 307
Apostolate of the Laity, Decree on, 111
Arcano Divinae Providentiae (Pius IX), 98-99
Arrupe, Rev. Pedro, 260-261
Assumption, dogma of, 174
Athanasius, Saint, 279
atheism, 258-259, 263
Auctorem Fidei (Pius VI), 330
Australia, Catholicism in, 454-456

Baker, Rev. Kenneth, xxvi
Balic, Rev. Carolus, 183
Bandas, Rev. Rudolph G., 123-124, 132
Baptism
of desire, 408-410; rite of, 373-374
Batanian, Patriarch Ignace Pierre XVI, 21-22
The Battle for the American Church (Kelly), 31, 116

Baum, Gregory, 90, 104, 318, 402
Bea, Augustin Cardinal, 165, 167, 393-394
Bell, Bp. George, 313-314
Beran, Josef Cardinal, 254
Blanch, Dr. Stuart, 77
Blessed Virgin Mary. *See* Our Lady
Bourne, Francis Cardinal, 416-417
Bouyer, Rev. Louis
liturgical renewal and, 27; Liturgy Constitution and, 334-335; post-conciliar Catholicism and, 9-10, 12; press and, 121, 125, 129-130, 132-135 Protestantism and, 144, 151-152
Broglie-Revel, Rev., 86-87
Browne, Michael Cardinal, 105-106
Brown, Robert McAfee
assessment of Vatican II and, 291-292; collegiality and, 92-93; *Dei Verbum* and, 197; Ecumenism Decree and, 95-96, 101, 102-103; and effects of Vatican II, 115; *Gaudium et Spes* and, 105, 106-107, 294-295; John XXIII and, 315; Liturgical Commission and, 337-338; papal authority and, 69-70; Paul VI and, 316, 317-319; Protestant observers and, 167-168; and Secretariat for Promotion of Christian Unity, 164-165; and separate schema on Our Lady, 185-186; and status of documents, 214; and titles for Our Lady, 194
Bruckberger, Rev. Henri, 8
Buckley, William F., 303

471

Bugnini, Rev. Annibale
    assessment of, 373-374; *Consilium* and, 337; Freemasonry and, 266-267, 274-275; Liturgical Commission and, 327-328; Liturgy Constitution and, 366; and preparatory schemata, 57
Bultmann, Rev. Rudolph, 146-147
Butler, Bp. B. C.
    infallibility and, 221; and purpose of councils, 210-211; and status of documents, 216, 219

Cabrol, Dom Fernand, 355-356
Campion, Rev. D. A., 293
A Canterbury Pilgrim (Cogley), 401-402
Carbone, Rev. Vincenzo, 56
Cardinal Moderators, of Vatican II, 49
Carli, Bp. Luigi, 88, 249, 398
Casini, Tito, 267, 275
Casti Connubii (Pius XII), 107-108
Castro Mayer, Bp. Antonio de, 246
Cavert, S. McCrea, 94, 97
Celada, Rev. Domenico, 371-372
Chambre, Rev. Henri, 234
The Changing Church (Küng), 132
Christian by Degrees (Hannah), 263
Christianisme et Démocratie (Maritain), 285
Christianity and Communism (Chambre), 234
Christian Order (periodical), xxvii
Church, Constitution on (*Lumen Gentium*), 82-84, 90-93
Church of England, 155-158, 175-176, 308-314
The Church of the Word Incarnate (Journet), 216
Clement of Alexandria, 201
clergy, in pre-conciliar Church, 26-27
Coetus Internationalis Patrum (International Group of Fathers), 191, 204-205, 246-248
Cogley, John, 121, 124, 140, 401-402
collegiality, *Lumen Gentium* and, 92-93
common worship, 319-320

Communio (periodical), 72
Communism
    Maritain and, 437-442; Mounier and, 285; Paul VI and, 298-305; temptation toward, 15-16; Vatican II and, 233-254
Concilium (periodical), 70-71, 124
Congar, Rev. Yves, 59, 402
Consilium, 337, 363-365
Constitution on Divine Revelation (*Dei Verbum*), 127-128, 197-207
Constitution on the Church in the Modern World. See *Gaudium et Spes*
Constitution on the Sacred Liturgy (CSL), 341-374; adaptation principle and, 361-366; debate on, 138-139; and evolving liturgy concept, 355-360; and instruction for faithful, 360-361; Latin and, 368-370; Liturgy Commission and, 333-338; and local ecclesiastical authorities, 367; and participation of faithful, 351-355; reaction to, 104; transubstantiation and, 348-351
contraception
    Gaudium et Spes and, 106-108
    Humanae Vitae and, 67-69, 212-213, 217, 319
Council of Trent, 197-198, 200
Counter-Reformation, Vatican II and, 163-164
Crane, Rev. Paul
    evangelisation and, 170-171; *Gaudium et Spes* and, 294; liberation theology and, 153-154; Maritain and, 286; and post-conciliar Catholicism, xxvii
Creed and Catechetics (Kevane), 150
Crehan, Rev. Joseph, 220-221
Cullmann, Oscar
    and ambiguity of Council texts, 85; Ecumenism Decree and, 101-102; Protestant observers and, 167; and titles for Our Lady, 192-193; Vatican II and, 162, 322
"curialists", 397-400

Index

Davis, Charles
  Gaudium et Spes and, 107, 108;
  Liturgy Constitution and, 336;
  liturgy schema and, 327; Vatican II
  and, 292
Declaration on Religious Freedom
  (*Dignitatis Humanae*) (Paul VI), 223
Declaration on the Unicity and Salvific
  Universality of Jesus Christ and the
  Church (*Dominus Iesus*), 91, 403-408
*The Decline and Fall of Radical
  Catholicism* (Hitchcock), 64, 111, 126
The Decomposition of Catholicism
  (Bouyer), 9-10
Decree on the Instruments of Social
  Communication, 110
Decree on the Renewal of the
  Religious Life, 103-104
Dei Verbum (Constitution on Divine
  Revelation), 127-128, 197-207
De Lammenais á Maritain (Meinvielle),
  285-286
De Smedt, Bp. Emile, 203-204
dialogue
  Communism and, 234-236, 252-253,
  302; vs. evangelisation, 169-172;
  Vatican II and, 289-291
Dignitatis Humanae (Paul VI)
  (Declaration on Religious
  Freedom), 223
Dillon, Rev. George F., 267-268
Divine Revelation, Constitution on
  (*Dei Verbum*), 127-128, 197-207
DO-C organization, 122
documents of Vatican II, and
  infallibility, 209-231
Dogmatic Constitution on the Church
  (*Lumen Gentium*), 82-84, 90-93
Dominus Iesus document, 403-408
Döpfner, Julius Cardinal, 49
Doronzo, Rev. E., 219-220
Duggan, Rev. G. H., 87
Dulac, Rev. Raymond, 103-104
Dulles, Avery Cardinal, 92
Duschak, Bp. William, 329-330, 335
Dutch Catechism, 150-151, 306

Dwyer, Abp. G. P., 156-158
Dwyer, Abp. R. J., 337
Dwyer, Archbishop R. J., 40

ecumenism
  and *avant-garde* aims, 36-39;
  Catholic form of, 158-159; of
  commissions, 51-52; Ecumenism
  Decree, 94-103, 159, 213; Marian
  dogma and, 194; progress of,
  172-177
Emmanuel, Père, 27-28
England, Catholicism in, 454-458
Epiphanius, Saint, 202
Esprit (periodical), 285
European Alliance. *See* Rhine Group
evangelisation, vs. dialogue, 169-172
evolving liturgy concept, 330, 355-360
extra ecclesiam nulla salus doctrine,
  412-416
Extraordinary Magisterium, 219-220,
  224-231
  See also Magisterium; Ordinary
  Magisterium
Extraordinary Synod, xxi-xxiii

faithful
  instruction for, 360-361;
  participation of in liturgy, 351-355;
  in pre-conciliar Church, 26-27;
  revolt of laity and, 111
Fatima, Our Lady of, 191-192
Fay, Bernard, 248
Felici, Pericle Cardinal, 23, 218-219
Fesquet, Henri
  Cardinal Moderators and, 49;
  commission candidates and, 42;
  Gaudium et Spes and, 112-113;
  IDO-C and, 124; as journalist, 134,
  398-399; Rhine Group and, 121;
  Russian Orthodox observers and,
  240-241; Turowicz and, 401; and
  United Nations speech of Paul VI,
  296

First Dogmatic Constitution on the Church of Christ (*Pastor Aeternus*), xxvii, 224-228
First Vatican Council. *See* Vatican I
Flanagan, Rev. Philip, 163-164, 310
Flood, Dom Peter, 400
Formosus, 279
Franco, Francisco, 303
Fraser, Hamish
   Integral Humanism and, 283; modern media and, 122; Paul VI and, 288-289, 291, 308; press and, 131
Freemasonry, 257-275, 323
French Revolution, 264, 268
Frings, Joseph Cardinal, 183
Fulda Conference, 47-48

Gallon, Rev. M., 132
Gamber, Rev. Klaus, 335
Garvey, Rev. Edwin C., 150-151
Gaudium et Spes (Constitution on the Church in the Modern World)
   assessment of, 293-296; banality of, 110, 209-210; Communism and, 247; equivocal nature of, 104-108; ethos of, 111-115; Sillonism and, 421-427; *See also* Communism
Geusau, Rev. Alting von, 136
Glorieux, Rev. Achille, 248
Godfrey, William Cardinal, 331
Graber, Bp. Rudolph
   Freemasonry and, 258-259, 263-266, 269-271, 274; and judgement of Vatican II, 229-230; and purpose of councils, 211; and spirit of Vatican II, 12-13
Greeley, Rev. Andrew, 8, 367
Gregorian chant, 354, 369-370
Gregory Nyssen, 202
Griffiths, Bp., 109-110
Grisez, Germain, 222
Grotti, Bp. Giocondo, 88, 183-184
Guéranger, Dom Prosper, 330, 447-451

Hallinan, Abp. Paul, 329

Hannah, Walter, 263
Hebblethwaite, Peter, 85-86
Heenan, John Cardinal
   ambiguity of Council texts and, 87; bishops at Vatican II and, 35; Bultmann and, 146-147; commission candidates and, 43-44; ecumenism and, 38-39, 172-173, 176, 194; first general congregation and, 41-44; *Gaudium et Spes* and, 112; John XXIII and, 14, 47; and judgement of Vatican II, 88-89, 114-115, 230-231; Liturgical Commission and, 331, 337; Liturgy Constitution and, 359; Magisterium and, 64, 71; Paul VI and, 64-65, 306; *periti* and, 55-56, 60-62; press and, 133; progressives and, 40; and purpose of councils, 211; Rationalism and, 149-150; Revelation debate and, 198-199; Roman Curia and, 399; and status of Catholicism, 9, 10
Hildebrand, Dr. Dietrich von
   Communism and, 243-244; and documents of Vatican II, 30-31; Liturgy Constitution and, 355; papal authority and, 250, 278-282; and pre-conciliar Church, 24-25; and spirit of Vatican II, 29-30
Hitchcock, James
   and fruits of Vatican II, 5-9; and *periti*, 64, 65-66; and revolt of laity, 111; and use of publicity, 125-126
Holloway, Rev. Edward, 81-84
Houghton, Rev. Bryan, 171
Howell, Rev. Clifford, 333
Hoyt, Robert, 66
Humanae Salutis (John XXIII), 22-23
Humanae Vitae (Paul VI)
   dissent from, 67-69, 217; as enigma, 319; status of, 212-213
Humani Generis (Pius XII)
   appeasement policy and, 168-169; ecumenism and, 174; and neo-modernism, 39; sources of Revelation and, 198

Index

Humanisme Intégral (Maritain), 287, 429-445
Humanum Genus (Leo XIII), 261-262, 264-265
Huyghe, Rev. Gerard, 125

Iam Vos Omnes (Pius IX), 99-100
IDO-C organization, 70-71, 122-124, 136, 401
Immaculate Conception, dogma of, 227
impeccability, of pope, 278
Index of Forbidden Books, 307
Index of Leading Catholic Indicators: The Church Since Vatican II (Jones), 458-463
Ineffabilis Deus (Pius IX), 227
inerrancy, of pope, 278
infallibility
 Liturgical Commission and, 338; nature of, 278-282; Vatican II documents and, 209-231; views of, 398
Institute for the Study of Conflict, 235
Instruments of Social Communication, Decree on, 110
Integral Humanism, 282-298, 429-445
International Group of Fathers (*Coetus Internationalis Patrum*), 191, 204-205, 246-248

Jewell, Walter, 419
John Chrysostom, Saint, 202
John Paul II, and assessment of Vatican II, 16
John XXIII
 Communism and, 242-243; and convoking Vatican II, 22-23; death of, 47; *Pacem in Terris* and, 239; Protestantism and, 314-315; Vatican II and, 14, 203-204
Jones, Kenneth C., 458-463
Journal du Concile (Fesquet), 42, 398-399
journalists. *See* press
Journet, Cardinal, 216

Kaiser, Robert
 buffet suppers of, 134-135; Cardinal Bea and, 393-394; Cardinal Ottaviani and, 139-140; Cardinal Suenens and, 395-396; communications document and, 140; IDO-C and, 124; Liturgy Constitution and, 344; and opening of Vatican II, 43; and praise for *periti*, 72; press and, 133-134; reports of, 398; Rhine Group and, 121, 122
Kelly, Rev. George A., 31-34, 116
Kevane, Rev. Eugene, 150
Khrushchev, Nikita, 243
Koenig, Abp., 136-137
Küng, Rev. Hans
 avant-garde aims of, 36; and book on Vatican II, 66-67; censure of, 402; description of, 394-395; and Sacred Congregation for the Doctrine of the Faith, 71-72, 74-78; and titles for Our Lady, 192-193; and view of Vatican II, 115-116, 132

La Croix (periodical), 133-134
laity, 26-27, 111, 351-355, 360-361
Lamentabili (Pius X) (Syllabus Condemning the Errors of the Modernists), 199-200
Latin, use of, 331-334, 368-370
Le Caron, H., 286-287
Lefebvre, Abp. Marcel
 and assessment of Vatican II, 4-5, 13, 88-89, 230, 249, 371; Bugnini and, 267; commission candidates and, 43-44; Communism and, 245, 246-248; and criticism of conciliar documents, 81-87; ecumenism and, 51-52, 176; evangelisation and, 169-170; *Gaudium et Spes* and, 104-106, 112; obedience and, 26; Paul VI and, 306-307; preparatory schemata and, 56-58; progressives and, 40; Protestant observers and, 166; and purpose of councils, 211; and status of documents, 215-216

Le Monde (periodical), 133-134
Leo, John, 124
Leo XIII
  Alta Vendita documents and, 267-268; *Humanum Genus* and, 261-262, 264-265; *Satis Cognitum* and, xxvii
Lercaro, Giacomo Cardinal, 49, 363-366
L'Humanisme (periodical), 270-271
Liber Accusationis in Paulum Sextum (Nantes), 297-298
liberation theology, 153-154
Liberius, 279
Liénart, Cardinal, 41-42
Lindbeck, George, 163
Liturgical Commission, 327-328
Liturgical Institutions (Guéranger), 330, 447-451
liturgical renewal, need for, 27-28
Liturgy Constitution. *See* Constitution on the Sacred Liturgy (CSL)
The Liturgy Revived (Bouyer), 9-10
local ecclesiastical authorities, and Liturgy Constitution, 367
Lucey, Bp. C., 35
Lumen Gentium (Dogmatic Constitution on the Church), 82-84, 90-93

Magisterium, 64, 71, 216-217, 220-221
See also Extraordinary Magisterium; Ordinary Magisterium
Manning, Henry Cardinal
  and convoking general council, 3-4, 210, 245; infallibility and, 280-281; papal authority and, 250-251; Rationalism and, 144-146, 148-149; and role of press at Vatican I, 387-392; and workings of Holy Spirit, 410-416
Maritain, Jacques, and Integral Humanism, 284-287, 429-445
marriage, and *Gaudium et Spes*, 105-106
Martin, Rev. Malachi, 134
Marty, François Cardinal, 8
Marxism. *See* Communism

Mary. *See* Our Lady
Mascall, E. L., 263
Mass, 175-176
  See also Constitution on the Sacred Liturgy (CSL); Liturgical Commission
Mass attendance, decline in, 370-371, 462-463
Maximos IV Saigh, Patriarch of Antioch, 332
May, Georg, 323-324
McBrian, Rev. Richard, 76
McCready, William, 8
Mchedlov, M., 241-242
McKee, Rev. John, 147-148
McLaughlin, Denis, 454-455
McNaspy, Rev. C. J., 328
McVinney, Bp. Russell, 112
Mediator Dei (Pius XII), 342-344, 351-353
Mediatrix of All Graces, as title for Our Lady, 186-189
Meinvielle, Rev. Jules, 285-286
Mellor, A., 259-260
Mesnil St. Loup, France, 27-28
Mikulich, Rev. Milan, 194
Mindszenty, Jozsef Cardinal, 236-237, 238, 254, 300
Mingo, Abp. Corrado, 189
Ministry and Life of Priests, Decree on, 104
Mitterand, Jacques, 271-273
Modernism
  neo-modernism and, 39; Paul VI and, 305-307; Pius X and, 11, 199-200, 330; Rationalism and, 144-152; secret societies and, 265
Mondin, B., 167
Montini, Rev. Giovanni Battista. *See* Paul VI
Moorman, Bp. John
  and division at Vatican II, 39; *Gaudium et Spes* and, 110, 209-210; Paul VI and, 316-317, 319-320; Protestant observers and, 166, 167; and separate schema on Our Lady,

Index

186; and titles for Our Lady, 187, 193-194
Mortalium Animos (Pius XI), 101-102, 158, 416-417
Mother of the Church, as title for Our Lady, 189-192
Mounier, Emmanuel, 285
Mueller, Bp. Joseph J., 119
Murphy, Rev. Francis X., 134
Murray, Dom Gregory, 354
Mysterium Fidei (Paul VI), 318, 349-350
Mystical Body of Christ (Pius XII), 177

Nantes, Rev. Georges de, 29-30, 296-298
National Catholic Register (periodical), xxvi
Naturalism, nature of, 260-261
Nau, Dom Paul, 221-222
Nelson, J. O., 104
neo-modernism, and *periti*, 39
Nevins, Rev. Albert J., 67
Newman, John Cardinal, 215, 408-410
New Yorker (periodical), 133-134
Nichols, Peter, 240
La Nouvelle Messe (Salleron), 341
Novak, Michael
  Cardinal Suenens and, 131-132; and fruits of Vatican II, xxvi; Integral Humanism and, 289; as journalist, 134, 396-397, 400; Paul VI and, 299-300; *periti* and, 140; Rev. Küng and, 394-395; Rhine Group and, 121
Nowell, Robert, 260

obedience, concept of, 25-26
observers at Vatican II
  Protestant, 165-168, 173-174; Russian Orthodox, 239-242
O'Carroll, Rev. Michael, 185, 190
"On Baptism of Desire" (Newman), 408-410
The Open Church (Novak), 134, 289
Open Letter to Jesus Christ (Bruckberger), 8

oral tradition, as source of Revelation, 197-207
Ordinary Magisterium, 217, 221-223, 224
  See also Extraordinary Magisterium; Magisterium
Ordination, rite of, 373
Origen, 201-202
Orthodox churches, 98-99, 184-185, 239-242
Ottaviani, Alfredo Cardinal
  Communism and, 242-243; and debate on Liturgy Constitution, 138-140; description of, 400; Freemasonry and, 271; and schema on Our Lady, 182
Ott, Dr. Ludwig, 222-223
Our Apostolic Mandate (Pius X), 421-427
Our Lady
  and Mediatrix of All Graces title, 186-189; and Mother of the Church title, 189-192; separate schema devoted to, 182-186
Outler, Dr. A. C., 92

Pacem in Terris (John XXIII), 239
Pallavicini, Pietro Cardinal, 3
papal authority, 69-70, 250-251, 278-282
  See also infallibility
Pascendi Gregis (Pius X)
  contemporary theologians and, 72-74; elitist attitudes and, 128-129; and evolution of worship, 330; Modernism and, 11; press and, 140-141
Pastor Aeternus (First Dogmatic Constitution on the Church of Christ), xxvii, 224-228
Paul, Saint, and Tradition, 201
Paul VI
  assessment of, 323-324; and assessment of Vatican II, 2-3, 5, 13-16, 379-380; Cardinal Mindszenty and, 238; collegiality and, 93; Communism and, 252-253, 298-305; contraception and, 107-108;

Dignitatis Humanae and, 223;
Integral Humanism and, 282-298;
Masonic tribute to, 323; Modernism
and, 305-307; Mother of the Church
title and, 191-192
Mysterium Fidei and, 318, 349-350
orthodoxy and, 64-65; post-conciliar
Catholicism and, 10-12; procedural
rules and, 49; Protestantism and,
307-322; Revelation schema and,
205-207; and status of documents,
218; United Nations speech of,
295-296; *See also Humanae Vitae*
Pawley, B.
councils and, 155-156; ecumenism
and, 174-175; Mass and, 176,
329-330; Paul VI and, 312-313; and
titles for Our Lady, 186; Vatican II
and, 161
The Peasant of the Garonne (Maritain),
288-289, 431
Pelikan, Jaroslav, 336
Père Emmanuel, 27-28
periti (experts)
neo-modernism and, 39; policy
formulation and, 48, 49; press and,
119-141; Protestant observers and,
168; role of, 55-78
Pistoia, Synod of, 330, 346-347, 349
Pius VI, 330, 349
Pius IX
Arcano Divinae Providentiae and,
98-99; *Iam Vos Omnes* and, 99-100;
Vatican I and, 391-392
Pius X
and condemnation of Modernism,
11, 199-200; Freemasonry and, 274;
Our Apostolic Mandate and, 421-427;
Pascendi Gregis and, 72-74, 128-129,
140-141, 330
Pius XI
Mortalium Animos and, 101-102, 158,
416-417; *Quas Primas* and, 283-284

Pius XII
Casti Connubii and, 107-108; *Humani
Generis* and, 39, 168-169, 174, 198;
Mediator Dei and, 342-344, 351-353;
Mystical Body of Christ and, 177;
nature of Church and, 90; and
views about Our Lady, 182
Poletti, Cardinal, 252
post-conciliar Catholicism, 16, 31-34,
291-296, 371, 379-380
post-conciliar commissions, and *periti*,
60-62
preparatory schemata, and *periti*, 56-59
press
and Vatican I, 387-392; and Vatican
II, 119-141
Prestige, Rev. L., 312
Protestantism
Church of England and, 155-158;
dialogue and, 169-172; ecumenism
and, 172-177; fragmentation in,
143-144; John XXIII and, 314-315;
liberation theology and, 153-154;
and observers at Vatican II, 165-168,
173-174; Paul VI and, 307-322; Pius
IX and, 99-100;
Rationalism and, 144-152;
and Secretariat for Promotion
of Christian Unity, 164-165;
temptation toward, 15-16; Tradition
and, 202
public opinion, and Vatican II, 125-126
Pusey, Rev. E. B., 410

Rahner, Rev. Karl
and *Humanae Vitae*, 68; and separate
schema on Our Lady, 182; and titles
for Our Lady, 187-188
Ramsey, A. M., 308-309
Rationalism, and Protestantism,
144-152
Ratzinger, Joseph Cardinal
Communio and, 72; and judgement
of Vatican II, 17, 231; and post-
conciliar Catholicism, xxiii-xxiv,
xxvii

Index

Reformation. *See* Protestantism
The Reform of the Roman Liturgy (Gamber), 335
Religious Freedom, Declaration on (Paul VI) (*Dignitatis Humanae*), 223
Religious Life, Decree on Renewal of, 103-104
Rennings, Rev. H., 358-359
Revelation, sources of, 197-207
The Rhine Flows into the Tiber (Wiltgen), 30, 44-45, 122
Rhine Group
    commission candidates and, 44-45; preparatory schemata and, 56-59; press and, 121; second session and, 47-51; and separate schema on Our Lady, 183-184; and titles for Our Lady, 190-191
Richard-Molard, G., 178
Ripley, Rev. F. J., 36-37, 456
Roberts, Abp. T. D., 133
Roman Curia, 397-400
Ross, Bp., 35
Ruffini, Ernesto Cardinal, 89, 112
Russian Orthodox observers, at Vatican II, 239-242
Rynne, Xavier
    Consilium and, 337; influence of, 134
    Latin and, 333; Liturgical Commission and, 328; Liturgy Constitution and, 336, 361; and *periti*, 48; press and, 132; and pressure for modernization, 35-36; Rhine Group and, 121; and second Pentecost concept, 126-128; and separate schema on Our Lady, 184; Social Communication Decree and, 110

Sacred Congregation for the Doctrine of the Faith, and Küng, 71-72, 74-78
Sacred Liturgy, Constitution on. *See* Constitution on the Sacred Liturgy (CSL)
Sacred Scripture, as source of Revelation, 197-207

Salleron, Louis, 287, 341, 369, 429-445
"Salvation of Non-Catholics" (CTS Pamphlet), 418-419
Santamaria, Bob, xxiv-xxv
Satis Cognitum (Leo XIII), xxvii
Schillebeeckx, Rev. Edward
    and preparatory schemata, 59; Protestant observers and, 168; Revelation schema and, 202-203
Schutz, Roger, 161-162
Scripture, as source of Revelation, 197-207
Secretariat for Promotion of Christian Unity, 164-165, 203-204
secret societies. *See* Freemasonry
Sergius III, 279
Shaw, George Bernard, 313
Sigaud, Abp. Geraldo de Proenca, 246
Sillonism, 421-427
Singleton, Ronald, 74
"sister Church" controversy, 309-312
Skydsgaard, K. E., 161, 162-163, 168
Slipyi, Josyf Cardinal, 254
slogans, and Vatican II, 124-125
Sloyan, Rev. Gerard, 126
Social Communication, Decree on the Instruments of, 110
Solzhenitsyn, Alexander, 240, 302
Southard, Rev. Robert, 7
Spain, Catholicism in, 453-454
Spellman, Francis Cardinal, 188
Staffa, Dino Cardinal, 347-348
Stephen VI, 279
Stepinac, Alois Cardinal, 254
Stourm, Abp. René, 137
"subsists" controversy, 90-92, 403-408
Suenens, Leo Cardinal
    as Cardinal Moderator, 49; description of, 395-396; humanism and, 292-293; and Mediatrix of All Graces title, 188-189; Michael Novak and, 131-132; press and, 135-136; purpose of marriage and, 105-106

Syllabus Condemning the Errors of the Modernists (*Lamentabili*) (Pius X), 199-200
Synod of Pistoia, 330, 346-347, 349

Taizé community, 161-162
Tardini, Domenico Cardinal, 213
Telford, Rev. George, 454, 456
Theodore II, 279
Theophanes of Nicea, 185
The Tablet
   Cardinal Ratzinger and, xxiii-xxiv; Communism and, 244-245; Rev. Arrupe and, 260; and separate schema on Our Lady, 184-185; Vatican II and, 162
This Is the Faith (Ripley), 456
Tisserant, Cardinal, 247
Tito, Marshal, 304-305
traditional Catholics, and Paul VI, 319-320
Tradition, as source of Revelation, 197-207
transubstantiation, and Constitution on the Sacred Liturgy, 348-351
Trent, Council of, 197-198, 200
Trochata, Cardinal, 253
Trojan Horse in the City of God (Hildebrand), 24-25, 29-30
Turowicz, M., 401

United Nations, and Paul VI, 295-296
United States, Catholicism in, 456-463
The Universe (periodical), 21
UNO. *See* United Nations

Van der Ploeg, Rev. J. P., 12
Vatican I, 197-198, 200-201; and *Pastor Aeternus*, xxvii; role of press at, 387-392; *See also* infallibility
vernacular, use of, 331-334, 368-370
Vietnam war, 237-238

Wales, Catholicism in, 456-458
The Wanderer (periodical), 303-304
Wegner, Rev. Antoine, 121, 398

Weigel, Rev. Gustave, 213
Wells, David F., 87
Wheeler, Bp. Gordon, 130-131
Willebrands, Jan Cardinal, 165, 239-241
Wiltgen, Rev. R. N.
   Cardinal Moderators and, 49; commission candidates and, 44-45; Communism and, 248; Council texts and, 30; as journalist, 122; *periti* and, 48; preparatory schemata and, 58-59; Rhine Group and, 50-51
Woodruff, Douglas, 55, 113, 143
World Council of Churches, 77, 154, 322
Wynn, Terence, 378
Wyszynski, Stefan Cardinal, 189-190, 245-246, 253-254

Yu Pin, Abp. Paul, 246
Yzermans, Rev. V. A., 138

ZNAK organization, 401